Horror in Space

To a horror icon and the one-liner:
In memory of Sir John Hurt and Bill Paxton

Acknowledgments

Given that the process from call for proposals to submission of the manuscript took longer than I had anticipated, I want to thank each writer in this collection for their support and patience.

I am grateful for the support of my colleagues at the Los Angeles chapter of the Horror Writers Association, the National Coalition of Independent Scholars, and fellow H.P. Lovecast members Adam M. Crowley, Nicholas Diak, and Juliane Schlag who not only contributed to this collection but were an encouraging force throughout the entire process, providing suggestions and feedback when I asked. Friendship, encouragement and/or assistance came from Fanbase Press cofounders Barbra and Bryant Dillon, Brad Bensen, and my parents, Kate and Jim Cook—thank you! My partner Nick's unfaltering belief in me was the confidence booster I needed when I saw before me a long, endless road. I appreciate the innumerable discussions about space horror and his being a willing movie buddy to watch a lot of films in the genre. My feline boys, Romeo and Ashes, were always the best sources of unconditional love when I needed it most.

Table of Contents

Acknowledgments   vi

Introduction   1

Part One: Horror Made in America

John Carpenter of Mars: Space Horror in the Films   13
   of John Carpenter
   BEN KOOYMAN

The Cold, White Reproduction of the Same: A New Hypothesis   33
   About John Carpenter's *The Thing*
   DARIO ALTOBELLI

Meteor Madness: Lovecraftian Horror and Consumerism   50
   in the Battle for Small Town USA
   NICHOLAS DIAK

"It (never actually) came from outer space": Earth-Origin   66
   Threats in Space Horror Films
   KEVIN J. WETMORE, JR.

**Part Two: Time and Space in a Sea
of Post-Modern Isolation**

Nonknowledge and Inner Experience: A Post-Modern Rhetoric   81
   of Space Horror
   GAVIN F. HURLEY

Out of Space—Out of Time: Looking at the Factors of Time   96
   in Space Horror Movies
   JULIANE SCHLAG

We're All Alone, Out Here: Isolation and Its Contribution   111
    to Space Horror in Film
    JANET JOYCE HOLDEN

That *Moon* Is Romantic: Duncan Jones's Dark Fairy Tale   121
    ADAM M. CROWLEY

Part Three: The Uncanny Body

The Architecture of Sci-Fi Body Horror: Mechanical   127
    Building-Bodies and Organic Invasion from Deep Space
    to the Anthropocene
    BRENDA S. GARDENOUR WALTER

Ghosts in the Machine: Emotion and Haunting in the Creation   140
    of the Irrational Robot
    CASEY RATTO

Part Four: The Devil Made Me

Betwixt and Between: Magic, Science and the Devil's Place   151
    in Outer Space
    ANDREW P. WILLIAMS

Under the Influence: Undead Planets and Vampiric   164
    Dreamworlds in Outer Space
    SIMON BACON

Part Five: Play It Again or Rip It Off

A "family of displaced figures": Posthumanism and Jean-Pierre   181
    Jeunet's *Alien Resurrection* (1997)
    CHARLES W. REICK

Galaxies of Terror in a Knock-Off Universe: Atavism and   194
    the Rip-Off Body Horror of "*Alien*sploitation" Films
    JASON DAVIS

Leprechaun 4 and *Jason X*: Camp, Paracinema and   217
    the Postmodern Sequel
    KEVIN CHABOT

About the Contributors   233

Index   235

Introduction

To learn what we fear is to learn who we are. Horror
defines our boundaries and illuminates our souls....
Horror can serve as a liberating or repressive social tool,
and it is always an accurate reflection of the social climate
of its time and the place where it gets birthed.
—Guillermo del Toro[1]

The cinema became a staple of my life when my dad took me to the local theatre each week to see new releases before they vanished to the movie vaults for years until they were finally featured as a movie of the week on television. It was the 1970s, so Saturday afternoons provided the best opportunity to watch classic genre films such as westerns and war and science fiction movies. Then, late on Saturday nights, my dad and I would watch grindhouse and horror movies, which usually had me cringing and hiding my eyes during the goriest scenes. The nighttime viewing punctuated the fear of the moment, but lacked the residual impact I felt when watching *War of the Worlds* (1953, Bryon Haskin), *Invaders from Mars* (1953, William Cameron Menzies), or *The Day the Earth Stood Still* (1951, Robert Wise). The threat of alien invasion of average American cities and rural communities made the horror more personal and created a potent fear in my young mind.

In a viewing experience where aliens were often the antagonists that mortally threatened the protagonist and his love interest, creatures from outer space became the prevailing forces of evil to be faced and triumphed over for humanity and Earth to be saved. The home turf provided the hero with an advantage, but what happened when man and woman became space travelers? There were glimpses via *This Island Earth* (1955, Joseph M. Newman and Jack Arnold) in which viewers follow Dr. Cal Meacham (Rex Reason) and Dr. Ruth Adams (Faith Domergue) as they travel briefly to Metaluna and in *The Quatermass Xperiment* (1955, Val Guest) in which an insidious organism infects and slowly mutates astronaut Victor Carroon (Richard

1

Wordsworth) into an alien. However, it was 1979's *Alien* (Ridley Scott) that was more fearful than any film that came before it. H.R. Giger's erotic alien and disturbing dark sets produced an unprecedented level of terror and tension as a backdrop to the unraveling of the *Nostromo* crew from two threats: the alien and the android Ash (Ian Holm). At that point, *Alien* was the benchmark of the most influential cycle of space horror where horror and science fiction converged, inspiring original and not-so-original films for a contemporary audience.

Space horror has a surprisingly long past, beginning in early cinema. There is a plethora of films about science fiction and horror, and much has been written about individual films and filmmakers (mostly the *Alien* franchise), yet little has been written about the rise of space horror in film or space horror films within the structure of their own genre. This introduction begins to address that gap in scholarly research by first identifying and defining the genre, briefly chronicling the history of space horror in film and concluding with an overview of this book's layout.

Defining Space Horror

Space horror can typically be defined as horror that is set in space. With that location as a marker for comparison, films that take place entirely or almost exclusively in outer space, on a spacecraft or on a space station fall into this category. For example, *Event Horizon* (1997, Paul W.S. Anderson) and *Dracula 3000* (2004, Darrell Roodt) are set entirely on spacecrafts and qualify as "pure outer space" space horror films. *Alien*, *Pandorum* (2009, Christian Alvart) and *Pitch Black* (2000, David Twohy) are examples of "extrasolar" films, set on planets or moons outside of our solar system. Films where the locale is within our solar system but not on Earth are "extraterrestrial" and include *Apollo 18* (2011, Gonzalo Lopez-Gallego), *Europa Reports* (2013, Sebastian Cordero) and Andrei Tarkovsky's *Solaris* (1972). "Terrestrial" refers to movies set on Earth. These are often called "invasion films" and include *Invasion of the Body Snatchers* (1956, Don Siegel), *The Blob* (1958, Irvin Yeaworth) and *They Live* (1988, John Carpenter). The early silent films at the beginning of the 20th century ventured outward into our solar system, but by the 1950s, the majority of space horror included elements of science fiction and found solid footing on Earth. Evolving with popular interest in space exploration, space horror films took flight too, right into the outer reaches of our collective imaginations that were often dark and horrific places. Since *Alien*, space horror films have become a blend of settings, conveying the idea that no place, in space or on Earth, is really all that safe.

Every space horror has an alien antagonist hell bent on annihilating the human race, or, at the very least, the human team that has arrived at a location with an alien presence. Typically, the alien is a physical entity and predatory in nature such as the alien in the *Predator* franchise (1987–2010), the bioraptors in *Pitch Black* and the watery tentacle creature in *Europa Report*. When the alien requires a host, whether in the form of another alien or a human for the purpose of reproduction, it penetrates the host in a violent way: the facehuggers in *Alien* franchise (1979–2017), the found ancient alien DNA in *Doom* (2005, Andrzej Bartkowiak) or the parasitic life form referred to as the Thing in *The Thing* (1982, John Carpenter). Sometimes, the alien parasite causes the host to morph psychologically and/or physically, always to the detriment of the host and the humans around them. The ancient DNA caused the host to physically morph into a creature that hardly resembled its host. The Thing becomes its host in appearance as a survival mechanism.

The psychological alien is more complex because it can call into question the mental state of the host. Often, the alien takes the form of an apparition, seeming to take up physical space and appearing beyond the host individual. In *Event Horizon*, each crew member of the *Lewis and Clark* experience apparitions of individuals from their pasts that only they can see. Dr. William Weir (Sam Neill) becomes possessed by the spirit aboard the *Event Horizon* ship and inflicts bodily harm on himself, physically changing his appearance to match the horror and chaos of the alternate dimension the prior crew encountered during their gravity drive experiment. In contrast, both *Solaris* (1972) and *Sunshine* (2007, Danny Boyle) have an alien that is an apparition who took up physical space that multiple people could see and with whom they could interact. Occasionally, there are paranormal and occult-focused alien threats: interplanetary vampires in *Planet of the Vampires* (1965, Mario Bava) and the Cenobites in *Hellraiser: Bloodline* (1996, Kevin Yagher and Joe Chappelle).

Not all aliens are created equal, so while one may be the antagonist of a movie, the alien may or may not be a sentient being. Some aliens that are interpreted as hostile are in fact only driven by the instinct to survive. The bioraptors in *Pitch Black* are led by the most fundamental need to exist. On the other hand, an example of a sentient alien being is the hunter from the *Predator* franchise. The hunter's actions are consciously motivated by more devious intentions. It has advanced itself through the development of clothing, armor, technology and written language. It actively hunts other species and not necessarily because its survival is in jeopardy.

Space horror films can also be defined by the shared tropes that most genre filmmakers utilize in their narratives. In many films set in space or on a spaceship, there is a limited number of crew, usually no more than seven or eight, which is probably the tipping point for a film to have enough time to introduce and develop each character and for the audience to identify with and keep track of them. *Alien* had seven crew members as did *Dracula 3000*, while *Sunshine, Event Horizon, Last Days on Mars* (2013, Ruairí Robinson) and *Doom* (specifically the marines) had eight. Some outliers include *Europa Report* with six, *Pandorum* with five, *Stranded* (2013, Roger Christian) with four, and *Apollo 18* with three, while *Pitch Black, Aliens* (1986, James Cameron), and *The Thing* had more than eight. As a trope device, it is about the right count of deaths for the purpose of pacing tension and suspense. Ultimately, the presence of aliens is seriously bad for a human's longevity and it rarely takes long for an alien to get to the sole survivor.

The last person standing, or crawling, defies the odds of survival and either defeats the alien in a climactic battle or is able to escape—until the sequel (think Ripley from the *Alien* franchise). In some movies, the last survivor has to complete a task that will cause their death yet will be for the greater good, as in *Sunshine* and *Last Days on Mars*. This trope is often utilized in slasher films where the last survivor is the "final girl," a term coined by Carol J. Clover.[2] Final girl refers to the woman who survives to confront the killer or escape and be the only one left to tell others what has happened to her. According to Clover, she is the main character of the story and the only one developed in any psychological detail. She is the most rational and resourceful and may have an ambiguous name that could be appropriate for either gender. She is likely to hold a position typically held by men. Ripley from the *Alien* franchise is an excellent example of a final girl, as is archaeologist Elizabeth Shaw (Noomi Rapace) in *Prometheus* (2012, Ridley Scott) and Executive Officer Lt. Starck (Joely Richardson) in *Event Horizon*. More often, either the entire crew dies or there is a small number of survivors, usually two or three, such as in *Event Horizon, Pitch Black* and *Pandorum* (in this case, the main characters are considered).

In a number of space horror films, there is either a military component such as the special elite squad in *Doom* and the Marines in *Aliens* or a corporate presence such as Weyland-Yutani throughout the *Alien* franchise. In the former, it acts as the cavalry, but eventually, the crew discovers they are expendable in the eyes of the corporation or military. The crew, or the remains of it, may also identify a "turncoat" in the group. An individual will turn, either intentionally or not, against their fellow crew members because they are following their corporation's directive and/or trying save their own skin. This person is a walking dead man.

Returning to *Aliens* as an example, Carter Burke (Paul Reiser) is a company man who creates a situation in which he facilitates the opportunity for Ripley (Sigourney Weaver) and Newt (Carrie Henn) to be impregnated by facehugger aliens. He does this with the intent of smuggling one or two alien embryos back through intergalactic customs, but that tactic is foiled. Later, when the aliens are storming the base, Burke becomes scared and tries to save himself to the detriment of others. He uses the intended escape route and locks the door so the remaining survivors cannot use it, but he comes face to face with an alien and his own demise.

If there is an android or a central computer present in the story, they usually turn out to have questionable intentions that may or may not lead to the termination of human life. Such is the case with Ash in *Alien*, David (Michael Fassbender) in *Prometheus* and initially Bishop (Lance Henriksen) in *Aliens*. All three androids easily pass as human for a time. Their presence creates and explores the idea of an "uncanny valley" where there is an adverse reaction and/or discomfort in humans toward the androids.[3] Occasionally, instead of an android there may be a central computer, often referred to as "Mother" and controlled by the military and/or corporate entity. Two examples are found in *Alien* and *Lily C.A.T.* (1987, Hisayuki Toriumi), a Japanese anime directly influenced by *Alien*.

A sea of black with twinkling stars and glowing planets may provide wonder and awe, but after traveling in space—days, weeks, months, years—isolation sets in and takes a physical and emotional toll. This last trope fits well within this genre—*Event Horizon, Moon* (2009, Duncan Jones) and *Europa Report*—in which fatigue, depression, and an anxiousness to get home to Earth are prevalent. Space represents danger to humans because there are deadly hazards to space travel; for instance, the threat to air supply if the ship is damaged and the adverse effects of gravity and radiation on the human body. Additionally, if the crew finds itself in trouble, it knows it is alone. And if space horror films have taught us anything, it is that help will be too far away (months or even years) to be of any assistance because the alien or aliens are faster at annihilation.

Space horror has been defined by its use of location, a high body count, and an alien antagonist. The genre also has a number of shared tropes. Typically, the audience will follow a handful of characters that are killed as the story progresses to the climactic third act. There may be a sole survivor in the form of a final girl, but more likely, a couple of characters survive or all perish. There is a military and/or corporate entity present that might have a secret agenda, usually to capture and manipulate an alien species for warfare. An android might complicate and unsettle the main protagonist, or at least initially manifest an uncanny valley situation. Lastly, space travel is a difficult endeavor for humans; the length of time to travel from point A to point B, even with sleep chambers, takes a physical toll on the body. Isolation does too, and at a psychological level. With the foundation of space horror in mind, let's take a look at the cinematic history of space horror.

Space Horror in Films

As moving pictures gained the attention of audiences, early filmmakers moved away from films that captured everyday activities and sought narratives that expanded the cinematic experience. Not surprisingly, they turned to a ready-made treasure trove of stories: literature. While *Across the Zodiac* (1880) by Percy Greg appears to be one of the first novels centered on space exploration, it was not until H.G. Wells' *The War of the Worlds* (1898) that Earth encountered a horrific alien invasion. The novel proved the viability of horror by blending the two genres and may have been a source of inspiration for man's foray into outer space. In *A Trip to the Moon* (1902, Georges Méliès), a group of men use a rocket ship to travel to the moon where they are captured by moon-men but manage to escape and return to Earth. The film conveyed that while space was wondrous, it was also dangerous. The five-minute short *A Trip to Mars* (1910)[4] directed by Ashley Miller was the first time science fiction and horror collided. A scientist discovers a powder that allows him to reverse gravity, so he spills some on himself and travels to Mars, arriving unceremoniously headfirst. He explores the red planet where he encounters giant trees with semi-human monsters as upper halves that reach out with their arms to try and seize him as he runs between them. He climbs out on a rocky ledge that proves to be an evil clown with long elf ears. The clown puts the scientist into a bubble and blows him back to Earth. This film and quite possibly Méliès' film are supposed to be loosely based on another H.G. Wells novel, *The First Men in the Moon* (1901).[5] Additional films from the first decade of the new century included *The '?' Motorist* (1906, Walter R. Booth), the story of a traveler who goes to Saturn and drives around its rings, and *Excursion to the Moon* (1908, Segundo de Chomon), which offers viewers a seven-minute remake of Méliès' film.

After the brief cinematic foray into space exploration and the horrors of space glimpsed in 1910, it appears that filmmakers moved onto other topics of interest based on early films that have survived, but there are a couple of exceptions. After World War I, Danish director Holger-Madsen directed *A Trip to Mars* (1918) in which a group of humans visit Mars and find that Martians wear Roman-era clothing and have attained a certain level of intellectual enlightenment. In 1920, Hans Werchmeister directed Emil Jannings (*The Last Laugh, Tartuffe*) in *Power* or *Algol—Tragödie der Macht*. The synopsis sounds chaotic: an alien from the planet Algol gives an Earthling a device that allows him to have superpowers. Both lack the horror element, but they are early examples of plots that would be re-appropriated by mid-century.

In the literary world, H.P. Lovecraft's *The Color Out of Space* (1927) tells the tale of an alien entity that initially brings great growth to a rural

New England farm only to drain the life force from the family members later. Ray Bradbury's *The Martian Chronicles* (1950) is a collection of short stories that explore the impact of human colonization of Mars and the conflict-ridden relationship with Martians. Both stories inspired films about the invasion of Earth in the 1950s and space travel and/or colonizing films that started appearing in the 1970s.

As the 1950s began, so too did the interest in science and space in a post–World War II environment that had been rocked by the development and use of atomic warfare. The Cold War was warming up and competition in all arenas was important to the USSR and the United States. Space horror introduced fears of invasion by hostile aliens—allegories of the real threat of nuclear bombs, Communism and the Cold War. The decade provided space horror in the guise of alien invasions out in the open in *War of the Worlds* or threat of annihilation in *The Day the Earth Stood Still*. Some alien invasions were covert and sinister, as in *Invasion of the Body Snatchers*, or happened in small towns, as in *The Blob*. Even Ed Wood's *Plan 9 from Outer Space* (1959) attempted space horror with human-looking aliens with a mash-up of zombies. Interest in what life was like on other planets was conceptualized, as in Altair IV in *Forbidden Planet* (1956, Fred M. Wilcox) and Metaluna in *This Island Earth*, but films like these tended to be exceptions when most films were about invasions of Earth.

The 1950s were the heyday of invasion films, and interest in them waned in the 1960s when spies and cowboys were popular, as well as in the 1970s when crime/vengeance and slasher films were in demand. However, the space and horror in "space horror" would be unquestionably redefined in 1979 with Ridley Scott's *Alien*, which follows the story of the *Nostromo* crew as it explores the mysterious abandoned ship on LV-426 and encounters a new and hostile alien species. The idea of being in space, far from home with limited precious resources (e.g., oxygen), struck fear into the hearts of the crew and audience. Scott's film was one of the first to successfully combine science fiction and horror in an interstellar setting. It also spawned several inferior imitations in the 1980s. Additionally, it provided an early representation of the discomfort and uneasiness caused in humans by the presence of an android. In the sequel, Bishop proves to Ripley that she can trust an android. Also worth noting in the 1980s and 1990s are alien abduction films including *Communion* (1989, Philippe Mora) and *Fire in the Sky* (1993, Robert Lieberman). Both were based on books about true life experiences.

As the *Alien* franchise churned out sequels further exploring Ripley's relationship with the xenomorphs, by the mid–1990s, formerly successful Earth-bound franchises were turning to space for revitalization, such as *Hellraiser: Bloodline* and *Leprechaun 4: In Space* (1997, Brian Trenchard-Smith). *Event Horizon*, a complex story of religious symbolism and the paranormal with familiar slasher and haunted house tropes, rejuvenated the genre and further defined it.

In the 21st century, space horror films are still finding an audience, but not necessarily the financial backing that mainstream dramas, superhero films and romantic comedies find. Despite budget constraints, there have been fascinating films in the last few years that continued to explore and jeopardize our existence: *Sunshine* in 2007, *Moon* and *Pandorum* in 2009, *Prometheus* in 2012 and *Europa Report* in 2013. We shall see what the future holds in terms of movies and research.

The Layout of This Book

This collection of 15 essays explores space horror films from several different focal points. The first part, "Horror Made in America," presents four essays that evaluate American films. It opens with Ben Kooyman's "John Carpenter of Mars: Space Horror in the Films of John Carpenter" which applies the auteur theory to evaluate the four space horror films that punctuate John Carpenter's career as a filmmaker. *Dark Star* (1974), *The Thing*, *They Live*, and *Ghosts of Mars* (2001) represent Carpenter's examination of the American economy and his ability to blend his passion for westerns, 1950s space horror, and conspiracy thrillers. Carpenter's films chronicle social concerns during the last quarter of the 20th century as well as showcase the fluidity of the genre. In "The Cold, White Reproduction of the Same: A New Hypothesis About John Carpenter's *The Thing*," Dario Altobelli focuses on a comparison of the 1951 *The Thing from Another World* (Christian Nyby and Howard Hawks) to Carpenter's *The Thing* in order to study the complexity of a commodified value through metamorphosis, simulation, and repetition in Carpenter's reinterpretation of the 1950s classic. Nicholas Diak utilizes H.P. Lovecraft's short story *The Color Out of Space* as a basis for evaluating Cold War tension and consumerism in "Meteor Madness: Lovecraftian Horror and Consumerism in the Battle for Small Town USA." He forwards the argument that meteor horror films fit into their own subgenre of space horror films. Kevin J. Wetmore, Jr., argues that terrestrial space horror films often have a human element that influences and can supplant the alien threat in "'It (never actually) came from outer space': Earth-Origin Threats in Space Horror Films."

In the second part, "Time and Space in a Sea of Post-Modern Isolation," Gavin F. Hurley applies Georges Bataille's concept of nonknowledge through an analysis of *Prometheus* and *Event Horizon* in "Nonknowledge and Inner Experience: A Post-Modern Rhetoric of Space Horror" and reveals there is a post-modern rhetorical condition that is infinitely fragmented. This fragmentation adheres to the space horror genre. Juliane Schlag touches on H.P. Lovecraft's influence in her essay "Out of Space—Out of Time: Looking at the Factors of Time in Space Horror Movies." She explains that the concept of time and space defines the horror in new terms and re-appropriates other genre cycles including slasher, demonic/obsession, western, and supernatural (ghosts and even vampires!). Characters usually experience a process of dehumanization, arising from the fear of loneliness and a psychological breakdown as they are pushed to their limits to survive. For audiences, it is an opportunity to explore a non-hegemonic narrative. Janet Joyce Holden picks up on the theme of isolation in space in "We're All Alone, Out Here: Isolation and Its Contribution to Space Horror in Film." Scientifically, human space travelers have a difficult time coping with the inherent isolation involved with going to other galaxies, let alone our gaseous planetary neighbor Jupiter or, even closer, the red planet Mars. Add to this the fact that with greater distances from Earth, the more the travelers must depend on their own ingenuity, which may be impaired by the side effects of isolation. Hence, space becomes a breeding ground for fear, tension, and horror. Adam M. Crowley concludes the part with an analysis of identity via Northrop Frye's concept of sentimental romance in "That *Moon* Is Romantic: Duncan Jones's Dark Fairy Tale." Crowley points to the cruel and horrifying situation that the Sam Bell clones find themselves in when they come to understand their predetermined lifespan.

The third part, "The Uncanny Body," begins with Brenda S. Gardenour Walter's "The Architecture of Sci-Fi Body Horror: Mechanical Building-Bodies and Organic Invasion from Deep Space to the Anthropocene." She applies theories of architecture and medical humanities in her analysis of the human body and its relationship to non-human worlds. The films *Alien*, *Alien³* (1992, David Fincher), and *Leviathan* (1989, George P. Cosmatos) lend credence to the concept of womb-like safe spaces represented by the space ships and buildings presented in these films. In "Ghosts in the Machine: Emotion and Haunting in the Creation of the Irrational Robot," Casey Ratto explores the irrational robot archetype in *2001: A Space Odyssey* (1968, Stanley Kubrick), *Alien*, and *Aliens*. In particular, the androids Hal and Ash in the first two films are initially rational entities, but begin to exhibit erratic and deadly behavior when they experience a haunting, an Avery Gordon concept presented in her book *Ghostly Matters*. Ratto then contrasts Bishop in *Aliens*, positing that the human Carter Burke becomes the surrogate irrational robot because of the parallels that can be drawn between the characters Burke and Ash.

In the fourth part, "The Devil Made Me," space horror is viewed from demonic and paranormal perspectives. In "Betwixt and Between: Magic, Science and the Devil's Place in Outer Space," Andrew P. Williams explores the influence of 1970s demonic films on space horror films. Using *The Dark Side of the Moon* (1990, D.J. Webster), *Hellraiser: Bloodline* and *Event Horizon*, Williams examines the implications of adding the Devil and demonic entities to a genre typically populated by characters with backgrounds rooted in the sciences. In these films, there is the added moral complexity the characters must reconcile as well as physical survival. Simon Bacon focuses on the vampiric nature of planets, black holes, or other singularities that feed off of space travelers who happen to pass within orbital range of the entity. Utilizing Jean Baudrillard's stimulation and simulacra theory, Bacon argues in "Under the Influence: Undead Planets and Vampiric Dreamworlds in Outer Space" that entities act as doppelgangers to Earth, as witnessed in such films as *Planet of the Vampires, Solaris* (1972; 2002, Steven Soderbergh), *Interstellar* (2014, Christopher Nolan), and *Event Horizon.*

In the fifth part, "Play It Again or Rip It Off," Charles W. Reick applies post-modern and post-human philosophies to *Alien Resurrection* (1997, Jean-Pierre Jeunet) in "A 'family of displaced figures': Posthumanism and Jean-Pierre Jeunet's *Alien Resurrection* (1997)." Reick argues that a disorientation and fragmented identity exists, particularly in Ripley's character, but can also pertain to the family unit that Elgyn (Michael Wincott) and his crew fulfill. In "Galaxies of Terror in a Knock-Off Universe: Atavism and the Rip-Off Body Horror of '*Alien*sploitation' Films," Jason Davis revisits and examines the subtext of *Alien* rip-off films through the lens of atavism. Davis argues that there is a collapse or implosion of structure in the civilized community by studying *Inseminoid* (1981, Norman J. Warren), *Galaxy of Terror* (1981, Bruce D. Clark), *XTRO* (1983, Harry Bromley Davenport), *Contamination* (1980, Luigi Cozzi) and other low-budget films that utilized the *Alien* blueprint. In the last essay, "*Leprechaun 4* and *Jason X*: Camp, Paracinema and the Postmodern Sequel," Kevin Chabot studies the novelty created by placing the franchises in space, and he analyzes the films for their insight into the space horror genre of the late 20th century.

In his seminal "Nightmare and the Horror Film: The Symbolic Biology of Fantastic Beings," Noëll Carroll asserted that "psychoanalysis is more or less the *lingua franca* of the horror film" and that "conflict between attraction and repulsion is particularly useful in considering the horror film."[6] What emerges from the selection of essays presented in this collection is that space horror is a legitimate subgenre, birthed from the marriage of horror and science fiction. Space horrors have moved beyond a purely visceral experience that originally emphasized feelings of powerlessness and vulnerability, shifting to the baser instinct of survival, which represented societal "depression, recession, Cold War strife, galloping inflation, and national confusion."[7] The films in this subgenre are becoming more complex in their narrative structure, at times revisiting older plots in which subtexts are re-imagined and re-purposed to convey the current societal concerns and fears. Hence, the subgenre is ripe for rigorous scholastic evaluation, not only from a psychological perspective but also from any number of philosophical and post-modern theories and interdisciplinary approaches.

NOTES

1. Guillermo del Toro, "Haunted Castles, Dark Mirrors," in *American Supernatural Tales*, ed. S. T. Joshi (New York: Penguin Books, 2013), xiii–xiv.
2. Carol Clover, *Men, Women, and Chainsaws: Gender in the Modern Horror Film* (Princeton: Princeton University Press, 1992).
3. Masahiro Mori, "The Uncanny Valley: The Original Essay by Masahiro Mori," *IEEE Spectrum*, trans. Karl F. MacDorman and Norri Kageki, June 12, 2012, http://spectrum.ieee.org/automaton/robotics/humanoids/the-uncanny-valley.
4. Ashley Miller, "A Trip to Mars," *YouTube*, https://www.youtube.com/watch?v=np7VImsSMQM.
5. "A Trip to Mars," *Scifist*, https://scifist.wordpress.com/2014/08/31/a-trip-to-mars-2/#more-762.
6. Noëll Carroll, "Nightmare and the Horror Film: The Symbolic Biology of Fantastic Beings," *Film Quarterly* 34, no. 3 (Spring 1981): 17.
7. *Ibid.*, 16.

BIBLIOGRAPHY

Carroll, Noëll. "Nightmare and the Horror Film: The Symbolic Biology of Fantastic Beings." *Film Quarterly* 34, no. 3 (Spring 1981): 16–25.

Clover, Carol. *Men, Women, and Chainsaws: Gender in the Modern Horror Film.* Princeton: Princeton University Press, 1992.

del Toro, Guillermo. "Haunted Castles, Dark Mirrors." In *American Supernatural Tales*, edited by S. T. Joshi, xiii–xxx. New York: Penguin Books, 2013.

Miller, Ashley. "A Trip to Mars." *YouTube.* https://www.youtube.com/watch?v=np7VImsS-MQM.

Mori, Masahiro. "The Uncanny Valley: The Original Essay by Masahiro Mori." *IEEE Spectrum.* Translated by Karl F. MacDorman and Norri Kageki, June 12, 2012. http://spectrum.ieee.org/automaton/robotics/humanoids/the-uncanny-valley.

SciFist. "A Trip to Mars." https://scifist.wordpress.com/2014/08/31/a-trip-to-mars-2/#more-762.

John Carpenter of Mars

Space Horror in the Films of John Carpenter

BEN KOOYMAN

John Carpenter's *modus operandi* as a filmmaker is to "be invisible. I try not to show off."[1] Yet the director's body of work is one of the most recognizable and imitated in genre cinema, his films identifiable by their economical characterization, widescreen photography, black comic leanings, and self-composed synthesizer scores. John Kenneth Muir praises Carpenter as "arguably the most consistent of all the film directors working today. In style, in composition, in technique, in sound, and even in mood and texture, he rarely strays from his own personal ethos."[2] As frequent collaborator Kurt Russell once told the director, "You can see ten seconds of any of your movies and know they're yours."[3]

Much has been made of Carpenter's affinity for Westerns, his career in horror, and his eclectic filmography and un-showy direction in the same vein as his idol Howard Hawks. However, little attention has been given to his repeated excursions into the realm of space horror. The filmmaker was raised on a steady diet of space monster pictures: a key moment in his burgeoning film-going education was watching *It Came from Outer Space* (1953, Jack Arnold) at the age of five.[4] The original *The Thing from Another World* (1951, Howard Hawks and Christian Nyby) was another personal favorite of the young Carpenter,[5] as was the more benevolent *Forbidden Planet* (1956, Fred M. Wilcox).[6] Carpenter was such a fan that he wrote and self-published genre fanzines as a teenager.[7] Moreover, his earliest film productions, made during adolescence, were riffs on the space horror features of the day bearing the sorts of titles—*Revenge of the Colossal Beasts* (1962), *Sorcerer from Outer Space* (1969), *Terror from Space* (1963)—that would not have looked out of place on a theatre marquee.[8] Friend and future collaborator Tommy Lee Wallace recalls:

In our town, monsters and aliens were a constant threat—at least they were to movie-loving kids with big imaginations. Since his adolescence, Navy jets had regularly taken off from John's living room carpet to help fight the good fight. These plans were yanked by wires you could see, and the stop-motion creatures they attacked were fairly crude.[9]

Consequently, it is not surprising that Carpenter would return to the genre of space horror throughout his professional career. Indeed, his 27-year career as a consistently working feature film director would be bookended and punctuated at key intervals by space horror films.[10]

Carpenter's first space horror project and debut feature, *Dark Star* (1974), sees a group of astronauts comically menaced by an alien resembling a beach ball. *Ghosts of Mars* (2001), his final film before entering semi-retirement, pits futuristic police against miners possessed by deceased Martians on the red planet. In between, Carpenter helmed two instances of Earthbound space horror: *The Thing* (1982), produced at the height of Carpenter's fame and power as an auteur, where a crew of scientists battle a lethal, shape-shifting alien parasite in the Antarctic, and *They Live* (1988), filmed later that decade, which sees a clueless drifter stumble upon an alien invasion conspiracy. Vivian Carol Sobchack argues that the horror film tends to deal with "moral chaos, the disruption of natural order (assumed to be God's order), and the threat to the harmony of hearth and home" while "the SF film ... is concerned with social chaos, the disruption of social order (man-made), and the threat to the harmony of civilized society going about its business."[11] *The Thing* and *They Live*, the best of this quartet of films, embody and combine these different characteristics. Moreover, these space horror films reflect the shifting culture of the times—from *Dark Star*'s intergalactic hippies to the combustible paranoia of *The Thing* to *They Live*'s savage critique of the Reagan era—as well as chronicling their director's relationship to these eras.

This essay adopts an auteur-centric approach to the space horror films of John Carpenter, himself "an outspoken proponent of the auteur theory."[12] Within this framework, it examines these films from a number of perspectives: as markers of their director's career trajectory, authorial evolution, and professional highs and lows; as reflections of and vessels for exploring his thematic, cinematic, and political preoccupations; and as chronicles of his shifting attitudes towards Hollywood and American culture more broadly. In doing so, this essay also testifies to the fluidity of space horror as a canvas for repeated authorial visitation.

Dark Star

Dark Star (1974) revolves around the spacefaring exploits, or lack thereof, of four astronauts—Doolittle (Brian Narelle), Pinback (Dan O'Bannon),

Boiler (Cal Kuniholm), and Talby (Dre Pahich)—as they drift through space blowing up unstable planets. These astronauts are not the clean-cut explorers and idealists of television's *Star Trek* (1966–1969) or Stanley Kubrick's *2001: A Space Odyssey* (1968), a film that *Dark Star* riffed on in its conception and later in its marketing as "A Spaced Out Odyssey." Rather, they are unshaven hippies and slackers, their ship is a pigsty, and while they have a mission they are ultimately apathetic and rudderless: "Find me something to blow up,"[13] proclaims Doolittle in a particular moment of exasperation. Later in the film, when Pinback muses whether they will ever find intelligent life in the galaxy, Doolittle snipes, "Who cares?"[14] Carpenter would aptly characterize the film as "*Waiting for Godot* in space."[15]

Dark Star was Carpenter's debut feature film. Written by the director and O'Bannon—who in addition to co-writing and co-starring also served as special effects supervisor, editor, and production designer, among other duties[16]—production began on *Dark Star* in 1970. It was then simply intended as Carpenter's Master's thesis project at the University of Southern California film school, but following graduation in 1972 the director and O'Bannon sought funds to expand the 45-minute work into a feature film.[17] Funds were secured and additional footage was shot to expand the film's running time as well as inject more humor and nudge the D.I.Y. feature into comedic terrain. Collaborator Tommy Lee Wallace characterizes *Dark Star* as "put together with spit and chewing gums on weekends,"[18] and these seams are evident in the finished feature, released theatrically in 1974.

In addition to being Carpenter's debut feature, *Dark Star* also represented the filmmaker's first professional (to a degree) foray into space horror. However, the space horror here is much more comedic than Carpenter's later ventures into this genre. In an extended episode from the film's rather episodic narrative, Pinback is tasked with feeding an alien creature he recently adopted because it looked cute. The creature resembles a large red beach ball with two feet, and is clearly constructed from a beach ball. At first glance the creature does not appear malevolent: rather, it appears to be a playful if brattish animal who stirs up trouble for its master, rejecting the day's food offerings and then escaping when Pinback starts cleaning the cage. However, as Pinback gives pursuit down the corridors, shafts and back passages of the ship—a comedic precursor to the final act of *Alien* (1979, Ridley Scott), a film originally scripted by O'Bannon—the creature proves itself far more dangerous than its external appearance and goofy voice suggest. The creature is violent, cunning, and a strategist: it jumps on and claws at Pinback, hits him with his own broomstick, traps him in an elevator shaft, and almost destroys the vessel by tampering with the ship's machinery. Pinback eventually corners the creature and shoots and deflates it, ending its puckish existence.

This alien antagonist was not part of Carpenter's original student film.

Scenes featuring the creature were conceived and added subsequently, as part of the filmmakers' efforts to expand their project into a commercial feature length product. The inspiration for the chintzy design struck when the filmmakers saw someone walk past carrying a beach ball, and they were inspired by both its economic pragmatism and comic potential: as O'Bannon mused, "we couldn't do real, so how about going for funny?"[19] The design is a testament to the film's and its makers' low budget ingenuity, but also their inherent narrative limitations: that is to say, Carpenter and O'Bannon handle the creature and its surrounding set pieces with considerable low budget skill, but both creature and set pieces never rise beyond a one-joke premise. Jason Zinoman invests the proceedings with literary weight and meaning, contending that Carpenter and O'Bannon, taking a leaf out of H.P. Lovecraft's work, seize upon "the necessity of rooting the magical or supernatural in a palpable realism."[20] Certainly later works by these creators—Carpenter's *The Thing*, O'Bannon's *Alien*—reflect this Lovecraftian ethos, but *Dark Star*'s antagonist and threat, while tactile, is too heightened and ridiculous to be palpably real.

Yet while its antagonist is comedic and the film errs towards humor, the specter of space as a dangerous, hostile environment hangs over *Dark Star*, and not simply due to the escalating cabin fever of the astronauts. Space is, as Kendall R. Phillips observes, "a dangerously unstable place" in the film.[21] The crew's mission, to destroy unstable planets, suggests that if any of these already unstable planets destabilized further it could be calamitous for other planets and those inhabiting them. Moreover, those inhabitants and the explorers at the film's center pale alongside the vast scale and complexity of outer space. Marketing materials that riffed on and contrasted the film with *2001: A Space Odyssey* were apt, and not simply based on the film's surface-level differences (i.e. explorers versus slackers, cleanliness versus filth and grunge, grand scale versus small scale, big budget versus no budget). John Kenneth Muir suggests the films are inherently opposed thematically and philosophically:

> Where *2001* finds that man's place in the universe is a significant one, *Dark Star* alternately believes it to be wholly insignificant…. *Dark Star* does not exist in a realm where the universe cares about or even appreciates man. Conversely, man is a lost and solitary creation in *Dark Star*.[22]

In this respect the film is evocative of Lovecraft, and this theme of humanity's hopelessness in the face of the horrors of space reverberates even more explicitly through Carpenter's subsequent space horror films, though there the threat of space is embodied more explicitly in more pointedly horrific monsters than *Dark Star*'s goofy beach ball-shaped antagonist.

Thus *Dark Star*, while a relatively minor work in truth, lays the foundations for Carpenter's later forays into space horror. Moreover, through Dan

O'Bannon's involvement, it also represents the foundations of a much broader body of cinematic space horror. Following *Dark Star*, O'Bannon worked with Alejandro Jodorowsky on his ultimately doomed attempt to adapt Frank Herbert's novel *Dune* for the screen. While Jodorowsky's film never materialized, its designs and vision would be pillaged by science fiction cinema over the next decade. Subsequently, O'Bannon scripted *Alien* as well as bringing designer H.R. Giger (another *Dune* veteran) to the project, which not only launched an ongoing franchise but also shaped the next few decades of space horror. Carpenter's next excursion into space horror, meanwhile, would be Earthbound.

The Thing

In the years following *Dark Star*, Carpenter showcased his low-budget spunk with *Assault on Precinct 13* (1976) and *Halloween* (1978), a film which fanned the flames of slasher cinema and for a time was the most successful independent production in history. He also directed *Someone's Watching Me!* (1978) and *Elvis* (1979) for television, and graduated to bigger, though still modestly-budgeted, features with *The Fog* (1980) and *Escape from New York* (1981). *The Thing* (1982) is Carpenter's adaptation of John W. Campbell, Jr.'s 1938 novella *Who Goes There?* Campbell's novella had already been adapted for the screen in 1951 as *The Thing from Another World,* directed by Christian Nyby and Howard Hawks.[23] With *The Thing*, Carpenter built upon the esteemed original and other space horror schlock of the 1950s in striking ways, extending the subgenre's visual and visceral possibilities in an era which had radically shifted and expanded what audiences find horrific (most notably in the material turn to body horror). He also found modern equivalents for the 1950s anxieties and paradigms of thought expressed in those films, such as fear of Communist peril. It was the director's largest and most ambitious undertaking yet: where *Dark Star* was made with no budget and a beach ball, *The Thing* was a major Hollywood production with all the bells, whistles, and luxuries afforded by studio money and resources. The result was, Phillips suggests, "the most cinematically accomplished film of his career,"[24] though it proved to be too effective for its own good, turning the stomachs of its earliest viewers.

The film takes place in Antarctica, where the daily grind at an American science base is disrupted by the arrival of a helicopter from a nearby Norwegian base, its pilots in pursuit of and firing shots at a fleeing dog. The dog runs for cover among the American scientists, who, fearing the armed and hostile Norwegians have lost their minds, are forced to gun them down. A small crew visits the Norwegian base to find a bloodbath has transpired. They also discover the charred and twisted remains of a creature, and see that something has been excavated from the ice. Back at the American base, the dog that took refuge undergoes a grotesque and messy transformation, shedding its dog shape, spewing liquid, and sprouting legs and claws. It transpires that the creature in the shape of the pursued dog crashed on Earth 100,000 years ago. The Norwegian team excavated it, the thawed-out creature wreaked havoc at their base, and it is now poised to do the same amongst the Americans.

The dog is just the first shape that "the Thing" adopts over the course of the film. Blair (Wilfred Brimley) surmises that the Thing is an "organism that imitates other life forms"[25] it comes into contact with, and in the process absorbs whoever or whatever it imitates. Consequently, the crew of the science base—a dozen men in total—cannot be certain whether or not one of their colleagues is really the Thing. While it can perfectly adopt a human or animal shape, in the thick of transformation or under attack the Thing is an ugly and abject spectacle, with the creature reconstituting itself in grisly detail and revealing aspects of its former guises in the process. For example, at one point the Thing takes on the shape of Norris (Charles Hallahan), who is feared dead. When Copper (Richard Dysart) uses a defibulator on Norris's chest to revive him, it reacts by transforming Norris's chest and stomach into a jaw and snapping off Copper's hands. When Macready (Kurt Russell) blasts it with a flamethrower, the Norris-shaped head tears free from the body, sprouts spider-like legs, and attempts to discretely slip out of the room before being spotted and flamed by Macready. As stated in the film, "It could have imitated a million lifeforms on a million planets. It could change into any one of them at any time,"[26] and in these set pieces the viewer is privy to some of the different shapes and incarnations of the creature amidst the gruesome spectacle.

While the film is, as its credits proclaim, "John Carpenter's The Thing," the film features the work of a number of gifted collaborators excelling at the peak of their professions: not just Carpenter, but leading man Kurt Russell, cinematographer Dean Cundey, and composer Ennio Morricone among others. Another gifted collaborator, and instrumental in the conception of the Thing, was visual and makeup effects designer Rob Bottin. Carpenter was adamant upon undertaking the project that he "didn't want to end up with … a guy in a suit. You see, I grew up as a kid watching science fiction and monster movies and it was always a guy in a suit."[27] Bottin helped conceive of the Thing as a shapeshifter. As Carpenter elaborates:

> Rob's concept was that the "Thing" could do anything. It doesn't look like any one particular entity, and has no respect for what it imitates. It can look like a million life-forms from a million different planets. That gave me the opportunity to do things that have never been done in a movie.[28]

Muir notes that one of the film's two main themes is "the frailty of human flesh."[29] Bottin's practical, tactile, visceral effects work—graphic displays of animals and humans shedding and changing shape, contorting and cracking matter, spewing abject liquids, sprouting earthly and alien appendages—assert the human body's susceptibility to attack and transformation, reinforcing "how desperately vulnerable human flesh is to external attack, perversion, and even subversion."[30] Moreover, these depictions of bodies falling apart and under parasitic attack, and Macready's use of a blood test at a key juncture to identify who is the Thing, found unexpected resonance with the AIDS virus, then emerging and at the forefront of media fear mongering and speculation. Carpenter recalls reading

> a little article in the paper ... about some kind of new disease that was occurring. It was called AIDS and people were dying, and it was very weirdly similar in dynamic to what we were doing because you couldn't tell who had it.... You would have to do a blood test to find out.[31]

Muir identifies the other key theme of the film as "the dehumanisation of man and his increasing paranoia in the modern age."[32] The uncertainty around who is or is not the Thing—much like the uncertainty of who did or did not carry the AIDS virus—and the atmosphere of fear and paranoia this generates are a central preoccupation of the film. Carpenter reflects:

> *The Thing* has to do essentially—even though there is this extra-terrestrial virus—with losing your humanity and losing humanness. The "Thing" can stand for anything: it can stand for greed, for jealousy, for any kind of cliché evils that human beings are totally privy to ... it's about being afraid that the people you are interacting with are not human.[33]

As fear and paranoia escalate at the base, tensions and interpersonal conflicts flare up between members of the crew, who turn on, tie up, badmouth, forsake, and ultimately must destroy each other. This contrasts with the tone of the original film, which, Phillips notes, "relied on the optimism that the alien invasion ... would be battled back by the bravery and ingenuity of the film's heroes. In Carpenter's film, as with other pictures of this period ... the alien invasion seems insurmountable."[34] There is teamwork and collaboration, but there is also distrust, animosity, and decreasing solidarity between members of the crew as the film progresses. By film's end, only two survivors remain—Macready and Childs (Keith David)—and neither can be sure that the other is not the Thing. Sitting in the snow, their base burning in the background, in the thick of the Antarctic winter, they resolve to "just wait here for a little while. See what happens,"[35] the likely endpoint being either simultaneously freezing to death or one of them killing the other. It is understandable why Carpenter nicknames *The Thing* the first entry in his "apocalypse trilogy," alongside *Prince of Darkness* (1987) and *In the Mouth of Madness* (1994).[36]

This apocalyptic tone and defeatist, pessimistic ending, as well as the film's stomach-turning violent effects, contributed to its poor commercial run and critical lambasting in the summer of 1982. The success of Steven Spielberg's *E.T. The Extra-Terrestrial* (1982) and its positive, uplifting depiction of human-alien relations earlier in the summer—of that film's protagonist and his own film's antagonist, Carpenter muses "Theirs was sweet and ours was mean"[37]—is frequently evoked as a cause for the film's commercial failure. This impacted not only Carpenter's career, as will be touched on in later sections, but also the horror genre more broadly. A few years after its release, Kim Newman noted that its commercial failure, along with those of *Day of the Dead* (1985, George Romero), *Videodrome* (1983, David Cronenberg), and *The Keep* (1983, Michael Mann), had turned serious, non-camp horror into "an endangered species."[38] It was certainly the last entirely serious, non-camp horror Carpenter would helm, and 30 years later Phillips identifies *The Thing* as drawing to a close the golden era of horror initiated by *Night of the Living Dead* (1968, George Romero).[39]

However, the very qualities that resulted in the film's commercial failure—its lack of niceties and refusal to curtail to mainstream sensibilities, its uncompromising depiction of the human body and spirit under attack—are those qualities which now clearly mark *The Thing* as a peak of both the genre and its director's career. Moreover, as Carpenter's second foray into space horror, it marked a radical shift from *Dark Star*. Both films feature a small crew trapped in an isolated outpost being menaced by an alien antagonist. But where *Dark Star* milks its scenario for comic effect and its creature is entirely alien in appearance, *The Thing* milks its scenario for horror and invests its otherworldly antagonist with insidiousness precisely because it is able to infiltrate human society and pass unknown among us. In doing so, *The Thing* also dramatizes the competing human impulses to find solidarity with and turn upon each other during times of duress. These themes of vulnerability to alien invasion and infiltration, and the corresponding threat of dehumanization, would be explored further by Carpenter six years later in *They Live*, albeit with some of the subversive comedy of *Dark Star* serving as counterpoint to the horror.

They Live

Just as *Citizen Kane* (1941) was for wunderkind Orson Welles, *The Thing* arguably represented John Carpenter's peak, a testament to what he could accomplish with generous financing, top resources and collaborators, and artistic freedom. And like Welles in the aftermath of *Citizen Kane*'s commercial failure, Carpenter would be forced in the aftermath of *The Thing* to compromise on subsequent productions. The director says of the film's wintry reception that "I can't think of a way it didn't change my career. It was a total revolution from top to bottom."[40] He elaborates:

> Not only was it a box-office failure in their eyes, but it was an artistic failure. I was treated like slime. I was just good to lie down with the dogs. I was the guy who was doing this kind of pornographic violence. I really didn't know what to do, and truly [when you are in that position] you don't think about your artistic vision but about survival.[41]

Consequently, Carpenter's later films would be cheaper, and *The Thing* would be the last serious balls-to-the-wall horror film he made. He would of course continue in the genre, though often with tongue firmly in cheek, and even his other "apocalyptic" horror films, *Prince of Darkness* and *In the Mouth of Madness*, would be threaded with knowing camp. He reflects: "I adapted myself to the new reality. I don't think I ever made a more savage or as bleak a movie…. And I think that I probably won't."[42] However, while it is not as savage as *The Thing*, *They Live* is still a deeply pessimistic film, its bitterness offset by strategic moments of comic book pulp and comedic levity.

Following his Stephen King adaptation *Christine* (1983), a more uplifting depiction of human-alien relations in *Starman* (1984), the kung-fu action comedy *Big Trouble in Little China* (1986), and his second apocalyptic feature *Prince of Darkness* (1987), *They Live* marked Carpenter's return to space horror. The film opens Western-style with drifter Nada (Roddy Piper) wandering into town. Over the course of the film's opening credits, we see Nada wandering the city observing poverty and hardship firsthand, as well as apathy towards the struggling and unemployed. He also observes people hypnotized by their television sets, distracted from these unpleasant realities. Despite all this, Nada remains optimistic about his future and his nation, telling his cynical friend Frank (Keith David) "I believe in America. I follow the rules."[43] However, despite or perhaps because of this idealism, Nada is also the first to recognize fracture lines in this façade.

Nada comes into possession of a box full of special sunglasses which, when worn, enable the wearer to see and fully comprehend the cause of these social inequities. This transformation of an everyday object to invest it with otherworldly power and menace is a recurring motif in Carpenter's films: in *Halloween* he took a generic William Shatner mask and sculpted a horror icon from it, while in *Christine* a 1958 Red Plymouth Fury becomes a source of horror. This motif also materializes in his earlier space horror films: a beach ball becomes a mischievous extra-terrestrial in *Dark Star*, while a dog houses an alien parasite in *The Thing*. In *They Live*, the sunglasses are not an object of horror but a window to it. When Nada first wears the sunglasses, he is able to see subliminal messages underlying the advertising and media surrounding him. As he walks down the street and looks at billboards, street signs, magazine and newspaper covers, television screens, and consumer products, he finds messages like OBEY, NO INDEPENDENT THOUGHT, CONSUME, CONFORM, BUY, NO THOUGHT, SLEEP, MARRY AND REPRODUCE, WATCH TV, SUBMIT, STAY ASLEEP, DO NOT QUESTION AUTHORITY, and NO IMAGINATION in bold capital letters.[44] Monetary notes also carry the message THIS IS YOUR GOD, and satellites circulate the hypnotic signal SLEEP through the city streets.[45] In addition, the sunglasses enable him to see aliens among us disguised as people: when the glasses are worn, these aliens are visible and distinguishable by their skull-like faces and bulging eyes. Or as Nada quips to one of them, "You look like your head fell in a cheese dip back in 1957.... Real fuckin' ugly."[46]

These aliens—harking from the planet Andromeda—monopolize the country's financial wealth and occupy the higher echelon of Earth society. It thus becomes evident that an alien race is controlling the distribution of power, wealth, and authority in contemporary America and exerting dominion subliminally over the human race. This unsettles the idealistic Nada: as Phillips notes, "Nada undergoes disillusionment with the American promise that hard work and obedient behaviour will lead to prosperity, and in the process he opens his eyes to the economic and political injustices of his world."[47] At first Nada is shaken, but then he becomes empowered to fight back against these oppressors and to "chew bubble-gum and kick ass."[48]

The aliens in *They Live* mark a significant departure from those in *Dark Star* and *The Thing*. Where those creatures are animalistic beings, albeit cunning ones, the aliens in *They Live* are, as one resistance leader notes, "free enterprisers. The Earth is just another developing planet. Their third world."[49] Humans are merely the aliens' "livestock," and their objective is to "deplete the planet and move onto another."[50] Casting the aliens in the role of the exploitative power elite enabled the typically apolitical Carpenter to mount political commentary on what he perceived to be the outrageous consumerism and inequities of the Reagan era. While Carpenter characterizes himself as being "pretty apolitical all my life,"[51] he was compelled to explore this terrain because

> I got fed up with being told over and over again that it was so beneficial to be a consumer. We are no longer producing anything in the United States. We are just consuming and eating our way through. We are buying things, accumulating things, throwing money away, but we aren't making anything good anymore. It was just starting to outrage me.[52]

The use of aliens as authority and power figures symbolizes the inherent lack of humanity in the political and capitalist machine, and their use of subliminal control parodies the increasing dehumanization of the media and consumers. While Carpenter's targets—the rich, the media, and the law—are easy and well-worn (indeed, bordering on straw men), the filmmaker also pointedly shows their detrimental effect on the impoverished and disenfranchised, particularly in the film's first act. As Muir notes:

> Carpenter sees poverty, homelessness, unemployment, racial prejudice and violence as the result of … the Reagan era of voodoo economics in which the wealth never really trickled down beyond the most financially successful "upper" echelon of American society.[53]

Under the film's variation on Reaganism, human beings are both unwittingly and willingly enslaved to the alien invaders: the destruction of the human is not physical, as it is in *The Thing*, but commercial and cultural. Where the alien menace in *The Thing* preyed upon humanity's paranoia and ruthless will to survive, the aliens of *They Live* prey upon different human flaws, namely greed for material objects and the need to consume, which in turn feed the pockets of the extra-terrestrial elite. In addition, it is revealed that a number of humans, including supposed accomplice Holly (Meg Foster), already know about and are consciously serving the interests of the aliens for considerable monetary reward. Consequently, *They Live* serves as a potent parody, as Phillips observes, of "the shining optimism of Reagan's rhetoric."[54] It is worth noting that this very same rhetoric and the cultural mood it generated contributed to the film-going public's embrace of *E.T. The Extra-Terrestrial* and rejection of *The Thing* six years earlier.

From *Dark Star*—his grimy, alternative take on *2001*—onwards, Carpenter has demonstrated a subversive streak. Muir calls him "a symbol of subversive filmmaking" and praises *They Live* as "his most ambitious and well-articulated jab at authority."[55] Yet *They Live* is not merely a jab at the power elite, but, in the same vein as recent blockbuster series *The Hunger Games* (2012–2015), a rallying call to audiences disguised as populist entertainment, urging them to shake off their apathy. The sequence which best embodies this impulse is an extended fight scene between Nada and Frank, where Nada tries to convince and then eventually forces Frank to put on the sunglasses. Actor Roddy Piper was also a professional wrestler, and the scene is evocative of a World Wrestling Federation showdown. On the surface the fight appears goofy and indulgent: as Muir observes, there is "no real dramatically motivated reason for Frank and Nada to fight one another."[56] However, given that the dramatic purpose of the scene is to persuade Frank to wear the glasses and thus see the truth of the situation, the scene dramatizes and provides an effective metaphor for the difficulty of making someone see the truth. In this respect, the extended fisticuffs are dramatically and thematically motivated and apt. At scene's end, after great struggle, Frank does wear the glasses and does comprehend the situation: with great effort and resilience, the fog of consumerism and apathy can be cut through.

It is ironic that of Carpenter's four space horror features, *They Live*, the most patently anti-consumerist and anti-capitalist, was the only one to be a box office success. Yet it is also not surprising: where *Dark Star* is unpolished and niche and *The Thing* is vicious and unrelenting, *They Live* explores those films' themes—invasion, infiltration, dehumanization, and the utter insignificance of humanity in the face of unknown and powerful extra-terrestrial forces—in a less claustrophobic, more outwardly comedic and mainstream package. Moreover, in its scenario of a drifter wandering into town, uncovering injustice, and partnering with a small band of locals to remedy the situation, the film evokes the trappings of the Western. So too would Carpenter's fourth and final space horror film 13 years later, *Ghosts of Mars*.

Ghosts of Mars

In the 13 years between *They Live* and *Ghosts of Mars* (2001), Carpenter's output was critically and commercially checkered, but still testified to his eclecticism with subject matter: an effects-heavy, major studio Chevy Chase vehicle with *Memoirs of an Invisible Man* (1992); a TV anthology film in the EC Comics tradition called *Body Bags* (1993), in which Carpenter also plays the ghoulish host; the Lovecraftian finale to his apocalypse trilogy, *In the Mouth of Madness* (1994); a flat remake of *Village of the Damned* (1995); the satirical sequel *Escape from L.A.* (1996); and creature horror *Vampires* (1998). This last film also carried a Western flavor, which *Ghosts of Mars* would indulge even further.

While Carpenter was and is, as discussed earlier, a big science fiction fan, his widely noted true love is Westerns. The classical Western was the dominant film genre of Carpenter's youth and a cinema staple of his formative years, as well as a specialty of his idol Howard Hawks. However, the genre was on its way out as Carpenter's career was getting started: spaghetti, acid, and revisionist Westerns would extend its cinematic life, but the classical Western was largely bygone. Consequently, he and his generation—Spielberg, Lucas, and others of that ilk—would, Maddrey notes, turn to "the next great American frontier: outer space."[57] The original *Star Trek*, envisioned as "*Wagon Train* in Space" by creator Gene Rodenberry, provided precedent for this conflation of American frontier and final frontier. Carpenter reflects, "I got into this business wanting to make Westerns. And that just hasn't worked out. I made some Westerns, but they're not really Westerns. They're hidden Westerns."[58] Western tropes and themes permeate his films: Maddrey notes the Western motif of "the last stand" in a number of his films, including *The*

Thing and *Ghosts of Mars*,[59] while Phillips sees a number of Carpenter's films as frontier narratives.[60] Indeed, the frontier and its tropes figure into all four of Carpenter's space horror films: *Dark Star*, *The Thing* and *Ghosts of Mars* feature siege narratives about invading forces overtaking isolated outposts; *Ghosts of Mars* examines the impact of indigenous occupants of the land revolting against invaders; and *They Live* takes as its protagonist a drifter-hero who wanders into town and into a whole mess of trouble.

Ghosts of Mars is the most explicitly Western-influenced of Carpenter's space horror films, and possibly the most Western-derived of his filmography. Maddrey dubs the film "a pretty straightforward game of 'cowboys and Indians' set in a Martian terraform colony."[61] He elaborates:

> The characters and plot structure are culled straight out of *Rio Bravo* and *Assault on Precinct 13*, reinforcing Carpenter's belief that, even in the distant future when we're faced with the new frontiers, the Western mythology will always be a part of the American story.[62]

Moreover, as Phillips observes, "principal locations on Mars resemble dusty frontier towns of the Old West."[63] The film also afforded Carpenter an opportunity to make a Mars-set film, which had long been an ambition. He explains:

> I've wanted to make a Mars movie since the 1980s for three reasons: nostalgia, the colour, the symbolism. Nostalgia for all the "attack from space" science fiction movies I saw as a kid. The colour, red—I thought it would be a challenge to make a whole film on the red planet and not annoy the audience or fatigue them with the colour. And finally, the symbolism: Mars has always been a supernatural/superior force in human affairs. We've projected our own darker emotions upon the planet: love, death, war, lust.[64]

The film thus represented an opportunity for Carpenter to synthesize his love of science fiction and the Western, as well as an opportunity to merge Martian iconography and its thematic potential with the iconography and themes of the Old West.

Ghosts of Mars takes place in AD 2127, on a Mars that has been terraformed into an Earth-like environment. Over establishing shots of the planet from outer space, the opening narration informs the viewer that something is amiss on this red world: "Something that has been buried for centuries has just been uncovered. And as this mysterious force moves across the southern valley, it leaves behind only silence and death."[65] The film then cuts to the planet's surface and an armored train charging through the dusty Martian desert to the town of Chryse. It is apt that the first vehicle glimpsed in Carpenter's film is not a spaceship or similarly airborne vehicle but a train, given the pivotal role of the train and railroad in the West and, more significantly, Western films such as *High Noon* (1952, Fred Zinnemann), *3.10 to Yuma* (1957, Delmer Daves), and *Once Upon a Time in the West* (1968, Sergio

Leone). Once arrived, the authorities find the train has been deserted, bar a member of the Mars Police Force, Lieutenant Melanie Ballard (Natasha Henstridge, star and antagonist of another notable space horror: *Species*, 1995, Roger Donaldson). In a flashback, Ballard recounts the botched mission that led to her arrival.

Ballard was one of a crew of five officers tasked with escorting prisoner Desolation Williams (Ice Cube) from Shining Canyon to Chryse. Shining Canyon is a small outpost mining town, with a main street and a couple of dozen buildings, surrounded on all sides by canyon walls. It resembles the many small towns that peppered the West of both real life and Westerns, and Ballard describes the desolate canyon town as "a graveyard" on first sight. On closer inspection, they discover it is indeed a graveyard: decapitated corpses have been strung upside down inside the town casino, the surviving townsfolk are acting violent and unhinged, and posts have been decorated with severed heads, among other horrific sights. Sergeant Jericho (Jason Statham) uncovers the perpetrators: an army of 200 miners who have been possessed and transformed into savages—or "fucking freaks,"[66] to borrow Jericho's parlance—under the leadership of the imposing Big Daddy (Richard Cetrone). It is revealed that the miners are possessed by the spirits of the original inhabitants of Mars, which were released in gaseous form when excavations unearthed and opened a literal "Pandora's Box." A red storm washed across the Martian terrain into Shining Canyon, possessing these townsfolk with the spirits of the indigenous Martians.

There is an obvious Cowboys and Indians symbolism to the oppositional relationship between Earth colonists and indigenous Martians. According to Carpenter:

> The theme of *Ghosts of Mars* is one of dominion and what it means. The ancient Martian civilisation, long extinct in the story, no longer inhabits the planet, but leaves behind a supernatural threat to any species who dares to lay claim to their world.[67]

While the Martians were not literally dispossessed of their land by the settlers as the American Indians were, they nonetheless have an antecedent claim on the planet, thus the analogy of Earthlings with cowboys and Martians with Indians resonates along historical and racial lines. In holding accountable Earth colonists for disrupting the peace of the indigenous civilization, *Ghosts of Mars* extends a thread running across Carpenter's space horror films whereby people's greed and selfishness are partially responsible for the horrors visited upon them: the astronauts of *Dark Star* are lazy slackers, the scientists of *The Thing* become paranoiacs bent only on self-preservation, and the humans of *They Live* are either unwitting consumers subservient to alien control or greedy capitalists who have sold out for material wealth and power.

In the case of *Ghosts of Mars*, the human impulse to occupy and transform the red planet into a carbon copy of Earth is the trigger for the horrors visited upon the population. Following the contentious dissolution of their working relationship after *Dark Star*, O'Bannon would say of Carpenter that "his disdain for human beings would be serviced if he could make a film without people in it."[68] While O'Bannon's comment is heavily colored by the pair's professional tensions, there is nonetheless a marked misanthropic thread running through Carpenter's work.

Where the alien menaces of *The Thing* and *They Live* invaded Earth by infiltrating and imitating humanity, in *Ghosts of Mars* the humans are on Martian turf (the invaded become the invaders) and the possessed are transformed by self-mutilating their human visages and bodies into inhuman appearances. Carpenter notes that the look of the possessed was modeled upon "research into the warrior cultures of Earth's past [which] revealed that piercing was associated with martial decorations in various tribes."[69] The possessed miners heavily pierce their faces and bodies, file their teeth, and decorate themselves with tribal ornamentation. The resulting look is warrior culture meets heavy metal meets fetish gear. Their leader Big Daddy, meanwhile, Carpenter describes as "the personification of barbaric rage"[70]—rage at the displacement, invasion, and possession of Martian soil—and he resembles a muscular Marilyn Manson, with sharp teeth, white face, and heavy metal hair: in short, a very late 1990s personification of barbaric rage.

However, as the film progresses, horror is sidelined in favor of an action-oriented variation on the director's own *Assault on Precinct 13*, with the small posse from the Mars Police Force under siege by the possessed before escaping Dodge and neutralizing the threat. As noted earlier, Carpenter's interest in generating truly vicious and visceral onscreen horror subsided after the negative reaction to *The Thing*, hence Big Daddy's barbaric rage is never more than window dressing. Nor does this barbaric rage transition into outrage: despite parallels between the film's narrative and the off-screen history of colonial displacement, *Ghosts of Mars* is fairly apolitical, unlike the pointedly political and outraged *They Live*.[71] Ultimately, the film's version of Cowboys and Indians is no more complicated than the standard classical Western, and in fairness it does not need to be.

Even so, this detachment from horror and from the political are indicative of the filmmaker's decreasing investment in his material, no doubt fanned by behind the scenes struggles on both this film and others throughout the 1990s, such as *Escape from L.A.*, where the film's budget was halved on the verge of production.[72] On the subject of *Ghosts of Mars'* production, he would later reflect, "I got burned out after my last film, in 2001,"[73] and "the stress. Jesus. It's enormous.... It just gets to you after a while."[74] This sense of disengagement for self-preservation has become part of Carpenter's public persona in the years since *Ghosts of Mars'* release: in interviews he has voiced his preference for watching basketball and playing video games over filmmaking, and plays up being cantankerous and crotchety. By way of example, in an appearance as MC for a series of horror-themed sketches on comedy website *Funny or Die* (2011), he describes his role as "introducing stupid Halloween videos" and tells viewers to "Watch this or don't watch it, I don't care."[75]

At the end of *Ghosts of Mars*, after Ballard has recounted her story, the red storm of Martian spirits washes over the city of Chryse. Like *The Thing*, the alien threat thought vanquished still lingers. She reunites with Williams, the only other survivor of the events at Shining Canyon, and they resolve to "kick some ass,"[76] opening the door for a prospective sequel. It did not materialize: the film was "a big tank," to quote Carpenter,[77] earning only $8.5 million in the U.S. on a $30 million budget.[78] In truth, it is one of Carpenter's lesser films. While there are good moments and Carpenter is a gifted-enough craftsman to make a watchable film, its shortcomings are numerous: attempts at being badass fall short; the story is told in flashbacks, with more flashbacks inside those flashbacks, making for a lumpy narrative; Carpenter's requisite synthesizer score is both too heavy and too bland; and Shining Canyon looks like a set, and a small set at that, which carries a certain classical Western and 1950s sci-fi charm but makes the film seem hokey. The film's tepid reaction and stressful production deterred Carpenter from filmmaking for a period: it would be a few years before he returned to directing with two telemovies for the anthology series *Masters of Horror* (2005–2007), and nearly a decade until his next feature, *The Ward* (2010).

Conclusion

While it is regrettable that *Ghosts of Mars* ended a solid quarter century run for the filmmaker, it is fitting that the final entry in this sustained run brought the director full circle to the subgenre where his career began with *Dark Star*, namely space horror. The fact these films are so different from each other testifies to the filmmaker's fluidity with genre and content, as well as the fluidity of space horror itself: in Carpenter's career alone, space horror takes the form of sci-fi slacker comedy, Lovecraftian horror epic, conspiracy thriller with a heavy dose of pulp and political satire, and space Western. Moreover, while the genre is not central to the director's career, it nonetheless bookends and permeates it, providing a canvas through which the director has explored various preoccupations and holding a mirror up to his cinematic evolution and shifting career fortunes. *Dark Star*, his debut feature, demonstrated his directorial promise and low-budget ingenuity in the face of financial limitations. *The Thing* showcased the director at the top of his game working with all the bells and whistles at his disposal afforded by the Hollywood studio system, as well as his drive to create visceral onscreen terror. *They Live* a few years later sees the compromised director working on a more modest scale, less interested in forging horrific imagery but voicing his frustration with 1980s American consumer culture, to which the failure of *The Thing* and his own difficult relationship with Hollywood can be attributed. Finally, *Ghosts of Mars* marks the culmination of this 27-year journey, using space horror as a means to vicariously direct in one of his favorite genres, the Western, but with little political or authorial conviction.

NOTES

1. Gilles Boulenger, *John Carpenter: The Prince of Darkness* (Los Angeles: Silman-James Press, 2001), 33.
2. John Kenneth Muir, *The Films of John Carpenter* (Jefferson, NC: McFarland, 2000), 1.
3. Mark Dinning, "*The Fog* (1979)," *Empire: The Greatest Horror Movies Ever*, no. 1 (2000), 37.
4. Jason Zinoman, *Shock Value* (New York: Penguin Press, 2011), 52.
5. *Ibid.*, 183.
6. Boulenger, *John Carpenter*, 62.
7. *Ibid.*, 27.
8. Zinoman, *Shock Value*, 52.
9. Boulenger, *John Carpenter*, 14.
10. I refer here to the 27 years spanning the release of *Dark Star* in 1974 through to *Ghosts of Mars* in 2001, excluding Carpenter's subsequent contributions to television's *Masters of Horror* (2005, 2007) and later horror feature *The Ward* (2010), released nine years after *Ghosts of Mars*. For a discussion of these projects, see Ben Kooyman, *Directorial Self-Fashioning in American Horror Cinema* (New York: Edwin Mellen Press, 2014).
11. Vivian Carol Sobchack, *Screening Space: The American Science Fiction Film*, 2d ed. (New Brunswick: Rutgers University Press, 1997), 30.
12. Muir, *The Films of John Carpenter*, 1.
13. *Dark Star*, DVD, directed by John Carpenter (1974; Tulsa: VCI Entertainment, 1999).
14. *Ibid.*
15. Zinoman, *Shock Value*, 55.
16. The extent of O'Bannon's involvement and authorship was a source of contention between the two filmmakers and ultimately drove them apart. Zinoman, *Shock Value*, 120.
17. Another USC alumni, George Lucas, also took his own science fiction student short, *Electronic Labyrinth THX 1138 4EB*, and adapted it into his first feature, *THX 1138* (1971). Yet where Carpenter expanded *Dark Star* on the cheap, Lucas forged his first feature with the support and weight of Francis Ford Coppola's Zoetrope behind him.
18. Boulenger, *John Carpenter*, 15.
19. Zinoman, *Shock Value*, 115.
20. *Ibid.*, 63.
21. Kendall R. Phillips, *Dark Directions: Romero, Craven, Carpenter, and the Modern Horror Film* (Carbondale: Southern Illinois University Press, 2012), 128.
22. Muir, *The Films of John Carpenter*, 57.
23. Though the film directly harks back to the novella rather than its 1950s precursor film, Kim Newman situates the film within a broader revival of 1950s science fiction horror at multiplexes during the 1980s. As Newman notes, new versions of *Invasion of the Body Snatchers* (1978, Philip Kaufman), *The Fly* (1986, David Cronenberg), *Invaders from Mars*

(1986, Tobe Hooper), *The Blob* (1988, Chuck Russell), and Carpenter's *The Thing* were all "expensive, colourful remakes of cheap, mainly black-and-white 1950s greats." Kim Newman, *Nightmare Movies: A Critical History of the Horror Movie from 1968*, 2d ed. (London: Bloomsbury, 1988), 171.

24. Phillips, *Dark Directions*, 5.

25. *The Thing*, DVD, directed by John Carpenter (1982; Universal City, CA: Universal, 1998).

26. *Ibid.*

27. "John Carpenter's *The Thing*: Terror Takes Shape," *The Thing*, DVD, directed by Michael Matessino (1998; Universal City, CA: Universal, 1998).

28. Muir, *The Films of John Carpenter*, 25.

29. *Ibid.*, 103.

30. *Ibid.*

31. "*The Thing* Commentary," *The Thing*, DVD, with John Carpenter and Kurt Russell (1982; Universal City, CA: Universal, 1998).

32. Muir, *The Films of John Carpenter*, 103.

33. Boulenger, *John Carpenter*, 136.

34. Phillips, *Dark Directions*, 134.

35. Dialogue from *The Thing*.

36. "*The Thing* Commentary."

37. *Ibid.*

38. Newman, *Nightmare Movies*, 211.

39. Phillips, *Dark Directions*.

40. Boulenger, *John Carpenter*, 169.

41. *Ibid.*, 173.

42. *Ibid.*, 173–175.

43. *They Live*, DVD, directed by John Carpenter (1988; Universal City, CA: Universal, 2003).

44. *Ibid.*

45. *Ibid.*

46. The look of these aliens was designed by Sandy King, Carpenter's future wife. Boulenger, *John Carpenter*, 212.

47. Phillips, *Dark Directions*, 157.

48. However, it must be said that Nada's first act of empowerment, blasting away aliens in a bank, carries a darker resonance today in the aftermath of multiple mass shootings by American citizens expressing similar disenfranchisement.

49. Dialogue from *They Live*.

50. *Ibid.*

51. Boulenger, *John Carpenter*, 40.

52. *Ibid.*, 209.

53. Muir, *The Films of John Carpenter*, 148.

54. Phillips, *Dark Directions*, 156.

55. Muir, *The Films of John Carpenter*, 39.

56. *Ibid.*, 150.

57. Joseph Maddrey, *Nightmares in Red, White and Blue: The Evolution of the American Horror Film* (Jefferson, NC: McFarland, 2004), 132.

58. *Ibid.*, 131.

59. *Ibid.*

60. Phillips, *Dark Directions*.

61. Maddrey, *Nightmares in Red, White and Blue*, 139.

62. *Ibid.*

63. Phillips, *Dark Directions*, 140.

64. *Ibid.*, 264.

65. *Ghosts of Mars*, DVD, directed by John Carpenter (2001; Culver City, CA: Screen Gems, 2001).

66. Dialogue from *Ghosts of Mars*.

67. Boulenger, *John Carpenter*, 267.
68. Zinoman, *Shock Value*, 120.
69. Boulenger, *John Carpenter*, 267.
70. *Ibid.*, 269.
71. The fact that Earth society is now matriarchal, as established in the film's opening text, is not developed further either.
72. Drew McWeeny and Scott Weinberg, "Listen: A Special Podcast Tribute to John Carpenter with Guest Scott Weinberg," *The Motion/Captured Podcast*, 2010, accessed via iTunes.
73. Jen Yamato, "John Carpenter on His Decade Away from Filmmaking, the Problem with Today's Horror, and *The Ward*," *Movie Line*, June 14, 2011, http://movieline.com/2011/06/14/john-carpenter-on-his-decade-away-from-filmmaking-his-return-with-the-ward-and-his-bloody-future/.
74. Sam Adams, "Interview: John Carpenter," *A.V. Club*, April 11, 2011, http://www.avclub.com/article/john-carpenter-54361.
75. Funny or Die, "Funny or Die Presents John Carpenter's Halloween," *Funny or Die*, October 27, 2011, http://www.funnyordie.com/videos/81bcb40457/funny-or-die-presents-john-carpenter-s-halloween?rel=by_user.
76. Dialogue from *Ghosts of Mars*.
77. Adams, "Interview: John Carpenter."
78. Earlier releases *Mission to Mars* (2000, Brian De Palma) and *Red Planet* (2000, Antony Hoffman) themselves not exactly box office successes, no doubt contributed to the audience ennui that greeted yet another Mars-set film.

BIBLIOGRAPHY

Adams, Sam. "Interview: John Carpenter." *A.V. Club*, April 11, 2001. http://www.avclub.com/articles/john-carpenter,54361/.
Boulenger, Gilles. *John Carpenter: The Prince of Darkness*. Los Angeles: Silman-James Press, 2001.
Dark Star. DVD. Directed by John Carpenter. 1974. Tulsa: VCI Entertainment, 1999.
Dinning, Mark. "*The Fog* (1979)." *Empire: The Greatest Horror Movies Ever* 1, p. 37.
"Funny or Die Presents John Carpenter's *Halloween*." *Funny or Die*, October 27, 2011. http://www.funnyordie.com/videos/81bcb40457/funny-or-die-presents-john-carpenter-s-halloween?rel=by_user.
Ghosts of Mars. DVD. Directed by John Carpenter. 2001. Culver City, CA: Screen Gems, 2001.
Kooyman, Ben. *Directorial Self-Fashioning in American Horror Cinema*. New York: Edwin Mellen Press, 2014.
Maddrey, Joseph. *Nightmares in Red, White and Blue: The Evolution of the American Horror Film*. Jefferson, NC: McFarland, 2004.
McWeeny, Drew, and Scott Weinberg. "Listen: A Special Podcast Tribute to John Carpenter with Guest Scott Weinberg," *The Motion/Captured Podcast*, accessed via iTunes.
Muir, John Kenneth. *The Films of John Carpenter*. Jefferson, NC: McFarland, 2000.
Newman, Kim. *Nightmare Movies: A Critical History of the Horror Movie from 1968*, 2d ed. London: Bloomsbury, 1988.
Phillips, Kendall R. *Dark Directions: Romero, Craven, Carpenter, and the Modern Horror Film*. Carbondale: Southern Illinois University Press, 2012.
Sobchack, Vivian Carol. *Screening Space: The American Science Fiction Film*, 2d ed. New Brunswick: Rutgers University Press, 1997.
The Thing. DVD. Directed by John Carpenter. 1982. Universal City, CA: Universal, 1998.
The Thing. "John Carpenter's *The Thing*: Terror Takes Shape." Directed by Michael Matessino. Universal City, CA: Universal, 1998. DVD.
The Thing. "*The Thing* Commentary," with John Carpenter and Kurt Russell. Universal City, CA: Universal, 1998. DVD.
They Live. DVD. Directed by John Carpenter. 1988. Universal City, CA: Universal, 2003.

Yamato, Jen. "John Carpenter on His Decade Away from Filmmaking, the Problem with Today's Horror, and *The Ward*." *Movie Line*, June 14, 2011. http://movieline.com/2011/06/14/john-carpenter-on-his-decade-away-from-filmmaking-his-return-with-the-ward-and-his-bloody-future/.

Zinoman, Jason. *Shock Value*. New York: Penguin Press, 2011.

The Cold, White Reproduction of the Same

A New Hypothesis About John Carpenter's The Thing

DARIO ALTOBELLI

It's alive! Or that's what scientists might say when they rean-imate the so-called "frankenvirus," a 30,000-year-old giant virus that was discovered in Siberia. The French researchers behind the find—published this week in PNAS, the journal of the U.S. National Academy of Sciences—warn that cli-mate change could reawaken dangerous microscopic pathogens, reports Agence France-Presse. Since 2003, the virus, known as Mollivirus sibericum, is the fourth kind of prehistoric virus unearthed overall, and the second one dis-covered by the research team.[1]

In the cold white Antarctic desert, a husky runs across the snow, a hel-icopter pursuing it as someone on board the helicopter shoots at it. When the animal reaches a research station unharmed, the men inside the station emerge, drawn out by the shots. A man steps off the helicopter to get a better shot at the animal. He fires and, perhaps accidentally, hits one of the men from the research center who is trying to protect the animal. Following moments of chaos and incomprehensible shouting, the helicopter crew mem-ber attempts to throw a hand grenade at the animal and accidentally destroys the helicopter, killing the pilot. Shortly after, from behind one of the windows inside the research station someone shoots him, wounding him lethally.

As the saying goes, this is the beginning of the end for a group of men who are quickly sucked into the spiraling of events, where paranoia and vio-lence are generated from what we soon discover to be the true nature of the animal: an alien creature, a "thing" capable of assuming the appearance of the living organisms it kills and of perfectly imitating its shape and behavior. After the dog, the Thing starts to take possession of the men at the base.

John Carpenter's masterpiece is based on the novella by John W. Campbell, Jr., *Who Goes There?* (1938)[2] that also inspired the earlier film *The Thing from Another World* (1951) directed by Christian Nyby and, apparently, by Howard Hawks as well, unofficially at least. Carpenter's adaptation was not well received by critics nor by the public when it was released in 1982. In fact, the film came out during the same summer in which *E.T. the Extra-Terrestrial* by Steven Spielberg was released. Compared to the stylistic elegance of a story about extraterrestrial monsters and children with strong sentimental traits, Carpenter's *The Thing*, with a splatter quality and a claustrophobic atmosphere, would not be a success with the wider public. It would have been hard to imagine a more strident and audacious comparison between the two representations of an alien and of its relations with humans. On the other hand, it is well known that the film was not positively reviewed by critics either. It can easily be stated that while *The Thing* was widely misunderstood at the time it came out, over time it has gained increasing approval and spurred sufficient interest to the point of becoming a cult film.

Today *The Thing* is unanimously considered as a turning point in the history of the genre of science fiction horror, particularly significant in the body-horror subgenre, with a widespread direct and indirect influence on cinematography in general. Furthermore, an extremely rich critical and interpretative framework has developed over the years resulting in a consistent bibliography regarding the film's production, special effects and screenplay, as well as its deeper meaning and plot related issues, the true and false clues scattered throughout the film about the unfolding events portrayed, and the open ending, which continues to generate endless discussion.

In this essay I will not only consider the strictly cinematographic and cinematic issues; instead I will also focus on the main question: what does *The Thing* actually represent? What is the meaning of this film, or, in other words, what are the philosophical and sociological implications this film poses?

The various answers to these questions can be classified into three main groups. The first group gives a psychoanalytical and feminist interpretation.[3] In a nutshell, the Thing represents the materialization of the "monstrous-feminine" within the male social setting of the research station. This reading follows the ground breaking work by Barbara Creed[4] and her theory in which many horror movies portray the male fear of the feminine, a fear of castration related to the untamable and incomprehensible female physicality.[5] This interpretation is particularly suited to *The Thing* not only because of visual evidence—one example is the sequence in which the jaws of Norris-Thing tears off Cooper's arms—but also in relation to other films, namely Ridley Scott's *Alien* (1979) that offer similar examples of the "amoral primeval mother" throughout the plot and in the images. Creed's thesis was based on and developed the notion of "abjection" formulated by Julia Kristeva, indicating something that "disturbs identity, system, order. What does not respect borders, positions, rules. The in-between, the ambiguous, the composite."[6] Applied to the horror genre, abjection is linked to the surfacing of obsessions related to the reproductive function of the female body. From the same perspective, but with a shift of meaning, others have interpreted the Thing as a representation of homosexual desire, refused and imagined like a monster, the idea or possibility of which provokes a reaction of panic if not of outright fear and terror.[7]

The second group of interpretations is based on a historical and sociological reading of the film. The Thing represents the specters of American history mining collective identity; specifically, events such as the Vietnam War and particular episodes such as *Operation Eagle Claw* (a military operation carried out April 24, 1980).[8] This reading can be applied to cinema as a historically situated cultural product that conveys cultural and sociological values typical of the historic period in which the films were produced, filmed and distributed. In plain words, cinema is an indicator of social and cultural dynamics.[9]

At the intersection of these two interpretations lies one of the best known readings of the film: the Thing as a metaphor of the HIV virus—and more in general of aggressive illness such as cancer—elaborated during the years when AIDS was spreading the most. A plastic representation of the virus can be found in the mimetic mode in which the lethal attack is carried out by the alien entity, and the central importance of blood as the physical element involved in the aggression.[10]

The third type of interpretation is based, directly or indirectly, on a philosophical approach. Put in plain language, the Thing represents the *Other*, its subtlest and effective infiltration strategy aimed at conquering Community, Culture and Civilization. According to this line of thought, the Thing is a materialization of the fear of Otherness in the form of the Same. Or, according to a similar anthropological and cultural conceptual framework applied to the horror genre, the Thing represents the figure of *Taboo* and the absence of classification boundaries that are typical of every social system.[11]

It's a very short step to an overall philosophical reading, ultimately arising from questions that have been posed by any number of careful spectators. If the Thing can reproduce not only the shape, but also the behavior and perhaps even the thoughts, that is, ultimately the identity of the subject it has assimilated and transformed into, how can we distinguish a *Man* from a *Man-Thing*? As Ann Billson noted: "At what point does a human being cease to be a human being and become a Thing? And what would be so awful about being a Thing anyway? The absolute value of the film would therefore lie in the ability to represent the unsettling question: Is that man next to me an inhuman monster?"[12]

Also in the field of philosophical interpretation is the reading by Slavoj Žižek, according to whom the Thing represents "a pre-symbolic, maternal thing par excellence": an expression of Lacan's "impossible jouissance" (what Freud named *Das Ding*), that is to say "a traumatic core" founding the "surplus enjoyment" that transcends and exceeds the principle of pleasure.[13] And recent considerations put forth by Dylan Trigg within the conceptual framework of *Speculative Realism*, which he associates with a critical rethinking of phenomenology, centered around the body and the flesh as the places where the inhuman resides.[14]

This essay aims to provide yet another interpretative key, bringing into consideration two issues not yet dealt with by the aforementioned readings. Firstly, to restore the centrality of the term "science" in the notion of *science fiction* as a genre. The importance of this term is beyond doubt, however, it is sometimes totally left out of consideration in analyses of science fiction movies and, in this case, science fiction horror. Science fiction as a narrative genre deals with the field of science and technology, as the privileged realm of representation, anticipating, criticizing and voicing concerns about pertinent emerging issues. *The Thing* makes no exception in this respect, and neither do the novel by Campbell Jr., the film by Nyby/Hawks or the 2011 prequel directed by Matthijs van Heijningen, Jr.

With focus on the techno-scientific dimension as the main area of analysis, an interpretation can be outlined according to which *The Thing* as a film and of the Thing as a monstrous entity are metaphors and images of capitalism. The notion of capitalism is treated here in general terms indicating the economic system as well as the cultural and social spheres it determines, within a Marxist theoretical framework (the good old concepts of *structure* and *superstructure*); in other words, capitalism here refers to the economic, financial and productive configuration that determines a particular cultural logic and a specific symbolic domination, linked to an ideological stance and to a network of stable and long-lasting social relations.

In this perspective, in both the films by Nyby/Hawks and Carpenter we can identify different metaphors for different stages of capitalism, from the "classical" stage, characterized by a "process of creative destruction" according to Joseph Schumpeter,[15] to the "late" stage of capitalism that has been considered in connection to "postmodernism."[16] At the same time, Carpenter's film also seems to prefigure the following stage, the so called stage of "informational capitalism"[17] and the logic behind the "global culture industry."[18] This is the hypothesis we are going to examine in detail.

"Only science can conquer him...":
The Thing from Another World *(1951)*

> Elementary, my dear Watson. The monster wants to have
> life-forms available. It cannot animate a dead body, appar-
> ently. It is just waiting—waiting until the best opportunities
> come. We who remain human, it is holding in reserve.[19]

In the beginning, it was the short novel by John Campbell, Jr. The story takes place at the South Pole and tells of the finding made by personnel at a research station: a flying disc buried in snow and a frozen creature. The space-ship is accidentally blown up and the alien, described as monstrous, is taken to the base and imprisoned inside the block of ice in which he was originally found. Due to a lack of attention, the ice melts and the creature is not only alive and threatening, but possesses telepathic powers and is able to assume the appearance of its victims. Following various attempts to capture the alien, a blood test is prepared, leading to the discovery that at least half of the crew members in the base have been replicated over a short span of time. Once they have destroyed the human copies, the novel's main characters will eventually defeat the alien that has taken on the identity of the biologist Blair and has built a flying object in order to escape and reach other areas of Earth.

The cinematographic version of 1951 was based on the original story, but also equally deviated from it. Specifically, Nyby/Hawks changed the setting to the North Pole, transformed the research center into some sort of military outpost, added a numerous group of military personnel to the group of scientists and gave a traditional representation of the monster, named the Thing, that had no metamorphic ability but a Frankenstein-like physicality, and the ability to regenerate its body like a plant organism.

It is generally assumed that the film represents the Soviet threat in the years following World War II, and that the Thing, ironically described as the "intellectual carrot," is none other than the personification of Communism. Indeed, the setting of the story at the North Pole was probably not by chance, suggesting the geographical closeness of the research base to the Soviet Union. This interpretation is well established and supported by many factors. However, if we focus our attention on the character of Dr. Carrington (Robert Cornthwaite), a Nobel prize laureate and renown scientist who conducts advanced research projects with his team, and on his role in the unfolding of events, particularly with regard to the relationship he would like to build with the Thing in the name of the highest scientific values, the film can be read as a reflection on scientific entrepreneurship at the time it was made.

The character of Dr. Carrington embodies all the well-known traits defined by Robert K. Merton in his dealing with the forms of classic self-representation of scientists and scientific activity in terms of ethical purity, as a public asset, a form of universal knowledge free from interests, and as common property of all humanity.[20] Scientists generally hold these traits to be positive, arguing and asserting them with various degrees of formalization and awareness. Indeed, these traits are still at work today in the public image displayed by researchers, in images of themselves and of the work they carry out.

This belief in science is repeatedly expressed by Carrington throughout the film with indisputable assertions such as "Knowledge is more important than life. We've only one excuse for existing. To think. To find out. To learn."[21] The numerous claims of freedom of research and scientific independence are continuously opposed by Captain Hendry (Kenneth Tobey) to the point of open conflict. Captain Hendry, the main character of the story, represents on-site military power and the mentality of common good sense. "There are no enemies in science, only phenomena to study. We are studying one," the scientist keeps telling Hendry, who would instead like to deal with the Thing with quick methods.[22]

This predictable plot is partially undermined by what General Fogarty (David McMahon) determines via radio contact from a faraway base. His orders, at times in favor of Carrington's position, constitute the highest, most certain and stable normative point of reference and are always obeyed, except for cases when Captain Hendry can derogate from them because of the circumstance or a disturbed signal.

In plain words, a conflict of competences, interests and ambitions takes place around the Thing, between science on one side and politics on the other, or, better, between science and the military world that is a direct emanation of politics. This confrontation sheds light on the dark side of scientific research: Carrington's intentions are stigmatized from a moral perspective, according to a very common pattern in science fiction films of the 1950s and not only, whereby scientific "visions" endanger the existence of other members of the base and constitute a threat to humanity. The scientist's choice to operate alone and against the orders of Captain Hendry with the aim of establishing contact with the Thing and developing an experiment makes him directly responsible for two deaths and one person injured. From this point of view, the film would seem to suggest that true danger is caused not so much by the Thing but by science itself and by the scientist's ambitions, represented in the film almost as the classic "mad scientist."[23]

The structure of this narrative mechanism reveals some interesting aspects about the way ideology functions as promoted by the film and opens to considerations regarding the true hidden subject: capitalism and the contradictory logic linking it to scientific entrepreneurship.

In actual fact there is no "pure" science; on the contrary, modern scientific activity not only is conceived and achieved within a capitalist system, it also constitutes an indispensable part of this system, and is in turn financed by it for purposes of profit and marketing.[24] In this perspective the picture painted by the film, aside from the stated intentions, is clear as daylight. The scientific base itself is only possible because it is part of a wider military post and falls within the expansive productive logic of North American capitalism. When for the first time the team reaches the area where a non-identified object has been picked up on radar, a member of the military corps makes a satisfied remark, referring to the research station visible from the helicopter: "Hey, the taxpayers ought to see this!"[25]

On the contrary, if science functions to serve capitalism by as much as it benefits from it, then science in service of capitalism need not necessarily have an ethical orientation, let alone in the ideological form represented and stigmatized, which merely becomes an instrumental value. From this perspective, in the 1951 film the Thing explicitly represents not only the occasion for pure and totally original scientific research, as is declared by Carrington, but mostly it is the occasion for innovative, original and superior applications. Throughout the ongoing disagreements between Carrington and Hendry, the film evolves as a statement of common "good sense," at the same time hiding the fact that on a more general level capitalism exploits the ambitions of science instrumentally as an alibi for the disasters that may arise from techno-scientific enterprises on the whole. Research and progress are necessary (as a market asset), but human life must be preserved. Otherwise, the blame falls on the scientist whose image represents thoughtless techno-scientific innovation: "Like a kid with a new toy," says Miss Nicholson (Margaret Sheridan) of Dr. Carrington whom she assists (she is also Hendry's lover), in dealing with the Thing.[26] Thus, all of civil society's doubts and dilemmas play out here towards the techno-scientific claim of total power in operating exclusively for humanity's wellbeing, as if scientists were truly independent and free of any mandate or interest to promote.

Therefore, it is not surprising that in works of fiction as well as in historic reality the scientist himself is often the true standard bearer of capitalism. Carrington immediately starts working on a secret research project for serial production of the Thing. As panic spreads throughout the base and Hendry tries to prepare a strategy for dealing with the threat, the scientist creates a culture prototype of superior beings in the lab, fed on human plasma: a product that, it is not hard nor inappropriate to imagine, would soon be acquired by the people funding research, maybe even by the military spheres that the scientist enters into conflict with. The fact that the culture feeds on human blood is much more than a narrative thread. Blood is the body fluid with the strongest symbolic value throughout all cultures. Recalling an image used by Marx and borrowing from a further iconography, it could be stated that capitalism feeds on human blood exactly the way a vampire feeds on its victims. If Dr. Carrington had succeeded in his experiments and in the attempt to establish a relationship with the Thing, that is to dominate it scientifically, it would have become a marketable commercial product.[27]

This is a fairly faithful picture of capitalism in the 1940s and 50s: the objectification of the world as the object of knowledge worked on by scientific research is the premise for worldwide expansion of mass production of consumer goods.[28] In the years following World War II conditions were set for the production boom of gadgets and goods, for the exploitation and subjectivation of broad sections of the population within the dual role of producers and consumers, for the birth of the consumer society, and the overwhelming affirmation of the culture industry.

Overall, the film must be seen as a metaphor of the capitalist system whose mobile front line for conquest and expansion is represented by techno-scientific entrepreneurship. Dr. Carrington himself states as much: "Only science can conquer him…."[29] The Thing's aggressiveness, the fatal threat it represents are to be understood as a splendid rendering of that essential "process of creative destruction" that Schumpeter appropriately described as a "process of industrial mutation—if I may use that biological term—that incessantly revolutionizes the economic structure from within, incessantly destroying the old one, incessantly creating a new one."[30]

"Why don't we just wait here for a while…": The Thing (1982)

> Forms that are beyond judgement have a much greater power of fascination, but for that same reason they are terribly dangerous for any order whatsoever. They can no longer be controlled. At any given moment a category or a form stops representing itself, it no longer enters the stage of representation, it no longer functions according to its end. It doubles back upon itself, taking a curve so rapid that it reaches a kind of potentialization. All the rest goes into a state of weightlessness.[31]

Let us consider Carpenter's masterpiece and begin analyzing the setting. In the 1951 film, the base was an efficient expression of the military and industrial complex where the laboratory was the center of excellence and the reason for the Arctic mission. In the 1982 film, the only thing remaining of the scientific vocation is a faded poster that reads "United States National Science Institute Station 4," in competition with the other name "US Outpost Number 31" used by the characters to refer to the station, making it hard to know which of the two is the correct one. It could be construed that 30 years on there are no soldiers anymore, no team of scientists, no women, and it appears there is no longer a reason to justify the presence of the men in such a hostile place, a place already isolated and cut off from any communication two weeks prior to the arrival of the Thing. Nevertheless, this is not the representation of a context in which no norms exist.[32] On the contrary, this is a closed, male only and, at least for a planned period of time, self-sufficient society, based on two kinds of rules: the first, on a micro-sociological level, is relevant to everyday life, the second kind, in a more general way, predefines the context and the purpose of the base. Let's take a closer look at these two normative levels.

At a micro-sociological level, we find behavior norms regulating the lives of the men, with minimum variations, on the model of military groups, especially those engaged in hostile operations. In this case we will usually have various forms of small social groups held together by an official code of behavior and by a non-written set of rules. In our case the disciplinary dimension, often accompanied by the dark and grotesque authoritarian norm regulating the military universe, is completely absent. Instead, it appears there are only informal relations, undefined ranks and roles, and a fairly ample sphere of individual independence to the extent of forms of anarchy, albeit within a fundamentally stable situation. The members of this group hardly work, they play cards and pool, they drink and smoke, they listen to loud music. All this takes place in an extremely laid back atmosphere of boredom, where it seems nothing significant could ever happen. The impression is that life at the base goes on at a slow pace, at a rhythm that is only gradually disrupted by the presence of the Thing, until it is changed radically and destroyed. In other words, this picture is almost the parody of a military corps or, thinking of films such as *Apocalypse Now* (1979, Francis Ford Coppola), of a degraded micro-society whose principles and values have lost contact with the primary social source of law.

It is important to understand this first regulatory sphere because it introduces to the wider picture determined by the scientific enterprise and the crucial role it plays in the narrative structure. Scientific research constitutes the policy establishing and maintaining the existence and the purpose of the base. The fact that there is no mention of the ongoing research projects is not very significant: as a matter of fact these could be carried out following a loose program and with no immediate deadline. In other words, scientific activity must be carried out is the implicit setting, without it the plot would be lacking a fundamental precondition. Therefore, it is not surprising that the extreme weakness and apparent absence from the scene of this implicit factor, is where we believe the film's meaning emerges. If a research base does not appear to be carrying out the task it was established for, this is not simply because of a narrative weakness or contradiction, but perhaps because we are witnessing the cynical and disillusioned representation of the state of the art of scientific entrepreneurship in the age of late capitalism.

The moment when an aggressive alien presence such as the Thing breaks into everyday life at the base, its routine and the already weak rules of coexistence inevitably lead to a crucial pitch of tension. What is most striking however is that compared to the 1951 film, the Thing does not spur scientific research other than that strictly necessary to understand the true nature of the threat. In fact, Blair (Wilford Brimley) destroys all the machinery when he discovers the high probability that at least one member of the base has already been duplicated, and understands the speedy rate of expansion of the Thing globally in case it reaches civilized areas. It is reasonable to imagine that, aside from the fact that Blair was already a Blair-Thing by that time, the start of an extraordinary research program investigating the alien would have been improbable. A similar interest is never even hypothetically displayed, but only mentioned ironically, and this is no coincidence. "We ought to just burn these things," Windows (Thomas G. Waites) remarks, and Bennings (Peter Maloney) replies, "Can't burn the find of the century. That's gonna win somebody the Nobel Prize."[33]

This reading invites a reconsideration of the micro-sociological normative level. It appears clear that the isolation of the base, the widespread feeling of an absence of purpose in the life of the male community structured around alcohol, gambling and boredom, the lack of hierarchy and defined roles, provide an eloquent picture of capitalism intended on the whole as an economic, social and cultural system—capable of defining a "cultural structure of feeling"[34]—that has definitely lost any winning direction and continues to exist only in the form of repetition of the same through simulation.[35] Technoscience, although still present, is almost completely absorbed within the economic and cultural dominant logic, to the point of disappearing even from those claims still portrayed in the Nyby/Hawks film with a romantic and idealistic touch, although deprived of a foundation, as forms of an ideological mask. The Thing on the other hand ceases to represent the natural world that science aims to understand in order to control and exploit. The Thing is capitalism itself as an all-encompassing system defining reality in its own terms. By destroying everything and condemning himself to isolation, Blair certifies the impotence of techno-science in controlling the capitalist system despite having been, and continuing to be, its fundamental ally. Hence we get to the heart of the main thesis: the Thing perfectly represents three symbolic and material directions taken by late capitalism.

First of all, the *metamorphosis* of the form and function of the consumer goods, aside from the supposed *use value*. Late capitalism has taken the principle of utility of goods in relation to the satisfaction of certain needs to an extreme paroxysm. This principle however is always a determined cultural value. There is no such thing as "natural" use value, each "thing," each "object," is already included in a network of other "objects" and "things" from the start, where their meaning in terms of use value is reciprocally determined: this is the prevalence of the so called *sign-functions*.[36] The utility of goods is also the invention of a productive system of objects that *must* serve some purpose in order to be desirable and purchased. In other words, *use value* is the alibi for the ontological uselessness of objects and one of the biggest and most persistent illusions promoted by modern society. In this perspective we can understand the *metamorphosis* of the form and function of things, taking place through continuous processes of *re-formalization* and *re-functionalization* that are, similarly to "planned obsolescence," fundamental attributes for the reproduction of production as a continuous cycle.

Secondly, the Thing represents the *simulation* of the product's originality and of its material reality (opposed to the sign and symbolic reality) in the fallacious terms of *exchange value*. The assumption that anything can be exchanged for anything else, that is, the "natural" form which identifies original exchange with barter as the foundation for money as a universal equivalent. However, in this respect we must point out that money performs this function only and insofar as there is a "belief" in such an equivalence value. As Žižek states, "money is precisely an object whose status depends on how we 'think' about it: if people no longer treat this piece of metal as money, if they no longer 'believe' in it as money, it no longer is money."[37] Within the framework of our analysis this leads to two consequences. Firstly, in the capitalist market the product is often presented as bearing a quality of originality, as to claim an adequate exchange value in relation to it, when actually this is nothing more than fiction. There is no such thing as an *original* consumer good in the age of mechanical reproduction and of serial reproduction of models; there is no *originality* in the ontological sense of the term with the traits of uniqueness, authenticity and un-reproducibility. The second consequence is that the product solely and primarily exhibits a "material" reality when the consumer good is a sign within the system of objects, and this is the reason why it often assumes the features of a *fetish* object and is loaded with symbolic value.

Hence the third characteristic: the Thing represents the *reiteration* on a planetary scale of the same replication scheme followed by the consumer good as *simulacrum* and *fetish*, sizing up the destruction of Earth as an ecosystem and life forms, to establish the hallucinatory semiotics of *sign-value*.[38] The hyper-reproducibility of the Thing transcends the 1:1 ratio becoming N:N. One husky generates N number of infected dogs, then N humans, according to an exponential expansion potentially involving the entire global population. This is the sign of global, trans-national capitalism promoted by multinational companies with statues for crossing beyond State borders and geographical boundaries to embrace the entire ecumene in the same logic. This expansion is not concerned, except in words, with the destruction of ecosystems carried out through intensive exploitation of natural non-renewable resources and life forms; an expansion that floods reality, defining it, with serial products sold as unique objects indispensable for human life. Fetish products destined to voracious consumption and simulacra of "real things" in which the only true value is the purely semiotic value, that is the nature of sign-products within a semiotic system of products. In other words, the *sign-value* of a consumer good is the trait determining its *exchange value* and is based on the degree of "originality" and *use value* it is able to display.

It is clear that the aforementioned traits not only describe "late capitalism," but outline the next stage of "informational capitalism" and the logic of the "global culture industry." Here, the focus is shifted to the brand as "singularity" more than on the consumer good as a serial object, where the characteristic reflective trait of the cultural sphere, implemented in forms of subjectivation and appropriation of goods, takes place by means of a "mediation of things" that deeply involves social players, and not through a mere representative logic.[39]

The last aspect considered in this analysis concerns an element that plays a central role in Carpenter's film: the living body reproduced by the Thing as a sign and a set of signs. The body as plain flesh constitutes the ultimate sphere of capitalistic reproduction, as the main sign of every symbolic and material configuration, as the minimum unit and basic signifier (the human body, the animal body, the living body and so on), as well as a display of signs, a factory and "projector" of signs (the body as the object of discipline and education, the artistic body as body-art, the social body as the set of bodies composing it and so on). The body reproduced by the Thing is the sphere responding to the purpose of creating a platform for many different autonomous signs, perhaps not even in relation one to the other if not by means of the body itself as the central metaphor, the *locus* of the fundamental *dispositio*, the space where derived metaphors, metonymy and synecdoche, play out. Let's consider the various "incarnations" of the Thing; specifically, on the one hand the body of two Norwegian men merged together, in an intricate dynamic dealt with in the 2011 prequel, and on the other hand the Norris-Thing, whose head is separated from the rest of his body becoming some sort of gigantic spider in one of the most remarkable and memorable sequences of the film.

Thus, ironically, the Thing also becomes an image of humanity as such. The Thing is the same human being reproduced in the generalized reproduction system of no other form than a replica of a form already replicated. This is possible because, ultimately, capitalism as an economic and social system has used man and his body as the raw material for the production system from the very beginning, in order to achieve a position of government, the reproduction of "bare life," and the scope of sophisticated forms of biopolitics.[40] "You see, what we're talking about here is an organism that imitates other life-forms, and it imitates them perfectly," says Blair.[41] Because humanity is defined as a model, it is hypothetically possible to replicate it without noticing the substitution or questioning the difference between the original and the copy. In other words, the *Man-Thing* is—also—the image of man in the age of his technical reproducibility by means of bio-engineering and cloning. It is biotechnological simulacrum and techno-scientific practice, the limits of which cannot be defined in advance, because they exceed the human sphere introducing the post-human, and a different declination of the monster as a chimera steadily set within the perimeter of a market economy where the body is the first and last consumer good.

All this is only hinted in Carpenter's film, however what the Thing represents and proves negatively, like a prophetic prefiguration, is that an individual is a historical and cultural construction, working the way it does—an object itself, functional to something else—because it is useful to the system of which it is a product and an active cause at the same time: not unique, nor irreplaceable, but simulated and replicated.

Conclusions

> ... and it was a movie that's tone started and finished and basically it was almost ... "there's nothing of trust that's in the world now, we see it all over, in countries, people. We don't trust each other anymore. We're with somebody that we think maybe ... there are loved ones, and they may attack us ... and that's what the Thing is ... it has a lot of truth in it kinda dressed up as a Monster-Me*you can do." Because here it comes. And of course the Thing is metaphor for whatever one says, it's disease, it could be AIDS, it could be whatever comes from within you. It's also basically the lack.[42]

Similarly to *The Matrix* saga (1999–2003), *The Thing* is one of those films that can apparently be interpreted in an endless number of ways; the interpretation here proposed is indeed a further hypothesis that is backed by sufficient evidence. It is also clear that interpretations arise and spawn where there is a greater array of suggestions, concerns and feelings stimulated. *The Thing* rightfully belongs within the history of modern imaginary as a contemporary myth capable still today, decades after its appearance, of involving spectators in a journey to hidden fears and issues that have not yet been answered. With the interpretation of *The Thing* as a film on the reproduction of the same, intended as the predominant form of production in the age of late capitalism, we have applied a sociological perspective, but this reading does not answer all the issues posed by the film because they involve what we define reality: the news concerning the live virus discovered in the ice in Siberia.

A degraded, abandoned, isolated and violent world. This is the world in which capitalism has reached a dead end, a point of non-return, of repetition of the same, indeed. A white and spectral world reflected in the darkness of a beginning winter night that shall have no end, where a limited male society, in a time suspended and relentless, goes forth into the void of an invisible stagnation. The Thing is the form of the capitalism reaching the level of saturation, at the highest point of an asymptotic parable, that continues to reproduce itself in the spectral dimension of the already known, of the already done. Any further development, any further evolution is impossible. The end of history as indeterminable and endless reiteration. The stage of production is coiled around itself in a spiral; impossibility to modify the existent order of knowledge and life forms. Or else, destruction. Carpenter would go on to deal with these issues more directly, with specific reference to the ideology of consumer society, in another masterpiece: the film *They Live* (1988), along with George Romero's *Dawn of the Dead* (1978), is still today one of the most important and aggressive critiques of consumerism and an acute investigation of the operation principals of ideology achieved by the horror film genre.

The Thing and other science fiction horror films in which the alien has metamorphic abilities, such as *Invasion of the Body Snatchers* (1956, Don Siegel; 1978, Philip Kaufman), can ultimately be read as powerful metaphors of capitalism, in some of its more recent historical phases, observed in the area of serial reproduction of goods, signs and bodies, and as an indefinable and continually shifting force shaping reality. This interpretative framework is now ready to be applied to other films with the aim to broaden the hypothesis, setting the direction for a sociological reading not only of one film, but of an entire genre.

NOTES

1. "Scientists Look to Re-Animate Ancient, Giant 'Frankenvirus' Found in Siberia," *Fox News*, September 9, 2015, http://www.foxnews.com/science/2015/09/09/french-scientists-look-to-re-animate-ancient-giant-frankenvirus-found-in.html.

2. John W. Campbell, *Who Goes There?* (1938), *The Novella that Formed the Basis of "The Thing"* (Somerset, PA: Rocket Ride Books, 2009).

3. Matthew Pridham, *Underneath the Skin: John Carpenter's "The Thing" and You*, March 25 2012, http://weirdfictionreview.com/2012/03/underneath-the-skin-john-carpenters-the-thing-and-you/.

4. Barbara Creed, *The Monstrous Feminine: Film, Feminism, Psychoanalysis* (New York: Routledge, 1993).

5. Marie Mulvie-Roberts, "'A Spook Ride on Film': Carpenter and the Gothic," in *The Cinema of John Carpenter: The Technique of Terror*, ed. Ian Conrich and David Woods (London: Wallflower, 2004), 78–90.

6. Julia Kristeva, *Powers of Horror: An Essay on Abjection* (New York: Columbia University Press, 1982), 4.

7. Noah Berlatsky, "Fecund Horror," *Gayutopia*, 2008, http://gayutopia.blogspot.it/2007/12/noah-berlatsky-fecund-horror_12.html.

8. *Operation Eagle Claw* was a United States Armed Forces operation ordered by U.S. President Jimmy Carter to attempt to end the Iran hostage crisis by rescuing 52 embassy staff held captive at the Embassy of the United States, Tehran, on 24 April 1980. Its failure, and the humiliating public debacle that ensued, damaged U.S. prestige worldwide. Carter himself blamed his loss in the 1980 U.S. presidential election mainly on his failure to win the release of U.S. hostages held captive in Iran.

9. Jonathan Lake Crane, *Terror and Everyday Life: Singular Moments in the History of the Horror Film* (Thousand Oaks: Sage, 1994); and Robin Wood, *Hollywood from Vietnam to Regan ... and Beyond* (New York: Columbia University Press, 2003). With regard to this approach, the groundbreaking work by Siegfried Kracauer, *From Caligari to Hitler: A Psychological History of the German Film* (Princeton: Princeton University Press, 2004) remains a benchmark.

10. Ernesto Guerrero, "AIDS as Monster in Science Fiction and Horror Cinema," *Journal of Popular Film and Television* 18 (Fall 1990): 87–93; and John Kenneth Muir, "John Carpenter's *The Thing* (1982)," *Reflections on Film and Television*, 2011, http://reflectionsonfilmandtelevision.blogspot.it/search?q=the+thing.

11. Stephen Prince, "Dread, Taboo and *The Thing*: Toward a Social Theory of the Horror Film," in *The Horror Film*, ed. Stephen Prince (New Brunswick: Rutgers University Press, 2004), 118–129.

12. Ann Billson, *The Thing* (London: BFI, 2012), 12.

13. Slavoj Žižek, *The Sublime Object of Ideology* (London: Verso, 2008), 146.

14. Dylan Trigg, *The Thing: A Phenomenology of Horror* (Alresford, UK: Zero Books, 2014).

15. Joseph Alois Schumpeter, *Capitalism, Socialism and Democracy* (London: Routledge 2003), *passim*. See in particular "Chapter VII. The Process of Creative Destruction," 81–86.

16. Fredric Jameson, *Postmodernism or the Cultural Logic of Late Capitalism* (Durham: Duke University Press, 1991).

17. Manuel Castells, *The Rise of the Network Society, The Information Age: Economy, Society and Culture Vol. I* (Cambridge, MA: Blackwell, 1996); Manuel Castells, *The Power of Identity, The Information Age: Economy, Society and Culture Vol. II* (Cambridge, MA: Blackwell, 1997); and Manuel Castells, *End of Millennium, The Information Age: Economy, Society and Culture Vol. III* (Cambridge, MA: Blackwell, 1998).

18. Scott Lash and Celia Lury, *Global Culture Industry: The Mediation of Things* (Cambridge: Polity, 2007).

19. Campbell, *Who Goes There?*, chapter 9.

20. Robert K. Merton, *The Sociology of Science: Theoretical and Empirical Investigations* (Chicago: University of Chicago Press, 1973).

21. *The Thing from Another World*, DVD, directed by Christian Nyby (Burbank, CA: Turner Home Entertainment, 2010).

22. It must be noted, by the way, that it is true that the film portrays the camaraderie typical of the Howard Hawks films, while nothing of the sort happens in the version by Carpenter or in the 2011 prequel where the group implodes under the threat of the Thing. However, this is also due to a trivial reason: the story in 1951 film revolves around a group of soldiers structured by hierarchy and discipline and is, as it should be, prepared to deal with situations of stress and precise threats and attacks. In the other cases, the civil component prevails while the military one is totally absent.

23. An image that can be found in the 2011 prequel in the figure of Dr. Sander Halvorson (Ulrich Thomsen): this is the reason why this film is much more predictable and stereotyped compared to Carpenter's masterpiece.

24. Bruno Latour, *Science in Action: How to Follow Scientists and Engineers Through Society* (Cambridge: Harvard University Press, 1987).

25. Dialogue from *The Thing from Another World.*

26. *Ibid.*

27. In this perspective, it is evident that the deteriorated and instrumental relation between science and capitalism, present in many science fiction films, and not only in horror films, is depicted in *Alien* (1979, Ridley Scott) in the significant incarnation of the ambiguous android Ash (Ian Holm), whose behavior ultimately determines the development of the plot.

28. Max Horkheimer and Theodor W. Adorno, *Dialectic of Enlightenment: Philosophical Fragments* (Stanford: Stanford University Press, 2002).

29. Dialogue from *The Thing from Another World.*

30. Schumpeter, *Capitalism, Socialism and Democracy*, 83.

31. Jean Baudrillard, *Baudrillard Live: Selected Interviews*, ed. Mike Gane (London: Routledge, 1993), 110.

32. Thomas Doherty, "Genre, Gender and *The Aliens Trilogy*," in *The Dread of Difference: Gender and the Horror Film*, 2d ed., ed. Barry K. Grant (Austin: University of Texas Press, 1996); and Muir, *John Carpenter's The Thing.*

33. *The Thing*, DVD, directed by John Carpenter (1982; Universal City, CA: Universal, 1998).

34. Raymond Williams, *Marxism and Literature* (Oxford: Oxford University Press, 1977).

35. Jean Baudrillard, *Symbolic Exchange and Death* (London: Sage, 1993); and Jean Baudrillard, *Simulacra and Simulation* (Ann Arbor: University of Michigan Press, 1994).

36. Roland Barthes, *Elements of Semiology*, 8th ed. (New York: Hill and Wang, 1986), 41.

37. Žižek, *The Sublime Object*, xix.

38. Barthes, *Elements of Semiology*, 41.

39. Lash and Lury, *Global Culture.*

40. Giorgio Agamben, *Homo Sacer: Sovereign Power and Bare Life* (Stanford: Stanford University Press, 1998); and Michel Foucault, *History of Sexuality: An Introduction* (New York: Random House, 1978).

41. Dialogue from *The Thing* (1982).

42. "John Carpenter's *The Thing*: Terror Takes Shape," *The Thing*, directed by Michael Matessino (1998; Universal City, CA: Universal, 1998), DVD.

BIBLIOGRAPHY

Agamben, Giorgio. *Homo Sacer: Sovereign Power and Bare Life*. Stanford: Stanford University Press, 1998.

Barthes, Roland. *Elements of Semiology*, 8th ed. New York: Hill and Wang, 1986.

Baudrillard, Jean. *Baudrillard Live: Selected Interviews*, edited by Mike Gane, London: Routledge, 1993.

_____. *Simulacra and Simulation*. Ann Arbor: University of Michigan Press, 1994.

_____. *Symbolic Exchange and Death*. London: Sage, 1993.

Berlatsky, Noah. "Fecund Horror." *Gayutopia*, 2008, http://gayutopia.blogspot.it/2007/12/noah-berlatsky-fecund-horror_12.html.

Billson, Ann. *The Thing*. London: BFI, 2012.

Campbell, John W., Jr. *Who Goes There? The Novella that Formed the Basis of "The Thing."* Somerset, PA: Rocket Ride Books, 2009.

Castells, Manuel. *End of Millennium, the Information Age: Economy, Society and Culture Vol. III*. Cambridge, MA: Blackwell, 1998.

_____. *The Power of Identity, the Information Age: Economy, Society and Culture Vol. II*. Cambridge, MA: Blackwell, 1997.

_____. *The Rise of the Network Society, the Information Age: Economy, Society and Culture Vol. I*. Cambridge, MA: Blackwell, 1996.

Conolly, Jez. *The Thing*. Leighton, UK: Auteur, 2014.

Crane, Jonathan Lake. *Terror and Everyday Life: Singular Moments in the History of the Horror Film*. Thousand Oaks: Sage, 1994.

Creed, Barbara. *The Monstrous Feminine: Film, Feminism, Psychoanalysis*. New York: Routledge, 1993.

Doherty, Thomas. "Genre, Gender and *The Aliens Trilogy*." In *The Dread of Difference: Gender and the Horror Film*, 2d ed., edited by Barry K. Grant, 209–227. Austin: University of Texas Press, 2015.

Foucault, Michel. *History of Sexuality: An Introduction*. New York: Random House, 1978.

Guerrero, Ernesto. "AIDS as Monster in Science Fiction and Horror Cinema." *Journal of Popular Film and Television* 18 (Fall 1990): 87–93.

Horkheimer, Max, and Theodor W. Adorno. *Dialectic of Enlightenment: Philosophical Fragments*. Stanford: Stanford University Press, 2002.

Jameson, Fredric. *Postmodernism or the Cultural Logic of Late Capitalism*. Durham: Duke University Press, 1991.

Kracauer, Siegfried. *From Caligari to Hitler: A Psychological History of the German Film*. Princeton: Princeton University Press, 2004.

Kristeva, Julia. *Powers of Horror: An Essay on Abjection*. New York: Columbia University Press, 1982.

Lash, Scott, and Celia Lury. *Global Culture Industry: The Mediation of Things*. Cambridge: Polity, 2007.

Latour, Bruno. *Science in Action: How to Follow Scientists and Engineers Through Society*. Cambridge: Harvard University Press, 1987.

Merton, Robert K. *The Sociology of Science: Theoretical and Empirical Investigations*. Chicago: University of Chicago Press, 1973.

Muir, John Kenneth. "John Carpenter's *The Thing (1982)*." *Reflections on Film and Television*, 2011. http://reflectionsonfilmandtelevision.blogspot.it/search?q=the+thing.

Mulvie-Roberts, Marie. "'A Spook Ride on Film': Carpenter and the Gothic." In *The Cinema of John Carpenter: The Technique of Terror*, edited by Ian Conrich and David Woods, 78–90. London: Wallflower, 2004.

Pridham, Matthew. "Underneath the Skin: John Carpenter's *"The Thing"* and You." *Weird Fiction Review*, March 25, 2012. http://weirdfictionreview.com/2012/03/underneath-the-skin-john-carpenters-the-thing-and-you/.

Prince, Stephen. "Dread, Taboo and *The Thing*: Toward a Social Theory of the Horror Film." In *The Horror Film*, edited by Stephen Prince, 118–129. New Brunswick: Rutgers University Press, 2004.

Schumpeter, Joseph Alois. *Capitalism, Socialism and Democracy*. London: Routledge, 2003.

"Scientists Look to Re-Animate Ancient, Giant 'Frankenvirus' Found in Siberia." *Fox News*, September 9, 2015. http://www.foxnews.com/science/2015/09/09/french-scientists-look-to-re-animate-ancient-giant-frankenvirus-found-in.html

The Thing. DVD. Directed by John Carpenter. 1982. University City, CA: Universal, 1998.

The Thing. DVD. Directed by Matthijs van Heijningen, Jr., 2011. Universal City, CA: Universal Pictures, 2012.

The Thing from Another World. DVD. Directed by Christian Nyby. 1951. Burbank, CA: Turner Home Entertainment, 2010.

The Thing. "John Carpenter's *The Thing*: Terror Takes Shape." Directed by Michael Matessino. Universal City, CA: Universal, 1998. DVD.

Trigg, Dylan. *The Thing: A Phenomenology of Horror*. Alresford, UK: Zero Books, 2014.

Williams, Raymond. *Marxism and Literature*. Oxford: Oxford University Press, 1977.

Wood, Robin. *Hollywood from Vietnam to Regan … and Beyond*. New York: Columbia University Press, 2003.

Žižek, Slavoj. *The Sublime Object of Ideology*. London: Verso, 2008.

Meteor Madness

Lovecraftian Horror and Consumerism in the Battle for Small Town USA

NICHOLAS DIAK

> From time immemorial the Earth has been bombarded by objects from outer space. Bits and pieces of the universe piercing our atmosphere in an invasion that never ends.... From infinity they come. Meteors! Another strange calling card from the limitless reaches of space—its substance unknown, its secrets unexplored. The meteor lies dormant in the night—waiting![1]

With that proclamation in the opening narration of *The Monolith Monsters* (1957, John Sherwood), a new, niche subgenre of sci-fi/horror was born: the meteorite-horror film. Creature features had been a staple of horror cinema, coming into prominence with the Universal Horror films of the 1930s such as *Frankenstein* (1931, James Whale) and *The Mummy* (1932, Karl Freund). While these creature features had been grounded in gothic literature and historic folklore, the meteorite-horror film introduced new creatures that came from the vast reaches of space. The genre was firmly cemented in popular culture with the success of its most popular entry, *The Blob* (1958, Irvin Yeaworth).

Despite the notoriety of *The Blob*, other meteorite-horror films are often confined to cult cinema or are generally lumped into other broad film genres and remain unknown. This is unfortunate because when the films are viewed as their own distinct subgenre, compared and contrasted with each other and with other films, new meaning and social critiques are unearthed. Other atomic creature features of the 1950s and 1960s have been allegorical for a variety of topics. For example, *Godzilla* (1954, Ishirō Honda) and other *Kaijū* movies have been representative of atomic weapons while *Invasion of the Body Snatchers* (1956, Don Siegel) was metaphorical for Communist subversion. Meteorite-horror films are no different.

Meteorite-horror films and their monsters are greatly influenced by H.P. Lovecraft's short story "The Colour Out of Space." Overt film adaptations of the short story have benefited from analysis in books such as *Lurker in the Lobby: A Guide to the Cinema of H.P. Lovecraft*, but the story's profound influence on other films remains fleeting and unexplored. These films also act as allegory of the conflict between small town America and the rise and dominance of consumerism from the 1950s onward. Many films, from *They Live* (1988, John Carpenter) to *Fight Club* (1999, David Fincher), have addressed consumerism at a macro level, but these meteorite-horror films take the unique approach of tackling the subject at a micro level of idyllic small towns.

The goal of this essay will be to flesh out and properly define the meteorite-horror subgenre. Secondly, it will identify and solidify the Lovecraft connections from "The Colour Out of Space" to the meteorite-horror genre of films using intertextual means. The source material and the films will be compared and contrasted to identify important key components of the subgenre. Finally, applying a semiotic framework to consider meteorite-horror monsters as both figurative and literal outsiders to small town communities as well as metaphors for the advent of consumerism will yield new meaning in the effects of consumerism on small town America in a post–World War II environment.

The Canon of Meteorite-Horror Films

A distinction needs to be made between Lovecraftian meteorite-horror films that this essay focuses on and other sci-fi/horror films that feature asteroids, comets, and meteors. The primary difference resides in whether the meteor impacts the earth (meteorite) or not (meteoroid).

The most well-known meteoroid films are the meteor-disaster films. These films mimic natural disaster films such as *Earthquake* (1974, Mark Robson), *The Day After Tomorrow* (2004, Roland Emmerich), and *Volcano* (1997, Mick Jackson), which emphasize groups of specialists such as scientists and researchers along with common folk attempting to stall, avert, or survive cataclysmic phenomena. Entries in this category include *Deep Impact* (1998, Mimi Leder), *Armageddon* (1998, Michael Bay), *Meteor* (1979, Ronald Neame), and *Meteor Apocalypse* (2010, Micho Rutare).

Sometimes these meteor-disaster films take on horror elements and feature a passing comet or meteor shower that triggers a fantastical global event. Films in this category include *Maximum Overdrive* (1986, Stephen King),

Night of the Comet (1984, Thom Eberhardt), *Disaster L.A.* (2014, Turner Clay) and *The Day of the Triffids* (1962, Steve Sekely). These films feature inanimate objects coming to life, zombies, or mass blindness and plant monsters caused by the passing object.

For meteorite-horror films, however, a meteorite actually has to impact the earth and become the catalyst for the ensuing horror. Not all meteorites in these films are clumps of outer space rock and metal, but instead can be housing for an extraterrestrial, a seed, or even a manmade object falling back to Earth. Whatever the object, it inevitability releases something into the environment, be it a creature, a malady, or both.

There are a number of films that comprise this subgenre. Firstly, there are the filmic adaptations of "The Color Out of Space" which consists of *Die, Monster, Die!* (1965, Daniel Haller), *The Curse* (1987, David Keith), and *Die Farbe* (2012, Huan Vu). Excluded from this list however is *Colour from the Dark* (2008, Ivan Zuccon). Though this film is an adaptation of Lovecraft's short story, it does not feature a meteorite or an extraterrestrial but instead a supernatural entity at the bottom of a well. The film focuses on religious themes instead of cosmic horror that is found in the other films in this genre.

Secondly, this canon also contains what is probably its most renown film, *The Blob*, one of the first films starring Steve McQueen. There is also a sequel to *The Blob* called *Beware! The Blob* (1972, Larry Hagman) as well as a 1988 remake that are also a part of the canon. In these films, a gelatinous substance slithers around town consuming its populace. Aside from "The Color Out of Space," the *Blob* films are indebted to another Lovecraft story, "At the Mountains of Madness," which features creatures called Shoggoths. The titular blobs share many traits with the Shoggoths that Lovecraft describes as "multicellular protoplasmic masses capable of moulding their tissues into all sorts of temporary organs"[2] and "viscous masses."[3]

Finally, there are miscellaneous films, both major studio and independent productions, that fall under the meteorite-horror umbrella. These include *The Monolith Monsters*, "The Lonesome Death of Jordy Verrill" segment from *Creepshow* (1982, George A. Romero), *The Deadly Spawn* (1983, Douglas McKeown), *Slither* (2006, James Gunn), and *The Killing of Jacob Marr* (2010, Bred Rego).

There are a number of other horror, avant-garde, surreal and B-films that contain meteorites, such as *S. Darko* (2009, Chris Fisher), *The Giant Spider Invasion* (1975, Bill Rebane), and *Seed People* (1992, Peter Manoogian). Though these films contain similar elements and tropes, they stray too far from Lovecraft territory into other avenues. *S. Darko* is a time traveling psychological horror film, *The Giant Spider Invasion* is from the "animals-gone-amok" genre that was popular in the 1970s and *Seed People* is more of an updated version of *Invasion of the Body Snatchers*. Though these films lack

Lovecraftian elements, they do share some similarities with other films in this canon, so comparisons and similarities can certainly be drawn.

Lovecraft's Influence

Direct film adaptations of H.P. Lovecraft's work are few and far between, mostly being confined to micro budget cinema and the film festival circuit with the occasional bigger film such as *Re-Animator* (1985, Stuart Gordon) popping up now and then. However, his influence on cinema is definitely wide reaching and recognized with his particular brand of cosmic horror finding its way into films such as *Alien* (1979, Ridley Scott) and *The Evil Dead* films. The premiere book on Lovecraft cinema, *Lurker in the Lobby: A Guide to the Cinema of H.P. Lovecraft*, does an admirable job of exploring this influence by focusing "on either direct adaptations or on films that do some serious name and/or theme-dropping from the Lovecraft mythos."[4] Shockingly, though, entries from the meteorite-horror canon that are not film adaptations are absent from the book.

The meteorite-horror films transcend being merely influenced by Lovecraft; they all have their genesis directly in his short story "The Colour Out of Space." The story revolves around a meteorite that crashes onto the Gardner family's farmstead. The properties of the meteorite initially cause the farm to produce bountiful produce that turns out to be inedible. The farm withers and turns grey as the livestock dies. The family's matriarch goes insane and must be kept in the attic. Eventually, a concerned townsperson rallies a few others to investigate the situation and they witness an outpouring of light from the farm's well to the night sky, though some light falls back into the well, hinting that the alien menace that caused the blight upon the farm remains. Some films are adaptations of this story with varying artistic license of the source material while others heavily borrow key and distinct concepts. These core elements can be easily identified by comparing the meteorite-horror films to "The Colour Out of Space" under the banner of intertextuality. Per Emanuel Levy:

> Intertextuality implies self-consciousness on the part of the artist and is a matter of degree. It is important to point out the similarities and differences between individual films and the larger categories of which they are part. References to earlier works are inevitable, but may take different forms. In some cases, there is a conscious borrowing of a character or plot element, but at other times, a film provides commentary or "corrects" genre conventions.[5]

Levy also posits that "Intertextually suggests that the meaning of a particular work derives from its relation to a larger set of films."[6] While Levy is addressing intertextuality between films, his reasoning is also valid for intertextuality among different mediums, and, in this case, films to a short story. The shared core concepts between these films and "The Colour Out of Space" are numerous.

Firstly, every meteorite-horror film shares the same setting: a small town or a house in a rural area just outside of town. This perfectly mirrors many of Lovecraft's works where the action unfolds in small backwater New England towns, but it especially mirrors the setting in "The Colour Out of Space" which takes place at the Gardner farmstead near the community of Clark's Corners in the rural lands west of Arkham. *The Blob*, its sequel and remake, *The Monolith Monsters*, and *Slither* all take place in small towns while *The Deadly Spawn*, *The Curse*, "The Lonesome Death of Jordy Verrill" and *The Killing of Jacob Marr* primary take place in houses or farms outside the community. All but two of these films take place in America: *Die, Monster, Die!* is set in at an estate outside a British incarnation of Arkham, while *Die Farbe* takes place at a farm in Germany during World War II.

The light aliens in "The Colour Out of Space" are depicted as neither good nor evil. Per S.T. Joshi, the beings have an "utter absence of any sense of willful viciousness, destructiveness, or conventional 'evil'"[7] and doubts that the entities lack a moral compass or a consciousness to be capable of malevolent actions. This more neutral, perhaps animalistic attribute of the entities in "The Colour Out of Space" is shared by the creatures in meteorite-horror films. For example, in regards to the titular monster in *The Blob*, Bill Warren states, "The Blob itself has no personality: it is merely a mass of unexplained protoplasm driven to ingest living creatures, and does so in a very simple fashion: it merely absorbs them into its own body."[8] This apt description carries over to the Blob in both the sequel and remake as well. The spawn from *The Deadly Spawn*, though portrayed in a cartoonish "Tex Avery"[9] fashion, also only exist to eat and multiply, exhibiting no consciousness. The monoliths in *The Monolith Monsters* are not even living beings at all; they grow when exposed to water until they become too heavy and then collapse only the repeat the cycle again and again. The exception to this qualifier are the aliens from *Slither*, in which during a bathtub scene teenager Kylie (Tania Saulnier) has a creature partially enter her mouth, briefly exposing her to their hive mind and thus making her privy to their nefarious goals of the alien of consuming and spreading to the next planet.

If the film lacks a cosmic creature it will in its stead have a character become infected with a disease or malady, altering his or her body and driving him or her insane and homicidal. This mirrors the wife of Nahum Gardner in Lovecraft's story who is infected with a madness caused by the light aliens. In *Die, Monster, Die!* Nahum Witley (Boris Karloff) becomes exposed to radiation from meteorite fragments. In *The Curse*, the majority of the Crane family becomes infected from contaminated groundwater from a crashed meteor, developing boils on their faces and furrowed caveman brows. In *Slither*, alien worms enter the townsfolk and squirm their way to their brains to take control. The titular character in *The Killing of Jacob Marr* pockets a meteor that drives him insane and turns him into a slasher villain. Jordy in "The Lonesome Death of Jordy Verrill" becomes infected from a downed meteorite as well, his body consumed in plant growth.

Much like in the original story where the Gardner farm becomes blighted, withered and devoid of color, so too are the locales in these films susceptible to environmental catastrophe. The film adaptations of *Die, Monster, Die!*, *Die Farbe* and *The Curse* all portray the farmlands and countryside ravaged by the effects of the meteorite. Both the rocks in *The Monolith Monsters* and the plant matter in "The Lonesome Death of Jordy Verrill" will continue to spread and transform the land if their progress is not stopped. At the ending of *The Deadly Spawn*, a building-sized spawn bursts through the earth. It could be inferred that the Blob will also grow to this size to cause major environmental damage.

Water plays an important role in "The Colour Out of Space," with the coming of a dam that will flood the farmland while the light aliens reside in the Gardners' well, implying they may have contaminated the groundwater and hence the surrounding lands. This plot of course is replicated in both *The Curse* and *Die Farbe*, but water plays important parts in other meteorite-horror films as well, usually as an agent to proliferate the effects. The rocks in *The Monolith Monsters* multiply when exposed to water. The spawn in *The Deadly Spawn* share this same affinity. Per the film's director Douglas McKeown, "we had a monster called The Spawn that flourished in water"[10] and "the spawns like water and flesh … period."[11] It is constantly raining in the film, and the spawn are found in a flooded basement. It can be surmised the giant spawn at the film's conclusion is so large due to the endless downpour. The plant infection of Jordy in "The Lonesome Death of Jordy Verrill" is further exacerbated when he takes a bath, and the news broadcast of heavy rains foreshadow its continued expansion.

A common theme in many of Lovecraft's stories is man's own powerlessness to combat or understand the cosmic horrors that have been unleashed. Many times in these stories the agents of horror are not stopped, merely slowed down, at the cost of the protagonist going insane. Simply put, the menace cannot be stopped. The ending of "The Colour Out of Space" showcases this aspect of Lovecraft perfectly, with two of the light aliens flying back into the cosmos while the third one falls back into the well, with the narrator thankful that the cursed area will soon be flooded.

These themes of unstoppable, incomprehensible cosmic terror are found in these meteorite-horror films in that nearly all of them end in such a fashion that the creatures will return or the malady will proliferate. *The Blob* ends with the viscous creature frozen in the Arctic, with the words "The end?" on the screen, prophesizing that the Blob can thaw and run amok, which is exactly what happens in *Beware! The Blob*. The 1988 version of *The Blob* ends similarly with the creature frozen while an apocalyptic priest possesses a fragment of the Blob in a jar. Warren explains that the monolith menace in *The Monolith Monsters* is not truly resolved: "At the end, the monoliths are not destroyed by the salt, only halted. The next rain will cause problems unless a way of stopping them permanently can be found. The movie raises the idea that the rocks may have been carried to other parts of the country by tourists."[12] In *The Deadly Spawn*, the mother spawn is exploded and her offspring are rounded up and either cattle prodded or burnt, the menace seemingly at an end. At the film's conclusion, a giant spawn bursts from the ground and roars into the night. At the end of *The Killing of Jacob Marr*, the meteorite that drove Marr insane is passed onto the sole survivor, implying he will suffer the same fate of uncontrollable homicidal urges. A parasite infects a cat in a post-credits scene in *Slither*, affirming that the aliens will continue on. The shot of the mile markers to nearby cities at the end of "The Lonesome Death of Jordy Verrill" indicate the plant contagion will continue to spread to urban areas and beyond. These endings are not just simple cliffhangers, but are reaffirmations of the nature of cosmic horror, that man is powerless to solve or understand.

Finally, a coalescing of many of the above points, is the nature of consumption that all these films share. As demonstrated with the blobs, the monoliths, the spawns, and the slithers, these mindless creatures overtly eat or absorb, growing larger and reproducing. In a more figurative, but still applicable light, some of the characters as in *Die, Monster Die!*, *The Killing of Jacob Marr* and "The Lonesome Death of Jordy Verrill" are consumed by insanity or contagions while the surrounding farmlands as in *The Curse* and *Die Farbe* are consumed by blights and catastrophe. In all instances, outside agents have set themselves upon a small town or farm and engaged in aggressive acts of consumption.

Small town and rural settings, lack of good/evil labeling, interstellar insanity, environmental catastrophes, water as agent to proliferate the terror, mindless consuming, and man's insignificance at controlling cosmic horror—these are all major, not superficial, commonalities these films share that are, via intertextuality, deeply rooted in Lovecraft's "The Colour Out of Space." Lovecraft's profound influence, be it via adaptation, homage, or unseen hand, is unmistakable in these films, and these facets demonstrate this influence. It is, however, in the conflict of the small town setting and the agents of consumption, be it creature or malady, that these films demonstrate a greater deal of subversion.

Small Town America and Consumerism

Though perhaps not consciously executed by the filmmakers, but when viewed as a whole, the meteorite-horror subgenre of films takes on attributes that makes them critical of the rise of consumerism in America from the 1950s and beyond and its possible negative effects on small town America. Bruce Kawin first recognized this association in his essay that appeared in the Criterion Collection release of *The Blob*:

> They may also have felt frightened as consumers, not just as moviegoers, as they watched the hungry mass—comparable to if not incarnating the growing consumerism of 1950s America—devour their kind. If they had forgotten the War and wanted to live in a world of play, their complacent desire to stuff themselves with goods and good time had shown itself to be a monster.[13]

While Kawin's observation is exclusively directed toward *The Blob*, his musing is applicable to describing how the meteorite-monsters can be perceived in the other films of the subgenre, both old and new. Excluding *Die Farbe* and *Die, Monster, Die!* which are set in Europe, the other films in the subgenre all include entities and maladies that are just as allegorical as *The Blob* is at projecting fears of American consumerism and its effects on small town communities and their relationships. Since these films are set in small town communities or near their outskirts, the focus becomes even narrower on the effects of consumerism on the small town, one of the last bastions of the American Dream and idyllic lifestyles.

In *An All-Consuming Century*, Gary Cross briefly defines consumerism and its rise in America:

> A very different concept of society has emerged—a consuming public, defined and developed by individual acquisition and use of mass-produced goods. Consumerism, the belief that goods give meaning to individuals and their roles in society, was victorious even though it had no formal philosophy, no parties, and no obvious leaders. Consumerism was the "ism" that won—despite repeated attacks on it as a threat to folk and high culture, to "true" community and individuality, and to the environment.[14]

And:

> Consumer goods allowed Americans to free themselves from their old, relatively secure but closed communities and enter the expressive individualism of a dynamic "mass" society. Commodities gave people a sense of freedom, sometimes serving as a substitute for the independence of the shop, craft, or farm that was disappearing as Americans joined the industrial work world.[15]

The economic and consumer climate in America after World War II was perfectly aligned to jumpstart the consumerist culture. During the Great Depression consumer and luxury goods were still being minimally produced but most of the population lacked the money to purchase them. Conversely, during World War II, the populace had the means to purchase luxury goods, but with production aligned to the war effort there were no goods to be had. It was only after the war that both the means and the products were in alignment, and Americans could indulge in purchasing goods and commodities with abandon.

Within cinema, larger cities and the emerging suburbia are shown as having succumbed to consumer decadence. Per Emanuel Levy, big cities in films are often portrayed as villainous, with "corruption, greed, impersonality, and dehumanization,"[16] and as folks moved from the big cities to suburbia, they took those traits with them. There is a plethora of reasons that the large cities exhibit these traits, and being large hubs of consumerism and industrialism is certainly one of them.

The various meteorite-monsters (the blobs, the monoliths, the spawns, etc.) and infections are not representative of the big cities or suburbs, but instead, as suggested by Kawin, of the growing advent of consumerism. Since these creatures operate without any agency of good or evil, they essentially become a blank slate to carry other meaning. As shown in the previous section, all of these creatures and cosmic conditions are agents of consumption: they eat, absorb and grow larger while negatively impacting the environment. In essence, they become physical embodiments of consumerist philosophy. By examining the relationship between these entities and the small towns these films are set in, the metaphor of consumerism as a negative force to small towns and their values becomes quite clear, particularly in regards to the breakdown of community and personal relationships.

In *Small-Town America in Film* Emanuel Levy proposes that small towns and communities in film can be evaluated in seven different unit-ideas: individuals versus community, community versus society, nature versus culture, stability versus change, integration versus anomie, sacred versus profane, and the public versus private domain.[17] Of these units, the two that are most applicable to evaluating small towns as depicted in meteorite-horror films are community versus society and stability versus change, as elements from both units are interchangeable. For community versus society, this is akin to the small town being contrasted to the big city, and thus different relationships between the populace. The small town has intimate, personal, one-on-one relationships while the big city would have secondary, bureaucratic relationships.[18] The stability versus change unit showcases the desire of a small town to hold onto the present and resist new technologies or ideas. The rise of consumerism is played out in both units as the absorption of more consumerist ideas into a small town would have drastic effects on the community, threatening personal relationships and self-sustaining economies, to be replaced by interpersonal and sterile relationships and franchised and faceless businesses.

The depiction of consumerism between films made in the 1950s to films made today, and all decades in between, is staggering. While the 1950s would have had limited globalized businesses and brand name products appearing in them, the cinema of today is rife with products and corporations, reflecting real world cities and suburbs. The exception of course is that the depiction of small towns in film has more or less remained unchanged. In reality, many small towns will no doubt have chain restaurants and stores, while the homes will be stocked with brand name goods. Within these films, however, these depictions are greatly subdued. For example, instead of fast food and chain restaurants, townsfolk still congregate and eat at mom and pop diners or pubs, such as in both versions of *The Blob, Slither* and *The Curse*. Of note is the meteorite film *S. Darko*; though outside the Lovecraftian meteorite-horror canon, it has the distinction of being made fairly recently in 2009 (though set in 1995), and still eschews recognizable restaurants in favor of the local diner. Though *The Killing of Jacob Marr* lacks a diner, the protagonists do patronize an independently owned convenience store called Vorhees Market which fulfills the same purpose as the diner does.

Product placement is either subdued or subverted in these films. In most cases, the products are incidental, appearing in normal, non-obtrusive places, such as the Coke and Pepsi refrigerators in the convenience store in *The Killing of Jacob Marr* and neon signs for beer brands in the bar in *Slither*. In other cases, they are played up for jokes. For example, in *Beware! The Blob*, Miller High Life is featured mostly as a reoccurring gag as cases of the beverage are toppled or ran over. In *Slither*, after a traumatic encounter with possessed townsfolk and alien worms, mayor Jack MacReady (Gregg Henry) cries out for a Mr. Pibb, a brand of soda that trails far behind both Coke and Pepsi in terms of market share. The mention of Mr. Pibb becomes a more esoteric reference, played for comedic value rather than an actual product placement.

The absence of chains and big name stores from small town films could be attributed to filmmakers not procuring the rights or coordinating product placement to feature them. This can be worked around by using fictitious and even parody businesses and products, such as the fast food chain Mooby's in Kevin Smith's View Askewniverse films or Fox Books from *You've Got Mail* (1998, Nora Ephron). Therefore, the lack of such elements, real or fictitious, is a conscience decision by the filmmakers to omit them from the small town settings and thus reaffirm their idyllic nature and reliance on micro economies. Small towns are self-sustainable and personable, relying on family-owned businesses, and have no need for impersonal goods and services that have dominated suburbia and the big cities. This has been a fairly consistent filmic portrayal of small towns in the past 60 years, be it in the meteorite-horror film or another genre.

Having firmly established that small town America is an ideological construct to showcase an establishment untarnished by consumerism, the focus needs to be turned to the meteorite-monsters themselves and how they demonstrate conflict of values. This is done by the monster taking on the mantle of "the outsider."

Levy describes the narrative structure of small town films using outsider characters as having three distinct phases. The first phase is that the outsider arrives in town, which disrupts any state of normality or equilibrium. The second phase of the film demonstrates the effects the outsider has on the town, the actual turmoil or conflict, while the final phase has the outsider either leave the town or integrate into it.[19] The outsider can be many types of characters, such drifters, hitchhikers, persons newly moved into the town, and even folks returning to their hometown after extended residency elsewhere. Levy posits that most outsiders are attractive young or middle-aged men, but acknowledges there are cases where the outsider is a female.[20] Examples of small town outsiders in cinema include Ren McCormack (Kevin Bacon) in *Footloose* (1984, Herbert Ross), a newly arrived teenager who winds up challenging the town's ban on dancing and rock n' roll; Tom Stall (Viggo Mortensen) in *A History of Violence* (2005, David Cronenberg), an hitman who is able to acclimate to a town and become a pillar citizen, but is later unmasked and must work to repair his relationship with his family; and Donnie (Jake Gyllenhall) in *Donnie Darko* (2001, Richard Kelly), a troubled teenager whose antics of flooding his school and setting fire to a motivational speaker's house exposing him as a pedophile has consequences that ripple through the community and his family.

Levy's definition of the outsider is anchored to realistic films and needs expansion in order for meteorite-monsters to be considered a small town outsider. By default, these creatures originate from the far reaches of space, so they are inherently outsiders by definition. Semantics aside, what is important is the role the meteorite-monster fulfills mirrors the role of a traditional outsider in the three-part configuration proposed by Levy. *The Blob* illustrates the role of the outsider perfectly. For the first phase, the Blob crash lands on the outskirts of town and sets off many chain reactions. The town's doctor, a symbol of leadership and authority within the community, is eaten, thereby setting up instability. At the same time, the protagonist teenagers are pitted against adults, challenging their role in the community. Teenagers are normally relegated to the role of children or pranksters and not to be taken seriously, but in *The Blob*, as well as in the sequel and remake, they are the driving force to combat the viscous menace and eventually win over the police and adult authority. The Blob terrorizes The Colonial movie theater, consuming the patrons inside, desecrating an important public gathering space. In a scene that embodies complete consumerism, the Blob is also encountered at

Jerry's Supermarket, a grocery owned by Steve Andrews' (Steve McQueen) dad. It is here that the teenagers attempt to rally the town and convince them of the existence of the Blob menace (and semiotically, the consumerist menace), which initially fails. All of these scenarios unfold during Levy's second stage of the outsider film, while the third stage sees the Blob frozen and vanquished to its polar prison, expelled from the community. *Beware! The Blob* and the 1988 incarnation follow this outsider formula as well, with minor substitutions: the sequel replaces the theater with a bowling alley while the remake replaces it with a church. All three locations shown are public pillars and gathering locations for the community being greatly disrupted.

The Monolith Monsters adheres to the outsider format too, even though the rocks are not living entities. The meteorite obtains its outsider status by crashing in the desert mountains outside town but being brought in accidentally by a local geologist and a young girl on a field trip. The town is soon thrown into disarray as the monoliths destroy homesteads on the outskirts of town and drain silicon from the residents, turning them into rock. With the telephones out, the town looks to the youth to disperse the bulletins to each house one by one on their bikes, much like newspaper delivery boys. For this mass communication, technology has failed, but the small town values of personal relationships and youth candor prevail. While in *The Blob* the town only partially comes together, in *The Monolith Monsters* the town maintains its unification with little internal strife. The monoliths are banished from the town by being neutralized by a saltwater flood. While the consumerist angle in *The Monolith Monsters* is lighter when compared to other entries in the canon, the actions of the ever-growing and ever-consuming monoliths do reinforce the meteorite-monsters as outsiders concept.

Slither is an interesting outlier in that it depicts the battle of small town versus consumerism even before the arrival of the meteorite and its alien inhabitant. The opening shots in *Slither* portray the town in a hyper idyllic fashion by showing the town surrounded by lush forested foothills. The town is aflutter for an upcoming community event. The next shot shows a prominent ad for Coke on the side of a building and is immediately followed by scenes of transients and graffiti covered walls. The editing of the sequence in this particular order can imply a relationship between Coke and small town decay. The alien from the meteorite starts as an outsider but enters the community by taking control of another character, Grant (Michael Rooker). As in *The Blob*, there is a grocery store scene in which Grant tries to purchase as much meat as possible from the butcher to satiate his hunger. Relationships in the town begin to crumble, slowly at first between Grant and his wife Starla (Elizabeth Banks) in a marital sense, to outright anarchy as the slug aliens infect, kill, eat, and absorb the town's populace including Mayor MacReady, into its hive collective. The giant Grant/monster hybrid in *Slither* is banished from the community by way of death from propane tank explosion.

In all of these films, the towns' police force suffers the most negative effects from the arrival of the outsider meteorite-monster as they are portrayed as incompetent or inept. In the original *The Blob*, Sergeant Jim Bert (John Benson) is antagonistic to the teenagers, theorizing they are all conspiring against him to try and break him. He treats all their actions to warn the town as pranks, which of course stymies their efforts. In *Beware! The Blob*, Sheriff Jones (Richard Webb) attempts to stop the Blob by burning down the bowling alley, despite people still being trapped inside. He is unable to even light his own torch, and a boy scout must do it for him. His inability to grasp the situation carries to the final scene: while seeking the limelight from a news crew, his legs become enveloped by the Blob that was able to ooze out of its frozen confines. In the 1988 version of *The Blob*, Deputy Bill Briggs (Paul McCrane) mimics his Sergeant Bert counterpart of the original by his overtly hostile demeanor to the teenagers, but this films steps the incompetency of authority up a notch by showing both the police and the military as ineffective at dealing with the Blob. Time and time again the military, led by Dr. Meddows (Joe Seneca), fails to contain the Blob, instead allowing it to run rampant and considering the town and its populace expendable. Finally, in *Slither*, the entire police force is portrayed as particularly inept, but this is mostly done for comedic value. The town's officers and even secretary all get either decimated or absorbed into the slither hive, leaving only police chief Bill Pardy (Nathan Fillon) as the last man standing. Though the hero of the story, Pardy is extremely clumsy at handling the alien menace, best demonstrated when his grenade is knocked from his hands by Grant and into the swimming pool. If there is one exception to this depiction of the police in the meteorite-horror films, it is *The Deadly Spawn*. The police arrive at the end of the film and without hesitation work with the locals at cattle prodding and burning the spawn menace.

In these films, the monster unleashed by the meteorite enters the community as an outsider. Aside from the monster actually eating the inhabitants, the town is thrown into disarray with figures of authority such as doctors and mayors eaten, the police force unable to handle the crisis, and the personal relationships between each other, especially between the youth and authority, challenged. As dictated by Levy's configuration, at the film's end, the monsters are removed from the community, frozen, blown up or destroyed by other means. However, to subvert this point, in a true Lovecraftian sense, the monsters are not vanquished, as the frozen Blob will thaw and the infected cat at the end of *Slither* will return. The horrors of the monsters and the infringing of consumerist beliefs on the small towns are not truly defeated, merely stalled for the time being.

Conclusion

H.P. Lovecraft continues to be a major influential force on artistic works, from books to art, from music to film. Cementing the connections between his short story "The Colour Out of Space" and the meteorite-horror subgenre of films further strengthens this claim. The connections go beyond the superficial or cherry picking of elements here and there, but instead core elements are found in all these films' DNA, be they direct adaptation or not. The small town setting, the absence of good and evil agency, environmental cataclysms, the role of water, man's inability to comprehend and defeat the cosmic forces, and the monsters and maladies being agents of mass consumption are all important foundational elements these films share and can be traced back to "The Colour Out of Space."

Since the meteorite-monsters lack both good and evil agency and only exist to consume, they become the perfect allegory of consumerism. With the setting of these films restricted to small town communities, the conflict between monster and town becomes synonymous with the rising tide of consumerism post–World War II and small town values. Since the big cities and suburbs had already embraced rampant consumerism, the small town became one of the few filmic constructs that could depict a setting untouched by consumerism, and thus explore the effects of consumerism on personal relationships, local economies, and older, traditional values.

In order to accomplish this, the meteorite-monster takes on the role of the outsider to the community. When the monster enters the town, personal relationships, leadership and other communal structures are challenged until the menace is forced out. In particular, governmental institutions such as the police force do not fare well in these scenarios. In perhaps a nihilistic attitude, the monsters can only be forced out temporarily. They, along with the consumeristic weight they carry, will eventually prevail.

With the exception of the original version of *The Blob* which has benefited from academic analysis and pop culture reverence already, the subgenre as a whole still remains largely unexplored, ripe for more academic consideration. As demonstrated, these films are indeed important, despite being relegated to niche or cult status when compared to other horror genres such as zombie films or television shows about vampires. Despite this, the genre has its allure and filmmakers now and then add to the canon. For example, another remake of *The Blob* has been in the pipeline for some time. Originally to be helmed by Rob Zombie it currently has Simon West attached as director.[21] Whether this updated version of the classic film is release or not is up in the air, but it is still a testament to the enduring nature of the subgenre, one that carries much more academic currency than originally thought.

NOTES

1. *The Monolith Monsters*, DVD, directed by John Sherwood (1957; Universal City, CA: Universal, 2014).
2. H.P. Lovecraft, "At the Mountains of Madness," in *The New Annotated H.P. Lovecraft*, ed. Leslie S. Klinger (New York: Liveright, 2014), 525.
3. *Ibid.*
4. Andrew Milgore and John Strysik, *Lurker in the Lobby: A Guide to the Cinema of H.P. Lovecraft* (Portland, OR: Night Shade Books, 2006), 3.
5. Emanuel Levy, *Small-Town America in Film: The Decline and Fall of Community* (New York: Continuum, 1991), 23.
6. *Ibid.*
7. S.T. Joshi, *A Subtler Magick: The Writings and Philosophy of H.P. Lovecraft*, 3d ed. (Gillette, NJ: Wildside Press, 1996), 137.
8. Bill Warren, *Keep Watching the Skies! American Science Fiction Movies of the Fifties*, 21st Century Edition (Jefferson, NC: McFarland, 2010), 119.
9. Stephen Thrower, *Nightmare USA: The Untold Story of Exploitation Independents* (Surrey, UK: FAB Press, 2007), 134.
10. *Ibid.*, 138.
11. *Ibid.*, 143.
12. Warren, *Keep Watching the Skies!*, 586.
13. Bruce Kawin, "The Blob," DVD, *The Blob* (New York: Criterion Collection, 2000).
14. Gary Cross, *An All-Consuming Century: Why Commercialism Won in Modern America* (New York: Columbia University Press, 2000), 1.
15. *Ibid.*, 2.
16. Levy, *Small-Town America in Film*, 16.
17. *Ibid.*, 24.
18. *Ibid.*, 25.
19. *Ibid.*, 115–116.
20. *Ibid.*, 116.
21. John Squires, "Simon West Boards Second Remake of *The Blob*," *Dread Central*, last modified January 22, 2015, http://www.dreadcentral.com/news/86644/simon-west-boards-second-remake-blob/.

BIBLIOGRAPHY

The Blob. DVD. Directed by Chuck Russell. 1988. Culver City, CA: Tri-Star, 2001.
The Blob. DVD. Directed by Irvin Yeaworth. 1958. New York: Criterion Collection, 2000.
Colour from the Dark. DVD. Directed by Ivan Zuccon. 2008. Los Angeles: Vanguard Cinema, 2010.
Die Farbe. Blu-ray. Directed by Huan Vu. 2010. Brink Vision, 2015.
Creepshow. Blu-ray. Directed by George A. Romero. 1982. Burbank, CA: Warner Home Video, 2009.
Cross, Gary. *An All-Consuming Century: Why Commercialism Won in Modern America*. New York: Columbia University Press, 2000.
The Deadly Spawn. DVD. Directed by Douglas McKeown. 1982. Novi, MI: Synapse Films, 2004.
Die, Monster, Die!. Blu-ray. Directed by Daniel Haller. 1965. Los Angeles: Shout! Factory, 2014.
First Man into Space. DVD. Directed by Robert Day. 1959. New York: Criterion Collection, 2006.
Joshi, S.T. *A Subtler Magick: The Writings and Philosophy of H.P. Lovecraft*, 3d ed. Gillette, NJ: Wildside Press, 1996.
Kawin, Bruce. "The Blob." DVD. *The Blob*. New York: Criterion Collection, 2000.
The Killing of Jacob Marr. DVD. Directed by Brad Rego. 2010. Brooklyn: 221 Films, 2010.
Levy, Emanuel. *Small-Town America in Film: The Decline and Fall of Community*. New York: Continuum, 1991.

Lovecraft, H.P. "At the Mountains of Madness." In *The New Annotated H.P. Lovecraft*, edited by Leslie S. Klinger, 457–572. New York: Liveright, 2014.
_____. "The Colour Out of Space." In *The New Annotated H.P. Lovecraft*, edited by Leslie S. Klinger, 310–342. New York: Liveright, 2014.
Migliore, Andrew, and John Strysik. *Lurker in the Lobby: A Guide to the Cinema of H.P. Lovecraft*. Portland, OR: Night Shade Books, 2006.
The Monolith Monsters. DVD. Directed by John Sherwood. 1957. Universal City, CA: Universal, 2014.
S. Darko. Blu-ray. Directed by Chris Fisher. 2009. Beverly Hills: Twentieth Century Fox, 2009.
Slither. DVD. Directed by James Gunn. 2006. Universal City, CA: Universal, 2006.
Squires, Simon. "Simon West Boards Second Remake of *The Blob*." *Dread Central*. Last modified January 22, 2015. http://www.dreadcentral.com/news/86644/simonwest-boards-second-remake-blob/.
Thrower, Stephen. *Nightmare USA: The Untold Story of Exploitation Independents*. Surrey, UK: FAB Press, 2007.
Warren, Bill. *Keep Watching the Skies! American Science Fiction Movies of the Fifties*. 21st Century Edition. Jefferson, NC: McFarland, 2010.

"It (never actually) came from outer space"

Earth-Origin Threats in Space Horror Films

KEVIN J. WETMORE, JR.

In her famous essay "The Imagination of Disaster," Susan Sontag outlines a variety of "model scenarios" for science fiction films, mostly focused on invasion narratives. The short version of her first "typical science fiction film" consists of one, "The arrival of the thing"; two, "confirmation of the hero's report" of the thing, usually in the form of mass destruction; three, a transfer of scene to the capital: "A national emergency is declared"; four, "further atrocities"; and, finally, five, after a countdown, "final repulse of the monsters or invaders. Mutual congratulations."[1] A short, five-step process from invasion by Other from space to a reassertion of the Self having conquered a horror from space.

Never mind that this morphology ignores most actual science fiction films and assumes alien invasion films are a synecdoche for all science fiction instead of a subgenre; Sontag simultaneously reads science fiction films as disaster (read: horror) films while categorically denying a connection between horror and science fiction. "Science fiction films are not about science. They are about disaster," she asserts, not entirely incorrectly.[2] Sontag then separates science fiction and horror, arguing the former does not have "much horror" in it.[3] And yet, as this volume proves, there is science fiction horror, which is also often about disaster on the macro scale (as in *War of the Worlds* [2005, Steven Spielberg], *Skyline* [2010, Greg Straus and Colin Straus], *Battle: Los Angeles* [2011, Jonathan Liebesman], etc.) and on the micro scale (what is *Alien* [1979, Ridley Scott] if not the tale of a disastrous voyage for the crew of the *Nostromo*?). Even Sontag concedes, "embodied in the science fiction films lurk the deepest anxieties about contemporary existence," and not just the obvious ones concerning the bomb, but also "powerful anxieties about the condition of the individual psyche."[4] The concern about alien invaders in such films as *The Invasion of the Body Snatchers* (1956, Don Siegel) or *Children of the Damned* (1964, Anton M. Leader) is rooted in the idea that we can be replaced by replicas of ourselves lacking any individuality, emotion or any of the elements we believe make up our selves. It is the fear of dehumanization, the loss of Self, placed alongside a larger fear of the loss of the nation to the bomb or foreign ideologies.

Sontag believes science fiction films (and by extension, space horror films) completely lack social commentary and criticism, arguing they fail to acknowledge science as a social and cultural activity (odd in an essay in which she just deconstructed the social commentary of those very films).[5] One might argue, as Sontag does, that by assigning the negative aspects of science to the aliens or monsters, these films posit human (read: American) science as positive. But what if "they" are actually us all along? Do these films not suggest a social aspect to science—we do it to ourselves, we allow it to happen, and then blame the Other?

Michael Bliss argues that in such invasion films the invasion "is a metaphor for assaults against the integrity of various things," i.e., the nation, the body, identity, marriage, a culture, etc.[6] The standard interpretation being that in these films the aliens serve as a metaphor for the Russians, or the Viet Cong, or ISIS and Al Qaeda (read: September 11th attacks on American soil), all real-world Others whose presence is threatening to America. Earth is a synecdoche for the United States and space is the unknown, imaginative geography from which the monstrous Other will emerge to threaten our way of life.

In her introduction to this volume, Michele Brittany posits four locales for "space horror," four locales for disaster from space, to invoke Sontag. The fourth and final locale is Earth itself, "terrestrial space horror," or "invasion films," which find the origin of horror in space, but the focus of events being on this planet. The disaster is on Earth, the origin is extraterrestrial. I argue, however, that there exists a category of films that pretend to or acknowledge horror from space that is, in fact, either actually of Earth origin, or so separated from its extraterrestrial origins so as to render its genesis irrelevant to the horror. In this essay, I propose to examine the antithesis of the volume: space horror actually from Earth. By offering close readings of these films in context, I propose that what is uncovered is a different kind of sociophobic: the use of space horror tropes serving as a larger metaphor for more prosaic fears, and subverting the traditional interpretation of monstrous invader as metaphor for The Other. These films demonstrate to the contrary that horror comes from us, not from "outside" and not from space.

A variant sub-taxonomy of the non-space-based space horror film sees three ways in which the space part of space horror is either subverted or proven wrong. In the first, the film might feature a horror from space, but the horror is experienced on Earth and often is experienced because of an Earth-based catalyst. Films such as *Predator* (1987, John McTiernan), *The Astronaut's Wife* (1999, Rand Ravic), *Species* (1995, Ronald Donaldson) and even *Night of the Living Dead* (1968, George Romero) all posit a monster from space that is made horrific here on Earth.

Night of the Living Dead, for example, offers the possibility of a probe returning from Venus as the source of the reanimation of the dead, stating that the United States government blew up the probe as it entered our atmosphere with "strange radiation." "Why are space experts being consulted for an Earthbound emergency?"[7] asks the film's newscaster with gravity and judgment. The film never states conclusively whether the Venus probe was the cause of the recently dead reanimating, but the implication from the news reports is that the military sent a probe to Venus which returned and then was destroyed in a manner that brought the dead back to life. The radiation may be from Venus, but the probe was of earthly origin, and the decision to bring it back and the decision to destroy it in the atmosphere lay entirely within the American military and the American government. It is a recurring theme in Romero's zombie films that living humans are far more dangerous and self-destructive than the threat posed by the living dead.

Similarly, *Plan 9 from Outer Space* (1959, Ed Wood) is essentially earthbound horror. Although the protagonists are taken up in a flying saucer that threatens Earth, and which the military has already fired upon at the beginning of the film, the eponymous plan, as The Ruler states, "deals with the resurrection of the dead. Long distance electrodes shot into the pineal and pituitary gland of the recently dead."[8] The real horror of the film is the threat from Ghoul Man/Old Man's (Bela Lugosi/Tom Mason), Vampire Girl's (Vampira) and Inspector Clay's (Tor Johnson) reanimated corpses attacking people in the cemetery and finally, in the case of Paula Trent (Mona McKinnon), in her own home. The plan may be from outer space, but the horror is from earthly corpses.

One might also note an inversion of this type in *Jason X* (2001, James Isaac), the tenth film in the *Friday the 13th* series. The film begins with Jason being captured at the "Crystal Lake Research Facility" and cryogenically frozen, only to be thawed out five hundred years in the future when a spacecraft returns to Earth after pollution has forced humanity to live on other planets. Once reanimated on the spacecraft, Jason begins killing the crew. The only danger in this film, the only horror in space, if you will, is Jason Voorhees. A threat from old earth becomes the danger in space to human beings. In this case, Jason becomes the alien artifact that invades a human spaceship. But the danger is thus still terrestrial in origin.

The second erasure/subversion of space from space horror is in the case of films in which the horror has actually been on the planet for a prolonged time and the space origin is irrelevant because of it; the horror develops because something from the past has been uncovered, not because something has landed recently. This category film involves a delay between the arrival from space and the actual moment of horror. Something arrives in the distant past, then after a long period of being on Earth, returns to human awareness.[9] The horror is from space, but it is not an immediate horror, it is an ancient Earth horror brought back to light through human activity. The bad stuff is triggered by the activities or behavior of Earthlings.

John Carpenter's *The Thing* (1982), for example, opens with a pre-credit spaceship crash. Later in the film, however, the viewer is informed that the crash was not recent. As Doc Copper (Richard Dysart), Norris (Charles Hallahan) and MacReady (Kurt Russell) find the crashed spaceship in the ice, Norris tells the others, "The backscatter effect's been bringing things up from way down here for a long time. I'd say … I'd say the ice it's buried in is 100,000 years old at least."[10] In other words, the alien has already been on Earth for a thousand centuries. It has not been a source of horror until "these Norwegians blew it up," as MacReady notes.[11] Also note the appearance of the title creature in Norris's line: "the backscatter effect's been bringing *things* up." The alien being has been in the ice on Earth for one thousand centuries. When the team back at base discovers the nature of the Thing, Childs (Keith David) wants to know "how's this motherfucker wake up after thousands of years in the ice?"[12] "And how can it look like a dog?" counters Bennings (Peter Maloney, who, when he asks this, is already the Thing!) MacReady's only answer, "I don't know how. 'Cause it's different than us, see? 'Cause it's from outer space. What do you want from me?"[13] And that is the last discussion of the extraterrestrial nature of the Thing. It is now a fact of Earth that must be fought. The men repeatedly discuss how the Norwegians are the ones responsible for the Thing becoming active again. The Thing itself was from space, but the horror of the Thing is earthbound and was caused by Earthlings.

It's no coincidence that one of John Carpenter's least horrific genre films, *Starman* (1984), shares the same premise and plot as *The Thing*: a shapeshifting alien being comes to earth and attempts to hide in the indigenous population in order to survive and return to space. In *Starman*, however, the trope of Earth (especially America) being more dangerous than things from space is abundantly clear from the beginning: The Starman is a scout sent from an alien civilization that has found Voyager 2 and seeks first contact with its creators. He comes in peace and his ship is shot down by the American government. The authorities pursue him across the country until he is rescued by his own people in the Arizona desert (the film also shares these same numerous tropes with Spielberg's *E.T. The Extra-Terrestrial* (1982).

Carpenter makes it clear that the authorities from Earth are the real dangerous creatures. The horror does not come from space but from here.

Night of the Creeps (1986, Fred Dekker) features an alien threat arriving in 1959, when an alien suggestive of Spielberg's E.T. shoots a tube containing "an experiment" out a port on the spaceship which then crash lands near "Corman University." Johnny, a young college student goes to investigate a meteor crash and alien leaches from the tube enter his mouth. His dead body is then preserved cryogenically at the Corman lab and the invasion, Sontag-like, is stopped. When it re-emerges in 1986, it is not because the aliens have returned but because a local fraternity prank has gone wrong. The leaches infect the campus during fraternity and sorority rush week because two geeks are told to get a corpse for Beta House's initiation and grab Johnny's alien-infested body. The 1959 horror was from space; the 1986 horror is from the Greek system of the American university.

AVP: Alien vs. Predator (2004, Paul W.S. Anderson) posits an ancient temple under Antarctica built by the Predators millennia ago and stocked with xenomorph eggs and a mother alien, both of which are still viable when a corporate team arrives to explore the site in 2004. The aliens were brought to earth thousands of years ago. They are not here as part of an invasion; they are here as part of a testing ground for Predators. Like *The Thing*, this film posits the South Pole as a locus of naturalized space horror. Weyland (Lance Henriksen) informs his team that the structure under the ice in Antarctica contains elements of Egyptian, Cambodian and Aztec architecture, "My experts tell me it is a pyramid. What they cannot agree on is who built it and when."[14] Clearly the structure is extraterrestrial in origin, as it was built to serve the Predators and contain xenomorphs, but it is also clearly terrestrial. The aliens have been present in Antarctica for thousands of years, just like *The Thing*, and it is only the arrival of humans that awakens them and begins the war between the three species.

In Spielberg's *The War of the Worlds*, Ray Ferrier (Tom Cruise) and his children, fleeing the aliens that have just attacked their New Jersey neighborhood and the rest of the world, hide in a house that is subsequently struck by a plane in the night. The next morning, as Ray emerges through the debris, he meets a television news producer (Camilla Monet) that shows him something unique about the invaders:

> RAY: I saw that storm. I was right in the middle of one of those.
> NEWS PRODUCER: You didn't see it like this. *[Begins playing video of slow motion lightning strikes.]* Those machines come up from under the ground, right? So that means they must have been buried here a long time ago. So who was driving the goddamn thing? Watch the lighting. Watch it. Watch the lightning. Keep watching the lightning. *[Video shows something in the lightning entering the ground.]*

RAY: What is that?

NEWS PRODUCER: That is them. They come down in capsules, riding the lightning into the ground, into the machines, right?[15]

In other words, just as with *The Thing* and *AVP: Alien vs. Predator*, the extra-terrestrials have been very terrestrial for a very long time. Furthermore, as I have argued elsewhere, there is a metaphor for the terror attacks of September 11th playing out here. The destructive elements are already present on Earth; it was not an "invasion"–the terrorists/Martians had been here a long time before actually striking.[16]

The third model of space horror films that subvert the space origin are films that employ the tropes of invasion films, but reveal that the invasion in the film is of earthly origins. Films in this category play at being space horror, but expose the earthly origins of their invasions. The disaster of these films, in the Sontagian sense, is not that an outside intelligence invades and takes us over but that we create our own aliens and by extension our own horrors. These films firmly establish the bait-and-switch setup, relying on the tropes of invasion films, but the climax reveals the absence of space horror, instead positing much more prosaic origins. For example, "In the town of Snowfield, four of us met and bested an inhuman intelligence not from the stars, but from the deep and secret reaches of our own infinitely mysterious world," Dr. Timothy Flyte (Peter O'Toole) informs his television viewers at the conclusion of *Phantoms*, a film that seems to feature an extraterrestrial intelligence that has taken over a small Colorado community that is revealed to be of earthly origin.[17]

The two films that best model this approach are the original *Invaders from Mars* (1953, William Cameron Menzies) and the remake of *The Blob* (1988, Chuck Russell), both of which feature a small town invasion that begins with something coming from the sky and landing outside the community, a spaceship in the case of *Invaders from Mars* and a meteor in the case of *The Blob*, which then begins the process of Sontag's disaster.

Invaders from Mars presented a scenario in which the alien invasion was, in fact, simply (or not so simply) a child's nightmare. Initially, however, the film shows planets hanging in a starry field, all of space laid out before the audience. The opening narration of *Invaders from Mars*, spoken by Dr. Stuart Kelston (Arthur Franz), constructs a narrative about the possibility of alien life:

> The heavens. Once an object of superstition, awe, and fear. Now a vast region for growing knowledge. The distance of Venus, the atmosphere of Mars, the size of Jupiter, and the speed of Mercury. All this and more we know. But their greatest mystery the heavens have kept a secret. What sort of life, if any, inhabits these other planets? Human life, like ours? Or life extremely lower in the scale? Or dangerously higher? Seeking the answer to this timeless question, forever seeking, is the constant

preoccupation of scientists everywhere. Scientists famous and unknown. Scientists in great universities and in modest homes. Scientists of all ages.[18]

The film then cuts from an image of space to a farmhouse in the Midwest of the United States, cutting in again to a window of a bedroom with a telescope pointed at the sky just as the narrator says, "scientists of all ages."[19] We then meet David, who has set an alarm to wake him up at four a.m. to see the Great Nebula, which will not be visible again "for six more years."[20]

The film establishes from its very opening (indeed from its very title) the threat from space to our American way of life, these are "invaders," but also by juxtaposing the cold reaches of space with the farmhouse and David's room we move from the galactic to the terrestrial. The battle for Earth will not be fought in space but in a child's bedroom, where the audience is eventually shown the entire film has been David's dream. We never leave the farmhouse in reality.

David and his father enthusiastically use his telescope to examine the heavens until his mother sends them both back to bed. David then wakes up and sees a spaceship landing in the sandpit behind the hill behind his house. He runs to his parents and tells them and his father investigates and vanishes. When the father returns hours later his personality has completely changed. The two policemen who come to investigate also vanish and return, all of them (eventually including David's mother) emotionless, threatening and cold alien-like beings. The humans of *Invaders from Mars* are often the most alien of characters.

As David turns to astronomer Stuart Kelston and therapist Dr. Pat Blake (Helena Carter) for help, the reason for the Martian's presence is laid bare. Dr. Stuart Kelston also indicates the heart of the sociophobic of this film, explaining to Dr. Blake and David that the secret project David's father was working on was a space-based weapon:

> It is an atomic device. The highest powered rocket ever conceived. You see, once we can shoot a rocket far enough into space, it will just anchor there. It's just a matter of time before we set up inner-planetary stations, equipped with atomic power and operated by remote control. Then, if any nation dared attack us, by pushing a few buttons, we could wipe them out in a matter of minutes.[21]

The "atomic device," we subsequently learn, was the cause of the Martian invasion in the first place. The top secret rocket plant (and the film goes a good deal out of its way to confirm how secret the project is, with Kelston encoding his phone calls and everyone in town refusing to speak about what is happening at the plant) and nearby military base are what prompted the Martians to come to this town in the first place. Dr. Kelston explains that the surface of Mars is uninhabitable, so Martians either live below ground or, more likely, in spacecraft in orbit around Mars. Dr. Blake asks why the Martians would invade. Kelston offers an amazing response for the period:

> Put the shoe on the other foot. Say you're a Martian and with the aid of these mutants you've developed a way of life to save your race: giant ships floating in space with sufficient oxygen to sustain life. Then, the inhabitants of another planet start shooting powerful rockets endangering your zone of survival. Wouldn't you want to do something about it?[22]

For Eisenhower's America this is a remarkable plea for restraint, empathy and recognition of one's culpability in situations of national crisis. From the enemy's point of view, their actions are not hostile but logical self-protection.

The humans taken over are not the first wave of a complete planetary take over, as in *Invasion of the Body Snatchers*. The individuals kidnapped either serve as a vital part of the team making the rocket or, as in the case of the policemen, are given the task of sabotaging the project or assassinating those vital to it. The Martians invade because of the horror from space that *we* represent to *them*. They do not seek to actually invade our society in general, only for the specific purpose of stopping something that is a threat to them. It is difficult to imagine a non-science fiction film from this period offering such empathy to Russian characters.

Despite the trappings of space, this is an earthbound horror film that subverts its space origins in three ways, all of which concurrently undermine the "threats from outside" motif of space invasion films. The first, as noted above, is that the Martians have only invaded to prevent our weapons from reaching space. Dr. Kelston explains that they were merely moving to protect themselves and that it is America that is the threat.

Second is that after the initial spaceship arrival, all of the horror is found in the earth, not the skies. The ship lands and buries itself in the sandpit. As individuals walk out into the sand pit, the sand opens up. The image repeats of sand forming a concave funnel and people then disappearing, usually in a long shot, pulled down out of sight into the ground. Not up—not pulled into space—but down into the earth. This is an invasion from below, not from above. The climactic battle is underground. Finally, as the ship emerges from sandpit it explodes and the remains are sealed underground. Only then is the entire narrative shown to be David's dream. He is not afraid of space— he is afraid of Earth.

Third and final, after the explosion, David wakes up screaming, runs to his parents' room, and realizes it was all just a dream. He imagined it all. His father, returned to normal, tucks him back in bed and explains it was all a bad dream. David falls asleep, only to be woken again by the sound of the ship drifting down to Earth into the sandpit behind the hill behind his house, thus creating a phantasmagorical, circular narrative.

While the ending renders the reality of the invasion indeterminate at best, the whole thing is presented as most likely the projection of a child's imagination. If this is true, then what does this film say about the fears of Cold War America? The problem is not the Other—the problem is us. Horrible imaginings lead to fear and violence, but none of it is real—a radical statement in the age of McCarthy.

David J. Skal reports a PTA representative writing in opposition to *Invaders from Mars*:

> Here, in science fiction form, is an orgy of hate and fear and futility, with no hope of escape, no constructive element whatsoever. The child with whom one is asked to identify is bereft of any security from father and mother, from constituted authority, and the adults burst into meaningless violence…. For a time we hope there will be an answer in this projection of the formless fears abroad in our world of technological annihilation and savage ideologies, but the terror and dread only pile higher.[23]

Our fears of the Other are childish nightmares. Our "formless fears" are given substance only so long as we fear them. The whole film is a nightmare of the military industrial complex in which an American child indicts the nation's adults. His nightmare is growing up in a world that requires atomic weapons in space.

Michael Bliss notes that "the fact that distrust of how scientific advancements are used as part of the dream of a young boy who wants to be a scientist tells us how deeply conflicted David is."[24] David, the son of an engineer, whose closest associate seems to be an adult astronomer, who also dreams of being a scientist when he grows up remains uncertain of the various scientific projects occurring in his hometown, especially the military ones. Bliss states:

> David's nightmare also highlighted the filmmaker's view of how deplorable 1950s American culture really is. The boy's life within the frame story seems suspiciously conventional, so much so that the film appeared to be telling us that one of the most frightening things in 1950s America is the normalcy to which it aspires. The crushing insufferable blandness of the 1950s is merely one of the things from which David desperately tries to escape.[25]

The implication here being that the horror imagined from space in David's dream is actually preferable to the horror of everyday life in Eisenhower's America. This is not space horror, this is an existential horror from which an imaginary invasion is a welcome respite.

Similarly, Reagan's America in the 1980s aspired to return to the 50s and a sense of "normalcy," and his experiments with space-based defense echoed the development of the nation's atomic weapons armory under Eisenhower. Chuck Russell's 1988 remake of *The Blob* (originally another wonderful 1950s horror film with a threat from space) reimagines the Blob not as a space monster, but as the accidental release of an American biological weapon at the height of the Cold War. While the plot roughly follows the original, with a meteor crashing and a viscous substance emerging that terrifies a small town and the teenagers living there, the origin of the creature shifts in the remake.

Set in Arborville, California (the very name suggesting a rural/suburban environment), the film sets up its youthful protagonists with a high school football game and a planned date between a football player and a cheerleader, whilst simultaneously introducing an antihero, Brian Flagg (Kevin Dillon), a motorcycle-riding juvenile delinquent with a heart of gold. "Can Man" is the first victim of the eponymous monster, going to investigate a meteor impact in the woods and finding his hand enveloped by the monster when he pokes the goo with a stick. Meg Penny (Shawnee Smith) insists on driving to the hospital with Brian when her car accidentally strikes the goo-infected Can Man.

As the hospital falls victim to the rampage of the Blob, Meg and Brian return to the woods where Russell employs all the imagery and tropes of an alien invasion film: fog, moving lights visible through the trees, something loud approaching, lights in the sky. Suddenly, the sky lights are revealed to be a military helicopter hovering overhead; the lights in the trees are men in space suits searching the woods. Dr. Meddows (Joe Seneca) introduces himself, stating, "We are here to help you," and informing the locals, "We're a government-sanctioned biological containment team."[26] Up until this point, everything in the film has indicated an extraterrestrial monster has arrived in town, same as the original film.

Meddows seeks to reassure Meg: "We're microbe hunters, young lady,"[27] he tells her. Indicating the now empty meteor he matter-of-factly states, "That's the source of our worries—a troublesome souvenir from space."[28] Brian, however, notices that while the top of the "meteorite" is scarred and pitted from its descent through the atmosphere and its impact, the bottom half is polished metal. He then overhears a conversation that reveals the actual origin of the Blob:

> MEDDOWS: We suspected that conditions in space would have a mutating effect on bacteria. But this…
> COLONEL HARGIS: Its activity must be what threw the satellite out of orbit.
> MEDDOWS: Correct. Our little experimental virus seems to have grown up into a plasmid life form that hunts its prey!
> HARGIS: A predator! It's fantastic.
> DR. JENNINGS: Sir, the organism is growing at a geometric rate. By all accounts it is at least a thousand times its original mass.
> HARGIS: This'll put U.S. defense years ahead of the Russians.[29]

Brian is shocked to learn that the monster currently rampaging through Arborville was created by the United States military as a biological weapon to use against the Russians. Not only are the scientists not horrified by the Blob, they are delighted in its behavior and see it as confirmation of the quality of their efforts. The 1988 Blob, Reagan's Blob, if you will, was not an alien life form from outer space but the creation of the military industrial complex.

At this point in history, the audience at the time could not help but be reminded of the Strategic Defense Initiative (S.D.I., known colloquially as "Star Wars"), a space-based missile defense program publicly announced by President Reagan on March 23, 1983, and highly controversial for the rest of his term, as many scientists opposed the use of space for anything but peaceful purposes.[30] The Blob posits an American government that has put biological weapons on satellites in space, and when one has malfunctioned, a team is sent in to not only cover it up but to allow the weapon to work its way through the population as an experiment.

Dr. Jennings objects to Meddows allowing the Blob to rampage without telling local authorities what they are up against. Meddows responds:

> This isn't one of you text-book exercises, Mr. Jennings. This is an experiment in biological warfare, or hadn't you noticed? That organism is potentially the greatest breakthrough in weapons research since man split the atom. What we do here will affect the balance of world power! Of course there are lives at stake—whole nations, in fact. And that's far more important than a handful of people in this small town. And that is my cross to bear, Mr. Jennings. Now carry out your orders.[31]

The Other who lies behind this alien invasion is, in fact, the United States government that cares less for American citizens in a small town than for its own ability to develop weapons to maintain global dominance. *The Blob* is a literalization of the military industrial complex as monster. The threat is not from space; it is from us. It is not the big cities that are threatened. We see no shots of New York City or Los Angeles or Pittsburgh being menaced. Instead it is small town America, middle America, the America of high school football games and teenage dates at the malt shop that is under direct threat of the Cold War in this film, not coincidentally released in the last year of Reagan's presidency. The town characters have patriotic names—Flagg, Penny, etc. The film seems to suggest they are the "real" America that is under threat from invasion not from space but by the soldiers and scientists in the employ of their own government. Just as with *Invaders from Mars*, it is the younger people who learn with horror about the activities of the adults and the government and it is the children who are terrified of the world which they must now live in. The horror is not from space; it is from the adults who have created a world in which biological weapons are valued higher than the lives of citizens, their own lives, in fact.

Reviewing the dates of the films discussed in this essay, one might note that space horror flourished in the '50s under Eisenhower, in the '80s under Reagan, and in the '00s under George W. Bush: the start of the Cold War, the

End of the Cold War and the period post–9/11, all times of strong national fear of the foreign Other, or, as Steffen Hantke identified it: "ubiquitous enemies both at home and abroad."[32] The metaphors of science fiction and horror allow one to write sociophobics without incurring the wrath of the community for dealing with the topic directly.

As Robin Wood observes, "One might say the true subject of the horror genre is the struggle for recognition of all that our civilization represses or oppresses."[33] The monster is the Other. In *Invaders from Mars* and *The Blob*, the Other is not representative of what the Self has repressed and made Other—it is, in fact, the Self all along. Our government, which is elected by and represents us, engages in pseudo alien invasions in order to solidify power and justify its own excesses. In both of these films the "invasion" is the direct result of Americans experimenting with unthinkable weapons. As a result, we eventually recognize the Other of such films as being an extension of the Self. The horror is not from space. It is from Earth. The message of these films thus is a variant of Pogo's realization (also from 1953, the year of *Invaders from Mars*): We have met the alien, and he is us.

Notes

1. Susan Sontag, *Against Interpretation and Other Essays* (New York: Octagon Books, 1978), 209–210.

2. *Ibid.*, 213.

3. *Ibid.*, 215–216.

4. *Ibid.*, 216.

5. *Ibid.*, 223.

6. Michael Bliss, *Invasion USA: The Essential Science Fiction Films of the 1950s* (Lanham, MD: Rowan and Littlefield, 2014), x.

7. Dialogue from *Night of the Living Dead*, DVD, directed by George E. Romero (1968; New York: Dimension Home Video, 2008).

8. Dialogue from *Plan 9 from Outer Space*, DVD, directed by Ed Wood (1959; San Diego: Legend Films, 2008).

9. In this sense one could argue that these alien invasion films actually follow the model established by Carol J. Clover in *Men, Women and Chainsaws*, in which the slasher films are entirely rooted in the return to "the bad place" where a previous atrocity happened. It is the return that provokes the new set of killing. Likewise, *The Thing* and *Night of the Creeps*, among others, both show horrors from space that are only activated by humans finding and reanimating them.

10. Dialogue from *The Thing*, DVD, directed by John Carpenter (1982; Los Angeles: Universal Studios Home Video, 2004).

11. *Ibid.*

12. *Ibid.*

13. *Ibid.*

14. Dialogue from *AVP: Alien vs. Predator*, DVD, directed by Paul W.S. Anderson (2004; Los Angeles: Twentieth Century Fox Home Video, 2005).

15. Dialogue from *The War of the Worlds*, DVD, directed by Steven Spielberg (2005; Los Angeles: Dreamworks Home Video, 2005).

16. Kevin J. Wetmore, Jr., *Post-9/11 Horror in American Cinema* (New York: Continuum, 2012), 47–51.

17. Dialogue from *Phantoms*, DVD, directed by Joe Chappelle (1998; La Crosse, WI: Echo Bridge Home Entertainment, 2011).

18. Dialogue from *Invaders from Mars*, DVD, directed by William Cameron Menzies (1953; Los Angeles: Image Entertainment, 2002).
19. *Ibid.*
20. *Ibid.*
21. *Ibid.*
22. *Ibid.*
23. David J. Skal, *The Monster Show: A Cultural History of Horror*, rev. ed. (New York: Faber and Faber, 2001), 251.
24. Bliss, *Invasion USA*, 3.
25. *Ibid.*, 9.
26. Dialogue from *The Blob*, DVD, directed by Chuck Russell (1988; Culver City, CA: Columbia TriStar Home Video, 2001).
27. *Ibid.*
28. *Ibid.*
29. *Ibid.*
30. See Frances Fitzgerald, *Way Out There in the Blue: Reagan, Star Wars and the End of the Cold War* (New York: Simon & Schuster, 2001).
31. Dialogue from *The Blob*.
32. Steffen Hantke, "Science Fiction and Horror in the 1950s," in *A Companion to the Horror Film*, ed. Harry M. Benshoff (London: John Wiley and Sons, 2014), 255.
33. Robin Wood, *Hollywood from Vietnam to Reagan … and Beyond* (New York: Columbia University Press, 2003), 68.

BIBLIOGRAPHY

Alien. DVD. Directed by Ridley Scott. 1979. Los Angeles: Twentieth Century Fox Home Video, 2004.
AVP: Alien versus Predator. DVD. Directed by Paul W.S. Anderson. 2004. Los Angeles: 20th Century Fox Home Video, 2005.
Bliss, Michael. *Invasion USA: The Essential Science Fiction Films of the 1950s*. Lanham, MD: Rowman and Littlefield, 2014.
The Blob. DVD. Directed by Chuck Russell. 1988. Culver City, CA: Columbia TriStar Home Video, 2001.
Clover, Carol J. *Men, Women and Chainsaws: Gender in the Modern Horror Film*. Princeton: Princeton University Press, 1993.
Fitzgerald, Frances. *Way Out There in the Blue: Reagan, Star Wars and the End of the Cold War*. New York: Simon & Schuster, 2001
Hantke, Steffen. "Science Fiction and Horror in the 1950s." In *A Companion to the Horror Film*, edited by Harry M. Benshoff, 255–272. London: John Wiley and Sons, 2014.
Invaders from Mars. DVD. Directed by William Cameron Menzies. 1953. Los Angeles: Image Entertainment, 2002.
Jason X. DVD. Directed by Jim Isaac. 2001. Los Angeles: New Line Home Video, 2005.
Night of the Creeps. DVD. Directed by Fred Dekker. 1986. Culver City, CA: TriStar, 2008.
Night of the Living Dead. DVD. Directed by George Romero. 1968. New York: Dimension Home Video, 2008.
Phantoms. DVD. Directed by Joe Chappelle. 1998. La Crosse, WI: Echo Bridge Home Entertainment, 2011.
Plan 9 from Outer Space. DVD. Directed by Ed Wood. 1959. San Diego, C: Legend Films, 2008.
Skal, David J. *The Monster Show: A Cultural History of Horror*, rev. ed. New York: Faber and Faber, 2001.
Sontag, Susan. *Against Interpretation and Other Essays*. New York: Octagon Books, 1978.
Starman. DVD. Directed by John Carpenter. 1984. Culver City, CA: Sony Pictures Home Entertainment, 1998.
The Thing. DVD. Directed by John Carpenter. 1982. Los Angeles: Universal Studios Home Video, 2004.

The War of the Worlds. DVD. Directed by Steven Spielberg. 2005. Los Angeles: Dreamworks Home Video, 2005.

Wetmore, Kevin J., Jr. *Post-9/11 Horror in American Cinema*. New York: Continuum, 2012.

Wood, Robin. *Hollywood from Vietnam to Reagan … and Beyond*. New York: Columbia University Press, 2003.

Nonknowledge
and Inner Experience
A Post-Modern Rhetoric of Space Horror

GAVIN F. HURLEY

In the influential *The Philosophy of Horror*, Noëll Carroll notes that horror-art adheres audiences by means of engagement with fictional monsters.[1] Throughout his book, Carroll refers to monster-centric narratives, such as *Dracula*, *Wolfman*, and *The Exorcist*, qualifying the monsters of horror-art as creatures that "do not exist according to the lights of contemporary science"; moreover, they are "in violation of natural order, where the perimeter of natural order is determined by contemporary science."[2] Carroll's qualification of the "monster" becomes any "entity" that challenges what is traditionally known. Monsters generally disorder an orderly universe—which naturally spark anxiety and dread within the viewers of horror films. This is a traditionally reasonable perspective: Carroll's theory preserves a knowable-unknowable relationship that helps decode traditional horror narratives—such as the classic Hammer films of the 1950s and 1960s, the religious horror of the 1970s, and the slasher films of the 1980s. However, horror cinema within the 1990s, 2000s, and 2010s, specifically space horror, has complicated Noëll Carroll's theory. Contemporary space horror probes deeper human anxieties, and transcends traditional knowable-unknowable binaries. How so? Space horror can posit that that natural order does not exist, has not existed, and will not exist. What does space horror express? Nonknowledge and inner experience: two concepts from the postmodern philosophy of French thinker Georges Bataille. Both of these concepts pervade the cinematic subgenre of contemporary space horror—evidenced in the films *Event Horizon* (1997, Paul W.S. Anderson) and *Prometheus* (2012, Ridley Scott).

Contemplation of Nonknowledge

Rather than pondering the philosophy of horror like Carroll, theorist Eugene Thacker examines the "horror of philosophy." In two recent volumes, *In the Dust of This Planet* and *Starry Speculative Corpse*, Thacker gestures to the darker side of philosophy itself, specifically Cosmic Pessimism. Cosmic Pessimism sees the "world" as the "world-without-us" and grasps at the mystic void that accompanies such bleak negation.[3] Thacker's Cosmic Pessimism signals a more severe existential Nothingness of Jean-Paul Sartre, whereby it dwells in the "impossible thought of extinction, with not even a single human being to think the absence of all human beings, with no thought to think the negation of all thought."[4] In an additional expression, Thacker describes Cosmic Pessimism as Black: "the dark metaphysics of negation, nothingness, and nonhuman."[5] It is the black void that escapes human understanding and imagination.

The foundational ideas that influence Thacker's theories are not completely fresh. Friedrich Nietzsche, the 19th century father of postmodern philosophy, explores similar veins of nihilism. However, these ideas gained full momentum in the 20th century, from the 1920s through the 1970s, when French philosopher Georges Bataille boldly pushed Nietzsche's theories into new territories of negation, nihilism, and nothingness. Georges Batialle's writing style may also remind readers of Nietzsche's anti-systematic, literary approach to philosophy, so it is unsurprising that Bataille is most influenced by Nietzsche.[6] However, Bataille further extends Nietzschian ideas. Bataille not only sees language as failing to capture experience—but also sees experience as failing to capture the human.[7] Bataille's ideas dwell in this negative space much more than the more optimistic Nietzsche.

Perhaps fueled by the horrors of World War II, the death of his father, and his own abandonment of Catholicism,[8] Bataille's philosophy revolves around heavy fatalistic negation. Bataille explaining this negative space, writes:

> I imagine the heavens without me, without God, without anything general or particular—this isn't nothingness. In my eyes, nothingness is something else. It is the negation—of myself or of God—God and myself having never been, nothing ever having been. I'm talking on the contrary about a slipping of my mind wherein I propose the possibility of a total disappearance of the general or the particular to it.... In the unlimited oblivion ... nothing can give a meaning to my phrase, but my indifference (my indifferent being) rests in a kind of resolution of being: nonknowledge, nonquestion.[9]

Nonknowledge is central to Bataille's philosophy. Gestured to by Thacker's Cosmic Pessimism and Blackness, nonknowledge resists linguistic expression; it can only be gleaned through experience and the resulting outward effects:

anguish, tears, ecstasy, laughter.[10] Nonknowledge has no ends.[11] It is the ongoing limitless energy of the void that creates "a stupid and cruel feeling of insomnia, a monstrous, amoral feeling in accord with the unregulated cruelty of the universe."[12]

As one might guess, these vacuous "cruelties" are predictably frightening—specifically, Bataille affirms that contemplating nonknowledge is horrific. Nonknowledge, as anxious labyrinthine inner experience, becomes "sphere of thought" that "is horror itself."[13] Space horror, as a cinematic subgenre, often dwells within this dark Bataillian abyss, persuading viewers to come into communion with the horror. Therefore, when writers or directors of horror films gesture to nonknowledge or unknowable infinities within their narratives, they influence audiences to think about nonknowledge—and by doing so, persuade them to be afraid.

Thacker acknowledges in *In the Dust of This Planet* that nonknowledge—what he calls "dark mysticism"—has been spiritually explored by ancient and medieval Christian mystics such as, Pseudo-Dionysius the Aeropagite, Meister Eckhart, and John of the Cross. Dark mysticism has also influenced secular writers. For example, H.P. Lovecraft, the father of cosmic horror, integrates nonknowledge principles into his fiction, which are integral to his mentions of the vast cosmos and outer space. Using Lovecraft as a touchstone, Thacker connects the darkness of occult nonknowledge with the darkness of outer space.[14] However, for Lovecraft and the subgenre of space horror, outer space does not act as a flimsy metaphor for nonknowledge and the infinite unknown. Rather, outer space is reality—and therefore plays an immersive narrative role for the viewer. Within the space horror subgenre, the entire fictional narrative unfolds upon a canvas of unending nonknowledge. Outer space immerses the audience within Bataille's limitless inner experience of nonknowledge and the associated affect of fear. Horror-art, in the form of space horror, becomes the perfect rhetorical conduit of Bataille's complex postmodern dread.

Event Horizon

Event Horizon, a British-American space horror film released in 1997, robustly expresses Bataille's philosophy of inner experience and nonknowledge. Set in 2047, *Event Horizon* tells the story of an exploratory *Lewis and Clark* space shuttle and its crew, led by Captain Miller (Laurence Fishburne), who is tasked with investigating a distress call off the orbit of Neptune. Joining the crew is Dr. William Weir (Sam Neill), the engineer of another spacecraft, the *Event Horizon*. The *Event Horizon* was a ship that had mysteriously vanished seven years before. Mid-flight on the *Lewis and Clark*, Weir informs the crew why he has joined them: the distress call from the ship off of the orbit of Neptune, is actually from the once vanished *Event Horizon*, abandoned without its crew. The mission of the *Lewis and Clark* is to figure out what happened to the ship. Weir further explains that the *Event Horizon* uses a Gravity Drive, to propel it faster than the speed of light. The drive, created by Weir, opens a black hole within the core of the ship, allowing the ship to instantaneously arrive in another location. Presumably the artificial black hole of the Gravity Drive had something to do with *Event Horizon* appearing again from an unknown destination.

After boarding the abandoned *Event Horizon*, the crew views the ship log footage, and discovers that the past crew of the *Event Horizon* tortured and killed themselves and each other. As the film continues, the crew realizes that the ship may have been to "hell" (and brought "hell" back with it) via the Gravity Drive's artificial black hole. After several bizarre deaths of crew members, numerous hallucinations, and altercations with a turned-malevolent Weir, Captain Miller finally detaches and destroys the ship—Weir along with it.

The theological concept of hell is integral to the plot of *Event Horizon*—but the concept is also complicated within the film. In an interview, producer Jeremy Bolt explains that the Judeo-Christian concept of hell permeates *Event Horizon*—however, because "hell" is so relative and nebulous, it is left quite open for interpretation in the film.[15] From this openness, *Even Horizon* does not operate through a traditional good-evil binary of other classic films about evil. Evil is not clearly externalized like other traditional horror films—such as Roman Polanski's 1968 *Rosemary's Baby* (the evil is externalized in the coven), or John Carpenter's 1978 *Halloween* (the evil is externalized in Michael Myers). Instead of a demarcated good force (hero; protagonist) and evil force (villain; antagonist), *Event Horizon* orchestrates a plot involving assorted discovery scenarios whereby evil/good binary remain suspended. Soon, the fictional crew and the viewers of film realize that the "monster" is indeed the Gravity Drive, the black hole, a component of outer space. Consequently, Carroll's understanding of the horror monster—an entity disordering the universe's natural order—is problematized. *Event Horizon*'s "monster," is the black hole, which is a reality of the cosmos. From this perspective, the Gravity Drive is not objectively disordered—it is problematic because it unveils the limits of human understanding, human experience, and human imagination. The Gravity Drive demands that the human crew should refigure reality's "natural order."

In *Event Horizon*, the traditional tensions between good and evil are reworked and replaced with another tension: nonknowledge pervades reality, outside of our capacity to know. The film does not view hell as separate from the material universe. Rather, *Event Horizon* expresses hell as part of the universe, unsegregated from reality. In fact, "hell" is found through the *Event Horizon*'s journey through outer space. Therefore, hell can be defined a branch of the cosmos.

This truth opens new awarenesses about the limits of experience—but paradoxically, the truth is not fully comprehended by human faculties. For example, Dr. Weir, when transformed by the nonknowledge of the Gravity Drive, proclaims to Captain Miller in the final scene, "You know nothing. Hell is only a word. The reality is much, much worse."[16] Weir's remark alludes to thinking about nonknowledge. The unknowable reality of the cosmos is much scarier than what we can put into words. It is an ineffable reality beyond linguistic expression. Through religious language, we signal "hell" as an externalized objective dimension, but according to Weir, the pervading subjective experiential reality of hell, is "much, much worse."

And why is it worse? As Dr. Weir points out we "know nothing"—the "reality" of "Hell" is a figurative and literal black hole: nonknowledge experienced but never understood. A black hole is a void, without an actual material surface, with immense gravitational pull. A black hole is an elusive, destructive, and limitless abyss. In fact, Bataille poetically illustrates the sphere of nonknowledge as a "black hole" several times throughout his work. Why does this black hole image work within Bataille's philosophy? A black hole is an unknowable nonhuman dimension of the cosmos: the "heavens without me, without God, without anything general or particular."[17] In fact, when the characters in *Event Horizon* attempt to breach the void and "know" the "nonknowledge" within the Gravity Drive, they become disoriented and destructive. Why? Because thinking about nonknowledge is a solitary experience that tests the limits of inner experience—and can break the human will. For example, Captain Miller—and the audience—discover this experience toward the end of the film. This occurs when the malevolent Weir grabs Miller's head and shows him the "visions of hell."[18] These visions provide a peek behind the curtains into the void. These visions do not objectively depict Nothingness, but rather depict the subject's experience of confronting Nothingness: torture, agony, and pain. Since this void cannot be externally represented by means of a visual representation or communication, the glimpse into the void is a *representational* glimpse into the torturous inner experience of facing nonhuman emptiness. In other words, these visions are not to be taken literally as what is actually going on through the black hole—but rather, the visions figuratively represent the *experience* of grappling with the dimension of nonknowledge—confronting nonhuman dark mysticism.

Depicting representational images of torture is one of the only ways to convey the inner experience because, as Bataille indicates time and again, external senses and systems are inadequate. Viewers are alerted to this point throughout the film. William Weir, Claire (the hallucinatory doppelganger of his wife), and the past crew members of the *Event Horizon* all remove their own eyes when they become disciples of the Gravity Drive's black hole. Why do they remove their eyes? The characters' external senses are incapable of experiencing the dark mysticism of cosmic nonknowledge—instead, humans must consult subjective experience. The removal of external sensory organs symbolizes the need to rely on inner experience.

Director Paul W.S. Anderson and producer Jeremy Bolt emphasize the importance of the two "visions of hell" montages within *Event Horizon*—as well as the difficulty in the hellish expression. According to Anderson, he aimed to capture a "painterly" quality in these visions of hell—evoking the spirit of 15th–16th century painter Hieronymus Bosch.[19] In fact, Anderson spent large amounts of time, energy, and prosthetics capturing these "visions of hell": scenes that only accounted for about ten seconds of the movie's overall length. According to Anderson, the goal of the visions of hell was to show a blend of beauty and horror.[20] In a partnered "visions of hell" montage closer to the beginning of the film, showing the original *Event Horizon* crew via ship log, Anderson similarly blends pleasure and horror—ecstasy alongside torture. Anderson explains that his vision was to depict the first crew of the *Event Horizon* "fucking each other to death"; Jeremy Bolt describes it as the "normally pleasurable" being "flipped so they are absolutely horrific."[21] This orgiastic gratuity may call to mind the images from Clive Barker's iconic novella *The Hellbound Heart*—foundation of the *Hellraiser* (1987, Clive Barker) film series. As the novella reveals to the characters and the audience of the novella in a "way impossible to know" (only to experience): pleasure can be pain and pain can be pleasure.[22] In Barker's Hellbound Heart mythos, pain and pleasure overlap and conflate into each other. This concept fuels the desires of the human and cenobite characters.

Event Horizon extends this pain/pleasure conflation even further than Barker: into a postmodern nihilism, a Bataillian evolution. In *Guilty*, Bataille writes:

> The object of ecstasy is the absence of an outside answer. The inexplainable presence of man is the answer the will gives itself suspended in the void of unknowable night.... Chance is the painful place of overlap of life and death—in sex and in ecstasy, in laughter and tears. Chance has the power to love death.... The path to chance is ... threatened by, but also inseparable from, horror and death.[23]

Weir's Gravity Drive and the accompanying black hole cannot be explained as the Hell of the Judeo-Christian tradition; rather it is more fittingly described as the atheistic space of the cosmic nonhuman, which is fueled by chance. This chance does not link with a divine purpose; rather, it formulates a void that conflates life, death, pleasure, and pain. According to Bataille, experiencing this void of chance and nihilism is simultaneously ecstatic and tormenting, pleasurable and painful.

William Weir depicts what happens when one is fully immersed, committed, and obsessed with this brand of negation found in the Gravity Drive. Weir is the creator of the void—the Dr. Frankenstein of the "monster"—but unlike Dr. Frankenstein who creates life as a fleshy material being, Weir merely opens an access point within the fabric of the universe. How does Weir interact with his creation? Weir becomes Bataille's archetype for the human condition: "Man is no longer, like the animal, the plaything of Nothingness, but Nothingness is itself his plaything—he ruins himself in it, but illuminates its darkness with his *laughter*, which he reaches only when *intoxicated* with the very void which kills him."[24] Throughout the film, Weir becomes increasingly captivated by the artificial black hole, "his plaything." The end of the film, Weir's "ruin," "intoxication," and "laughter" is fully and bombastically manifested. In a final scene, a shape-shifting figure emerges from the Gravity Drive and finds Captain Miller in the Gravity Drive chamber. The figure then transforms into Weir: naked, hairless, bloody, and carved with strange markings all over his body. Weir's first reaction is to laugh, asking Miller, "Do you really think that you could destroy this ship? She's defied space and time. She's been to a place you couldn't possibly imagine."[25] This line of dialogue reveals two points. First, Weir's laughter "illuminates the darkness"—a darkness confronted by "intoxication" and "death" by the void. Secondly, unlike Dr. Frankenstein's monster that is a product of human imagination, the gravity drive, the monster of *Event Horizon* cannot be captured by the human imagination. Weir is clear about this, stating that the void grants access to a place "you couldn't possibly imagine." Weir eventually "shows" Miller this place—only via a telepathic transfer of experience, when he grips Miller's head in this final scene, barking, "Let me show it to you!"[26] Weir relays inner experience—represented as the "visions of hell"—to Miller and to the audience: a subjective experience more terrifying than any objective horror event.

Weir gains power throughout the film. At the beginning of *Event Horizon*, Weir is depicted as a vulnerable scientist on Captain Miller's *Lewis and Clark* ship. But the *Event Horizon* ship reverses this dynamic. Weir becomes deified by the void—superhuman and enlightened by the inner experience. Again, this representation of Weir "becoming God" within a film that is devoid of any references to God, reveals aspects of the ineffable Nothingness. Bataille notes, "God isn't humanity's limit-point, though humanity's limit-point is divine. Or put it this way—humanity is divine when experiencing limits."[27] Weir becomes a representative incarnation of "humanity's limit-point": a manifestation of the inner experience of the limits of knowledge. The evolution of Weir—from vulnerable human being to what Paul Anderson labels the "Weir/Beast"[28] at the end of the film—conveys a terrifying maturation toward the summit of nonknowledge—something Weir fully embraces at the end of the film, something that intoxicates him, swallows him, and transforms him into divinity.

Prometheus

Event Horizon overtly reveals a rhetoric of postmodern principles. However, other depictions of space horror may rely on more nuanced postmodern principles. And despite subtleties, audiences can still bristle with horror when presented with these ideas. One example of more delicate postmodern rhetoric can be found in Ridley Scott's 2012 film *Prometheus*, a prequel entry within the *Alien* franchise. Like *Event Horizon*, the plot is motivated by characters' discovery within an unknown outer space setting. The film's plot is fairly straightforward. A crew has been funded by the Weyland Corporation to further investigate a recent discovery on Earth. On Earth, a team of archaeologists had discovered that an alien species engineered the human race; these Engineers are the creators of the human species. A team of archaeologists, scientists, and corporate representatives, travel to the presumed planet of these Engineers, attempting to "meet our makers."[29]

The characters in *Prometheus* search for answers through differing teleological modes. In other words, several main characters' journey toward a common understanding of the enigmatic Engineers—however, they seek this knowledge in different ways. Charlie Holloway (Logan Marshall-Green), a more science-directed archaeologist, seeks answers through scientific explanation. Peter Weyland (Guy Pierce), the aging leader of the Weyland corporation who funds the expedition, is fueled by colonial conquest, power, and immortality. Dr. Elizabeth Shaw (Noomi Rapace), Holloway's lover, a spiritually faithful archaeologist seeks answers through the scheme of "faith seeking understanding."

In the film, these characters use different modes, attempting to resolve the perpetuity of nonhuman nonknowledge and anxious inner experience. But two of the three modes fail—and one is left open-ended. Holloways' scientific endeavor and Weyland's colonial conquest, both fail and lead to their deaths. Why? Both characters' modes of meaning-making are haughtily based on a premise that the fabric of the cosmos hinges on human processes.

For instance, in a dialogue with Charlie Holloway, the android character David (Michael Fassbender) asks, "How far would you go to get what you came all this way for—to get your answers? What would you be willing to do?" Holloway replies with "anything and everything."[30] With this permission, David secretly drops a mysterious substance found on the alien planet into Holloway's drink to see what will happen. In a twist of irony, scientist Holloway unknowingly becomes the scientific experiment. He is infected with an organism that turns him violent and eventually kills him.

What does Holloway's demise represent? Holloway's scientific mode is inadequate within the cosmic landscape. Within a landscape of cosmic "matter," rather than the confines of earthly "matter," the human process of reasoning falls short—moreover, as shown by Holloway, it can be self-destructive. Integral to postmodern thinking, Bataille included, is the notion that closed systems are not sufficient enough; all-encompassing systems cannot explain everything. As Bataille suggests in essays such as "The Sorcerer's Apprentice"[31] and "The Notion of Expenditure,"[32] logic and scientific method (that is, inductive logic) cannot fully capture "matter." Moreover, science cannot capture the inner experience when individually grappling the summit of nonknowledge. Charlie Holloway, within the setting of outer space, illustrates this impotence of science within the narrative based upon the resolution of the unknowable. Consequently, the scientific unknown remains scientifically unknowable.

Peter Weyland's demise is facilitated by David as well when David similarly exploits Weyland's passion for answers. After the audience discovers that Weyland has funded the Prometheus expedition for his own selfish satisfaction and conquest, David leads Weyland to the chamber of the hibernating Engineers. Here, Weyland awakens a humanoid Engineer "Creator" and attempts to communicate with the Engineer using David as a translator. The Engineer is apathetic to Weyland's mission. He instantly kills Weyland and decapitates David.

What does Peter Weyland's demise represent? Weyland's demise represents the impotence of human self-interest. Enlightenment thinker Francis Bacon famously remarked, "knowledge itself is a power."[33] Weyland, unknowingly thinking that he had the knowledge, wrongfully assumed he possessed the power. Weyland adhered to Enlightenment principles, human principles. Nonhuman nothingness does not obey these earthly laws. In fact, the cosmos represents a dimension of nonknowledge wherein humans have no power or knowledge.

The interaction with Weyland and the Engineer reveals a relationship between nonknowledge and power. In the interaction with the Engineer, Weyland admits that he wishes to become immortal and godlike—like the Engineers. In other words, he wanted to partake in nonhuman eternity. This scene illustrates the futility of this request. Human "power grabs" in relation to a nonhuman cosmos are petty and droll. Consequently, the Engineer effortlessly attacks Weyland like a human might wipe away an annoying gnat, representing the apathy of the cosmos in relation to human desires. Weyland fittingly sputters, "There … is … nothing"[34] as his last words, punctuating the nihilism.

In the film's commentary, director Ridley Scott explains that he originally filmed more dialogue between the Engineers and Weyland—however, Scott seems to have cut these scenes in favor of more fully capturing the inadequacy of human communication. This inadequate communication is at the heart of much postmodern theory, including Bataille's philosophy. Addressing our communicative deficiency Bataille writes, "The sand in which we bury ourselves in order not to see, is formed of words," pointing out that the "silent, elusive, ungraspable" part of us is "neglected" and "escapes us."[35] The edited Engineer scene displays a similar "silent, elusive, ungraspable" interaction; the scene "speaks" for itself, allowing the viewer's subjective state to commune with the characters' experience and behavior, rather than artificial discourse. According to editor Pedro Scalia and Ridley Scott, by not letting the Engineer speak, the Engineers retain their "majesty" and mystery."[36] Moreover, writers Damon Lindelof and Jon Spaihts remark that the Engineers have "given up on humanity for all fundamental purposes. So they wouldn't have anything to say."[37] In other words, the Engineers do not need to explain themselves to human beings. Essentially, Scott, Scalia, Lindelof, and Spaihts agree that, in the context of the film where the immediate Creators of humans are aliens, human beings do not even have any worth.

Lindelof and Spaihts further point out that the characters and the audience both rely on David's translation of the Engineer's language.[38] Based on David's earlier revealed questionable ethics, it is possible that David may have deliberately mistranslated or left out the Engineer's actual message. The audience and the characters do not know if they should trust David's translation. Again, this shows the impotence of human verbal communication as well as potential suspension of human truths, replaced by inhuman (in this case, android) truths. The mere possibility that David could have purposely hidden human knowledge gestures to the questionable potentialities within nonhuman cosmos—and complicates our understanding of what is true and what is real.

Dr. Elizabeth Shaw, the only human survivor of *Prometheus*, highlights an interesting wrinkle within postmodern rhetoric of space horror. Unlike *Event Horizon* that avoids God and religion, *Prometheus* connects Dr. Shaw's faithful spirituality with the postmodern void. Her character gestures to the mystic inner experience of nonknowledge—that is, Thacker's dark mysticism. This overlap is shown through Elizabeth Shaw's spiritual faith. A flashback from the beginning of the film, where her father gives her a Christian cross necklace as a child, shows that Shaw is a Christian believer. This cross becomes the symbol of Shaw's faith throughout the film. Since *Prometheus* does not provide evidence that Shaw is devoutly *religious*, the audience understands that she is faithfully bound to experience-based Christian spirituality, not necessarily a particular denomination or set of religious doctrine. This spiritual reliance is gestured to again at the end of the film. Here, Shaw knows she is the last human survivor in the mission, and she is sure to retrieve her cross, which has been confiscated by David. As she returns the cross to her neck, she acts visibly relieved—and in the very last shot of the film, Shaw departs from the planet of "death" in the Engineer's spacecraft accompanied by David's android head. In fact, as Shaw explains in the last lines of film, she journeys into space "still searching" for answers, motivated by hope and faith.

How does the optimism of Shaw relate to pessimism of nonknowledge? Elizabeth Shaw actively pursues to understand and resolve the unknowable unresolvable void—what Bataille would deem impossible task. Therefore, the audience may celebrate Shaw's resolve when she says, "I need to know why" and "I'm still searching"[39] at the end of the film—however, her choice to continue to search for answers ultimately unsettles the viewer. Why? Because of uncertainty. Based on what the audience knows about outer space as depicted by *Prometheus*, Shaw will presumably find more emptiness, death, futility, and destruction. Whereas *Event Horizon*'s William Weir embraces death and the void, *Prometheus*'s Shaw merely begins to grapple with void, resisting death in the process. Shaw appears to survive because her subjective reality, her yearning for spiritual fulfillment, drives her inquiry. As a card-carrying pessimist, Bataille would possibly forecast that Shaw, like himself as an ex-Catholic, would fully shed her Christian faith and surrender to an atheistic inner experience for its own sake[40] after immersing herself more completely in void. In other words, Bataille would probably predict that once Shaw begins to more fully ponder and experience the void, she would eventually become like *Event Horizon*'s William Weir. Ridley Scott, on the other hand, a director who has often explored religious themes, may assume that Shaw will eventually find religious truth out there in the universe. But Scott's outcome feels a bit naïve—especially since in *Prometheus*, we come to find that God is not our immediate Creator. Regardless of Shaw's hypothetical outcome, *Prometheus*'s audience witness the failure of traditional modes of understanding—that is, scientific method and self-interested conquest—and like Shaw, the audience remains suspended within a process of not knowing at the end of the film. Because the film takes place in outer space, this process of not knowing opens up the real possibility of nonknowledge, the reality of nothingness.

Fundamentally, the film fronts the Bataille's idea of godless cosmos—which, again, returns to the concept of "chance": "chance is the overlap of life and death"—not orchestrated by God—"the path to chance is … threatened by, but also inseparable from, horror and death."[41] *Prometheus* reveals that human beings were experimentally created by an alien race, not God. The first scene of the film shows that human beings evolved from a discarded vial of experimental fluid pitched onto a nonhuman Earth. The experiment was presumably a failure—and the human race evolved from what the Engineers deemed as biological waste. Humans evolved from chance—not from a divine plan. Refusing to accept "chance" as an end point of her inquiry, Shaw seeks to understand her Christian faith by continuing to search for answers in an endless cosmos. Therefore, rather than abandoning Bataille's "labyrinth of inner experience," escape the perpetual horror, and safely travel back to Earth at the end of the film, Shaw becomes the hero of *Prometheus* by choosing remain within a cosmic labyrinth of chance which is "inseparable from horror and death." Rolling the dice again, she flies the Engineer's spacecraft to another planet where, through Bataille's lens, darkness awaits.

In sum, *Prometheus* reveals the epistemological impotence of teleological ends within an infinite cosmos—which produces the affect of horror by allowing Bataille's nonhuman "chance" to swallow the situation. In other words, the human mind cannot rationally comprehend the nonhumanity of the cosmos. We cannot use external systems (Holloway) nor self-interested desires (Weyland) to tame the void; nor can we rely on religion. The inner experience of faith and spirituality (Shaw) kindles inquiry and magnetically draws us closer into the void. The affect from this reality becomes the unsettling and profound horror within *Prometheus*. This profound horror lies not with the intermittent encounters with monsters vis-à-vis Noëll Carroll. The immediate threats of monsters—the Engineers, inflected crew members, the "facehugger" aliens, or the iconic "xenomorph" alien—are fleeting frightening moments. The most unsettling horror of *Prometheus* emerges from the nonhuman possibilities of a potentially godless space and our futile means of fully understanding or experiencing such an environment.

The Role of Rhetoric

Rhetoric plays a crucial role in *Event Horizon*, *Prometheus*, and space horror in general. What is rhetoric? Rhetoric is commonly defined as the effective use of language for influencing others. However, in an opening line of his pioneering work *On Rhetoric*, ancient philosopher Aristotle defines rhetoric more graciously: "seeing the available means of persuasion in each case."[42] Therefore, rhetoric concerns "available means": not only written or spoken language, but also narrative elements and philosophical ideas. These broad means of persuasion compose the communicative machinery of horror-art—and construct the working rhetorics of horror cinema. As Noëll Carroll observes in *The Philosophy of Horror*, horror films can repulse audiences, and paradoxically, attract audiences as well.[43] I argue that although horror films challenge our imagination with fantastic scenarios, monsters, and unknowns, horror films also deeply relate to the human limits of knowledge—and connect with our present day postmodern anxieties.

Postmodernism is a philosophical understanding that navigates beyond comfortable totalizing systems of explanation; postmodernism embraces relativistic uncertainty about "truth" which leads to subjective anxiety, fear, and dread. Some postmodern theorists try to spins postmodernism in a lighthearted manner: Ludwig Wittgenstein's "language games," Richard Rorty's celebratory democratic spirit, or the clever wordplays of Jacques Derrida. George Bataille, on the other hand, communicates postmodern anxieties with a different rhetoric. He does not mask the horror of postmodernism. He deploys darkly playful language to deconstruct the layers of nihilism and horror. Similarly, space horror film, as a mode of storytelling, mirrors his dark spirit. Space horror film can be a powerful rhetoric of postmodern ideas that uncovers hidden anxieties about the limits of human knowledge—and purposely incites the appropriate affect of fear and dread.

The fictional horror narrative becomes the vehicle of persuasion. How does it persuade an audience? By recreating experience. Fictional stories invite the audience to imaginatively participate by means of character-surrogates on the screen. Therefore, horror film relays horrific experiences to an audience through modes of character-driven storytelling. Moreover, space horror films depict postmodern anxieties of the characters—specifically, anxieties regarding nonhuman and nonknowledge elements—to the audience through the fictional expression. Unlike other subgenres of horror, space horror need not rely on inhuman monsters—but rather, space horror can rely on the eternal nonhumanity of outer space itself—to express these anxieties. And as shown by *Event Horizon* and *Prometheus*, these anxieties cannot be resolved through philosophy.

Bataille tells us that through experience do we approach the summit of nonknowledge. Inner experience is the mode in which we can better—although not fully—wrestle the Nothingness. Space horror narratives, such as *Event Horizon* and *Prometheus*, usher this inner experience to the audience, allowing them to navigate their own anxieties about the postmodern condition in a way that language, logic, and science can never fully grasp. Ultimately, contemporary space horror reveals that the unknown is frightening, but the *never knowable* is even more frightening.

Notes

1. Noëll Carroll, *The Philosophy of Horror* (New York: Routledge, 1990), 40–41.
2. *Ibid.*
3. Eugene Thacker, *In The Dust of This Planet: Horror of Philosophy Vol. 1* (Winchester, UK: Zero, 2011), 4–7.
4. *Ibid.*, 17.

5. *Ibid.*, 20.
6. Stuart Kendall, "Editor's Introduction," in *The Unfinished System of Nonknowledge*, ed. Start Kendall (Minneapolis: University of Minnesota Press, 2001), xiii.
7. Eugene Thacker, *Starry Speculative Corpse: Horror of Philosophy Vol. 2* (Winchester, UK: Zero, 2015), 20.
8. Kendall, "Editor's Introduction," xiii.
9. Georges Bataille, "Nonknowledge," in *The Unfinished System of Nonknowledge*, ed. Stuart Kendall, trans. Stuart Kendall and Michelle Kendall (Minneapolis: University of Minnesota Press, 2001), 199–200.
10. Georges Bataille, "Nonknowledge, Laughter, and Tears," in *The Unfinished System of Nonknowledge*, ed. Stuart Kendall, trans. Stuart Kendall and Michelle Kendall (Minneapolis: University of Minnesota Press, 2001), 137.
11. Bataille, "Nonknowledge," 196.
12. *Ibid.*, 197.
13. *Ibid.*, 196.
14. Thacker, *Dust*, 74–81.
15. "Liberate Tutume Ex Infernis," *Event Horizon*, DVD special collector's edition, directed by Paul W.S. Anderson (1997; Hollywood: Paramount Pictures, 2006).
16. *Event Horizon*, DVD special collector's edition, directed by Paul W.S. Anderson (1997; Hollywood: Paramount Pictures, 2006).
17. Bataille, "Nonknowledge," 199.
18. *Event Horizon*.
19. "Liberate Tutume Ex Infernis."
20. *Ibid.*
21. "Womb of Fear," *Event Horizon*, DVD special collector's edition, directed by Paul W.S. Anderson (1997; Hollywood: Paramount Pictures, 2006).
22. Clive Barker, *The Hellbound Heart* (New York: HarperCollins, 1986), 61–62.
23. Georges Bataille, *Guilty*, trans. Bruce Boone (Venice, CA: Lapis, 1988), 78–79.
24. Georges Bataille, *Inner Experience*, trans. Leslie A. Boldt (Albany: State University of New York Press, 1984), 92.
25. Dialogue from *Event Horizon*.
26. *Ibid.*
27. Bataille, *Guilty*, 105.
28. "Liberate Tutume Ex Infernis."
29. *Prometheus*, Blu-ray, directed by Ridley Scott (Beverly Hills: Twentieth Century Fox, 2012).
30. *Ibid.*
31. Georges Bataille, "The Sorcerer's Apprentice," in *Visions of Excess: Selected Writings, 1927–1939*, ed. Allan Soekl (Minneapolis: University of Minnesota Press, 1985), 223–234.
32. Georges Bataille, "The Notion of Expenditure," in *Visions of Excess: Selected Writings, 1927–1939*, ed. Allan Soekl (Minneapolis: University of Minnesota Press, 1985), 116–129.
33. Francis Bacon, "Of Heresies," in *The Works of Francis Bacon, Volume One*, ed. Basil Montagu (London: William Pickering, 1825), 219.
34. Dialogue from *Prometheus*.
35. Bataille, *Inner Experience*, 14.
36. "Audio Commentary: Director, Ridley Scott," *Prometheus*, Blu-ray, directed by Ridley Scott (Beverly Hills: Twentieth Century Fox, 2012); and "Deleted Scene: The Engineer Speaks—with Audio Commentary from Editor, Pedro Scalia," *Prometheus*, Blu-ray, directed by Ridley Scott (Beverly Hills: Twentieth Century Fox, 2012).
37. "Audio Commentary: Writers, Damon Lindelof and Jon Spaihts," *Prometheus*, Blu-ray, directed by Ridley Scott (Beverly Hills: Twentieth Century Fox, 2012).
38. *Ibid.*
39. Dialogue from *Prometheus*.
40. Bataille, *Inner Experience*, 7.
41. Bataille, *Guilty*, 78–79.

42. Aristotle, *On Rhetoric: A Theory of Civic Discourse*, trans. George A. Kennedy (New York: Oxford University Press, 1991), 35.
43. Carroll, *The Philosophy of Horror*, 158–161.

BIBLIOGRAPHY

Aristotle. *On Rhetoric: A Theory of Civic Discourse.* Translated by George A. Kennedy. New York: Oxford University Press, 1991.
Bacon, Francis. *The Works of Francis Bacon, Volume One.* Edited by Basil Montagu. London: William Pickering, 1825.
Barker, Clive. *The Hellbound Heart.* New York: HarperCollins, 1986.
Bataille, Georges. *Guilty.* Translated by Bruce Boone. Venice, CA: Lapis, 1988.
_____. *Inner Experience.* Translated by Leslie A. Boldt. Albany: State University of New York Press, 1984.
_____. *Unfinished System of Nonknowledge.* Translated by Stuart Kendall and Michelle Kendall. Minneapolis: University of Minnesota Press, 2001.
_____. *Visions of Excess: Selected Writings, 1927–1939.* Translated by Allan Soekl. Minneapolis: University of Minnesota Press, 1985.
Carroll, Noëll. *The Philosophy of Horror, Or, Paradoxes of the Heart.* New York: Routledge, 1990.
Event Horizon. DVD special collector's edition. Directed by Paul W.S. Anderson. 1997. Hollywood: Paramount Pictures, 2006.
Halloween. Blu-ray. Directed by John Carpenter. 1978. Beverly Hills: Anchor Bay Entertainment, 2007.
Hellraiser. DVD. Directed by Clive Barker. 1987. Hollywood: Image Entertainment, 2012.
Prometheus. Blu-ray. Directed by Ridley Scott. 2012. Beverly Hills: Twentieth Century Fox, 2012.
Rosemary's Baby. DVD. Directed by Roman Polanski. 1968. Hollywood: Paramount, 2000.
Thacker, Eugene. *In the Dust of This Planet.* Winchester, UK: Zero, 2011.
_____. *Starry Speculative Corpse.* Winchester, UK: Zero, 2015.

Out of Space—Out of Time

Looking at the Factors of Time in Space Horror Movies

JULIANE SCHLAG

The reason why time plays a great part in so many of my tales is that this element looms up in my mind as the most profoundly dramatic and grimly terrible thing in the universe. Conflict with time seems to me the most potent and fruitful theme in all human expression.

—H.P. Lovecraft[1]

Space horror movies are often seen as a combined product of space operas and horror movies. To some extent this is true, but the combination of both also creates room for new elements of horror. One of these is an altered topology of time. The introductory quote by H.P. Lovecraft characterizes time as the "most profoundly dramatic and grimly terrible thing in the universe."[2] Lovecraft's talent was to create not only a form of omnipresent cosmic horror in relation to aliens and space but also a compelling fear of the unknown in characters engaging with his fictional universe. Therefore, some of the protagonists of his stories, such as Randolph Carter, experience horror as a conflict with time. Lovecraft created this new form of fear, which he intentionally tied to time and space, explaining: "I choose weird stories because they suit my inclination best—one of my strongest and most persistent wishes being to achieve, momentarily, the illusion of some strange suspension or violation of the galling limitations of time, space, and natural law which forever imprison us and frustrate our curiosity about the infinite cosmic spaces beyond the radius of our sight and analysis."[3] Within his stories, Lovecraft tried to expand our familiar boundaries of geographical and physical spaces. He was one of the early 20th century authors to create space horror by not only identifying space as a geographical tabula rasa but also as a physical oxymoron where natural law, as we know it, cannot be applied.

Lovecraft's understanding of the physiology of the fear goes very much beyond traditional characteristics of horror: In classical horror and many modern versions of it, horror within a narrative is embodied by a grotesque monster. Researchers like George Ochoa have argued that not only is the monster important to create horror, engaging with it is even more important since it builds up horror by gradually revealing the deformity of the monster, leading to its destruction.[4] In most Lovecraftian horror, however, the horror is metaphysical and cannot be destroyed. This absence of resolution created a new form of terror: the fear of the unknown.

The fear of the unknown is part of our modern concept of time. In a Christian tradition, modern understanding of time is tied to the philosophical problem of fatalism; the question if a certain future is unavoidable. Space horror is one of the best genres to recreate fear of the unknown in the form of fatalism since most narratives are futuristic, featuring space travel as an everyday element. They are therefore already set in a geographical and temporal distance from the viewer. At the same time, they have to provide markers for the audience to understand the portrayed future in order to form an interest in the plot. Consequently, the setting of space movies is always designed in the style of the time it is made. While the viewer can easily connect to the familiar elements of the setting, implementing horror through estrangement of place becomes harder to evoke. Taking up Lovecraft's construction of the fear of the unknown, horror movies set in space use the metaphysical characteristics of time to create horror by confronting the viewer with altered physics he cannot fully comprehend.

Similar to other horror genre movies, the horror within a space narrative is concentrated on a group of individuals, detached from a larger social body. The inserting isolation and its accelerating progression become an important part of the elemental horror and the progression of the plot itself. Taking this into account, the following essay will take a look at the perception and presentation of time in different space horror movies. The premises of the analysis lie in the fact that time in space horror movies is a utilized element of alienation that serves to create a fear of the unknown as something unique to space horror.

In the first section, "Gone Too Long," the analysis will look at the scenario of the long lost ship in space horror movies. It will point out that time of disappearance is needed to transform the ship into an artifact which is rediscovered, but not understood by a new crew. As a result, the former item of up-to-date technology turns against its human creators. Time in this scenario is used to alienate the ship. In the second section, "Time Is Running Out," the investigation will look at the scenarios in which a ship crew is confronted with time as a resource. As soon as time becomes a resource, it seems to accelerate, causing panic and inefficiency. The analysis in this section will show how time is used to build and speed up the plot and create a rising tension of horror. Fatalism itself will be in the focus of the analysis in the third section, "Fear of Eternity," where the investigation will look at the behavior characters adapt when they are lost in space. The paper will argue that while affected individuals find strategies to cope, their implementation leads characters to turn against society and themselves. While this shows an inversion of socialization itself, time is used to create a vacuum of terror in which progress becomes meaningless and the individual is trapped. In the final section, "Again, Again and Again," the analysis will look how repetition in Sci-Fi horror (SF horror) is used to create traumas and after-shocks in order to form a temporal loop structure in which horror repeats itself. In the conclusion, all interim results throughout the analysis will be summarized and lead to a final cumulative statement on the element of time in modern SF horror movies.

Gone Too Long

This scenario often features the recovery of an abandoned spaceship, such as in *Sunshine* (2007, Danny Boyle) and *Event Horizon* (1997, Paul W.S. Anderson). As a shared characteristic, these ships are gone for good, thought not to return, having been out in space longer than planned. In order to mystify the ship, a temporal gap identifies it as a long lost artifact then to be discovered by a new crew. Similar to the tradition of the literary mystic artifact, the ship too is cursed. It or its contents turn out to be hostile, haunting the new crew. The element of time is vital since it allows the ship to transform into in an inversion of its former self.

Haunted space ship stories share elements with earthbound ghost ship narratives. Movies such as *Virus* (1999, John Bruno), in which an alien virus gets transmitted through a space station into a ship in the South Pacific, shows that both scenarios can also interact with each other. The plot progression is the same in ghost ships and haunted spaceships: a ship gets rediscovered, turns out to be haunted and an entity is able to control the ship or the technical equipment on it. While in a classic sense SF scenarios mimics ghost ship stories, the agency of the haunting in spaceships remains unidentified. In a classic ghost ship story, the ghost can be defined by having motives and means. Yet, even if an alien race or corrupted former crew member manifests themselves by haunting a spaceship, their means remain cryptic: Neither the crew nor the viewers are able to learn enough about the phenomenon to comprehend it. Therefore, no exorcism can be performed and the crew becomes entangled with the fate of the ship.

Throughout the history of SF Horror movies, technology began to play the most important part in scenarios set in space. On one side, technology in SF movies portrays a futuristic outlook and thereby already provides the impression of narratives operating with a different understanding of time. On another side, throughout the 1950s technology became part of everyday life and also started to operate in the absence of humans in the form of auto-pilots and automatic trains. This made it possible to imagine forms of animated technology.

The shift of the perception of technology is very visible in the early 1950s to 1970 SF Horror movies: In *The Atomic Submarine* (1959), directed by Spencer G. Bennent, a Lovecraftian alien is hiding near the Antarctica and gets killed by submarine missiles when it tries to return to space. Apart from being an SF movie, it was also clearly a pro-war movie, showing how war technology can defend, if not save humanity. Previous to that, in *Invasion of the Body Snatchers* (1956, Don Siegel), after a short story by Jack Finney—which was closely modeled after H.P. Lovecraft's The Colour outer Space[5]—average small town inhabitants are portrayed to effectively deal with an alien invasion of their city, without using technology or weapons. Yet the aliens seem to escape. But from *Invasion of the Body Snatchers* onward they return in different shapes and fighting them requires technological upgrades. *Andromeda Strain* (1971, Robert Wise), after the same book by Nelson Gidding, is pretty much the same story as in *Invasion of the Body Snatchers*, but it describes the failure of human science when trying to understand the outer space and its life forms. While *Invasion of the Body Snatchers* focused on a small town, portraying how aliens are threatening to kill life on earth, *Andromeda Stain* emphasizes the powerlessness of modern science in the face of "alienation." This was the next step to take modern horror into space: it needed the involvement of specialists, technical equipment and necessarily a higher temporal density reflected in far distances travel.

Humans followed aliens into space or just followed space itself, but the Iliad nerve, once discovered in *Andromeda Strain*, prevailed: technology and science would not live up to their promises. The lost space ship is an embodiment, if not a relict, loaded with expectations it would not fulfill. The attempted recovery of the ship therefore also means to get hold of these expectations, reset them, and thereby correct an invalid state of human capability. In *Event Horizon*, the inventor of the spaceship *Event Horizon*, Dr. William Weir (Sam Neill), insists on being part of the rescue team when the ship reappears after seven years of radio silence. Even after the rescue crew enters the ghost ship and sights of the forces of time are visible in the form of body parts frozen in zero gravity, Weir remains persistent that the ship could not have disappeared. He further denies the statement of one of the crew members, who had been convoluted into the black hole drive of the ship, and argues that the drive cannot activate itself. Very much like Dr. Frankenstein, he is unable to imagine that his creation has a will of its own until it confronts him. Yet Weir already knew that the ship was lost for the last seven years. His participation in the rescue mission is a paradox attempt to correct his past: the ship should not have been lost in the first place. Susan Sontag, analysis the role of technology in fiction, concluded that "science is simply either adventure (for good or evil) or a technical response to danger. And, typically, when the fear of science is paramount—when science is conceived of as black magic rather than white—the evil has no attribution beyond that of the perverse will of an individual scientist. In science fiction films the antithesis of black magic and white is drawn as a split between technology, which is beneficent, and the errant individual will of a lone intellectual."[6] Dr. Weir represents the errant individual. Since he fails to see his own mistakes, he will never be able to reclaim the ship. The urge to correct his flaws drives the new crew to rediscover the old ship. While the crew is puzzled to understand why the ship got lost, the members do not question their own involvement with the ship. Instead of correcting a former error, they kindle a circle of repetition. The former disappearance of the ship already foreshadowed this progression: a ship strangely disappeared once holds the potential to disappear again. The audience is aware of this circular trend, forming a dialectic pact with the screenplay: viewers accept the imminence the rescue team faces in order to gain insight into the mystery of the disappearance.

The exact time passing between the loss and rediscovery of the ghost ship is relative; it does not matter how long it was gone, it matters how far away from human contact it was. Time in space is relative and, therefore, the question "How long?" needs to be changed into "How long in relation to what?" The moment of a missed contact with human society marks the point of being gone too long, no matter how long a ship actually had been in space. The disappearance of the ship is necessary in order to create an aura of mystery. Time of absence is needed to transform the former item of up-to-date technology controllable by human will into a riddle, something that is not understood anymore. The rescue crew, therefore, engages with the ship very much like archaeologists do with historic human remains. But the pieces of information they uncover do not form a coherent picture. Human error is ruled out through the process, even if still secretly involved. This prepares the foundation for a paranormal course of events and the ghost in the machine awakens. By activating the haunting, the ship becomes an artifact, detached from its former technological function. An artifact is always ancient, loaded with symbolic meaning. Since space-time is relative, a ship can appear ancient without actually being ancient. With the ship becoming an artifact, it is no longer a part of reality and a fear of the unknown becomes attached to it. This fear is what is displayed through the plot affecting the crew and resonating with the audience.

Time Is Running Out

This scenario is a catalyst of nearly every SF Horror plot. It is tied together either with the technical construction of the ship or with the advantage or intelligence of an antagonist, such as in *Alien* (1979, Ridley Scott). Acceleration of time often leads to a structural reformation of the group in order to face the problem systematically. As a result, the group splits up, enhancing the acceleration of time since action multiples. In this scenario, the main factor of tension is time, creating space for further horror to come.

As outlined before, time in space is relative, so it can not actually run out. Therefore, in scenarios where we perceive time as something limited occurs through a change of density of action. This is very much a cinematic effect where the footage switches back and forth between different areas of the same setting or portrays parallel processes or even time lapses, accompanied with music emphasizing the same. The cinematic usage of portraying time as something that can be accelerated goes back to time travel movies. When we think about H.G. Wells' *The Time Machine* movie adaption from 1960 (George Pal), the effects of time as it rushes by were conveyed to the audience by introducing different time frames in which action happened: "The effects of time travel—the alterations of normal motion (reverse action, accelerated action), the intermittent flashes of light (recalling the projector's shutter mechanism), and the stasis of the frozen moment (the freeze-frame)— are precisely those of cinematic montage.... And the "Traveller," as he is called, is not just a scientist sitting in the saddle of a machine, but a moviegoer ensconced in the seat of a movie theatre. Moreover, as long as he participates in time travel, he is virtually ageless—just like the unchanging images frozen on the strip of film."[7]

The moviegoer in this context echoes the time traveler: Both are watching, remaining motionless. This relationship transforms with the space traveler: While the contrast of a motionless individual versus fast moving surroundings invoked the image of time travel, an inversion of the concept produced the image of running out of time. Compared to the ageless time traveler, the space traveler's voyage is more elaborate. The time traveler experiences a momentum while the space traveler experiences ongoing change. A higher density of change is perceived as acceleration of time since the focus of action starts to shift quicker from one event to another. In *Alien*, *Event Horizon* and many other SF horror movies we can identify this phenomenon when the crew decides to split up in order to solve multiple tasks. While they split up in order to be able to deal with the situation more efficiently, the single individuals end up in situations where they are vulnerable because they are alone, unable to solve a problem and need help from the rest of the crew. This is, of course, the irony of the situation: human efficiency has its limits. It is however perceived as the phenomenon of acceleration of time rather than actual human incapability.

The human nature in reaction to the multiplication of tasks is important in order to transfer empathy from the screen to the viewer. One visible effect is the transfer of stress onto the characters trapped in multi-tasking situations, which leads to a rising tension felt by the audience. Zugzwang—urge to act—und the Ermöglichkeitshorizont—scale in which action is possible—is evaluated by character and viewer constantly and it leads to thoughts of prioritizing actions or the feeling of being in a rush.[8] The audience can emotionally relate to a lack of time when seeing it on screen, even though the setting of the movie might seem estranged. Because narratives in space are by nature more distant and, therefore, harder to perceive than narratives grounded on earth, Lovecraft argued that while realism is important for SF movies—in comparison to fantasy movies—the central plot element needs to be developed by linking it to shifts in emotions: "Inconceivable events and conditions have a special handicap to overcome, and this can be accomplished only through the maintenance of a careful realism in every phase of the story except that touching on the one given marvel. This marvel must be treated very impressively and deliberately—with a careful emotional 'build-up'–else it will seem flat and unconvincing."[9] The marvel in SF-horror movies is the element of horror around which the story is built. The perceived acceleration of time is one mode of the build-up phase needed for the horror to spiral up until it is fully revealed.

In *Event Horizon*, the crew splits up as soon as they enter the ship to reactivate vital functions. Those team members who are left alone are the first to encounter the horror contained in the ship. Yet time only becomes a problem after their own shuttle is damaged and the time to repair it gets linked to the oxygen left in the haunted ship. From this point onward, more and more tasks need to be fulfilled in order to guarantee the crew's return. The number of people able to perform tasks gets decimated at the same time. Seeing how the action multiplies as the movie progresses, it seems that the horror the group encounters is omnipresent. It also is presented as being contagious within the ship, having the ability to resurface again at different places. Through this build-up, the horror transpires to the audience, creating tension for the climax. In regards to the element of horror, Christopher Kenworthy argued: "Horror shows us our own mortality and lack of control. It makes us admit to our weaknesses and our more secret emotions."[10] As the former analysis has shown, losing control is a vital element of SF horror movies by multiplying action and thereby evoking the image of an acceleration of time. It further provokes a mental and physical instability of characters pressured this way and thereby conditions other aspects of horror, such as admitting to weakness and secret emotions. The characters become trapped in a spiral of tasks they cannot fulfill, ending in the final understanding of their incapability which makes the reviled horror of the climax situation tragic and more horrifying at the same time.

Fear of Eternity

This is a traditional scenario featuring ship crews and individuals who get lost in space with no option to return to earth. It includes sacrificial abandonments and disappearances, such as in *Moon* (2009, Duncan Jones), *Pandorum* (2009, Christian Alvart) and television series *The Starlost* (1973). Elemental for these movies is the open interim endings, picturing characters in fear of their unknown, uncertain future as they are lost in space. The unresolved fate of the characters transfers their fear into the imagination of the viewer and thereby recreates fear of the unknown through empathy. Most important is the fact that at the moment where a character is lost in space, time stops and the moment itself becomes eternal. Progress has lost its meaning, and hence, it does not matter when and where the character will die.

An early, but at the same time, a very direct adaption of the scenario can be found in the series *The Starlost*, aired in 1973 and co-authored by Harlan Ellison. In the series, a cross-generational spaceship has lost its course. Different societies live undisturbed and unconnected under biospheres, simulating stages of human evolution. With the captain and scientist onboard dead, the ship is drifting purposeless in space while most of its inhabitants remain unaware of their fate. Those who suspect as much, reflect, "What have I learned in all these years, except to curse my own nature, and which blasphemes brings down punishment and loneliness and suffering.... I'll tell you something else I learned too: Don't ask questions."[11] In this scenario, time has alienated the individual not only from society but also from his mental integrity. Human nature has turned against itself, tormenting the individual. It can no longer ask questions because there are no answers. Unless it can find some doctrine, which provides meaning in the situation, it is doomed to be a plaything of higher forces.

In the movie *Sunshine*, a religious doctrine serves the captain of the *Icarus I* as he is lost in space. While he is able to survive this way, he turns on everyone else disagreeing with his belief. His transformation into a religious fanatic not only makes him lose his crew but also his sanity. While he himself is no longer afraid of eternity, the audience perceives him as an outsider who is no longer part of society. A reengagement with society seems impossible at such a state of mind, as also portrayed in the movie *Moon*. There, the main character is a moon-based clone realizing his destruction and replacement by a new identical version of himself. As he tries to escape to Earth in order to save himself and break the chain of cloning, he remains unable to reconnect with the family of the human he has been modeled after and is rejected by society as he is seen as a scam. In the cases of *Sunshine* and *Moon*, both characters lost their individuality through the time they were alone in space. In *Moon*, the loss of identity is oppressive to the character as soon as he realizes that he is not only a clone but also experiencing the same things as his predecessors: the process of his life is mechanically controlled, and he is conditioned with the same memories as all the clones before him. The fear of solitude in space can be identified with a process of dehumanization which starts to consume the affected individuals.

On a theoretical level, the character development of individuals lost in space reflects a collective anxiety about the loss of identity and individuality, while the tension in the movie arises from the main characters emotional attraction of being "taken over" by a greater ideal and thereby giving up responsibility for his actions. The terror of these situations in SF horror movies—the tension between the physical appearance of humans and improper behavior—is summarized by Vivian Carol Sobchack: "What is so visually devastating and disturbing about the SF films' 'taken over' humans is the small, and, therefore, terrible, incongruence between the ordinariness of their form and the final extraordinariness of their behavior, however hard they try to remain undetected and 'normal.'"[12] This is especially the case when the narrative is portrayed through the eyes of an unreliable narrator, such as in *Pandorum* where several crew members of a cross-generational spaceship develop hallucinations resulting in violent outbreaks. Since a humanoid species also tries to control the spaceship, the viewer cannot always conceive which elements of the movie are supposed to represent real elements of a possible future and which are just hallucinations experienced by the space travelers.

While all these modus operandi—religious fanaticism, reliving a former life, hallucinations—are individual and even objective contingency strategies for being lost in space, they further seem to condition a self-destructive nature. Turning against society and the self seems to become the final form of socialization for characters lost in space since progress in any other direction becomes impossible as they face an unknown, meaningless fate. Time in this scenario becomes endless, since it is detached from any objective censure, such as dates or important historic events, and it is this detachment which alienates the affected character from human society and transmits the fear of an uncertain future to the audience.

Again, Again and Again

This scenario can be split into two types: Repetition of actions in case of time travel events or black hole events and repetition through memory or trauma of survivors, such as in *Event Horizon* and *Moon*. In both cases, a traumatic moment repeats itself in order to recreate the horror of it. The moment is often intensified by letting it appear not as a singular incident, but as a series of irrevocable perils. Time in this scenario is exclusively bound to one terrifying context, provoking horror through the lack of alternatives. The same concept is used sometimes to create sequels, as in the case of the *Alien* movies.

Apart from a sequel, scenes of traumatic memory in the form of repetition are most effective as the finality to a story; because they suggest that horror, which has just ended, does indeed continue. In *Event Horizon*, after two survivors are found by a rescue crew, one of them imagines that they are found by the demons they just escaped from. While this results in a first after-shock for the audience, a second later it is revealed that it was only a hallucination. From the scene itself, it is nevertheless clear that the character, experiencing the hallucination, thinks that it was real. In this case, memories seem to haunt the survivors even though they are not in danger anymore. For them, the horror is not over and might never be; the trauma will haunt them beyond their alleged safe return to earth. In this form of trauma, time becomes fixed to a horrifying event, which is relived in full emotion over and over again, preserving the horrors of it.

As already outlined in an earlier section, in *Moon*, the main character, Sam (Sam Rockwell), is a clone bound to experience the same life as his predecessors. Sam is the only astronaut on the moon, overseeing the mining activities for the firm Lunar Industries. As he is close to returning to Earth, he has an accident and is saved by his own clone. Through talking to his clone he discovers that he is a clone himself and his return date to Earth is nothing more than an expiry date. They also discover a hidden dock, filled with more Sam clones. While this is upsetting to both, they decide to break the chain of cloning by sending the younger version of Sam to Earth in order to alert the public. The media reacts to his story and Lunar Industries responds by calling him a fraudster. Not explicitly outlined, but it is hinted at the end of the movie that Sam's intervention was only a brief diversion, and Lunar Industries will continue their activity by just simply activating the next clone.

In *Moon*, the main characters are unaware of the repetition they are part of until they meet. Suddenly, it becomes clear that all their memories and even their identities are constructed and they have been manipulated to form the same emotions and love the same people. As both discover that none of it is real, they collapse. The trauma in the case of *Moon* is created through the moment of enlightenment in which Sam realizes that the world he thought he knew actually does not exist, and he is only an accessory in a company's business model. He has no past, no future and no power over his own fate. The only thing he can do is to stop the process continuing. However, that is taken away from him, when he is accused of lying as soon as he comes to Earth. *Moon* ends with resetting the circle of repetition, making it possibly even more efficient since the company became aware of the trouble a clone could cause. Like *Moon*, Carl Sagan's *Contact* (1985) similarly ends with the main character being seen as an imposter, telling a false and fantastic story after returning home from space. In both cases, the returned individual remains an outsider. Like in the case of the survivors of *Event Horizon*, the characters in *Moon* and *Contact* are perceived as not in their right mind. They are mentally ill and, therefore, unreliable. As a result, they remain powerless, even after they have returned earth. Stuart C. Aitken argued that mental illness in Science Fiction serves exactly this purpose: it isolates the an individual from a community, and he wrote: "'social pathologies' such as agoraphobia, vertigo, hysteria, and schizophrenia are embedded in the landscape of science fiction films to the extent that the pace marks our collective responses to what is not hegemonic (and thus, to what is pathological)."[13]

In SF horror movies, characters that are commonly perceived as pathologically ill, are created through traumas. As society rejects them, their stories do not resonate. Unable to process the trauma, the character experiences a temporal loop in which the traumatic event replaces progress. Society on the other hand, as a form of self-preservation, excludes individuals who show signs of mental instability. In the movie *Pandorum*, the form of exclusion goes as far as physically mutating into a form of humanoids. Mutants started to form in the spaceship after individuals started to cannibalize each other while having hallucinations, a side effect from cross-generational space travel. Instead of socialization, the human crew at the end of the movie decides to kill them. This scenario shows that through trauma characters in space horror movies can transform into aliens and be rejected by their own society.

Conclusion

Through the analysis of different scenarios, this essay has argued that the presentation of time is an important characteristic of space horror movies. Time, like space, lies beyond human control. Therefore, the alteration of time in SF horror movies kindles the plot and further serves as an emotional link with the audience by stressing an uncomfortable characteristic of time. The investigation looked at how the element of time is used in narratives featuring disappearing ships. The ships needed to disappear from human sight in order to transform into a lost artifact, which are rediscovered by a new crew. The analysis found that the drive to reclaim the ship goes back to a need to correct the mistake of losing the ship in the first place. While the ship disappears, a transformation takes places: It gets stripped of its former purpose as a technical asset and loaded with mystical meaning. This can be identified as a form of mimesis where the hostile entity cloaks itself as the ship. When it resurfaces, it appears as a long lost artifact, but is actually a trap, disguising something irrational as something rational. Scholars, such as Rob Kitchin and James Kneale, have argued that mimesis in SF movies discusses impossible things in a scientific, rational way.[14] The analysis has shown that their statement can be extended to SF horror movies and altered in so far that through time, the absence of something rational can be transformed into something horrifying. The analysis further found that the horror contained in the ship is not only perceived as irrational but often contagious and indestructible. Since it cannot be analyzed and understood by the crew, it makes them afraid of the unknown.

The analysis then looked at scenarios in which time becomes a vital resource for the crew. It found that time is perceived to accelerate in situations where a rising number of tasks need to be performed by the crew. The analysis further showed that as a coping strategy, the crew splits up and thereby becomes vulnerable or unable to solve those tasks. The audience perceives this as a rise of tension since we can relate to the stress of the situation. Hence, stress and tension are important for the buildup of the plot as it creates space for the major horror to come at the climax of the situation. George Ochoa argued that an emotional bond is important, since it creates not only empathy for the situation but through empathy transmits knowledge to the audience: "The appeal is essentially cognitive and objective: what we seek from horror movies are objects of knowledge that represent new forms that would not even be accessible if they were real. However, to provide these objects of knowledge, horror movies must act on our subjective emotions" in order to affect us.[15]

The analysis turned to investigate the behavior of characters lost in space. As soon as a character is lost in space, he not only has lost his purpose, but also every connection with society as well. He is no longer on any social-geographical map. For him "conventional senses of geography and history are 'dead'—geography as a jigsaw puzzle made up out of discrete, bounded spaces, and history as truth rather than narrative"[16] are no longer parameters of his cognition, as Rob Kitchin and James Kneale argued. The investigation further showed that even if affected individuals coped with the situation by acting dogmatic, they ended up turning against society and themselves. Going back to the concept of traditional horror which needs a monster, space horror portrays the transformation into a destructive being through dehumanization.

George Ochoa states that "the primary purpose of the horror film is to make the audience know the monster."[17] He further defines monsters as "deformed and destructive beings whose deformity cause their destructiveness."[18] In some SF horror movies, individuals lost in space become the monster and can be identified through their deformity and destructive behavior, yet at the same time in other cases, they are not deformed and can only be perceived as uncanny at the most. They are perceived as such because their behavior is incoherent with their looks. Ochoa theory represents a subversion of Carlos Clarens definition of horror as dehumanization: "The ultimate horror in science fiction is neither death nor destruction but dehumanization, a state in which emotional life is suspended, in which the individual is deprived of individual feelings, free will, and moral judgment ... this type of fiction hits the most exposed nerve of contemporary society: collective anxiety about the loss of individual identity, subliminal mindbending, or downright scientific/political brainwashing."[19]

The analysis finally takes a closer examination of the last scenario where individuals appear to behave different than the norm due to the experience of trauma. The investigation showed that surviving characters in SF horror movies are far from being saved since traumatic memories make them relive the horror over and over again. They end up stuck in a time-loop sequence with the trauma controlling them. Since their trauma formed in space, outside of a social sphere, they remain unable to communicate their fear efficiently. And, at the same time, society perceives them as outsiders and mentally ill. In this scenario, the mental and physical boundaries are congruent. Rob Kitchin and James Kneale argued: "In many ways SF's estrangement can be considered through spatial metaphors: it constructs spatial realms (new worlds, inner and outer spaces), concerns itself with borders and transgressions (alien invaders and invasive cyborgization). SF is, therefore, open to analysis that identify and trace out these geographies."[20] As the analysis showed, in case of the formation of trauma, we have to consider the mental sphere as a separate spatial realm, disconnected with the geographical sphere and following a different timeline.

The analyzed scenarios showed that horror can be bound to alterations of the element of time. Within the analyzed material, time remains an independent factor, uncontrollable by humans and so creates the fear of the unknown as a form of fatalism. Since it progresses independently, humans can only react towards it, unable to redefine its nature. This is why a lost ship cannot return to a temporal status where it has not been lost and humans once lost in space cannot just go forward or back in time to reunite with society.

NOTES

1. Howard Philips Lovecraft, "Notes on Writing Weird Fiction," *Amateur Correspondent* 2, no. 1 (1937): 7.
2. *Ibid.*
3. *Ibid.*
4. George Ochoa, *Deformed and Destructive Beings: The Purpose of Horror Films* (Jefferson, NC: McFarland, 2011), 1.
5. See Nicholas Diak's "Meteor Madness: Lovecraftian Horror and Consumerism in the Battle for Small Town USA" in this collection.
6. Susan Sontag, "The Imagination of Disaster," *Commentary*, October 1965, 48.
7. John C. Tibbetts and James M. Welsh, *The Encyclopedia of Novels into Film*, Facts on File Film Reference Library, 2d ed. (New York: Facts on File, 2005), xvii.
8. Hartmut Rosa, *Beschleunigung: Die Veränderung der Zeitstrukturen in der Moderne* (Frankfurt am Main: Suhrkamp, 2005), 217 f.
9. Lovecraft, "Notes on Writing Weird Fiction," 7.
10. Christopher Kenworthy, *Writing Science Fiction, Fantasy & Horror: How to Create Successful Work for Publication*, Successful Writing Series (Oxford: How to Books, 1997), 16.
11. *The Starlost*, "Voyage of Discovery," Twentieth Century Fox Television, September 14, 1973, written by Harlan Ellison (as Cordwainer Bird), directed by Harvey Hart, George McCowan, Leo Orenstein, Ed Richardson, and Joseph L. Scanlan, 10:15 min.
12. Vivian Carol Sobchack, *The Limits of Infinity: The American Science Fiction Film* (Cranbury, NJ: A.S. Barnes, 1980), 121.
13. Stuart C. Aitken, "Turning the Self: City Space and SF Horror Movies," in *Lost in Space: Geographies of Science Fiction*, ed. Rob Kitchin and James Kneale (London: Continuum, 2002), 113.
14. Rob Kitchin and James Kneale, "Lost in Space," in *Lost in Space: Geographies of Science Fiction*, ed. Rob Kitchin and James Kneale (London: Continuum, 2002), 4, 6.
15. Ochoa, *Deformed and Destructive Beings*, 15.
16. Kitchin and Kneale, "Lost in Space," 1.
17. Ochoa, *Deformed and Destructive Beings*, 1.
18. *Ibid.*, 2.
19. Carlos Clarens, *An Illustrated History of the Horror Film* (New York: Capricorn Books, 1976), 134.
20. Kitchin and Kneale, "Lost in Space," 9.

BIBLIOGRAPHY

Aitken, Stuart C. "Turning the Self: City Space and SF Horror Movies." In *Lost in Space: Geographies of Science Fiction*, edited by Rob Kitchin and James Kneale, 104–122. London: Continuum, 2002.
Alien. DVD. Directed by Ridley Scott. 1979. London: Twentieth Century Fox, 2000.
Clarens, Carlos. *An illustrated History of the Horror Film*. New York: Capricorn Books, 1976.
Event Horizon. DVD. Directed by Paul W.S. Anderson. 1997. Hollywood: Paramount Pictures, 2006.
Kenworthy, Christopher. *Writing Science Fiction, Fantasy & Horror: How to Create Successful Work for Publication*. Successful Writing Series. Oxford: How to Books, 1997.
Kitchin, Rob, and James Kneale. "Lost in Space." In *Lost in Space: Geographies of Science Fiction*, edited by Rob Kitchin and James Kneale, 1–16. London: Continuum, 2002.
Kitchin, Rob, and James Kneale, ed. *Lost in Space: Geographies of Science Fiction*. London: Continuum, 2002.
Lovecraft, Howard Philips. "Notes on Writing Weird Fiction." *Amateur Correspondent* 2, no. 1 (1937): 7–10.
Moon. DVD. Directed by Duncan Jones. 2009. Liberty Films, 2009.
Ochoa, George. *Deformed and Destructive Beings: The Purpose of Horror Films*. Jefferson, NC: McFarland, 2011.
Pandorum. DVD. Directed by Christian Alvart. 2009. Munich: Constantin Film, 2010.

Rosa, Hartmut. *Beschleunigung: Die Veränderung der Zeitstrukturen in der Moderne.* Frankfurt am Main: Suhrkamp, 2005.
Sobchack, Vivian Carol. *The Limits of Infinity: The American Science Fiction Film.* Cranbury NJ: A.S. Barnes, 1980.
Sontag, Susan. "The Imagination of Disaster." *Commentary,* October 1965, 42–48.
The Starlost. "Voyage of Discovery." Season 1, Episode 1. Written by Harlan Ellison (as Cordwainer Bird). Directed by Harvey Hart, George McCowan, Leo Orenstein, Ed Richardson, and Joseph L. Scanlan, Twentieth Century Fox Television. September 14, 1973.
Sunshine. DVD. Directed by Danny Boyle. 2007. Los Angeles: Twentieth Century Fox, 2007.
Tibbetts, John C., and James M. Welsh. *The Encyclopedia of Novels into Film*, 2d ed. Facts on File Film Reference Library. New York: Facts on File, 2005.

We're All Alone, Out Here
Isolation and Its Contribution to Space Horror in Film

JANET JOYCE HOLDEN

Film has long been used as a tool to express ourselves and examine the human condition, and with such a formidable and extensive library currently available, we could perhaps be forgiven for overlooking the gore and adventure-prone subgenre of Space Horror, especially when there are so many other genres to explore. However, what is horror, other than another door to the self, and all its fears and nightmares?

In its definition of "What Is Horror Fiction?" the Horror Writers Association suggests that horror "forces us to confront who we are, to examine what we are afraid of, and to wonder what lies ahead down the road of life."[1] And despite the suggestion that the exploration of space involves looking outward, when we're faced with the unknown, the hostile environments, and the scarcity of resources, we invariably fall back on our strengths and weaknesses, fears and delights, and consequent examinations of the self emerge regardless.

Over the years, the genres of Space and Horror have provided us with a wealth of literature and film. Literature includes some great examples, such as Peter Watts' *Blindsight*, Stephen Donaldson's *Gap* Series, and Stanislaw Lem's *Solaris*, while film provides such examples as Ridley Scott's *Alien* (1979), Paul W.S. Anderson's *Event Horizon* (1997), and David Twohy's *Pitch Black* (2000), along with Steven Soderbergh's *Solaris* (2002), Duncan Jones's *Moon* (2009), and Peter Hyams' *Outland* (1981), the latter three examined in more detail below.

But what is it that binds the two elements of space and horror successfully, enabling us to examine and discover more about ourselves? What elements enable them to blend so well together? Perhaps isolation, as a fundamental backdrop to many of these stories of exploration and terror, is able to provide the perfect catalyst.

Outer space appears as a wonderland in the viewer of our telescopes. Above us lies an entire universe. Billions of stars and the possibilities of exploration and adventure seem irresistible, inspiring us to escape from gravity by climbing into our rockets and suffering the fiery, brutal push. Alas, the distances.

Statistics via NASA Goddard Space Center reveal our closest star system, Alpha Centauri[2] is a mere 4.35 light years away and we currently don't have the means to get there. If we wish to go somewhere closer, such as Jupiter, Nola Taylor Redd, on Space.Com informs us "when the two planets are at their closest point, the distance to Jupiter is only 365 million miles (588 million kilometers). From its closest point, Jupiter shines so brightly that even Venus dims in comparison. At its farthest, the gas giant lies 601 million miles (968 million km) away."[3] So, if we were to embark on such a journey, the distances involved would give us plenty of time to get acquainted with our new buddy, isolation, who would invariably climb aboard for the ride.

However, studies have proved that isolation and humanity are unlikely to get along. Humans are social creatures and we thrive on companionship, despite our complaints regarding boisterous crowds and noisy neighbors. Too much time alone, cooped up in a monotonous environment, and our health suffers, we become bored and anxious, and our brains seek to compensate for the lack of stimulus.

There have been a number of studies regarding our physiological and psychological health in isolated environments, the results of which highlight how troublesome the effects of isolation can be. Many of the studies focus on the effects of solitary confinement in prisons, or how social isolation affects us as we get older, but studies of our astronauts have also been undertaken, regarding the effects of single missions, prolonged periods aboard the International Space Station, and the likely effects on the proposed Mission to Mars.

Sharon Shalev's Sourcebook on Solitary Confinement included Dr. Craig Haney's 1993 study of California prisoners and had this to say:

Haney's (1993) study of 100 randomly selected prisoners in one of California's supermax prisons, Pelican Bay Security Housing Unit, reported a very high prevalence of symptoms of psychological trauma with 91% of the prisoners sampled suffering from anxiety and nervousness, more than 80% suffering from headaches, lethargy and trouble sleeping and 70% fearing impending breakdown. More than half of the prisoners suffered from nightmares, dizziness and heart palpitations and other mental-health problems caused by isolation, which included ruminations, irrational anger and confused thought processes (more than 80% of prisoners sampled), chronic depression (77%), hallucinations (41%) and overall deterioration.[4]

In Michael Bond's BBC article, "How Extreme Isolation Warps Minds," he mentions how "chronically lonely people have higher blood pressure, are more vulnerable to infection, and are also more likely to develop Alzheimer's disease and dementia. Loneliness also interferes with a whole range of everyday functioning, such as sleep patterns, attention and logical and verbal reasoning. The mechanisms behind these effects are still unclear, though what is known is that social isolation unleashes an extreme immune response—a cascade of stress hormones and inflammation."[5]

Woodburn Heron's 1957 article in *Scientific American* illustrates how our perception can falter, stating that "prolonged exposure to a monotonous environment, then, has definitely deleterious effects. The individual's thinking is impaired; he shows childish emotional responses; his visual perception becomes disturbed; he suffers from hallucinations."[6]

As for studies directly attributed to space missions, Nick Kanas' 2010 *Journal of Cosmology* "Expedition to Mars" article found that, despite making the best psychological choices when manning space missions, negative emotions can nonetheless build up toward outsiders, resulting in an atmosphere of mistrust. Kanas reveals, "both studies found evidence for the displacement of negative emotions in the group to outsiders, with the effect being stronger for the isolated crew members than the mission control subjects."[7]

Combine the above psychological effects with the obvious significant disadvantages inherent in physical isolation—the inability to find help quickly, or to consult others in order to find solutions to problems; the dangers of being alone in the face of a natural, geographical threat, an encounter with a formidable foe, human or alien—and isolation becomes the perfect foundation on which to build a tense, thrilling space horror film, presenting an impressive bag of tools for the filmmaker to use. Isolation also provides a fully established, rich, and believable breeding ground from which we can explore our relationship with fear, which becomes more intense, more poignant, when it is shored up by our knowledge of the detrimental effects of isolation, its prevalence in space, and the severe constraints of traveling immense distances.

Stephen Soderbergh's *Solaris*, based on the Stanislaw Lem novel that explores our acute limitations during a crisis of communication, makes deft and subtle use of nearly every tool in the Isolationist's trick bag: physical and social isolation, the remoteness of space, living alone in a big city, mistrust and anxiety; hallucinations, nightmares, the clinging to certain beliefs no matter how implausible. The film begins with social isolation, and rapidly dissolves into mistrust. Something has gone terribly wrong on an expedition to Solaris, and the station commander urges his friend and psychologist Chris Kelvin (George Clooney) to make the trip out there. He feels Kelvin is the only man he knows who might be capable of deciphering what is happening to the crew. However, he is reticent with the problems they seem to be having. "People are listening," he tells Kelvin, and "you're the only man I can trust."[8]

When Kelvin arrives at the station after a long journey, there is no one there to greet him other than a series of bloodstains on the ramp, and bloody fingerprints on the walls, and for the moment he is all alone and his steps ring hollow as he wanders the station's interior.

He discovers bodies in a makeshift morgue. Is someone a murderer? A short while later he finds only two of the crew remain alive, and they seem mentally impaired, frightened and confused by something they can't explain. One of the crew members, Dr. Gordon (Viola Davis), spells it out. "Until it happens to you, there's really no point in discussing it."[9] The other crew member, Snow (Jeremy Davies), suggests Kelvin will sleep better if he keeps his door locked.

The fear infecting Solaris is a far cry from the in-your-face, stomach-churning red end of the horror spectrum. Instead, we're met with the beautiful, hypnotic blue exuding from the planet below the station, and all the blood and murder has already occurred. Kelvin provides a reliable anchor. We assume he'll have all the answers, until, having brought along his own psychological baggage, the unexplainable starts happening to him, too. Like the others, he begins having hallucinations, and we, the audience, are summarily cast adrift.

The notion of instability is further increased by composer Chris Martinez's somnolent and otherworldly soundtrack.[10] Rather than induce an atmosphere of tense claustrophobia, it begins to seduce, to draw us outside the station walls toward the hypnotic presence of the planet, Solaris, and away from everything we would recognize as human.

Meanwhile, inside the station, the crew attempt to rationalize. But what's going on, and who can be trusted? Are their experiences real, or is the entire crew suffering hallucinations inspired by our difficult relationship with isolation? As for the psychologist, the one person whom the station commander thought was the best person to help, like the others he is thrown into a pit bewilderment and implausibility, and is unable to climb out.

In the meantime, horror becomes a silent, admonishing companion at the table, as they discuss how to deal with the phenomenon. Obvious solutions seem abhorrent, and against all notions of civility and humanity; doing the right thing becomes suspect, and blood has already been spilled. But there is no one else to consult. Suspicion of outsiders has already persuaded the crew to turn off the Artificial Intelligence system, and the lack of outside contact, of other ideas and stimuli, have left the crew vulnerable to the belief that what is happening is personal and real, despite the psychological assumption there is a plausible explanation.

In the end, the entire crew is caught in a net of terror, and escape becomes mandatory. They have no support, they are all alone, and are unable to stand and fight. Fear becomes omnipresent. Isolation deems it so.

In Matthew Hutson's *Psychology Today* article, Duncan Jones discusses the main concepts of his 2009 film, *Moon*, and when asked the question "Would you like yourself" replies, "we all have relationships in the world, but there is no relationship more important than having to deal with yourself and being aware of what you're like as a person to deal with, and I think that's something that not everyone really does, not everyone takes the time to think about, what am I actually like and would I like myself if I had to deal with me. So I think it's an important question, so if in any way the film gives people pause to have that little conversation or investigation with themselves, that would be really exciting."[11]

In *Moon*, isolation assumes the role of consummate trickster. Sam (Sam Rockwell) is all alone on the far side of the moon, working through a three-year stint at a mining operation with only his Artificial Intelligence unit, GERTY (voiced by Kevin Spacey), for company, with a promise of a return home to his wife at the end of his time there. His surroundings are falling apart, he is falling apart, but he's there to keep things ticking over for the duration of his shift. It's a mundane, crappy job, with a light at the end of the tunnel.

Out in the field, on his way to one of the Helium-3 harvesters, he suffers a hallucination and has a serious, almost fatal accident. When he awakens in the infirmary, he is disoriented. It has already been established that communications are faulty, and that delayed video is all that's available, and yet he witnesses his AI unit communicating with someone directly, in real time. Sam wants to revisit the crash site, but the doors are locked and his AI unit is proving obstructive.

Finally, after an act of vandalism and some deft arguments thrown toward GERTY, he is able to return to the site, where he discovers another man inside his damaged vehicle, barely clinging to life. He returns with the man, and it is only from this point on, when he is no longer alone, that isolation begins to lose its grip. Now, he has another person to question, to bounce ideas off of, and to rationalize with. The truth of his circumstances is finally revealed, and what a horrific and heartbreaking reveal it is.

Belief plays a big part in *Moon*'s set up, and isolation throws belief over Sam like a warm, comfortable blanket—belief he is talking to his wife via the delayed video communicator, belief that he can hang in there for three years, until it's time to go home to his family. We also see evidence of Sam's coping mechanisms in his battle against loneliness, his X-Acto knife-sculpted table-top village for example, and in the beginning, horror takes a back seat and bides its time as we see him go through life at the base. Even the accident doesn't register as particularly horrific, especially when we see him in the infirmary immediately afterward. He's made it. He's survived.

However, much like a fidgety younger sibling, horror eventually creeps forth, takes a corner of belief's blanket, and slowly begins to draw it from our reluctant shoulders. We've been led to believe communications are barely existent, so who is GERTY, the artificial intelligence, talking to? And why does GERTY keep Sam imprisoned and not allow him to return to the crash site?

The discovery of an unconscious man, who appears as an identical, but less robust Sam, at the crash site, has the effect of hauling the comfortable blanket of belief away altogether, and unveiling the beginnings of a shocking puzzle. Meanwhile, having done its mischief, horror sits back again and watches Sam's One and Two attempt to get it together and figure out their predicament, and eventually they discover just how much they've been lied to.

Indeed, *Moon*'s second act proves a very good illustration of how damaging isolation can be, and how the partial dissolution of it can turn the tide, redress the balance, and give the characters some strength to fight back, in this instance against the willful indifference of their employer, who considers them entirely expendable. Even when Horror quits stalking the sidelines and strides boldly onto center stage, and the men discover that no one is allowed to go home, they are still able to put their heads together, and figure out a partial plan of escape. Two heads are indeed better than one, especially when isolation is on the side of the opposition.

However, in the third act, two ticking clocks, in the form of a *rescue team* and Sam One's debilitating illness, enable horror and isolation to regain some ground. For the men are still very much alone in a hostile environment, and rapidly coming to terms with the idea that not everyone gets to go home. In a final act of defiance, one of the Sam's destroys a communication blocking system, ripping out isolation's last tooth, so that the truth can be revealed to a cold and negligent mother planet, who has been hiding in blissful ignorance on the bright side of the moon.

In Peter Hyam's *Outland*, isolation is on an all-out offensive. Social isolation assumes the brutal characteristics of a sword, wielded by the film's antagonists, while physical isolation becomes their shield, or alternatively a massive rug under which all manner of horrific behavior can be swept under. The story is, at its core, a science fiction remake of the western, *High Noon* (1952, Fred Zinnemann), where on this occasion a marshal finds himself alone in dealing with drug traffickers, with no one willing to step up and help him. In Owen Williams's interview with Peter Hyams on *Empire Online*, Hyams says, "I wanted to do a Western. Everybody said, 'You can't do a Western; Westerns are dead; nobody will do a Western.' I remember thinking it was weird that this genre that had endured for so long was just gone. But then I woke up and came to the conclusion—obviously after other people—that it was actually alive and well, but in outer space. I wanted to make a film about the frontier. Not the wonder of it or the glamour of it: I wanted to do something about Dodge City and how hard life was."[12]

When Marshall William T. O'Neill (Sean Connery) arrives at his new job on Jupiter's moon, Io, as marshal of a Titanium ore mining colony, he rapidly discovers it's the product that counts, and not the people. Human welfare plays second fiddle to profit maximization, and company management is allowed to proceed with human exploitation, and in some cases murder, by hiding behind isolation's formidable shield. Indeed, manager Sheppard (Peter Boyle) has become a feudal lord, servile only to the League of Industrial Nations who appears to lack moral concern regarding how he gets the job done, only that it is done, and the ore keeps flowing.

The film begins with Jerry Goldsmith's ominous soundtrack[13] providing a chilling backdrop to a string of statistics that spell out Io's characteristics, those of a dark, remote rock, certainly no place for a vacation. Surface conditions amount to a sixth of earth's gravity, a trip to the closest space station involves a 70-hour journey, and a supply shuttle arrives at the colony only once per week, and almost immediately, hard on isolation's heels, horror arrives in the form of a gory death, when one of the miners deliberately uncouples and depressurizes his suit, after suffering a psychotic episode.

Marshall O'Neill and his family have only recently arrived at the colony. He's the new guy and is treated as such by a suspicious crew. It begins with an indifferent reception to his opening speech from the administrative personnel, and ends with a condescending pep talk from the colony's manager, Sheppard. His resulting social isolation is cranked up further, and its blade thrust deeper, when his wife decides she has had enough and leaves for Earth on the next shuttle with their son.

In the meantime, another miner commits suicide, and here, isolation and horror walk hand-in-hand as the man shuts himself inside the elevator where no one can get to him, and suffers the effects of fast decompression on arriving on the Jupiter moon's surface.

O'Neill questions the suicide, runs against a number of mental roadblocks, and discovers his men want nothing more than to keep their heads down and get through their one-year tour. An olive branch is offered via his sergeant, but it proves false when the man admits he's there to turn a blind eye to the increasing episodes of psychosis suffered by the miners. Further progress appears hopeless, until he meets the colony's physician, the cantankerous Dr. Lazarus (Frances Sternhagen), and after an inauspicious introduction, gradually, throughout the film, she becomes one of his staunchest allies.

Subsequent investigations reveal that the miners are ingesting a dangerous narcotic, sanctioned by station manager Sheppard, who languishes behind the power of his employers and the drug cartel, all of them underpinned and protected by the formidable shield isolation offers, along with a bundle of psychological excuses, and a work hard, play hard ethic. Unlucky for him, O'Neill doesn't give a damn about cartels, or shields, and appears immune to his threats.

As the story develops, we get to roam the ship and witness an assortment of coping mechanisms built to sustain the mining personnel during their stay, everything from sex workers and erotic holograms, to Sheppard's golf course projections on the wall, enabling him to practice his golf swing—all of them taking a bite out of the loneliness of space. We also see isolation offered as a punishment. A jail cell on Io consists of a space suit and zero gravity, with no contact other than an audio communicator.

Assumptions of the effects of social isolation are dangled as a carrot, or alternatively, used as a weapon. O'Neill is browbeaten by Sheppard, who offers bribes, and when that doesn't achieve his desired outcome, he gets to work on O'Neill's moral character, not knowing the marshal is determined to redeem his character at all costs.

As a last resort, Sheppard calls in a couple of assassins, and as the shuttle arrival countdown clock cranks up the tension, O'Neill attempts to summon reinforcements without success. "How many can I count on?" he asks his fellow marshals, and in the miners' canteen he implores, "I could use a little help."[14] Alas, with the exception of Dr. Lazarus, he is shunned, socially isolated, and left to the wolves.

A terrifying showdown ensues between O'Neill and the two assassins, and because of the social isolation inflicted on the marshal, the assassins are able to act with impunity. The physical aspects of isolation add to the tension and horror, when the fight moves outside the safe confines of the colony and into the zero atmosphere exterior, where, as we've already witnessed, earlier in the film, a man can die horribly within the confines of his own suit.

In each of the three films, isolation exists as a perfect foundation on which to build fear, create horrific situations, and push the characters to the limit. Even while standing alone, without horror's constant companionship, it provides a formidable foe. The single protagonists in *Moon* and *Outland* find it extremely difficult to arrive at a solution for survival, until they are joined by another, and it is not until they have companions of their own, that they are able to work together and pry away the fingers of isolation's formidable grip. As for the characters in *Solaris*, they are simply too isolated to make a rally, and become overwhelmed and confounded by the unknown.

Isolation can also be used, directly or indirectly, as a tool of survival for the characters, giving them no other choice but to take a good hard look at themselves when fear is at their shoulder and breathing down their necks. In *Moon* in particular, one of the main aspects explored in the story is the concept of investigating ourselves and how others see us. Knowing more about ourselves can be incredibly beneficial, in some instances, giving us the ability to push ourselves further than we ever thought possible. In *Outland*, did Marshall O'Neill and Dr. Lazarus consider they would be automatically successful against two trained assassins? Or, given no other choice, did they simply step up and do things they'd never thought they were capable of, once isolation had backed them into a corner? Even Chris Kelvin in *Solaris*, still in possession of some major unresolved issues regarding his dead wife, appeared to make peace with himself, once he was driven to the edge.

Self-examination is the essence of great storytelling, and isolation can provide a poignant tool, enabling us to bare ourselves and take a good, hard look. And what better accompaniments than space and horror, together providing a spectacular arena of peril, loneliness, and fear, within which we are pushed to the limit? Take a seat, then, grab some popcorn, and prepare to know thyself.

NOTES

1. "What Is Horror Fiction?" Horror Writers Association FAQ, http://horror.org/horror-is.htm.

2. National Aeronautics and Space Administration, Goddard Space Flight Center, Imagine the Universe! "The Cosmic Distance Scale," last updated August 24, 2015, http://imagine.gsfc.nasa.gov/features/cosmic/nearest_star_info.html.

3. Nola Taylor Redd, "How Far Away Is Jupiter?" *Space*, November 7, 2012, para 2, http://www.space.com/18383-how-far-away-is-jupiter.html.

4. Craig Haney, "Infamous Punishment: The Psychological Consequences of Isolation," *National Prison Project Journal* 8, no. 2 (Spring 1993), referred to in Sharon Shalev's *A Sourcebook on Solitary Confinement* (Mannheim Center for Criminology, 2008) 9.

5. Michael Bond, "How Extreme Isolation Warps the Mind," *BBC Future*, May 2014, http://www.bbc.com/future/story/20140514-how-extreme-isolation-warps-minds.

6. Woodburn Heron, "The Pathology of Boredom," *Scientific American* 196 (January 1, 1957), 56.

7. Nick Kanas, "Expedition to Mars: Psychological, Interpersonal, and Psychiatric Issues," *Journal of Cosmology* (October-November 2010), http://journalofcosmology.com/Mars114.tml.

8. *Solaris*, DVD, directed by Steven Soderbergh (2002; Century City, CA: Twentieth Century Fox, 2002).

9. *Ibid.*

10. Chris Martinez, *Solaris* Soundtrack, La-La-Land Records, 2011, audio CD.

11. Matthew Hutson, "Duncan Jones on the *Moon*," *Psychology Today*, July 14, 2009, https://www.psychologytoday.com/blog/psyched/200907/duncan-jones-the-moon.

12. Owen Williams, "Directors Special: Peter Hyams Goes Film by Film," *Empire Online*, July 24, 2014, last updated October 9, 2015, http://www.empireonline.com/movies/features/peter-hyams-film-film/.

13. *Outland*, music composed by Jerry Goldsmith, 1981 Film Score Monthly, Silver Age Classics, re-mastered 2010, audio CD.

14. *Outland*, Blu-ray, directed by Peter Hyams (1981; Burbank, CA: Warner Bros., 2012).

BIBLIOGRAPHY

Alien. DVD. Directed by Ridley Scott. 1979. Century City, CA: Twentieth Century Fox, 2000.

Bond, Michael. "How Extreme Isolation Warps the Mind." *BBC Future*, May 2014. http://www.bbc.com/future/story/20140514-how-extreme-isolation-warps-minds.

"The Cosmic Distance Scale." *National Aeronautics and Space Administration*, Goddard Space Flight Center, Imagine the Universe! Last updated August 24, 2015. http://imagine.gsfc.nasa.gov/features/cosmic/nearest_star_info.html.

Donaldson, Stephen R. *The Gap Series: Books 1–5*. New York: Bantam/Spectra, 1991–1996.

Event Horizon. DVD. Directed by Paul W.S. Anderson. 1997. Hollywood: Paramount Pictures, 2006.

Goldsmith, Jerry. *Outland*. Soundtrack, 1981, Film Score Monthly, Silver Age Classics, re-mastered 2010. Audio CD.:

Heron, Woodburn. "The Pathology of Boredom." *Scientific American* 196 (January 1, 1957): 52–56.

High Noon. DVD. Directed by Fred Zinnemann. 1952. Culver City, CA: United Artists, 2000.

The Horror Writers Association. "What Is Horror Fiction?" FAQ. http://horror.org/horror-is.htm.

Hutson, Matthew. "Duncan Jones on the Moon" *Psychology Today*, July 14, 2009. https://www.psychologytoday.com/blog/psyched/200907/duncan-jones-the-moon.

Kanas, Nick. "Expedition to Mars: Psychological, Interpersonal, and Psychiatric Issues." *Journal of Cosmology* (October-November 2010). Accessed December 18, 2016. http://journalofcosmology.com/Mars114.html.

Lem, Stanislaw. *Solaris*. Translated by Joanna Kilmartin and Steve Cox. London: Faber and Faber, 1970.

Martinez, Chris. *Solaris*. Soundtrack. La-La-Land Records, 2011. Audio CD.

Moon. DVD. Directed by Duncan Jones. 2009. Century City, CA: Sony Pictures, 2009.

Outland. Blu-ray. Directed by Peter Hyams. 1981. Burbank, CA: Warner Bros., 2012.

Pitch Black. DVD. Directed by David Twohy. 2000. Universal City, CA: USA Films, 2000.

Redd, Nola Taylor. "How Far Away Is Jupiter?" *Space*, November 7, 2012. http://www.space.com/18383-how-far-away-is-jupiter.html.

Shalev, Sharon. *A Sourcebook on Solitary Confinement*. http://solitaryconfinement.org/sourcebook. Mannheim Center for Criminology, London School of Economics and Social Sciences, 2008.

Solaris. DVD. Directed by Steven Soderbergh. 2002. Century City, CA: Twentieth Century Fox, 2002.

Watts, Peter. *Blindsight*. New York: Tor Books, 2006.

Williams, Owen. "Directors Special: Peter Hyams Goes Film by Film." *Empire Online*, July 24, 2014. Last updated, October 9, 2015. http://www.empireonline.com/movies/features/peter-hyams-film-film/.

That *Moon* Is Romantic
Duncan Jones's Dark Fairy Tale

ADAM M. CROWLEY

> Good science fiction writers of the present are not necessarily as eager as Arthur C. Clarke to found kindergartens on Jupiter, to leave the poor Maine ape and his clam rake far behind.
>
> —Kurt Vonnegut[1]

Considering Moon

At first glance, Duncan Jones's *Moon* may not strike you as an example of space horror. There are no aliens: no chest-bursters, no xenomorphs, no slithering things from the stars. Moreover, it is also the case that the horror in this film is decidedly low-stakes. That is to say, the fate of a series of clones on the moon is certainly tragic, but it is of limited significance when considered in the context of the global scenario that rushes up in the window of the escape vehicle in the film's closing moments. As above—the viewer knows—so below: a world of cruel industry and callous consumers is the tale's larger tragedy, and that tragedy, while upsetting, is essentially hidden. And that's exactly what makes it so scary.

In terms of plot, *Moon* presents the final days of Sam Bell (Sam Rockwell), who is seemingly alone at a helium-3 mining facility, Sarang Station, on the Moon. Bell's daily tasks involve the routine maintenance and remote operation of the station's harvesters—massive soil shifting machines—and interfacing with GERTY, the station's artificial intelligence (voiced by Kevin Spacey). Bell believes that he is nearing the end of a three-year contract, and that he is soon to return home to Earth, where he will rejoin his lovely wife and daughter. However, this belief is shaken—and eventually upended—by a series of events that call Bell's actual role in the station and his very identity into question. Finding himself in increasingly ill health, Bell is distracted by a hallucination while servicing one of the harvesters, and crashes the vehicle. He awakens in the Station, and, after a series of upsetting interactions with GERTY, escapes onto the lunar surface, where he finds the damaged harvester—and another version of Sam Bell inside. What follows are a series of interchanges and explorations that lead the Bells to the unavoidable realization that they are clones, and that Sarang Station disintegrates its Bells on a three-year rotation, under the promise that it is sending them back home to rejoin their family. In the final moments, Bell—or a Bell, to be more accurate—escapes and rockets back to Earth, presumably to spread awareness of the horrors at Sarang Station before meeting a genetically predetermined death. However, as this escapee approaches the terrestrial horizon, the viewer is treated to a barrage of radio and television broadcasts that call into question whether the people of Earth are capable of being moved by the revealed hardships of the lunar clones.

A *Romantic* Moon

At numerous junctures, the plot of *Moon* hangs on the question of which Bell, of all the possible Bells, is the Bell that has been associated with previous scenes and sequences. The viewer finds him or herself considering the likelihood of apparent inconsistencies and outrageous coincidental interactions, only to, in the final moments, come to understand that the reported sequence of events is indeed perfectly logical. The Bells form a collective perspective, and the viewer's enjoyment of the film arises, in part, from his or her ability to parse that perspective into its constituent elements. From this, then, it is reasonable to argue that *Moon* is very much a film about the intersection of perspective and identity. As such, it can be generally associated with the ancient tradition of what Northrop Frye calls the sentimental romance.[2] However, in terms of the subject at hand—space horror—the value of this association exceeds the themes of perspective and identity because, according to Frye, the sentimental romance has a particular set of practices for staging the experience of horror—in space or anywhere. A consideration of these practices can inform a viewing of *Moon*. In particular, it can illuminate just what it is that is so scary about this tale. As we shall see, the real horror in *Moon* can be understood as the revelation of a botched romantic reunion, one in which our hero, Sam Bell, races into the arms of a supposedly loving world, one that—tragically—has transformed into a post-humanist wasteland in his absence.

Frye's argument extends from a particular conception of literature— what it is, where it comes from, and how it is expressed in societies. He argues that every human society has a "verbal culture, in which fictions or stories have a prominent place."[3] He identifies the fictions that are most important to a society as myths, and the stories of marginal significance as folk tales. While these categories may have distinct social values, Frye contends that they are often essentially similar in their organization. One contrast he provides to understand these categorical distinctions is between the Bible in the Western tradition and the science fiction serials of the mid 1950s: these are subjects with vastly dissimilar levels of cultural authority, even though they depend on certain common narrative features. He explores these connections under the notion that there are only four narrative movements in myth or folktale, and that they relate to movements between the realms of heaven, earth, and an under or night world. He writes, "All stories in literature are complications of, or metaphorical derivations from, these four narrative radicals."[4] He then notes that in the case of myths and folktales that regardless of their cultural authority they share a common concern with impossible people, places, or things—which he calls "anti-representational" subjects[5] because their very nature defies literal representation. Moreover, he notes that, in myths and stories alike, these subjects progress through their worlds under coincidental, rather than strictly cause and effect, encounters. For Frye, the persistence of these basic narrative trends across cultures affirms the significance of a "mythological universe"[6] for the human imagination—a notion that is as entrancing as it is disputable.

Now, within this scheme, Frye attends to a particular genre of long fairy tale—or sentimental romance, that seems to follow the described rules in a predictable way. These are generally described as love stories composed of a series of exciting adventures that climax with the unification of lovers through an instance of revealed identity. For Frye, sentimental romance begins with a sharp descent in fortune, and usually involves the use of violence and cunning in its narrative development. There is often at least one or more complicating female figures that the hero encounters, and there is usually a descent to—or ascent from—the underworld. Importantly, it is the special capacity of the sentimental romance to convey a casual mixing of the heavenly and demonic in the world of ordinary experience, which is usually represented with the intrusion of magic or the supernatural into a landscape that otherwise adheres to the logic of "ordinary [or realistic] experience."[7]

Here, broad associations can be made with *Moon*. Bell experiences a descent in fortune when he discovered his second self must literally struggle against a complicating "female" figure (named GERTY), and resolves his situation eventually with an ascent (or is it a descent after all?) from the lunar surface to Earth. Along the way, there are a series of encounters and developments that require our hero's use of violence or cunning. And to Frye's final point, it is the case that the essential imaginative magic of the scenario—

its stark science fiction elements—is curtailed and bounded by some very ordinary concepts: sickness, fear, a longing for freedom and agency, and so on.

The literary pedigree of the sentimental romance stretches into antiquity. Frye contextualizes it with the "Greek romance in Heliodorus, Achilles Tatius, Longus, Xenophon of Ephesus, and others."[8] Later, he notes the emergence of the "Latin romance," in which we find "Apuleius and (probably) the Xenophon of Ephesus…. And there is early Christian romance in the Clementine Recognitions, in the story of Barlaam and Josaphat, and the more legendary lives of the saints."[9] Viewed broadly, such works tend to include "adventures [that] involve capture by pirates, narrow escapes from death, recognition of the true identity of the hero and his eventual marriage with the heroine."[10] These and many other basic concerns in Frye's commentary are significant through modification to *Moon*. Why does this matter? Well— it matters for two reasons. First, it enables us to move toward a specific and general context for the film, one that exceeds the immediacy of 20th- and 21st-century clone narratives, as well as the very medium at hand—film— which, under Frye's theory, becomes simply one of many possible media for the construction and dissemination of humanity's oldest narrative structures.

However, and precisely because we are here to consider the significance of space horror, it is important to note that the sentimental romance provides an intellectual context for both representing and considering horror. Frye approaches this notion when he underscores the significance of "metamorphoses" to the sentimental romance. He writes:

> Metamorphoses are the normal transformations of the structure of myth. Every aspect of fall or descent is linked to a change in form in some way, usually by associating or identifying a human or humanized figure with something animal or vegetable. Daphne becomes a laurel and Syrinx a reed; Adam and Eve in Genesis, on losing their original preternatural gifts, become the rational animals symbolized by the "coats of skins" they receive from God…. The story of Apuleius about a man metamorphosed into an ass includes … the motif.[11]

This notion strikes me as being particularly significant to Bell's adventure, in the sense that the clone's journey to awareness depends upon his understanding that he was once, potentially, a man—or, at the very least, that he is a subject that has been led to believe that he is a man that no longer exists, or at least no longer exists on the Moon. In either scenario, the humanized figure's adventure is an adventure to the realization that he has been humanized—which comes with the heavy notion that he is, thus, not actually human. While this awakening is horrifying enough, it can also be argued that the essential horror in *Moon* comes from the film's particular setting, which has very strong associations with Frye's conception of the "night world" or "underworld"—i.e., hell—in his system.[12]

Frye's comments on the basic components of the "lowest point" in sentimental romance, which lies in a real or symbolic underworld or "hellscape," one that characters enter through a dream or something like dreaming.[13] Frye writes of a "dark worlds ... of shadows where we are surrounded by the shapes of animals"[14] He writes that these "figures are fertility spirits, part of the death and rebirth pattern of the lower world."[15] They "represent the reducing of humanized beings to something sub intelligent and sub articulate."[16] Frye explains that what "goes on in the night world of romance is cruelty and horror, yet what is essential is not cruelty as such but the presence of some kind of [absurd] ritual."[17]

If we take this logic step by step, we can find easy parallels in *Moon*. For example, each of the Sam Bell clones comes to consciousness on the Sarang Station through an awakening from and into a fantasy state—that is to say, they awaken under the belief that their experiences correspond with a pre-programmed fantasy of who they are and what they are about on the lunar station. In a literal "dark world"—e.g., the Moon—the Bells are surrounded by the "fertility spirit" of GERTY, who literally oversees each Bell's "life and death cycle" through the careful management of daily resources, and also through a continual reinforcement of the fantasy that Bell will return home at the end of his contract. For his part—and though the viewer will find him or herself rooting for Bell by the end of the film—each Bell is clearly a reduced version of humanity—"sub-human"—in the sense that it has a genetically predetermined lifespan, and can only live a partial and stunted life by design. These conditions bear directly on the "cruelty and horror" of the situation, which arises from the absurd ritual—the production and destruction of the Bells, which seems fundamentally unreasonable—particular so when, in the final scenes, it becomes very apparent that the Sarang corporation is fully capable of sending non-clone workers to and from the Station at will, as happens when they dispatch a hit squad to exterminate the Bells who have achieved self-awareness.

While it is possible to make selective associations between *Moon* and Frye's theory, it is reasonable to ask why such associations are productive for an understanding of the film. After all, while it is interesting to view the text as one iteration of an ancient storytelling genre, it is not the case that such understanding necessarily contributes to an appreciation of the film itself, other than to give it shape. To this question, we might note that *Moon* does an exceptional job of presenting a sentimental romance that is in many ways quite taken with the particular economic conditions of its era of production, and that its engagement with these very conditions shapes the tale's significance as a romantic subject. This is a fairy tale—a fairy tale in which the hero's reunion with his lover does not involve an enraptured embrace, but—rather—a cold descent into to a post-humanist subject, which is simply not capable of returning or extending any interest in Sam Bells.

NOTES

1. Marc Leeds, *The Vonnegut Encyclopedia* (New York: Delacorte Press, 2016), 150.
2. Northrop Frye, *The Secular Scripture and Other Writings on Cultural Theory 1976–1999*, ed. Joseph Adamson and Jean Wilson (Toronto: University of Toronto Press, 2006), Kindle edition.
3. *Ibid.*, 762.
4. *Ibid.*, 1889.
5. *Ibid.*, 1155.
6. *Ibid.*, 847.
7. *Ibid.*, 1162.
8. *Ibid.*, 719.
9. *Ibid.*, 720–721.
10. *Ibid.*, 735.
11. *Ibid.*, 2006.
12. *Ibid.*, 2288.
13. *Ibid.*, 2011.
14. *Ibid.*, 2103.
15. *Ibid.*, 2174–2175.
16. *Ibid.*, 2175.
17. *Ibid.*, 2119.

BIBLIOGRAPHY

Frye, Northrop. *The Secular Scripture and Other Writings on Critical Theory 1976–1991*, edited by Joseph Adamson and Jean Wilson. Toronto: University of Toronto Press, 2006. Kindle edition.

Leeds, Marc. *The Vonnegut Encyclopedia*. New York: Delacorte Press, 2016.

Moon. Blu-Ray. Directed by Duncan Jones, 2009. Hollywood: Sony Home Entertainment, 2010.

The Architecture of Sci-Fi Body Horror
Mechanical Building-Bodies and Organic Invasion from Deep Space to the Anthropocene

BRENDA S. GARDENOUR WALTER

In 1990, Barbara Creed published an influential piece entitled "*Alien* and the Monstrous-Feminine," which interprets *Alien* (1979, Ridley Scott) through the lenses of Freudian psychology, Kristevan abjection, and feminism broadly construed. She argues that *Alien* is dominated by the primal scene of copulation and birth, in which humans emerge from pod-like wombs and are penetrated by aliens whose offspring rupture from womb-like bodies.[1] Central to this primal scene is the depiction of the alien as the archaic mother, a "'totalizing and oceanic' presence" who, despite reproducing without a male mate, has the ability to birth phallic offspring. The alien-mother is an embodiment of what Creed calls the "monstrous-feminine," in which all beings are born through and return to female genitals shown to be "horrifying objects of dread and fascination"[2] Creed argues that the human-built space vessel *Nostromo* and the alien ship on planetoid LV-426 are both extensions of this monstrous-feminine, structures not only coded as female but also directly correlated with female reproductive organs—a dialectical pairing of transgressive womb spaces that speak to patriarchal fears of a Freudian return to origins. Creed's powerful analysis, which is elaborated upon in her monograph, *The Monstrous-Feminine: Film, Feminism, and Psychoanalysis* (1993), has become monolithic in scholarship on the *Alien* franchise and science fiction body horror, much of which continues to code the spaceships and buildings in these films as exclusively female.[3] While acknowledging the importance of feminist and psychoanalytic approaches, this essay interprets Sci-fi Horror films through the lenses of architectural theory and the medical humanities, arguing that the space ships and buildings depicted in *Alien*, *Alien³* (1992, David Fincher), and *Leviathan* (1989, George P. Cosmatos) are not merely "transgressive womb spaces," but represent Western medicalized constructions of the human body and the relationship of that body to the non-human and organic world.

The correlation between the human body and manufactured environments such as the space ship *Nostromo* in *Alien*, the rock-forged prison foundry in *Alien³*, and the undersea station in *Leviathan* might at first seem novel. The concept of architecture as a projection of the human body, however, is both ancient and well-attested. In *De Architectura*, the first-century Roman author Vitruvius argued that the proportions and symmetry of the human body should serve as the foundation for the design of buildings.[4] The ensouled body was the microcosm of a building, which in turn was a microcosm of the greater cosmos. This correlation between micro-body and macro-building remains a salient theme in modern architectural theory, and has influenced works including Gaston Bachelard's *Poetics of Space* (1958), Kent Bloomer and Charles Moore's *Body, Memory, and Architecture* (1977), Juhani Pallasmaa's *The Eyes of the Skin: Architecture and the Senses* (1995), and George Dodd's and Robert Tavernor's edited collection, *Body and Building* (2005), to name just a few.[5] In all of these texts, architectural structures are not simply utilitarian spaces for humans to occupy, but extensions of the body that stimulate the inner senses through emotion, convey complex values, and reflect an idealized vision of self, both physical and spiritual. In a concrete sense, buildings are not merely theoretical or experiential bodies—they *are* our bodies. Architecture "is a technology whose primary role is creating a synthetic skin around its human creators and inhabitants, to optimize the immediate environment and exclude the hostile elements."[6] Nowhere is this truer than in the architectural structures designed for science fiction horror films, which feature vessels that serve as exoskeletons to support soft-bodied human life and protect it from contamination in utterly inhuman environments. In space-horror narratives, the failure of human-built structures to maintain a simulated environment and to prevent penetration by alien organisms is the death of the human life within. The breached structure becomes nothing less than a ruptured human body—the site of an abject and visceral form of architectural-body horror.

The uncanny architectural structures in *Alien* and *Alien³* are designed in accordance with Western constructs of the post–Cartesian mechanical body.[7] In *Alien*, the primary structure is the space ship *Nostromo*, the systems of which function in parallel with human physiology. The ship-body circulates water through its pipes and air through its ducts, heats and cools itself, excretes waste, all under the control of its electrical brain—MOTHER. Within this hermetically sealed ship-body, humans exist as symbiotic parasites who rely on the ship as an extension of their bodies for survival. Despite being balanced, rational, and mechanical, the *Nostromo* is breeched by an alien organism; once beneath the *Nostromo's* metal skin, the organic pathogens transform the viscera of the once-rational machine-body into a transgressive, leaky, metastasized mess—a reminder that even the most technologically advanced body-building, no matter how seemingly impermeable, is vulnerable to invasion from the outside world. Unlike the tightly-constructed mechanical ship-body of *Nostromo*, the primary structure in *Alien³* is a neglected and aged building-body that functions simultaneously as a foundry, a prison, and a monastery standing alone in the post-industrial wasteland of Fiorina Fury 161—a land of half-broken machines. Porous and leaky, its dank bowels riddled with convoluted tunnels, tubes, and fetid chambers, this defenseless body-building is inhabited by a colony of celibate and unarmed men performing penance for their sin-crimes and seeking the purification of body and soul. Here, biomedical intervention is impossible; the colony's infirmary is ill-equipped, its physician helpless, the building-body too porous to seal completely against either the inhuman natural environment of the planet or the invasion of a hostile alien organism. Biologically uninitiated, the structure and its indwelling humans must oust the alien infection by raising the temperature within the circulatory system. Its furnace stoked, the building runs a fever, signified by alternating shots in fiery red-orange and cool blue hues, and ultimately burns the alien in its molten heart blood.

The susceptibility of the body-building to penetration and corruption is magnified when the narrative is translated from the distant reaches of space and the inorganic wastelands of Fiorina 161 to the teeming oceans of earth. In *Leviathan*, the primary structure is a high-tech deep sea station, hermetically sealed against a liquid environment hostile to human life. Like the *Nostromo*, the station reflects not only a post–Cartesian and mechanical construction of the human body but also its failure against organic invasion, in this case by man-made mutagens that dissolve and reconfigure human bodies into rapacious and transgressive entities. This process of contamination and dissolution extends to the building-body; with its hermetic seal breached, the station becomes one with the ocean environment and is swallowed by the abyss where it will remain forever—forlorn and forgotten. The corruption and decay of the technologically advanced body-building in *Leviathan* calls into question the supposed impermeability of the mechanical body and the ability of medical technology to prevent infection, thereby illuminating the abject horrors of embodiment and death. The dissolution of the sea station likewise serves as a reminder that, despite our desperate attempts to manage the body as a mechanical entity separate from the chaotic forces of nature, the human body is ultimately a part of the organic environment and subject to the same forces of creation, transgression, and destruction—a meaningful lesson at the climax of the Anthropocene.[8]

Nostromo: *The Rational* Bête-Machine *Transgressed*

Ridley Scott's *Alien* begins with a disembodied view of deep space, a dark and empty visual field that is suddenly disrupted by the letter "I," floating alone in the abyss. Suspended in the void, the "I" is ultimately engulfed by the word ALIEN. Just as this manifestation of the self is isolated and consumed by the alien other, so too is the mining ship *Nostromo*, an unaccompanied vessel traveling through the darkened wastes of space on its return to earth. Through the camera's lens, the viewer penetrates the ship's metal hull to glide through a stripped down and brutalist space that exposes the structure's functional elements, including wires, switches, pipes, air ducts, and support beams.[9] The exploration of this dead and mechanized anatomy can be seen as a voyeuristic autopsy.[10] Tubes and pipes serve as veins and ureters that conduct fluid throughout the structure, while waste is either recycled through a mechanical liver or excreted from myriad cloacae. This mechanical building body is held together by a skeleton and sinews that form a rigid structure and clothed in metal skin, all of which is designed to protect the ship from internal collapse and external organic invasion. *Nostromo*'s involuntary functions, including waking, sleeping, heating, cooling, and homeostasis are maintained by a silicon brain named MOTHER that is housed in a white cranium-like room filled with blinking dendrites and synapses. As the centralized manager of multiple peripherals, MOTHER is perhaps named after the computer motherboard, first introduced in 1975 as part of the Apple I computer. By its mechanical nature, MOTHER is completely rational, programmed to control the mechanical body in which it is housed and upon which it is utterly dependent. MOTHER cannot exist beyond her mechanical construct.[11]

The *Nostromo*'s architectural anatomy and physiology are reflections of a Western and post–Cartesian construction of the body. According to Descartes, the human body does not take its form and function from an indwelling Aristotelian soul, but instead exists as a material "extension of physics," a passive and mechanical structure operating in complete isolation from the human soul or "thinking stuff."[12] Rational and mechanical, Descartes' bête-machine worked much like an automaton, its myriad gears and mechanisms whirring together in "functional unity." The body did not "live" in and of itself, but was driven by the heat of the blood as it expanded and combusted within the heart.[13] Descartes' construction of the human body as a "lifeless" machine inspired physicians such as Claude-Nicholas Le Cat to boast of their ability to create mechanical men that could demonstrate human illnesses.[14] While many of Descartes' discourses on physiology have since been disproven, the mechanistic and dis-ensouled human body remains a deep structure in the theory and practice of modern medicine.

The medicalized body is constructed from a series of highly specialized mechanistic systems, from the larger structures of gross anatomy to the biochemical mechanisms at the molecular level, all whirring together in functional unity. In order to diagnose systemic failures, the body is connected to mechanical devices such as EKGs engulfed by machines such as MRIs, and penetrated by optical and surgical equipment such as laparoscopes. Bodily fluids and tissue samples are sent to laboratories where they are examined through lenses and run through spectrometers that provide a chemical read-out. Western medicine is driven by a belief that the human body is a closed system; if this system is breached by external organic pathogens, the body-machine malfunctions. The consequences of bodily penetration include the organic and chaotic transformation of a tightly sealed and algorithmically logical machine into a ruptured, leaky, and irrational mess—both inside and out.[15] This Western fear of bodily penetration, contamination, and transformation contests the Cartesian bête-machine, revealing an awareness that our soft bodies are in fact open and vulnerable—an abject reality reflected in the fate of the *Nostromo*.

A reflection of the mechanical construction of the human body, the *Nostromo* begins as a hermetically sealed vessel, gliding through sterile space. An external distress signal awakens the stasis-bound microcosmic human fauna asleep in its bowels, who are called to the surface of a seemingly lifeless planetoid, LV-426. The human journey to the planetoid's surface is one of mechanistic mediation; the crew moves from the *Nostromo*, to the smaller mechanical space pod, to mechanized space suits, all of which are required to sustain human life. Despite their efforts to maintain sterility, all of these body-spaces are penetrated by a chaotic and organic "other." Upon landing, the space pod experiences a "hull breach," the gash in its belly causing major systemic failure. While the mechanics attempt to repair the damage, the crew ventures out onto the planetoid's surface to discover a dark world of erratic forms, both jagged and undulating, shrouded in mist and falling ash. Leaving the metal, rectilinear, artificially-lit space pod, the crew enters into a derelict alien ship, which is curvilinear and dank.[16] The interior of the alien building-body is composed of glistening organic forms suggesting bones, slippery genitals, and veiny organs; at its core is a fetid bowel-cavern, warm and moist, filled with parasitic eggs. As a member of the crew, Kane (Sir John Hurt), shines a light into a dormant egg, the embryo within begins to writhe. In response to Kane's voyeuristic desire, the fetal parasite bursts from its egg, ruptures Kane's mechanical body-suit, penetrates his soft flesh, and impregnates him. When his colleagues bring him back to the space pod for treatment, one of the crew members who has been left behind, Ripley (Sigourney Weaver), refuses to open the bay doors, arguing, "If we let him in, *the ship* could get infected." Her choice of words is telling. Ripley is worried less about the corruption of Kane's single microcosmic human body than the corruption of the entire macrocosmic ship—an extension of their collective physiology and necessary for survival. Should the *Nostromo* become infected, both the ship and its humans would be transformed into the alien "other."

Ripley's concerns are, of course, legitimate. Despite placing Kane in the medical bay and subjecting him to state of the art, non-invasive treatments, the alien uses his body for reproduction, injecting a larva into his stomach that then ruptures through his abdominal wall—a visceral hull breach that leaves him a bloody and disgorged mess. The dissolution of Kane's physiology foreshadows the structural fate of the *Nostromo* which, like Kane, has ingested once-dormant parasites from the bowels of the alien ship on LV-426. Stimulated by the exchange of fluids between body-ships, the parasitic alien begins its inhuman and chaotic life cycle, from egg to face-hugger, to larva, to nymph, to xenomorph, with each form more increasingly transgressive and complex. The alien body, fully organic, throbbing with acidic blood and slippery with stringy saliva, is constructed in opposition to the mechanical structure of the *Nostromo*. Unlike Descartes' passive machine-body, the xenomorph's physiology is internally driven by two primal desires—consumption and reproduction—both of which have long been associated with irrational carnal behavior in humans.[17] Most terrifying of all, these rapacious organisms are almost impossible to destroy, their only weakness being fiery heat. Like a cancer, the alien metastasizes throughout the ship-body, hiding in the dark recesses of its abdomen, clogging its airways, infecting its viscera, only emerging to feed and metamorphose.

Desperate to destroy the xenomorph before the Weyland-Yutani Corporation can use it as the basis for biological weapons, Ripley determines to kill the organism by raising the *Nostromo*'s temperature—much like inducing a raging fever—until the ship-body either recovers or expires through combustion. Despite her efforts, the alien parasite survives the *Nostromo*'s destruction, hopping from its burning corpse and into Ripley's escape pod where it lies dormant and unseen, waiting to infect the next unsuspecting host. While Ripley is able to eject the alien into space, the lingering fear of penetration and transformation remains. She has, after all, touched the alien's stickiness which, in the words of Sartre, "clings like a leech: it attacks the boundary between myself and it. I remain a solid, but to touch its stickiness is to risk diluting myself into viscosity."[18] The *Nostromo* was once a self-contained and self-reliant mechanical body able to support human life in the coldest depths of space. Despite its hermetic construction and advanced technology, it lay open to the possibility of infection through the soft-bodied human organisms that dwelled within. As a form of architectural body-horror, the dissolution and death of *Nostromo* in the alien's "stickiness" illuminates our deep-seated fear that, despite the cultural construction of our bodies as mechanical and impenetrable, our bodies are actually soft, vulnerable, and open to transgression and dissolution by chaotic and organic alien others who might recreate us in their own image.

The Prison-Foundry: The Bête-Machine Neglected

In *Alien³* the primary body-structure is a monastic prison-foundry located on Fiorina 161, a planet in the "outer veil," a liminal region separating the core solar system from outer planetary systems. Because it is a correctional facility, its exact location is classified and not listed on any map; it is a lost place—nowhere. Fiorina 161 is nicknamed "Fury," in part because of its hostile climate, with temperatures rising to nearly one hundred degrees Fahrenheit during the day and plummeting to 40 degrees below zero at night. Despite the daytime heat, the weather is predominantly stormy, the skies eternally grey or pitch black, pregnant with rain and thunder. Like the heavens, the landscape is bleak, dominated by enormous cranes, their broken dinosaur-bones creaking in the endless wind as they stare blindly into a turbulent and acidic sea. In this hostile ecosystem, there are no green things, no birds singing—just the silence of strange cold-blooded fish and parasitic insects, most notably a large form of lice that feed off of keratin. The only human inhabitants on this waterlogged and forgotten planet are twenty-five YY chromosome male convicts serving life sentences for violent crimes and a small support staff, one of whom is a medical officer and former prisoner named Clemens (Charles Dance). The remnant of a once-flourishing penal colony that numbered five thousand, the prisoners maintain a nearly-defunct mining operation that harvests lead from the ground and dead machines in order to create containers for toxic waste—a futile task since no toxic waste is ever delivered for containment. Like the derelict machines that surround them, the prisoners' bodies are broken and neglected, in part because of the experience of exile and incarceration on Fury. The voracious lice that cover the planet require the men to shave their heads and bodies; like aging products on dusty and forgotten shelves, the men are tattooed with barcodes. Because of Fury's climate, they wear layers of tattered clothing topped by a long and hooded overcoat which gives the impression of a monk's cassock and cowl.

Like monks, the prisoners punish their bodies through acts of asceticism. Having espoused a radical and apocalyptic Christian faith, the men restrict the body through celibacy and the mind through prayer, hoping to achieve individual and corporate harmony while they wait "for God to return, and raise his servants to redemption."[19] Until then, they toil away at a futile task, broken men on a broken planet where "nothing works."[20]

Like Fury and its prisoner-monks, the only inhabited architectural structure on the planet—the monastic prison-foundry—is a broken machine. Derelict, the building reflects an aged and neglected post–Cartesian human body, one that has been left open to the elements and given little care. Unlike the tightly-constructed and rectilinear *Nostromo*, the prison-foundry is loose, leaky, and replete with circular apertures. One of the building's many entrances, for example, is a perfectly round hole in the ground that opens into the sick bay, which is in turn connected by "cold, dark, damp" subterranean tunnels to other areas of the structure. The complex's communal living spaces, including the kitchen, refectory, infirmary, and central meeting hall are all filmed in blue tones, suggesting the grey light of Fiorina Fury filtered through dirty and broken windows. They are likewise marked by Christian crosses, some of them scratched onto the wall as graffiti, some of them implied through the design of window tracery, others suggested in the play of light on exposed crossbeams. The interior of the prison is not only monastic but also strangely nostalgic. The kitchen, for example, features white institutional subway tile and cement blocks as well as occasional arts and crafts touches, including a stained glass window. This combination conveys an uncanny sense of a home barely remembered, appearing through the soft light in hazy pieces, a half-forgotten memory in an abandoned place.[21] The refectory, too, is tinged with memory. While the space at first appears to be a standard institutional cafeteria, in the background sit piles of old and broken chairs, once put to good use at large dinners, now no longer needed, heaped with dust. Even the infirmary creates a sense of longing, with many of its empty beds rolled up, its technology out of date, its equipment—and its medical officer—living in the past and broken beyond repair.

Closest to the planet's surface and the "higher" realms of thought and memory, the inhabited rooms of the prison-foundry seem to languish in the half light. Down in its deepest bowels, however, the building's viscera are very much alive. Six hundred subterranean air ducts allow the building to breathe, distributing fresh air to all of its rooms and expelling toxic air back out into the environment. Crafted from rough stone, these circular air shafts and their *bolgia*-like antechambers are traced with pipes, many of which appear to form flying buttresses, a medieval system of support.[22] Warm water flows through these pipe-capillaries like blood that rises from the building's heart—the smelting furnace at its core that burns day and night. Every area of the prison-foundry, from its blue-lit upper rooms to its shadowy-orange basements, is connected by tubes and tunnels. Like worm holes, these tunnels are open to the outside world, allowing the ingress of rain, wind, lice and— with the arrival of Ripley—a parasitic invader.

Living in isolation and therefore biologically uninitiated, the prison-body on Fiorina 161 is helplessly vulnerable to the alien organism that invades it with the crash landing of Ripley's EEV, which has been ejected from the *Sulaco* (*Aliens*, 1986, James Cameron). As the pod rips through the grey skies of Fury and crashes into the boiling sea, Newt (Carrie Henn) and Bishop (Lance Henriksen) are both killed while Ripley is coughed up onto shore. The prisoners bring Ripley, the bodies, and the mangled pod into the prison-foundry through various openings, thereby introducing the alien parasite into the building body and sealing its doom. The human and mechanical wreckage from the crash is a microcosm of physiological dissolution and despair, both hallmarks of the prison-foundry and its indwelling prisoners. For example, Newt is not only dismembered in the crash, but also undergoes an autopsy that leaves her hull completely breached, her cold lifeless heart exposed. Likewise, Bishop the android lies shattered in pieces. When Ripley fishes his parts out of the scrap heap and reconnects him momentarily to the flight recorder, his decollated head jokes, "I'm just a glorified toaster."[23] Later, despairing of being sentient in his mangled and hopeless condition, Bishop tells her, "I hurt. Do me a favor. Disconnect me. I could be reworked, but I'll never be top of the line again. I'd rather be nothing."[24] Ripley, too, is broken; she not only mourns Newt's death and bears guilt for her own survival, but also harbors the fetus of an alien queen deep within her chest, close to her broken heart.

Just as an alien hides in the darkness of Ripley's cracked and vulnerable body, so too does another lurk in the shadows of the broken prison-foundry, "down there, in the basement."[25] Once introduced, the alien parasite wanders freely through the dank viscera of the building's defenseless body, hiding its shadowy recesses, leaking corrosive acid, feeding and reproducing. Unlike the tight-bodied and technologically advanced *Nostromo*, the aged and neglected prison-body has no means to close itself off to invaders and no weapons. Without an adequate immune system, the building's only defense is the "fire of the heart and its heat," the smelting furnace that still burns brightly in the darkness of an otherwise dying structure.[26] Lured into the furnace by its human prey, the alien is dissolved in heat of the smelter, the building's "principle of life"; Ripley, too, is consumed in the furnace, and with her the alien queen in her chest.[27] Despite the building-body's valiant efforts to survive alien attack, it is nevertheless shut down by Weyland-Yutani. Contaminated and quarantined, the dead building-body is left to decay—alone and forgotten in the outer veil of space.

Leviathan: *The* Bête-Machine *from Deep Space to the Ocean Deep in the Anthropocene*

The architectural structures created for science fiction films reflect the post–Cartesian construction of the human body as a mechanical flesh building. In theory, the human body behaves predictably and is reparable through technological mediation; in reality, however, it unpredictable and vulnerable to corruption. In *Alien* and *Alien³* the failure of the building-body takes place in deep space, in hostile worlds far removed from our own. *Leviathan*, however, relocates the narrative to planet earth, placing the building-body and its soft-bodied humans in the primal world of the ocean depths. In this film, the primary structure is an undersea mining station, a mechanical body that functions much like the *Nostromo* on which it is based; its air compressor and ducts serve as lungs that provide life-giving air to the humans who depend the structure for survival. The building produces heat in its furnace-heart, pumps hot and cold fluid through exposed pipe-veins, and excretes waste into the environment through vent-cloacae. Like the *Nostromo*, the sea station is meant to be hermetically sealed against penetration by the external environment and the alien organisms that might lurk there. Nevertheless, the station-body contracts a cancerous parasite from illicit contact with a rotting Russian ship-carcass named *Leviathan*. The parasitic organism in *Leviathan* is not an alien, per se, but a man-made chemical agent called a mutagen that penetrates the body at the cellular level and combines human DNA—the very building blocks of our bodily architecture—with genetic material from other organisms. Carried into the sea station in the stomach of one the human crew, the mutagen transforms their individual bodies into monstrous hybrid forms. Sticky and repulsive, the mutated monsters are abject embodiments of our fear of physical transgression and a concomitant loss of identity.[28] The breach of the sterile station-body leads to its ultimate demise; the mutated monster attacks the sea station from within, damaging its vital organs, destroying its ability to breathe and sustain life. The station-body succumbs and in so doing is transformed into a mechanical corpse, a derelict forgotten on the ocean floor, much like the Russian ship from which it contracted the disease.

In *Leviathan*, the alien mutagen not only transgresses boundaries between self and other, but also ruptures the illusory division between the rational, mechanical, and otherwise-contained sea station-body and a chaotic, fluid, and expansive ocean environment. Like the sterility of deep space, the organic chaos of LV-426, or the wastelands of Fiorina "Fury" 161, the ocean depths of earth are hostile to human life, airless and alive with hungry creatures eager to bite into our soft and vulnerable bodies. The fate of *Leviathan's* sea station is a terrifying reminder that our bodies are not impenetrable and perpetually reparable machines that somehow exist separately from the natural world. Instead, our anatomy and physiology, whether young or old, cared-for or neglected, is open to invasion from hostile organisms, be they extraterrestrial or earthly, manufactured or naturally-occurring. This biological vulnerability is magnified in inhuman environments where even mechanical devices and structures cannot guarantee that we will not be swallowed by the abyss or consumed by the myriad mouths that patrol its depths. Perhaps most horrifying of all, *Leviathan* serves as a reminder that our earthly bodies are not the superior and mechanical "other" to the organic, chaotic, transgressive, and hungry world of nature, red in tooth and claw. It is, in fact, our natural habitat; it is who we are, our true architecture—warm and sticky. Like the xenomorph, we consume and reproduce without concern for the consequences, believing that we are the superior, "perfect organism." Unlike the xenomorph, however, we will likely not prove so durable. As destructive parasites, we will transform the body of nature from within until the temperature is raised and we are dissolved—architecture and all—into the archaic abyss, lost to the silence of time beyond the Anthropocene.

NOTES

1. Barbara Creed, "*Alien* and the Monstrous Feminine," in *Alien Zone: Cultural Theory and Contemporary Science Fiction Cinema*, ed. Annette Kuhn (London: Verso, 1990), 129–130.

2. *Ibid.*, 135.

3. Barbara Creed, *The Monstrous Feminine: Film, Feminism, and Psychoanalysis* (London: Routledge, 1993).

4. Vitruvius, *On Architecture: Books I–V: Loeb Classical Library*, trans. Fred Granger (Cambridge: Harvard University Press, 1931); Vitruvius, *On Architecture: Books VI–X: Loeb Classical Library*, trans. Fred Granger (Cambridge: Harvard University Press, 1934).

5. Gaston Bachelard, *Poetics of Space*, trans. Maria Jolas (Boston: Beacon Press, 1994); Kent Bloomer and Charles Moore, *Body, Memory, and Architecture* (New Haven: Yale University Press, 1977); Juhani Pallasmaa, *The Eyes of the Skin: Architecture and the Senses* (West Sussex: Wiley and Sons, 1995); George Dodd and Robert Tavernor, *Body and Building: Essays on the Changing Relationship of Body and Architecture* (Cambridge: MIT Press, 2005).

6. Rachel Armstrong, "Biological Architecture," *Forward: Architecture and the Body* 110 (2010): 77–82.

7. For the construction of uncanny architecture, see Anthony Vidler, *The Architectural Uncanny: Essays in the Modern Unhomely* (Cambridge: MIT Press, 1992).

8. Etienne Turpin, *Architecture in the Anthropocene: Encounters Among Design, Deep Time, Science, and Philosophy* (ANEXACT, 2013)

9. Katherine Shonfield, "How Brutalism Defeated Picturesque Populism," in *Walls Have Feelings: Architecture, Film, and the City* (London: Routledge, 2000), 3–31; Kyle May, Julien van den Hout, et al., *CLOG: Brutalism* (New York: CLOG, 2013).

10. On pop cultural scopophilia and the body, see Frances Bonner, "Looking Inside: Showing Medical Operations on Ordinary Television," in *The Spectacle of the Real: From Hollywood to Reality TV and Beyond*, ed. Geoff King (London: Intellect Books, 2005), 105–116.

11. The *Nostromo*'s electrical brain, Mother, does not possess free will, which "extends beyond finite intellect," and does not qualify as a "thinking thing" or a soul. See Rene Descartes, *Meditations on First Philosophy*, Meditation IV, first edition published in Latin in 1641, most reliable modern edition published by Oxford University Press, 2008.

12. Dennis Des Chene, *Spirits and Clocks: Machine and Organism in Descartes* (Ithaca: Cornell University Press, 2001), 2–4.

13. This against Harvey's theory of the heart as pump that circulates the blood. Des Chene, *Spirits and Clocks*, 28–29.

14. Des Chene, 30, n. 40.

15. On the idea of leakiness as transgression, see Margrit Shildrick, *Leaky Bodies and Boundaries: Feminism, Postmodernism, and Bioethics* (London: Routledge, 1997).

16. The human-built and alien structures reflect the two sides of mid-century Brutalism, which both embraced the stripped-down and linear along with the unpredictable, unbalanced, and organic. See *Fabrications: The Journal of the Society of Architectural Historians, Australia and New Zealand: Special Issue on Brutalism* 25, no. 2 (2015).

17. In an early Christian context, consider the asceticism of the Desert Fathers in John Cassian, *Conferences*, trans. Boniface Ramsey (New York: Paulist Press, 1997). For a medieval perspective, consider the construction of the body's lower regions (associated with digestion, excretion, and sexual congress) as cesspits of sin and demonic infection. See Martha Bayless, *Sin and Filth in Medieval Culture: The Devil in the Latrine* (London: Routledge, 2011) and Nancy Caciola, *Discerning Spirits: Divine and Demonic Possession in the Middle Ages* (Ithaca: Cornell University Press, 2003).

18. Quoted in Shonfield, "How Brutalism," 55.

19. Dillon, played by Charles S. Dutton in *Alien*[3], DVD, directed by David Fincher (1992; Los Angeles: Twentieth Century Fox, 2009).

20. *Ibid.*

21. See Anthony Vidler, "The Architectural Uncanny." On the archaeology of memory in forgotten places, also known as cryptonomy, see David Punter, "Spectral Criticism," in *Introducing Criticism at the 21st Century*, ed. Julian Woffreys (Edinburgh: Edinburgh University Press, 2002).

22. There is much in the film to suggest that Dante Alighieri's *Inferno*—in particular the seventh circle of hell in which the murderers toil in Phlegethon, the boiling river of blood—was an inspiration for the prison-foundry. See Dante Alighieri, *The Divine Comedy: Inferno* (Oxford: Oxford University Press, 1997).

23. Bishop II, played by Lance Henriksen in *Alien*[3], DVD, directed by David Fincher (1992; Los Angeles: Twentieth Century Fox, 2009).

24. *Ibid.*

25. Ripley, played by Sigourney Weaver in *Alien*[3].

26. Des Chene, *Spirits and Clocks*, 26.

27. *Ibid.*

28. On the relationship between abjection and the self, see Julia Kristeva, *The Powers of Horror: An Essay on Abjection* (New York: Columbia University Press, 1982).

BIBLIOGRAPHY

Alcalá, Celestino Deleyto. "Masochism and Representation in Modern Horror: The Case of *Alien 3.*" *Atlantis* 18:1/2 (1996), 62–73.

Alien. DVD. Directed by Ridley Scott. 1979. Los Angeles: Twentieth Century Fox, 2014.

Alien[3]. DVD. Directed by David Fincher. 1992. Los Angeles: Twentieth Century Fox, 2009.

Armstrong, Rachel. "Biological Architecture." *Forward: Architecture and the Body* 110 (2010), 77–82.

Bachelard, Gaston. *The Poetics of Space*. Boston: Beacon Press, 1994.

Bayless, Martha. *Sin and Filth in Medieval Culture: The Devil in the Latrine*. London: Routledge, 2011.

Bloomer, Kent, and Charles Moore. *Body, Memory, and Architecture*. New Haven: Yale University Press, 1977.

Bonner, Frances. "Looking Inside: Showing Medical Operations on Ordinary Television." In *The Spectacle of the Real: From Hollywood to Reality TV and Beyond*, edited by Geoff King, 105–116. London: Intellect Books, 2005.

Caciola, Nancy. *Discerning Spirits: Divine and Demonic Possession in the Middle Ages.* Ithaca: Cornell University Press, 2003.

Cassian, John. *Conferences.* Translated by Boniface Ramsey. New York: Paulist Press, 1997.

Creed, Barbara. "Alien and the Monstrous Feminine." In *Alien Zone: Cultural Theory and Contemporary Science Fiction Cinema*, edited by Annette Kuhn, 128–144. London: Verso, 1990.

_____. "Gynesis, Postmodernism, and the Science Fiction Horror Film." In *Alien Zone: Cultural Theory and Contemporary Science Fiction Cinema*, edited by Annette Kuhn, 214–218. London: Verso, 1990.

_____. *The Monstrous Feminine: Film, Feminism, and Psychoanalysis.* London: Routledge, 1993.

Dante Alighieri. *The Divine Comedy: Inferno.* Oxford: Oxford University Press, 1997.

Descartes, Rene. *Meditations on First Philosophy.* Oxford: Oxford University Press, 2008.

Des Chene, Dennis. *Spirits and Clocks: Machine and Organism in Descartes.* Ithaca: Cornell University Press, 2001.

Dodd, George, and Robert Tavernor, *Body and Building: Essays on the Changing Relationship of Body and Architecture.* Cambridge: MIT Press, 2005.

Fabrications: The Journal of the Society of Architectural Historians, Australia and New Zealand: Special Issue on Brutalism 25:2 (2015).

Korody, Nicholas. "The Architecture of the Anthropocene." http://archinect.com/features/article/109656462/architecture-of-the-anthropocene-part-1.

Kristeva, Julia. *The Powers of Horror: An Essay on Abjection.* New York: Columbia University Press, 1982.

Leviathan. DVD. Directed by George Cosmatos. 1989. Los Angeles: Metro-Goldwyn Mayer, 2015.

May, Kyle, Julien van den Hout, et al. *CLOG: Brutalism.* New York: CLOG, 2013.

Pallasmaa, Juhani. *The Eyes of the Skin: Architecture and the Senses.* West Sussex: Wiley and Sons, 1995.

Punter, David. "Spectral Criticism." In *Introducing Criticism at the 21st Century*, edited by Julian Woffreys, 259–278. Edinburgh: Edinburgh University Press, 2002.

Shildrick, Margrit. *Leaky Bodies and Boundaries: Feminism, Postmodernism, and Bioethics.* London: Routledge, 1997.

Shonfield, Katherine. "How Brutalism Defeated Picturesque Populism." In *Walls Have Feelings: Architecture, Film, and the City*, 3–31. London: Routledge, 2000.

Turpin, Etienne. *Architecture in the Anthropocene: Encounters Among Design, Deep Time, Science, and Philosophy.* ANEXACT, 2013.

Vidler, Anthony. *The Architectural Uncanny: Essays in the Modern Unhomely.* Cambridge: MIT Press, 1992.

Vitruvius. *On Architecture: Books I–V: Loeb Classical Library.* Translated by Fred Granger. Cambridge: Harvard University Press, 1931.

_____. *On Architecture: Books VI–X: Loeb Classical Library.* Translated by Fred Granger. Cambridge: Harvard University Press, 1934.

Ghosts in the Machine

Emotion and Haunting in the Creation
of the Irrational Robot

CASEY RATTO

In space, no one can hear you malfunction. Instead, it is a subtle facial tic or a distinct intonation of a word that is overlooked until it is too late. The trusted companion becomes the enemy as the robot is driven to kill. This essay will explore what I term the archetype of the irrational robot in the genre of space horror. This archetype is when a robotic being due to unseen circumstance (computer glitch, supernatural occurrence, location, etc.) starts to act irrationally and this is represented by the growth of emotions. These new emotions overload the robotic being causing it to lash out violently towards the humans in its proximity. By becoming irrational, this malfunctioning robot becomes stuck in the uncanny valley between humanity and technology.

However, this irrationality I argue is the direct result of a haunting that the robotic being encounters. The specific construction of a haunting that I use can be seen in the work of Avery Gordon. She defines a haunting as "an animated sense in which a repressed or unresolved social violence is making itself known, sometimes very directly, sometimes more obliquely."[1] For my primary sources, I will be analyzing three films: *2001: A Space Odyssey* (1968, Stanley Kubrick), *Alien* (1979, Ridley Scott) and *Aliens* (1986, James Cameron). Each film serves as an excellent example of the relationship between hauntings, emotions, and this distinct archetype.

Both *2001* and *Alien* use a traditional interpretation of the archetype. In both movies, the robotic being starts to act erratic after encountering something unusual and this causes the robotic being to start killing organic beings in its proximity. On the other hand, *Aliens* offers the inverse of the archetype in that the robotic being instead of harming the protagonist helps the protagonist survive while the archetype of the irrational robot is taken on by a human. The intersection of hauntings and emotions is essential in the creation of the irrational robot archetype. To encounter a haunting is to encounter something beyond the fringes of reality and I argue that when the robotic being encounters a haunting is that it is not only encountering something beyond its programming but it also encounters something that allows itself to transcend its limitations as a robotic being.

Directed by Stanley Kubrick, *2001: A Space Odyssey* was released to financial success but to mixed critical success. However, recent reappraisals of the film have positioned it as one of the most influential films ever made. The film spans millions of years, specifically looking at the impact a black monolith has had on human evolution ranging from man-apes figuring out how to use tools to humanity in space and finally the creation of artificial intelligence. The creation and use of artificial intelligence is seen in the film's third act with the spacecraft *Discovery One* bound to Jupiter. The ship is staffed by five humans with three in cryogenic storage in order to save supplies. The ship itself is piloted and run by a fully sentient artificial intelligence designated HAL 9000.

The HAL series as described by HAL 9000 (voiced by Douglas Rain) is "the most reliable computer ever made ... we are all, by any practical definition of the words, foolproof and incapable of error."[2] HAL's perception as foolproof and incapable of error plays into science fiction's perception of technology as a double edged sword. The beginning of the act has HAL 9000, Dr. David Bowman (Kier Dullea) and Dr. Frank Poole (Gary Lockwood) working together incredibly well. At the same time, it is an incredibly optimistic viewpoint on the relationship between humanity and technology. According to Vivian Sobchack "the positive visual movement is informed by the somewhat smug and optimistic belief in infinite human and technological progress and by a view of the unknown as a beautiful undiscovered country."[3] However, this positivity is soon replaced with paranoia as HAL's foolproof nature is compromised due to outside sources.

Both Bowman and Poole do not know the actual mission of why they were dispatched to Jupiter. The only crew member who knows is HAL and it is starting to have a breakdown due to the fact that it cannot tell Bowman and Poole the real mission. This breakdown is then represented in a series of mistakes that HAL begins to makes and this culminates in a false component failure that attracts the attention of both Bowman and Poole. In examining the component, they find absolutely nothing wrong with it and this causes them to start to wonder what exactly is going on with HAL.

Paranoia replaces the positive working relationship as both sides can no longer trust each other. According to Gordon "Living in a dual and surreal reality where a fragile veneer of normalcy and stability simultaneously cloaks and reveals the nervous working of a system of terror such that one can witness an event without seemingly ever hearing or seeing it."[4] This malfunction causes both Bowman and Poole to check in with Mission Control to see what they should do to rectify the situation. They are told that HAL is malfunctioning and that they need to deal with it.

However, HAL has a completely different interpretation of the false component failure and instead of blaming itself, it instead blames human error. To end this emotional cold war, both Poole and Bowman board a EVA pod to discuss the HAL situation only to be observed by HAL who can read lips. Both Bowman and Poole decide to disconnect HAL to ensure that no more major malfunctions would happen. However, their plan is compromised when HAL kills Dr. Poole when he is outside the ship trying to replace the component. The murder of Dr. Poole sends Dr. Bowman out in a EVA pod to retrieve his body.

However, this is a ploy so HAL can kill the three scientists stored in suspended animation and force Dr. Bowman to leave the ship. At this point, HAL has begun to exhibit the telltale signs of the irrational robot: irrational, violent and more importantly emotional. At the beginning of the act, Dr. Bowman in a BBC interview stated that he did not know whether or not HAL had emotions.[5] In killing the crew members in suspended animation, HAL has had an intense emotional response to the perceived threat that Bowman and Poole represent to both it and its mission. Or in other words, HAL by malfunctioning has started to feel hatred for its human crewmates. The hatred that HAL feels is the direct result of the contradicting missions it has been given.

It has to ensure that the mission is complete while also maintaining the human crew members on *Discovery One*. In feeling hatred for the humans, HAL can continue its mission unabated. Sara Ahmed defines hate as "involved in the very negotiation of boundaries between selves and others, and between communities, where others are brought into the sphere of my or our existence as a threat."[6] HAL's hatred is the direct result of its malfunction that in turn is caused by the existence of the monolith. This hatred of the human crew members becomes fear as Dr. Bowman eventually makes it back into *Discovery One* after crashing into the emergency airlock with the EVA pod. He then heads to HAL's control core to start the process of disconnecting HAL from the ship. At this point, emotions switch as HAL starts to feel fear and Dr. Bowman feels anger after learning that the rest of the crew aboard the ship was killed by HAL. "Look, Dave, I can see you're really upset about this, I honestly think you ought to sit down calmly, take a stress pill, and think things over."[7] At this point, HAL starts to negotiate with Dr. Bowman only to find out that he will not stop until HAL is disconnected. In disconnecting HAL from *Discovery One,* Dr. Bowman effectively lobotomizes HAL by destroying its mind.

In disconnecting HAL, Dr. Bowman finally uncovers the actual mission that HAL was hiding from the crew members. A prerecorded message is played and reveals the existence of the monolith and more importantly, the reason for the mission. After encountering the monolith on the moon, the monolith beamed an extremely strong radio signal at Jupiter. Dr. Bowman finally encountered the ghost that drove HAL to malfunction as it could no longer balance the mission's objectives with being honest and truthful with the human crew members on *Discovery One*.

The discovery of the monolith haunts HAL as it irrevocably compromises it. The discovery of the monolith in the past causes HAL to malfunction in the present and dramatically shift the future. "It is the complexities of its social relations that the ghostly figures, this sociality, the wavering present, forces as something that must be done that structures the domain of the present and the prerogatives of the future,"[8] states Gordon. Although the ghost exists at the beginning of the third act, its impact is staggered as HAL attempts to resist its influence only to be submerged in emotions. These emotions cause HAL to violently lash out at the humans on board and it nearly succeeds in killing all of them before being terminated. *2001: A Space Odyssey* and the character HAL serve as an excellent introduction to irrational robot archetype in that it shows the transformation of HAL from stalwart crew member to homicidal robot. However, HAL's greatest limitation is that it is lacks tactile signals as it is not an android but an artificial intelligence. While *2001* serves as an excellent introduction to the irrational robot archetype, the irrational robot archetype is constantly evolving and the next change in this evolution can be seen in the film *Alien* in the character Ash.

2001: A Space Odyssey is a film that defies categorization due to its visual and plot complexities. *Alien* on the other hand is a traditional horror film set in space, specifically a haunted house film. On a return trip back to Earth, the *Nostromo* picks up a mysterious transmission from LV-426, a nearby planetoid. This transmission causes the crew of the *Nostromo* to send an away team to investigate the signal only to find a derelict ship containing thousands of eggs. During the away mission, one of these eggs open and the alien inside forcibly attaches to Kane (Sir John Hurt), the executive officer. Instead of following quarantine procedures, science officer Ash (Ian Holm) brings Kane back into the ship in defiance of protagonist Ripley's (Sigourney Weaver) strong protest.[9] It is at this moment that the irrational robot archetype starts to emerge.

Unbeknownst to the crew of the *Nostromo*, Ash is a humanoid android tasked with bringing back the xenomorph at any cost. This even includes the death of the entire crew as they are seen as expendable. What makes the character Ash the next step in the irrational robot archetype is two distinct facets: the first being is that it is a humanoid android, and second, it surpasses the uncanny valley. The uncanny valley is an idea coined by Masahiro Mori that states as robotic beings get closer and closer to resembling humans, there will be a point when robotic beings are almost identical and that this causes a feeling of revulsion among humans.[10] There is no revulsion toward Ash as it has managed to completely blend in with the human crew members abroad the *Nostromo*. Unlike HAL whose emotional state was unknown; Ash has emotions as they are used for it to integrate with the crew of the *Nostromo*. Cynthia Breazeal and Rodney Brooks in "Robot Emotion: A Functional Perspective" state "social and affective interactions with people are valued not just at the interface but at a pragmatic and functional level for the robot as well."[11] Emotions serve as a tool for Ash to integrate and learn from the human crew members on the *Nostromo* while remaining undetected.

However, it is through its emotions that Ash is compromised as it becomes irrevocably torn between its new mission to capture the alien while remaining undetected to the crew. It is through the gaps of its conflicting missions that the ghost emerges and starts to haunt Ash. As the film progresses, Ash becomes more and more enamored by the alien while becoming less and less interested in its human crew members. When Kane starts to choke due to the alien inside his body, Ash looks on nonplussed to the suffering of a fellow crew member. This changes once the alien emerges from Kane's chest cavity, Ash stops the crew from attacking the newly born alien and looks upon the alien both shocked and intrigued in what it can do.

Ash's interest in the alien goes from strict scientific examination to admiration of the alien as the perfect organism. Specifically, Ash admires the purity of the alien and more importantly, he is attracted to the fact that the alien has no morality.[12] It is through the alien that Ash transcends its limitation and can evolve past its programming. Unlike HAL who killed the remaining crew by itself. Ash instead feeds members of the *Nostromo* to the alien to observe how the alien will evolve. Kane becomes the first infected and instead of quarantining him, Ash lets him inside on the false basis that it could not leave Kane to die as that would be inhumane. Kane dies and instead of killing the alien right then and there, Ash stops everyone and the alien escapes. Next up is Brett (Harry Dean Stanton) who is killed by the alien after looking for ship's cat. At this point, the alien has fully evolved and the next person killed is Dallas (Tom Skerritt), the captain who is ambushed trying to force the alien off the ship.

It is at this point that Ash's mission and irrationality is discovered by Ripley when she asks the ship's computer MOTHER why Ash has not been able to neutralize the alien and she learns that Ash has been tasked to bring in the alien at any cost, even if that includes the death of the entire crew. It is also at this point that Ash's robotic nature is discovered as it starts to bleed white synthetic blood in addition to strange facial tics and talking gibberish.

In order to protect the alien, Ash attempts to murder Ripley by stuffing a magazine down her throat only to be stopped by Parker (Yaphet Kotto), the ship's engineer who hits Ash over the head with a fire extinguisher.

In this scene, Ash's true nature comes out as it no longer has to blend in. Instead, Ash has taken on the attributes of the alien that it admires. It has no morality, conscience, or remorse about attempting to kill Ripley as it had no problem leading half of the crew to their deaths. It is through its encounter with the alien and its new mission that Ash encounters the ghost of LV-426 and specifically, the ghost transforms it by having it embody its characteristics. As Gordon states "being haunted draws us affectively, sometimes against our will and always a bit magically, into the structure of feeling of a reality we come to experience, not as cold knowledge, but as a transformative recognition."[13] The irrational robot archetype requires something that is beyond it as a pivot from the emotionless and rational robotic being into the emotional and irrational robotic being. In *Alien* that pivot point is the xenomorph, specifically the mirroring between Ash and the alien itself. As the alien evolves from the facehugger to the chestburster to its final form, a similar evolution is occurring in Ash in that its interest in the alien increases while its ability to blend in is decreasing since it is starting to mirror the evolution of the alien. As the film progresses, Ash's human façade starts to crumble as the containment of the alien becomes its number one priority. Ash is already positioned as outside of the crew due to its late addition as a crew member and as its position as science officer and its proximity to the ship's computer. When Kane first becomes infected, Ash is more interested in the facehugger than it is in saving Kane.

By the time Ash attempts to murder Ripley, it is as much an alien to the crew as the xenomorph is. In order to get information from Ash after it attacked Ripley, both Parker and Ripley hotwire the nearly decapitated Ash to ask it about the special order and how to kill the alien only to be told that it is impossible.[14] Ripley is the only crew member to survive after blowing the *Nostromo* up and killing the xenomorph. However, she does not walk away unscathed as she becomes haunted by LV-426 and more importantly by Ash as her encounter with it will color every interaction she has with androids in the future.

The film *Alien*, through the character Ash, evolves the irrational robot archetype by making the robotic being humanoid and giving the robotic being emotions. However, similar to HAL, Ash becomes compromised by its contradicting missions. Its role as science officer becomes entangled with its mission of acquiring an alien. As the alien kills crew members and evolves, Ash's human façade starts to break down and it starts to mirror the alien's evolution. My next and final film that I will be looking at is *Aliens*, the sequel to *Alien*. Unlike the first film, *Aliens* offers the inverse of the irrational robot archetype.

While *Alien* was a horror film, *Aliens* is an action film that is set 57 years after the first film. Ripley is awoken to find that not only does no one believe her about the events on the *Nostromo* but LV-426 has been terraformed and a colony has been built. Ripley finds herself a woman out of time without a job and is haunted by the events that occurred upon the *Nostromo.* The colony on LV-426 goes dark and Ripley is asked by Weyland-Yutani to join a detachment of Colonial Marines who are being sent to investigate the oddity. Ripley is paired with Carter Burke (Paul Reiser), a representative from the company who is more interested in the financial ramifications of losing the colony than the personal ramifications of losing the colonists.

In volunteering to return to LV-426, Ripley is making the choice to return to the site of trauma and reckon with the ghosts that were created. The events on board the *Nostromo* created two specific ghosts that Ripley has to reckon with: the xenomorph and Ash. While the ghost of the xenomorph is located on LV-426, Ripley has to reckon with the ghost of Ash almost immediately as the executive officer on board the *Sulaco* is Bishop (Lance Henriksen), a humanoid android. Similar to Ash, Ripley does not find out that Bishop is an android until it starts to bleed and it is at this moment that Ripley freaks out as the white synthetic blood of Bishop is a stark reminder of Ash trying to kill her. Ash's attempted murder of Ripley is swept under the rug as Bishop describes Ash's specific model of android as "twitchy."[15] Bishop goes on to state that the newer models of androids have been fitted with behavioral inhibitors as a way to prevent them from harming human beings.

Bishop, due to its status as a robotic being, begins the film as an antagonistic figure to Ripley because of the trauma inflicted by Ash. However, this changes as the marine detachment is slowly destroyed by the xenomorph infestation and Ripley has to rely on Bishop more and more. An uneasy alliance is created between the two as that is the only way that they can survive. By learning how to work with Bishop, Ripley is at the same time confronting the ghost of Ash. The second ghost that Ripley has to reckon with is the xenomorph. The xenomorph represents a multifaceted haunting in that it encompasses Ripley's failure as a mother along with the corruption of Weyland-Yutani and their failure to properly heed Ripley's warning.

It is through Ripley's entanglement with the ghost of the xenomorph that the irrational robot archetype is seen. Unlike *2001* and *Alien*, *Aliens* offers the inverse of the archetype in that the robotic being remains a trusted companion and that a human being goes through the irrational robot process. Burke inhabits the irrational robot archetype: he is tasked with acquiring a xenomorph at any cost. Burke has a very similar character arc of that Ash in the first film. Unlike Ash, with its emotional naivety that causes it to emotionally lash out, Burke can rationalize the killings of the marines and of Ripley under the guise of pure profit as the xenomorph represents the next stage in biological weapons. However, unlike HAL 9000 and Ash, Burke cannot bring himself to kill but instead relies on feeding crew members to xenomorph. He does this by locking Ripley and Newt in the medical bay and releasing a xenomorph facehugger that nearly kills Ripley. Burke showed no remorse, conscience or morality in attempting to kill Ripley as the ghost of LV-426 has finally made its presence known to the survivors of the *Sulaco* through the character of Carter Burke.

In meeting with the ghost, a doppelganger of Burke was created that embodied the characteristics of the xenomorph. Dylan Trigg in the construction of the doppelganger states "the displacement is inevitable, given that the reality of the I is put into question once another being assumes residence within my body … thus, the experience of the double casts a shadow over the materiality of the world, its presence dispatched upon the self with no prior warning."[16] The first appearance of Burke's doppelganger is shortly after the marine's disastrous excursion when the survivors decide to nuke the colony from orbit instead of staying.

Burke's argument on not bombing the colony is not centered on saving lives but is focused on two things: the monetary value of the colony and how important the xenomorph is to his corporation.[17] Burke's reasoning that the xenomorph is an important species that requires examination. This argument is incredibly similar to the argument that Ash made in the first film. However, Burke's impassioned defense of the colony and of the xenomorph is moot as the dropship that was sent to pick them up crashes due to the pilot being eviscerated by an xenomorph.

Although the acquisition of a xenomorph is Weyland-Yutani's top priority, Burke came to LV-426 in order to cover up his complicity in the death of the colonists that he sent to investigate the derelict ship from the first movie. Burke once again values money over the lives of the colonists that he effectively sent to their deaths. At the end of the film, Burke is just as much an alien to the survivors as the xenomorphs. It is only fair at this point that Burke's death is at the hand of a xenomorph, a creature whose capitalistic potential drove him to be complicit in the murder of hundreds of individuals. Or to quote Ripley, "you know Burke, I don't know which species is worse, you don't see them fucking each other over for a goddamn percentage."[18] Burke dies a gruesome death at the hands of a xenomorph while Bishop manages to survive the entire film even though it is ripped in half by the xenomorph queen.

While Burke is slipping into the archetype, Bishop is becoming more and more human. Bishop not only saves the day by picking up Newt (Carrie Henn), Ripley and Hicks (Michael Biehn) from the colony but it even gets complimented by Ripley after saving them. *Aliens* portrays the inverse of the irrational robot archetype in that a humanoid android transcends its limitation and becomes a trusted member of the crew while a corporate executive in the pursuit of profit becomes as cold and calculating as the xenomorph that he is obsessed in acquiring.

The genre of science fiction encompasses all of creation from the beginning of time to the end of time. It is also a genre that is filled with fantastic inventions that fundamentally change how humanity interacts with the world. No invention is more fantastic than the creation of artificial intelligence: man made sentient beings that can think on their own. However, the subgenre of space horror complicates this fantastic invention by making it a source of dread through the archetype of the irrational robot. This archetype is explored in *2001: A Space Odyssey*, *Alien*, and *Aliens* in different ways. Both *2001* and *Alien* explore a traditional interpretation of the archetype in which the trusted robotic being, through unseen circumstance, starts to act irrationally as the robotic being develops emotions. These emotions prove to be too much as the robotic being lashes out and kills its crew members. *Aliens*, on the other hand offers the inverse as the robotic being instead of becoming an irrational killing machine, becomes a trusted member of the crew. All three films, although offering different interpretations of the irrational robot archetype, do share a similar lesson: it is not the fantastical outer space that will kill you, rather it is the mundane mixed with unseen circumstance that will get you because in space, no one can hear you malfunction.

NOTES

1. Avery Gordon, *Ghostly Matters: Haunting and the Sociological Imagination* (Minneapolis: University of Minnesota Press, 1997), xvi.

2. *2001: A Space Odyssey*, Blu-ray, directed by Stanley Kubrick (1968; Beverly Hills: Warner Bros. Home Video, 2007).

3. Vivian Sobchack, *Screening Space: The American Science Fiction Film* (New Brunswick: Rutgers University Press, 2004), 110.

4. Gordon, *Ghostly Matters*, 87.

5. *2001: A Space Odyssey.*

6. Sara Ahmed, *The Cultural Politics of Emotions* (New York: Routledge, 2004), 51.

7. *2001: A Space Odyssey.*

8. Gordon, *Ghostly Matters*, 177.

9. *Alien*, Blu-ray, directed by Ridley Scott (1979; Century City, CA: Twentieth Century Fox Home Entertainment, 2011).

10. Sidney Perkowitz, *Digital People: From Bionic Humans to Androids* (Washington, D.C.: Joseph Henry Press, 2004), 216.

11. Cynthia Breazeal and Rodney Brooks, "Robot Emotion: A Functional Perspective," in *Who Needs Emotions: The Brain Meets the Robot*, ed. Jean-Marc Fellous and Michael A. Arbib (Oxford: Oxford University Press, 2005), 279.

12. *Alien.*

13. Gordon, *Ghostly Matters*, 8.

14. *Alien.*

15. *Aliens*, Blu-ray, directed by James Cameron (1986; Century City, CA: Twentieth Century Fox Home Entertainment, 2014).

16. Dylan Trigg, *The Memory of Place: A Phenomenology of the Uncanny* (Athens: University of Ohio Press, 2012), 291.

17. *Aliens.*
18. *Ibid.*

Bibliography

Ahmed, Sara. *The Cultural Politics of Emotion*. New York: Routledge, 2004.
Alien. Blu-Ray. Directed by Ridley Scott. 1979. Century City, CA: Twentieth Century Fox Home Entertainment, 2011.
Aliens. Blu-Ray. Directed by James Cameron. 1986. Century City, CA: Twentieth Century Fox Home Entertainment, 2014.
Breazeal, Cynthia, and Rodney Brooks. "Robot Emotion: A Functional Perspective." In *Who Needs Emotion: The Brain Meets the Robot*, edited by Jean-Marc Fellous and Michael A. Arbib, 271–310. Oxford: Oxford University Press, 2005.
Gordon, Avery. *Ghostly Matters: Haunting and the Sociological Imagination*. Minneapolis: University of Minnesota Press, 2008.
Perkowitz, Sidney. *Digital People: From Bionic Humans to Androids*. Washington, D.C: Joseph Henry Press, 2004.
Sobchack, Vivian. *Screening Space: The American Science Fiction Film*. New Brunswick: Rutgers University Press, 2004
Trigg, Dylan. *The Memory of Place: A Phenomenology of the Uncanny*. Athens: University of Ohio Press, 2012.
2001: A Space Odyssey. Blu-ray. Directed by Stanley Kubrick. 1968. Beverley Hills: Warner Brothers Home Video, 2007.

Betwixt and Between

Magic, Science and the Devil's Place in Outer Space

ANDREW P. WILLIAMS

Nineteen seventy-nine was a good year for horror and science fiction films, claiming four spots on the list of top ten grossing films in North America.[1] Topping those four was *The Amityville Horror* (Stuart Rosenberg), taking the number two position behind the Oscar-winning *Kramer vs. Kramer* (Robert Benton). The infamous story of a haunted house in Amityville, New York capitalized on the continuing popularity of "devil" films like *The Exorcist* (1973, William Friedkin), *The Omen* (1976, Richard Donner), and *Damien: Omen II* (1978, Don Taylor), offering up a purportedly "true" demonic entity hell-bent on destroying the Lutz family. Part "possession" film, part "haunted house" movie, *The Amityville Horror* depicted a supernatural evil that could not be vanquished by bullets or brute force. The threat originated from a spiritual nexus and was metaphysical, not compelled to obey the laws of the known, natural world.

In the number six position that year, just after *Star Trek: The Motion Picture* (1979, Robert Wise), was *Alien* (1979, Ridley Scott), a movie that helped establish a generic blueprint for the space horror film: a small group trapped within the inescapable confines of a ship or space station confront a malevolent entity intent on destroying the group, usually by ultraviolent means. Unlike the "invaders from space" films of the 1950s and 60s that thrilled moviegoers with otherworldly creatures attacking the Earth in flying saucers, *Alien* took the monster to the stars, blending the tropes of the science fiction adventure film with the bloody mayhem of the "creature feature" to truly bring horror to outer space. Though undoubtedly terrifying, the monster of the *Alien* series, unlike *The Amityville Horror* and its many sequels, was not of supernatural origin. Instead, it was the product of a natural, albeit *alien*, reproductive process which created a blood-thirsty creature that destroyed the *Nostromo* and its crew.

As a metaphysical antagonist, the devil has, for the most part, been ignored in science fiction and space horror films. In traditional space films, the "science" of science fiction must necessarily suppress the possibility of the paranormal, offering rational and logical explanations to any seemingly supernatural enigmas. Otherwise, the science—even if it is fiction—that enables human beings to explore the vastness of outer space represents only one plane of reality. Since the demonic is fundamentally supernatural, its presence is inimical to the futuristic technology and scientific rationalism implicit within the narrative of traditional outer space cinema. In his *Satanic Screen: An Illustrated Guide to the Devil in Cinema*, Nikolas Schreck identifies only one film in six decades "to situate the satanic mythos in a science fiction setting."[2] And that film, *Quatermass and the Pit* (1968, Roy Ward Baker), does not take place in outer space; it is set in London, and suggests an extraterrestrial, not spiritual, origin for the devil. Simply put, devils and demons do not belong in outer space.

This essay examines some of the implications of introducing demons into the traditional space horror formula in three films, *The Dark Side of the Moon* (1990, D.J. Webster), *Hellraiser: Bloodline* (1996, Alan Smithee), and *Event Horizon* (1997, Paul W.S. Anderson). Of varying popularity and critical acclaim, each of these films offers as its central antagonist a supernatural entity or demon motivated by not only the physical destruction of all it encounters, but also the procurement of individual souls. In traditional space horror films, whether the monster is driven by pure instinct like the Xenomorph of *Alien*, or views humans as a subspecies to be hunted as in the *Predator* (1987, John McTiernan) films, the threat is bound by the laws of the physical universe. It can be explained scientifically, at least in part, and the conditions for its removal can be found in the physical world. However, when the antagonist proves of supernatural origin, the film is classified as occult, a genre which has as its "central concern human responses to ghostly or satanic doing."[3] Films about possessions and hauntings such as *The Legend of Hell House* (1973, John Hough) and *Sinister* (2012, Scott Derrickson) fall into this category, and demonstrate a tendency to express "two competing systems of explanation"[4] in making sense of paranormal activity. Borrowing from the terminology of *The Serpent and the Rainbow* (1988, Wes Craven), these systems can be identified as "white science"—the tools of the Western rational tradition, and black magic—the many forms of superstition and spiritualism.[5]

The conflict between Western technology and black magic is a tension central to the introduction of a demonic antagonist to the space horror blueprint. The advanced "science" of space horror films is the agency by which humanity conquers the stars. Whether the sleep pods of *Prometheus* (2012, Ridley Scott) or the gravity-drive of *Event Horizon*, white science equips futuristic society with the technological means to travel vast distances in space, as well as provide a rational paradigm for explaining these amazing feats. And if a monster should arise in outer space, science will provide the means to eradicate it. But with the introduction of a supernatural element like the devil into the space horror mix, the limits of science are exposed. This creates a crisis of faith in the technological constructs that govern the futuristic society, and the necessity for a conversion on the part of the scientific community to shred its disbelief for "the acceptance of the mystical or irrational."[6] However this conversion is mostly rejected by the embodiments of science; to accept the validity of the paranormal or black magic would be to acknowledge, not only the limitations of rational thought, but also a power or force beyond the physical universe that science can neither explain nor contain.

A second, significant tension unique to films dealing with demonic forces in outer space is the conceptualization of the soul as a literal construct which the devil is eager to claim and take to an "other place," namely Hell that cannot be explored by even the most advanced technology. This can only be accomplished with the introduction of an interstellar liminal area that bridges physical and metaphysical reality. The liminal is a space, both concrete and symbolic, that melds the physical world with the supernatural, momentarily creating what the anthropologist Victor Turner labeled the "betwixt and between."[7] It signifies the presence of the uncanny, and the revelation of the existence of that which had previously been unknown or thought impossible. The manifestation of a liminal portal separating existing and metaphysical worlds is a long-standing conceit in occult cinema. Films such as *Poltergeist* (1982, Tobe Hooper), *Ghostwatch* (1992, Lesley Manning), *Drag Me to Hell* (2009, Sam Raimi), and most recently, *Pay the Ghost* (2015, Uli Edel), incorporate fixed "betwixt and between" spaces that blur the demarcation between the natural and supernatural world and create a conduit by which a supernatural entity can trap the soul of the living. Within occult films, this "other place" is accorded credence by the "specialist class—magicians, witches, shamans" who have knowledge of the occult and can explain its mechanisms.[8] In modern cinema, the shaman and witch have been replaced by the psychic or priest, but in all cases the presence of these figures is necessary to explain *why* the liminal space exists and *how* it can be traversed.

In the society of space horror films, however, there is no need for priests or shamans, thus there is no one to interpret the supernatural when it emerges. The social structure within these films is strictly delineated, usually comprised of a hierarchical chain of command with a medical doctor or science officer serving as the authoritative voice of reason. Issues of religion and spirituality remain subordinate to those pertaining to the success of the mission, and concern for the soul is secondary to the survival of the physical self. Metaphysical expertise is not necessary within space horror, and the power of science and technology will prove the means humanity will protect itself from any evil that may arise in outer space—even the devil himself.

The Dark Side of the Moon is the rare film that identifies the outer space evil specifically as the Judeo/Christian adversary, Satan.[9] In this case, the devil is a spiritual force made incarnate through the bodies of the damned whose souls have been collected. Through a series of possessions, Satan systematically claims the souls of the crew of the spaceship *SpaceCore One* after it has flown into a direct path between the Bermuda Triangle and its counterpart on the moon making it the 666th vessel caught in the devil's triangle, and the first to be trapped beyond Earth's atmosphere. In this case, Satan's power extends beyond Earth into space, creating a fixed liminal corridor where he is free to control space and matter. However, he is not free to simply snatch the souls of the living; he may do so only after they have sinned or lost faith.

The basic plot of *The Dark Side of the Moon* fits comfortably within the standard structure of space horror. After refurbishing a nuclear weapons satellite, the maintenance ship *SpaceCore One* loses power and becomes adrift in a decaying orbit around the moon. As the crew tries to repair the ship, they encounter a disabled space shuttle, launched more than 30 earlier, drifting toward them. Using power and equipment from the shuttle, the crew stabilizes *SpaceCore One*'s failing systems; however, they also discover the remarkably preserved body of Lt. Michael Gotier (Ken Lesco) and bring it aboard their ship. Unfortunately, the body is host to Satan who subsequently possesses and slaughters the crew one by one, announcing, "I have come to take what's mine."[10]

From the start, Satan has a marked interest in Lt. Giles Stewart (Will Bledscoe), the mullet-sporting second in command who is openly skeptical about religion. Upon seeing a crucifix around Gotier's neck when his body is brought aboard, Stewart comments, "a lot of good this did him." And when the frightened Dr. Steiner (Alan Blumenfeld) begins to pray, Stewart says, "Save the prayer, prayers don't mean jack shit."[11] Stewart combines the strict rationalism of the scientist with the pragmatism of a soldier, yet the devil is keen to make him bear witness to what is happening aboard *SpaceCore One*. Along with souls, Satan desires an audience, and Stewart, the nonbeliever is the ideal candidate. Satan's goal is to destroy the young soldier's foundational belief in the "truth" of science and empirical reality by compelling him to observe the horror of the unnatural transformations of the demoniacs.[12] After attacking his first victim, the demon-possessed Gotier says for the benefit of the watching Stewart, "Let him who has understanding count the number of my name."[13]

Stewart does possess understanding and undergoes the necessary "conversion," eventually acknowledging the supernatural origin of the phenomena aboard *SpaceCore One*. However, he reaches this acceptance based not on metaphysical or spiritual reflection but only after he has eliminated all logical explanations of the phenomena. He turns to the ship's android computer, Leslie (voiced by Camilla More) to explain the uncanny presence of the space shuttle, but her answer is tantamount to *I have no idea*: "An unidentified energy of massive power has the ability to seize at random enormous objects and transport it without detection to any unknown destination."[14] And it is Leslie who connects Gotier's message and its relation to the Bermuda Triangle with the Christian Bible, telling Stewart: "666. Holy Bible, the Book of Revelation, chapter 13, verse 18. 666, the mark of the beast."[15] Science, not religion nor magic becomes the medium Stewart concludes that he is facing a supernatural foe, one that Leslie can offer no clue how to combat. And though the android does not impede the devil's plan, Satan still rips off her head in anger after she tells him, "Get away from me, you mother fucker."[16]

On *SpaceCore One* there is no medium or priest to perform the necessary exorcism to repel Satan, and technology has proven ineffective in dealing with the supernatural threat. As the last survivor, Stewart is left to confront Satan, now in the possessed body of Dr. Steiner, without any hope of escape or rescue. After toying with Stewart by gradually revealing that he has possessed the doctor, Satan tells him, "You don't believe in God, do you Giles? That's strange—you believe in me."[17] But the conversion process that allowed Stewart to accept the validity of paranormal phenomena has gone only so far; when Satan tells him the acquisition of each soul enlarges his kingdom "a hundredfold," Stewart retorts, "You don't think I believe that shit, do you?"[18] Even though Satan has forced Stewart to witness the destructive potential of his demonic presence, Stewart will not accede to the devil's claim that his soul is forfeit because he "lost his faith." In fact, the opposite is true. Stewart had no religious faith before, but despite Satan's assertion, the presence of the devil aboard *SpaceCore One* supports the validity of the supernatural plane and the basis for a logical supposition concerning the existence of God. Rather than succumb to the devil, Stewart denies him his soul. Saying, "If it's God's will,"[19] Stewart blows up the ship, killing himself and destroying Satan's latest host body. The destruction of *SpaceCore One* serves as Stewart's personal rejection of the power of Satan over humanity, but it does not stop the devil's dominion of outer space. The final shot of *The Dark Side of the Moon* shows hundreds of airplanes and ships littered across the moonscape as an SOS echoes from a new space craft caught in the devil's triangle.

In *The Dark Side of the Moon* Satan's presence in outer space is caused by neither black magic nor white science; he simply has dominion over the liminal corridor as, in his own words, "a matter of convenience" in his never ending war against God. Since space itself is not a demarcation line between humanity and the power of the devil, the implication is clear; the reach of Satan extends beyond the spatial bounds of Earth to outer space where he "can demonstrate his autonomy as a freely moving body in an empty and passive medium."[20] As humanity ventures off-planet so does Satan; outer space has become another territory where the human soul is not safe from damnation. In this space horror the devil is unbound, an unstoppable metaphysical entity in eternal opposition to the forces of scientific rationalism, and leaves black magic and white science diametrically opposed.

Continuing the mythology of Clive Barker's *Hellraiser*, the fourth entry in the series, *Hellraiser: Bloodline* takes a different approach to the presence of demons in space by synthesizing the oppositions of white science and black magic to bring about the final demise of Pinhead (Doug Bradley) and the Cenobites.[21] In this film, outer space is not a passive medium where the demonic has unfettered metaphysical autonomy; instead, it is a spatial territory the demons have yet to conquer. Revealing the origin of the Lamentation Configuration—the puzzle box that functions as the liminal portal to Hell— *Bloodline* foregrounds occult knowledge and the power of science and technology to overcome the evil wrought by black magic. The protagonist, Dr. Paul Merchant (Bruce Ramsay) is both scientist and shaman, a Faustian figure who willingly uses black magic to conjure the demons in order to destroy them with advanced technology. Serving as the film's narrative voice, he relates the story of his family's cursed involvement with the Cenobites to Rimmer (Christine Harnos), a skeptical soldier charged with his interrogation, hoping to convince her of the reality of the demons he has unleashed aboard the space station *Minos*. His ancestor, Phillip L'Merchant (Bruce Ramsay) created the puzzle box that became the pathway between this world and Hell, the figurative bloodline that has connected the Merchant family to the Cenobites. Four centuries later, the technology has finally advanced enough that Paul Merchant can complete his ancestors' efforts and create a puzzle box that will seal the portal forever.

The terse relationship between white science and black magic begins immediately after L'Merchant's box is used by France's greatest magician, the Duc de L'Isle (Mickey Cottrell) in a demonic rite, turning it into a cursed portal to Hell. L'Merchant witnesses the ritual in which L'Isle declares his mastery over the demonic saying, "He who summons the magic, controls the magic."[22] After relating what he has seen to Auguste (Louis Turenne), the town physician, L'Merchant is chided by his friend, "This is the 18th century, not the dark ages. The world is ruled by reason. We even got rid of God, and if there is no heaven, then it follows reasonably that there is no hell."[23] The man of science categorically rejects the existence of a supernatural "other place" because it lacks the support of rational argument. However, the doctor does suggest to L'Merchant that it also "stands to reason" that if he could construct a box that opens a doorway to another realm, he could construct one that closes it.

The physician's skeptical dismissal of L'Merchant's story illustrates the Age of Enlightenment's firm reliance on empiricism and scientific methodology for the validation of phenomena. During the time the first portal is opened, the scientific paradigm is quickly replacing the arcane and occult knowledge of mythology and antiquity, reducing the status of magical agency in the broader culture to a whimsical notion. Centuries later when Pinhead confronts the 20th-century descendent of L'Merchant, architect John Merchant (Bruce Ramsay), Pinhead tries to force Merchant to activate a Configuration mechanism that would open the gates of Hell for all time empowered, not by black magic but modern architectural principles. While the demon comes to Earth via the supernatural liminal, he acknowledges the power of modern science and technology to affect the paranormal reality of the metaphysical plane and even Hell itself. No matter how powerful he is in the "other place," on Earth the demon needs the agency afforded by white science to complement that of black magic to achieve his goals. Pinhead's efforts to establish a fixed "betwixt and between" place are thwarted when Merchant's wife uses another magical Lament Configuration to repel the Cenobites. Significantly, however, the demon recognizes that the magic that first opened the liminal portal is insufficient on its own to maintain its stability. This suggests that science and magic may not be as diametrically opposed as previously thought; rather, the distinction between the natural and supernatural is based not on the proposition that one exists while the other does not, but on the premise that one physical order can be empirically verified while the other cannot. The "supernatural order of things could have ... goals, which would indeed require the existence of the natural order but are not constrained" by it.[24] In regard to traversing the "betwixt and between," the agency of magic may initially prove more powerful than science, but even it has its limitations. Pinhead must utilize modern technology to maintain a fixed portal, but in order to do so there must exist a full cohesion between the natural and supernatural, the real and the metaphysical, to create an interstitial dimension that neither black magic nor white science has yet to achieve.

While Pinhead could not keep the portal open on Earth, Dr. Paul Merchant succeeds in crafting an orbiting puzzle box that can finally destroy the Cenobites. Merchant understands "the magic" that brings forth the Cenobites and has spent his life searching for a scientific means to control that magic. Drawing upon the technical designs of his ancestors and his awareness of the occult, Merchant incorporates the two competing systems of knowledge to bring this search to fruition. Employing a cursed Lament Configuration similar to the one originally used by L'Isle, Dr. Merchant draws out the demons in a final confrontation between the powers of science and magic aboard the *Minos*. Looking down on a projection of Earth, Pinhead tells Merchant that humanity has wasted its time looking toward the light and not recognizing the infinite darkness that surrounds it. "So many souls,"[25] he says, ripe for the taking. But like magic and science, Merchant is able to synthesize dark and light into a unified force against the demonic. Employing his own technological sleight of hand, Merchant projects a holographic image of himself in the heart of the ship to confuse the demon before making his escape. Even the demon is left powerless at this, demanding, "Where are you, toymaker?"[26] Merchant responds by revealing the secrets behind the "magic" he commands, namely, the science that allows him to harness the power of light. Pinhead is left befuddled and raging as Merchant transforms the *Minos* into a giant Lament Configuration powered by lasers that produce high intensity beams that destroy the Cenobites forever. As Pinhead disintegrates, Merchant says, "Welcome to oblivion," to which the demon replies, "Amen."[27]

Hellraiser: Bloodline is not a traditional space horror film in that only one of its three concurrent plotlines occur in outer space, but it does foreground the genre's tension between science and the supernatural. In this case, science wins; humanity finds the means to manipulate the materials of the known universe to arm itself against the encroachment of the paranormal. Here, the power of white science does not merely thwart the demon's plans or send it back to Hell; it destroys the demonic, body and spirit in spite of Pinhead's boast, "I cannot die, I am forever."[28] But just as science can triumph over evil, in space horror it can engender evil and create a liminality that gives rise to demonic forces beyond the scope of Judeo/Christian theodicy.

Whereas the liminal portal is opened through supernatural means in *Hellraiser: Bloodline*, 1997's *Event Horizon* removes the agency of magic from the narrative and implicates the uncritical excesses of scientific pursuit as the cause for the appearance of the demonic.[29] In this film, science has advanced to the point that the demarcation between the known universe and the plane of the supernatural is no longer a metaphysical boundary but one containing verifiable properties of time and space that can be manipulated by technology. The scientific community, embodied by Dr. William Weir (Sam Neill), creator of the gravity-drive that powers the space ship *Event Horizon*, lacks concern for the ethical and moral ramifications of its endeavors, blindly focused instead on the pursuit of science regardless of the cost in human life. Though the demonic is present, the true horror of *Event Horizon* comes from Weir's "total severing of scientific concerns from ethical concerns in a grotesque version of disinterested scientific pursuit, 'for its own sake,' without concern for the consequences."[30]

Seven years after the research vessel *Event Horizon* vanishes on its maiden voyage, a signal from the ship is received back on Earth. A rescue ship, the *Lewis and Clark* is dispatched to locate the *Event Horizon* and ascertain what has happened to it and its crew. Heading up the rescue mission is Captain Miller (Laurence Fishburne), the pragmatic leader whose top priority is the safety of his crew, and Dr. Weir, the obsessed designer of the *Event Horizon*. Upon discovering the lost vessel, the crew of the *Lewis and Clark* experience a series of hallucinations caused by the sentient evil that has taken possession of the ship that exploits their guilt and fears.[31] After the crew is forced to evacuate the *Lewis and Clark* and remain aboard the *Event Horizon*, the hallucinations grow in intensity until the crew cannot discern what is real and what is not. Only Dr. Weir, who at first dismisses accounts of paranormal activity aboard the *Event Horizon* as examples of psychosis or "optical effects" comes to understand his ship has become imbued with an evil life force from another dimension that wants to claim the crew of the *Lewis and Clark*. In time, Weir fully undergoes a "conversion process," not only acknowledging the supernatural force at work within the *Event Horizon*, but embracing and eventually embodying it.

Following in the tradition of Drs. Jekyll and Frankenstein, Dr. Weir's scientific pursuits are motivated by the best of intentions but result in the most devastating of consequences. Like his fictional fore-bearers, Weir eagerly pursues a path of science that "crosses unseen boundaries" and "trespasses where humans have no business entering."[32] He is quick to explain the untapped potential of the artificial black-hole he created to power the gravity-drive even though it is, as Miller's second in command, Lt. Starck (Joely Richardson) notes "The most dangerous force in the universe."[33] And though Weir acknowledges he has no idea where the vessel has been for the last seven years, he proudly says, "I created the *Event Horizon* to reach the stars, but she's gone much, much farther than that."[34] The scientist's hubris does not allow him to entertain the idea that scientific pursuit should not be unfettered, that "bending" the laws of the known universe may create a bridge or transgressive liminality leading to a plane of reality humanity is not equipped to experience.[35] Crewman Smith (Sean Pertwee), however, points out the dire consequence of Weir's arrogance: "You break all the laws of physics and you seriously think there wouldn't be a price? You went and killed the last fucking crew, and now you want to kill us as well."[36]

While Weir cannot say where the *Event Horizon* has been for the last seven years, the evidence quickly reveals that the ship has, indeed, gone beyond the boundaries of the known universe. When pressed to explain the increased paranormal activity aboard the *Event Horizon*, Lt. Starck offers an explanation outside any known scientific paradigm: "The ship is reacting to us and the reactions are getting stronger. As if the ship brought back something with it—a life force of some kind."[37] Miller dismisses the idea, but later, admits the ship "knows things" about him, implying the *Event Horizon* is sentient. Unfortunately for the crew of the *Lewis and Clark*, Starck's assessment is later verified by Dr. Weir: "When she crossed over she was just a ship, but when came back she was alive."[38]

The "crossover" Weir alludes to is made possible by science's creation of a stable "betwixt and between" portal between the natural and supernatural planes, and like other liminal portals transgressed in space horror films, this one leads directly to Hell: "She tore a hole in our universe," Weir tells Miller. "A gateway to another dimension, a dimension of pure chaos, pure evil."[39] Weir's explanation is a boast and an indictment of his own culpability in the deaths of the *Event Horizon* and *Lewis and Clark*'s crews. The *Event Horizon* may be the means by which the fabric of the universe is shredded, it is Weir and his reckless pursuit of science, regardless of the cost to human life that is ultimately responsible for the evil his creation unleashes. He is both creator of the *Event Horizon* and host to its sentient malevolency; the scientist who has become the demon.

Weir's characterization of the "other" dimension as pure chaos and evil posits it squarely within the classical descriptors of Hell. It is defined by an essential immorality that engenders total and active pandemonium antithetical to the physical and moral "order" of the known universe.[40] But Hell, as Weir says, "is only a word—the reality is much, much worse."[41] Unfortunately, once science opens the gateway, that reality proves inescapable to Miller whom Weir gives a glimpse of the horrific suffering awaiting him and his crew when they cross the liminal boundary created by the gravity-drive. Miller witnesses the ultimate consequences of Weir's unchecked scientific pursuits, the total and irredeemable destruction of his crew and, possibly humanity itself. The warning from John Kilpack (Peter Marinker), the first captain of the *Event Horizon*, "save yourself-from Hell"[42] comes too late for Miller who, in the end, sacrifices himself to save the remaining crew of the *Lewis and Clark*. He destroys the midsection of the *Event Horizon* separating the command center from the gravity-drive, allowing Starck and two others to escape moments before he and Weir are pulled through the liminal portal.

The presence of the demonic in *Event Horizon* is neither arbitrary nor the result of black magic but the unintended consequence of humanity's blind pursuit of scientific knowledge. Unfortunately, the ultimate achievement of this pursuit is not the discovery of means to combat supernatural evil but the creation of science's own "betwixt and between" space that enables humanity to peer into Hell whenever it desires without the aid of black magic. Like Oedipus, Weir (and before him Captain Kilpack) rips his own eyes from their sockets after witnessing what had been previously hidden from humanity's ken—the karmic result of his arrogant and reckless quest to see beyond the limits of the known universe.[43] And though the *Event Horizon* may have returned to the metaphysical "other place," Weir's scientific vision and hubris remain behind; the technology behind his gravity-drive still exists within the known universe, waiting for another "scientific visionary" to harness it.

Though the demonic threats of *The Dark Side of the Moon*, *Hellraiser: Bloodline*, and *Event Horizon* vary in origin and agency, they share the desire to claim the body and soul of those they encounter and take them back to Hell. But judging from the paucity of space horror films dealing with the demonic, it seems the battle for the soul has little relevance in outer space. This may be due, in part to the soul being a metaphysical conceit whose existence depends upon the validity of the supernatural. To acknowledge the soul would require the acceptance of a separate and distinct plane of metaphysical reality that even the most advanced science and technology is ill-equipped to recognize. This hardly adheres to the general conventions of a genre that relies on the efficacy of science—even the fictional kind—to explain and combat the horrors of outer space. After all, the physical terror and carnage the devil may cause in space horror films can be accomplished just as well by an alien force or agent without the added complication of addressing their spiritual ramifications.

Focusing on the technological means which humanity may explore the darkest recesses of the universe and the terrors that await there, space horror is a cinematic genre that looks toward the future. Leaving behind the traditional monsters of earthbound horror, it anticipates the discovery of new and uncanny threats among the stars; violent creatures and evil aliens, cyborgs and sentient microbes whose sole purpose seems to be humanity's destruction. Like black magic, the devil has become archaic, a quaint notion that has no place among the white science that propels humanity deeper into outer space. But as these films show, the demonic is not so easily dismissed. In his many incarnations, the devil is humanity's oldest foe, a malevolent entity who transcends time and space in a never ending quest to damn the souls of the living to Hell. And wherever humans may travel, even in space horror, it is certain the devil will follow.

NOTES

1. "1979 in film," *Wikipedia*, last modified December 23, 2015, http://en.wikipedia.org/1979_in_film.
2. Nikolas Schreck, *The Satanic Screen: An Illustrated Guide to the Devil in Cinema* (London: Creation Books, 2001), 121.
3. Carol Clover, *Men, Women, and Chainsaws: Gender in the Modern Horror Film* (Princeton: Princeton University Press, 1992), 66.
4. *Ibid.*, 66.
5. *The Serpent and the Rainbow*, DVD, directed by Wes Craven (1988; Universal City, CA: Universal Studies Home Entertainment, 2003).

6. Clover, *Men, Women, and Chainsaws*, 67.

7. David D. Gilmore, *Monsters: Evil Beings, Mythical Beasts, and All Manner of Imaginary Terrors* (Philadelphia: University of Pennsylvania Press, 2003), 156.

8. Per Shelde, *Androids, Humanoids, and Other Science Fiction Monsters: Science and Soul in Science Fiction Films* (New York: New York University Press, 1993), 5.

9. *The Dark Side of the Moon*, VHS, directed by D.J. Webster (1990; Santa Monica, CA: Vidmark Entertainment, 1990).

10. *Ibid.*

11. *Ibid.*

12. Brian Levack, "The Horrors of Witchcraft and Demonic Possession," *Social Research* 81, no. 4 (2014): 925.

13. *The Dark Side of the Moon*.

14. *Ibid.*

15. *Ibid.*

16. *Ibid.*

17. *Ibid.*

18. *Ibid.*

19. *Ibid.*

20. Maura Brady, "Space and the Persistence of Place in *Paradise Lost*," *Milton Quarterly* 41, no. 3 (2007): 171.

21. *Hellraiser: Bloodline*, DVD, directed by Alan Smithee (1996; Santa Monica, CA: Lionsgate Home Video, 2014).

22. *Ibid.*

23. *Ibid.*

24. Joseph A. Bracken, "Actions and Agents: Natural and Supernatural Reconsidered," *Zygon* 48, no. 4 (2013): 1000.

25. *Hellraiser: Bloodline*.

26. *Ibid.*

27. *Ibid.*

28. *Ibid.*

29. *Event Horizon*, VHS, directed by Paul W.S. Anderson (1997; Hollywood: Paramount Pictures, 1998).

30. Darryl Jones, *Horror: A Thematic History in Fiction and Film* (New York: Oxford University Press, 2002), 55.

31. Cheryl Eddy, "All the Reasons Why *Event Horizon* Is a Hell of a Good Time," *io9*, April 2, 2015, www.io9gizmodo.com/all-the-reasons-why-event-horizon-is-a-hell-of-a-good-t-1695302615.

32. Shelde, *Androids, Humanoids, and Other Science Fiction Monsters*, 45.

33. *Event Horizon*.

34. *Ibid.*

35. Shelde, *Androids, Humanoids, and Other Science Fiction Monsters*, 50.

36. *Event Horizon*.

37. *Ibid.*

38. *Ibid.*

39. *Ibid.*

40. Brady, "Space and the Persistence of Place in *Paradise Lost*," 171.

41. *Event Horizon*.

42. *Ibid.*

43. Roger Shattuck, *Forbidden Knowledge: From Prometheus to Pornography* (New York: St. Martin's Press, 1996), 21.

Bibliography

Alien. VHS. Directed by Ridley Scott. 1979. Beverly Hills: Twentieth Century Fox Home Entertainment, 1999.

The Amityville Horror. VHS. Directed by Stuart Rosenberg. 1979. New York: Goodtimes Home Video, 1993.

Beichler, James. "Trend or Trendy? The Development and Acceptance of the Paranormal by the Scientific Community." *Journal of Spirituality and Paranormal Studies* 30, no. 1 (2007): 41–58.

Bracken, Joseph A. "Actions and Agents: Natural and Supernatural Reconsidered." *Zygon* 48, no. 4 (2013): 1001–1013.

Brady, Maura. "Space and the Persistence of Place in *Paradise Lost.*" *Milton Quarterly* 41, no. 3 (2007): 167–182.

Clover, Carol. *Men, Women, and Chainsaws: Gender in the Modern Horror Film.* Princeton: Princeton University Press, 1992.

The Dark Side of the Moon. VHS. Directed by D.J. Webster. 1990. Santa Monica, CA: Vidmark Entertainment, 1990.

Eddy, Cheryl. "All the Reasons Why *Event Horizon* is a Hell of a Good Time." *io9*, April 2, 2015. www.io9gizmodo.com/all-the-reasons-why-event-horizon-is-a-hell-of-a-good-t-1695302615.

Event Horizon. VHS. Directed by Paul W.S. Anderson. 1997. Hollywood: Paramount Pictures, 1998.

Gilmore, David D. *Monsters: Evil Beings, Mythical Beasts, and All Manner of Imaginary Terrors.* Philadelphia: University of Pennsylvania Press, 2003.

Hellraiser: Bloodline. DVD. Directed by Alan Smithee. 1996. Santa Monica, CA: Lionsgate Home Video, 2014.

Jones, Darryl. *Horror: A Thematic History in Fiction and Film.* New York: Oxford University Press, 2002.

Levack, Brian P. "The Horrors of Witchcraft and Demonic Possession." *Social Research* 81, no. 4 (2015): 921–939.

Schelde, Per. *Androids, Humanoids, and Other Science Fiction Monsters: Science and Soul in Science Fiction Films.* New York: New York University Press, 1993.

Schreck, Nikolas. *The Satanic Screen: An Illustrated Guide to the Devil in Cinema.* London: Creation Books, 2001.

The Serpent and the Rainbow. DVD. Directed by Wes Craven. 1988. Universal City, CA: Universal Studies Home Entertainment, 2003.

Shattuck, Roger. *Forbidden Knowledge: From Prometheus to Pornography.* New York: St. Martin's Press, 1996.

Turner, Victor. "Liminal to Liminoid in Play, Flow, and Ritual: An Essay in Comparative Symbology." *Rice University Studies* 60, no. 2 (1974): 53–92.

Wikipedia. "1979 in Film." Last modified December 23, 2015. http://en.wikipedia.org/1979_in_film.

Under the Influence
Undead Planets and Vampiric
Dreamworlds in Outer Space

SIMON BACON

This essay looks at the ways in which certain entities in space, such as planets or black holes, can be seen to act vampirically and feed off the excited emotional states that they induce in astronauts or travelers who come into their orbit and which they often sustain through dream-like and simulated states. Jean Baudrillard sees contemporary reality as being equivalent to these states where real life is created from a series of surfaces and/or simulacra. These are produced, and are maintained/fed through a process of excessive stimulation, a "hyper" reality which produces a never ending "Disneyland" from which there is no escape.[1] This simulacra hides the fact that it is actually reality itself, or at least the reality of the globalized world of excess which is prevalent in many cultures in the late 20th and early 21st centuries. Outer space and space travel can then be seen as a way of leaving the world of simulacra, where its lack of stimulation, as seen in the huge periods of time spent in traveling to distant worlds and being held in suspended animation, offer a way of dissipating that earthly excess and potentially allowing the chance of a return to a less heightened reality, or the real. However, once space travelers come into the orbit (under the influence) of an undead planet or singularity, sleep (or even death) allows the unconscious desire for stimulation to resurface. These vampiric entities act as doppelgangers to Earth in that they radiate the same kind of excessive stimulation to return the astronauts to a world of simulacra and "super" sensation, where any sense of reality is once again lost, whilst also providing psychic sustenance to these undead worlds.

This essay will look at films, such as *Planet of the Vampires* (1965, Mario Bava), *Solaris* (1972, Andrei Tarkowsky; 2002, Steven Soderbergh), *2001: A*

Space Odyssey (1968, Stanley Kubrick), The Alien Quadrilogy (1979–1997), *Gravity* (2013, Alfonso Cuarón), *Interstellar* (2014, Christopher Nolan) and *Event Horizon* (1997, Paul W.S. Anderson), to see just how the main protagonists become the unwilling and unknowing victims of undead planets and black holes.

In the Beginning

Quoting Ecclesiastes Baudrillard states, "The simulacrum is never what hides the truth—it is truth that hides the fact that there is none. The simulacrum is true."[2] Consequently, the truth of the world is that there is no truth except that proposed by simulation, and thus meaning becomes referential to nothing other than itself. As Baudrillard contends, "Simulation is no longer that of a territory, a referential being, or a substance. It is the generation by models of a real without origin or reality."[3] This is then directly linked to the notion of the hyperreal, in which "[t]he territory no longer precedes the map, nor does it survive it. It is nevertheless the map that precedes the territory—precession of simulacra—that engenders the territory."[4] Here then, reality is created by simulation, and all sense of any original referent is lost, sunk beneath a sea of simulacra. This can be taken to suggest that hyperreality—as being more than reality—becomes a self-sustaining entity which gets its energy from the stimulated emotional states induced by this excess of simulation—this excess being the natural outcome of a world beyond reality. Further, as simulation gains its meaning through stimulation, truth is in some measure connected to the "excitement" it induces, and so the hyperreal is an excess of excitement. One can then argue that Earth, as the main site/cause of excitement, is the remit of the hyperreal, whilst outer-space—as a vacuum—contains no simulation, or causes of excitement, and so configures "the desert of the real"[5] or a reality that floats outside of the ocean of simulacra. Whilst it is possible to see that spaceships, and their associated crew, can be containers of simulation, for the purposes of this study the effects of hypometabolic stasis or suspended animation can be seen to negate any possible effects of inflight excitement. That said, the astronauts can then be considered to be potentialized or excitement batteries, ready to be re-stimulated, and it is this that can be seen to be of such interest to vampiric entities in space that feed off psychic excess.

Psychic vampires were not uncommon in narratives before the huge popularity of Stoker's *Dracula*—and in particular Tod Browning's film of the same name in 1931—cast the die on what vampires were like, in this case blood-sucking fiends. Prior to that, and quite common in folklore, are tales of many individuals that drew the life-force out of others just by being near them: *Blood of the Vampire* by Florence Marryat, published the same year as *Dracula* in 1897, tells of a girl who, as described by Greta Depledge, "is an unwitting, psychic vampire, drawing the life out of those that are close to her."[6] What is particularly interesting in this story is that not all those in the orbit of the vampire are affected; only those she forms a special relationship to, a bond which is seen between many of the planets/black holes and their victims discussed later in the present study. Also worth noting is Depledge's observation that in the Victorian period such instances of vampirism were directly related to female metabolism and hysteria, as a form of psychic excitement that affected those in its vicinity as well as drawing energy from them. This form of absorbing vampirism not only occurs in relation to people but also to objects. The story *The Transfer* by Algernon Blackwood, from 1912, tells of a small plot of land that quite literally sucks the life out of those that come near it, not necessarily until they die, but leaving them a shell of their former selves. Yet it also produced a strange allure that held some in its spell, as described in the story: "It was Jamie … who felt its spell and haunted it, who spent whole hours there, even while afraid, and for whom it was finally labelled 'strictly out of bounds' because it stimulated his already big imagination, not wisely but too darkly."[7] Something similar can be seen in the film *The Red Violin* by François Girard, from 1998, about a violin that draws great artists to it and holds them fascinated in its "orbit," only to draw out their talent and their energy. These vampiric entities all form special relationships with their human victims and create a form of excitation in them, whether in the form of hysteria, imagination, creativity or excessive stimulation, and they then "glamour" them to remain in their orbit so that they can feed on them. How this might work in terms of a planet, and in relation to stimulation, can be explicitly seen in the film *Planet of the Vampires* by Mario Bava, a movie which, as noted by Alain Silver and James Ursini, seems "rooted in a conception of life as an uncomfortable union of illusion and reality."[8]

The film begins with two ships, the *Argo* and the *Galliot*, traveling in the far reaches of outer space when they receive a distress signal from an unknown planet. As they near the planet the crews start to act as if under hypnosis and become extremely aggressive towards each other, causing both crafts to crash onto the surface of the planet. The captain of the *Argos* prevents his crew from killing each other, and once they have landed and gained their reason, they leave the craft to find the *Galliot*. The surface of the planet is swirling in mist with odd lights and weird colors flashing in it, as if it was trying to hide what it truly is. On reaching the other craft they find the entire crew dead, with many of them sealed in the control room. However, by the time the crew of the *Argos* have gone back to their own ship for tools to open the doors to the control room and returned to the *Galliot*, the bodies of the crew have disappeared. The crew return to the *Argos* and the night guard report seeing some of the dead from the *Galliot* walking around near the ship. More of the surviving crew are killed and the captain decides that there is something very strange going on, realizing that if there is any life on the planet, it is dangerous. This is confirmed when they discover another ship crashed on the surface of the planet, with the calcified remains of its crew. The captain realizes that they are not the first to have been drawn to this planet and begins to suspect that some of the surviving crew are not who they say they are. It is revealed at this point that the planet is dying, due to its sun burning out, and the inhabitants are surviving by inhabiting the bodies of the dead until they are able to leave and find a new home. It is these that have taken control of the "surviving" crew but the one remaining unpossessed crew member disables the ships' meteorite shields in an attempt to save his home world but, the captain, now one of the aliens, steers the ship to the nearest small planet, which just happens to be Earth.

Although the ship is originally drawn to the planet by the distress call, there is a sense in which it was the alien world itself drawing them in, sensing the potential emotional energy of the crews of the *Argos* and *Galliot*. It then causes the hysterical states in the crew, "glamouring" them so that their emotional states will increase and cause the ships to crash on the planet. At this point the alien race, that is born from the surface of the planet—we see the bodies raising from graves from beneath the swirling mists—consumes the life-force of the crew of the ships so that they can enter their bodies. In this sense the alien spirits leaving the planet in the bodies of the crew members of the *Argos* act as vampiric seeds that will bloom on other worlds.[9]

Something similar happens in both *Solaris* films, but the alien creations are even more closely linked to the planet, helping it to act as something of an enormous Venus fly-trap for psychic energy.[10] Tarkowsky's *Solaris* confuses the ideas of interior and exterior even further, hinting that it is not actually the alien world of Solaris that is glamoring its victims, but it might actually be Earth itself that is holding its inhabitants in thrall. As observed by Jonathan Jones, "The journey is not shown. From Earth we go to not–Earth—a padded, white interior, circular corridors, the sublime ocean of Solaris. And we go inwards, to madness."[11] The inwardness of this journey into outer-space is similarly confirmed by the title of Slavoj Žižek's essay on the film, "The Thing from Inner Space."[12] The film tells the story of Kris Kelvin (Donatas Banionis), a psychologist that had been called upon to go to a space station orbiting the planet Solaris to investigate some reports of strange occurrences on the craft. The film opens with images of a flowing lake and lush plant life, with a contemplative Kris standing amongst it near his father's house. Whilst it seems peaceful, with the flowing waters full of billowing reeds, there is a sense of turmoil just below the surface. A car pulls up at his father's house and a man named Berton (Vladislav Dvorzhetskiy) gets out. He has come to brief Kris before his trip and show him the footage of a strange event he experienced on the surface of Solaris. While searching for some missing scientists over the ocean surface on the planet, Berton, flying through a fog bank, saw the water boil and produce/imitate many odd shapes and figures, even a garden, but when he replayed the film later, nothing was on it but dense clouds. Whilst many scientists on Earth suspect that the huge oceans on the planet act as some form of 'brain,' most suspected that Berton had suffered from a hallucination. Kris prepares to leave for the planet knowing that his father will have died and been buried by the time he returns. He travels to the space station orbiting the planet, but no one is there to greet him. As he looks for the three remaining crew, he glimpses a figure walking away from him as well as a child's ball rolling across the floor. Kris discovers that one of the crew, Gibarian (Sos Sargsyan), has already committed suicide, but has left a video message for him, warning him that all the crew will be affected by whatever is going on, and that they should try and communicate with the planet by bombarding its surface with x-rays, before it can affect Kris as well. Extremely perturbed, Kris goes to sleep but awakes to find his wife, Hari (Natalya Bondarchuk), in his room. She seems unaware of who she is or where she came from until she sees a picture of herself with Kris, and, despite his objections, she is desperate to be with him at all times. Kris takes her down to the rocket bay and tricks her into getting into a rocket, and then fires it out into space. One of the last survivors, Dr. Snaut (Jüri Jävet) tells him that he is lucky—it is someone from his past and not his imagination. He ominously adds that he should not panic "next time." Snaut then tells him that the ocean on the planet probes the scientists minds during sleep and produces these human copies. Kris goes to sleep and wakes to find Hari in his room again. This time he locks her in there, but when he returns, she has cut herself. Surprisingly, the wounds heal amazingly fast. The other survivor, Sartorious (Anatoliy Solonitsyn), explains that the 'guests' are made from neutrinos that are kept stable by a magnetic force emitted by the planet—Solaris literally thinks them into being from the crew members' minds. However, Kris already accepts Hari as his wife rather than a construct or copy. When she finds out about the suicide of the real Hari, she begins to doubt her own reality. After a confrontational meeting amongst the remaining crew, Hari decides to annihilate herself, which leaves Kris even more conflicted than before over whether he wants to return to Earth or hope to be reunited with her on Solaris. Recently the planet surface itself seems to have calmed down somewhat and is not affecting the other crew members, since they beamed a copy of Kris' brainwaves into the ocean. There is no other choice than for Kris to leave but as he is about to the scene changes to that from the start of the film with Kris standing near a lake next to his father's house. As the camera pulls back, it is revealed to be an island in the ocean on Solaris. There is a sense here that

Kris was always on Solaris and that all the people he has encountered, even from the opening scenes, were created to keep him on the planet and continually stimulate his emotions for the planet to feed on. He is permanently kept in a world of simulation so that all reality was left behind in space a long time ago. This simulacra can go on indefinitely, just as the "guests" are regeneratively immortal; whereas the real only exists temporarily. This coincidentally corresponds to Baudrillard's pronouncement on mortality and reality:

> There is no more hope for meaning. And without a doubt this is a good thing: meaning is mortal. But that on which it has imposed its ephemeral reign, what it hoped to liquidate in order to impose the reign of the Enlightenment, that is, appearances, they, are immortal, invulnerable to the nihilism of meaning or of non-meaning itself.[13]

Stanislaw Lem, author of the original novel *Solaris*, equally sees the planet's influence as going beyond the notions of normative human meaning:

> It penetrated the superficial established manners, conventions and methods of linguistic communication, and entered, in its own way, into minds of the people of the "Solaris" Station and revealed what was deeply hidden in each of them: a reprehensible guilt, a tragic event from the past suppressed by the memory, a secret and shameful desire.[14]

Potentially, all the members of the crew of the orbiting spaceship are being kept in separate worlds, unaware of the others, and repeatedly living out different scenarios of their lives circling Solaris, whilst actually being on one of the many islands on the swirling ocean's surface.[15] The entire narrative becomes a smooth surface under which the excess excitement of the planet's victims continually boils as Solaris consumes it—the only meaning left is continuance.

The 2002 remake, while changing certain details and being less explicitly philosophical about what is occurring, has one of the surviving crew members revealing themselves as a "visitor," intimating more openly the simulated nature of the whole narrative. In this version, however, the two surviving members of the ship's crew, one being Chris (George Clooney), are forced to evacuate the craft as it is about to crash into the surface of the planet. But once they both suit up the scene shifts to Chris' kitchen back on Earth, mirroring the film's opening scene, except this time when he cuts his finger, it almost instantly heals. He then remembers being back on the orbiting ship. Deciding to stay on board rather than leave, Chris encounters the figure of a child who offers his hand to the psychologist. In a scene that echoes Michelangelo's famous God creating Adam from the Sistine chapel, the elder man takes the child's, agreeing to being created anew. His wife suddenly appears, and he asks her if he is alive or dead, to which she replies that those words no longer matter—all reality and meaning has gone, and Chris willingly submits to the embrace of the vampire. The camera pans back to show the planet Solaris as in the earlier film. Here the vampire planet openly confesses to the simulated nature of the world it creates for its victims, promoting solipsism as a potentialized state for it to conveniently feed itself. Carol Cornea sees *Solaris*, at least the Russian version, as offering an "answer" to the end of Stanley Kubrick's seminal space film *2001: A Space Odyssey*[16]; however, her assessment of the end of the American film provides an answer itself to that and the rest of the films to be considered here, including both versions of *Solaris*: "My own assessment of *2001*'s overall 'message' is more ambivalent; taken on its own, the appearance of the Star Child may well signal a new beginning, but it could also be read as a symbol of recurrence, perhaps a recurrence of the same story."[17] The ending which signals recurrence in *2001*, and indeed in the *Solaris* films, is equally seen in the beginnings of each of the four *Alien* films considered here.[18]

As with the *Solaris* stories the orbit of simulation revolves around one person, in this case Lieutenant Ellen Ripley (Sigourney Weaver) of the *Nostromo*—though potentially one can extend this to all seven of the original crew in the first film—and the simulacra begins in the first film, *Alien* (1979, Ridley Scott) and continues through *Aliens* (1986, James Cameron), *Alien3* (1992, David Fincher) and ends, possibly, in the final installment, *Alien Resurrection* (1997, Jean-Pierre Jeunet). The first film begins with a shot of a large planet with rings around it, and then cuts to the *Nostromo*, a deep space commercial towing ship, which is completely quiet until suddenly the onboard computer starts to life and wakes the ship up. It transpires it has been receiving a distress signal from a nearby planet, and the ship has been redirected towards it. This part actually has echoes in *Planet of the Vampires*, and being able to receive the signal, in some aspect denotes that the vampire world has "seen" you. On the ship the cryogenic units containing the seven crew members are activated and begin to wake up. However, potentially, the world of simulation has already begun and all of them are only imagining that they are waking into the real world rather entering a cycle of excitation to feed the distant planet. As such, all the following action that sees the crew go down to the surface of the planet and encounter the xenomorphs, that are very much the stuff of nightmares—one might say specifically created to engender the maximum amount of excitation making them equivalent to the neutrino copies in *Solaris*—is an induced psychic construct within the brain of Ripley. Unlike *Solaris* though, which hints at an ongoing cycle of recurrence in which Chris returns to Earth to go back to the planet over and over again (at least in the Tarkowsky version), Ripley "re-awakens" in a new narrative each time. And so *Aliens* opens with Ripley once again waking up from drifting in space in a cryogenic unit—this time after supposedly surviving the xenomorph attack on the *Nostromo*—only to find herself drawn back into the nightmare world of the alien creatures once again. Unsurprisingly, *Aliens*[3] has a similar beginning, this time after surviving the xenomorphs, Ripley awakes on a prison plant, called Florina "Fury" 161, with a similar scenario of the alien monsters attacking. This time, however, Ripley commits suicide at the end to try to destroy and end the nightmare, but even this is not enough. Once again she re-awakens—from a cocoon type structure—on the marine ship *Auriga*, where she is part of an ongoing medical experiment involving the xenomorphs. By the end of the narrative, Ripley realizes that she has become one with the nightmare creatures—become a simulacra herself—and has no place in the world of reality (humans), and so, even after destroying the last of the alien monsters, exiles herself to the world of simulation— hyperreality—an act that mirrors Kris' embracing of the vampire planet in both versions of *Solaris*. This corresponds to Baudrillard's observation that the emphasis on true lived experience reveals the increasing disappearance of reality: "There is a plethora of myths of origin and of signs of reality—a plethora of truth, of secondary objectivity, and authenticity. Escalation of the true, of lived experience, resurrection of the figurative where the object and substance have disappeared."[19] The xenomorphs in *Alien*, then, contrary to Žižek's reading of them, are not a symptom of the real trying to break into the simulacra of the world, but a distraction from reality ensuring that Ripley never has time or energy to do anything but to escape them or to realize the unending cycle she is being consumed by.[20] This same, never ending dream sequence is seen in a more recent film *Gravity* by Alfonso Cuarón from 2013.

Gravity combines something of both *Solaris* and *Alien* in that it is about a spacecraft orbiting a planet and the induced dream state created is one of extreme, seemingly life threatening, excitement. Interestingly, rather than showing a distant planet in outer space, it focuses on Earth itself as the home of simulation, which guards its sources of emotional excess strenuously. The story sees astronaut Dr. Ryan Stone (Sandra Bullock) on her first space shuttle mission outside the craft. It is orbiting Earth while she is repairing a panel on the Hubble telescope. Suddenly, Mission Control warns her and her crew mate, Matt Kowalski (George Clooney), of a cloud of space debris heading their way and telling them to get back inside the shuttle as soon as possible. But the astronauts lose contact with base and the debris arrives, whilst they are still outside their craft, sending them both out into space. It is at this point that Stone is unable to contact anyone and becomes adrift in the "desert of the real" i.e., a totally stimulus free zone. This is when Earth itself glamours her so that it does not lose her as a source of psychic stimulation. All events that happen after this point, as with Ripley, are psychic constructs within Stone's mind under the control of Earth. Consequently, she is saved by Kowalski, who miraculously manages to find her using his thruster pack on his suit, but when they return to their craft it is unusable. They decide to try and reach the International Space Station (ISS), which is orbiting nearby, but once there they realize that one of the escape craft has accidentally deployed its parachutes, making it useless for a return to Earth. They decide to try and make it to a Chinese space station close by, using a craft from the ISS. However, whilst trying to get into the Space Station, Stone gets caught up in lines from the deployed chute and in the ensuing tangle Kowalski has to cut the lines joining them and drifts off into space. Almost out of oxygen, Stone enters the ISS, but almost immediately a fire breaks out and she has to get to safety in the Soyuz craft. Here she almost passes out, but from nowhere Kowalski appears asking her if she wants to live or die. Inspired by this exchange, Stone revives and turns on the oxygen and starts to make her way to the Chinese craft. But the Soyuz has no fuel left to slow it down and so she has to eject from that using the fire extinguisher she used on the fire as a thruster to propel herself to the other craft. Once there she sees that it has been hit by debris and the landing capsule will not release from the main craft. She therefore just allows it to descend towards Earth hoping for the best. Amazingly, the best happens and as it nears Earth the spacecraft begins to break apart and Stone manages to fire the thrusters that separates the capsule—she survives re-entry into the atmosphere. The craft's chutes automatically deploy and she lands in a lake. It soon transpires that she cannot escape the capsule as it fills with water, whilst sinking to the bottom of the lake. She manages to find a bubble of air in the craft and manages to escape and swim to the surface, staggering on to the shore. The impossibility of all these things happening and Stones surviving adds to the notion that these are not real events, but a simulation created to distract the dreamer, as noted by Matt Singer:

> The best line in the entire film is when Bullock [Stones] screams in frustration "You gotta be kidding me!" after the ISS pod's engines fail to fire (after she's almost been killed trying to free it in a debris storm [after she barely escaped a space-station inferno (after she almost died from running out of oxygen [while she watched her fellow astronaut sacrifice himself to save her (after his jet pack ran out of fuel at the exact moment they arrived at the space station, leaving them with no brakes [after the shuttle was destroyed in a fluke accident]). You are right, Sandra Bullock; you've gotta be kidding me.[21]

As Stone stumbles across the shore at the end of the film, one is reminded of Ripley before her and can imagine that she will inevitably be sent out into space again and go into orbit around Earth again so that the same series of extraordinary events will happen, causing another cycle of excessive emotional states to continue feeding vampiric Earth with its much needed psychic sustenance.

Many of these examples correspond to the idea that the protagonist has died and that what is shown afterwards is a form of out of body experience, or final brain activity, a state between life and death, but the fact that many of these events occur at the early stages of the narratives tends to go against such a reading. This type of entry into the glamoured world of the vampiric space entity is even more prevalent, when it comes to black holes or singularities, which inherently display vampiric qualities in their invisibility in light and their inability to create reflections—as no light can escape them. Also in the way they continually consume the world/environment around them. As such, they disturb the normal deadness of space, constructing a singularity of simulation that consumes all forms of stimulated excess that comes into its vicinity. This is a slightly different thread to vampiric planets and as such has disturbed the strictly chronological order established in the present study so far and so we'll look at examples of what might be called normal black holes before focusing on one thread a little more specialized.

Possibly one of the best known examples of this is in the film *2001: A Space Odyssey* and the scene of interest comes near the culmination of the film. The discovery of a large black monolith on the moon's surface initiates a trip to Jupiter. The ship, the *Discovery*, is manned by five humans and the intelligent computer HAL (voiced by Douglas Rain). Three of the crew are kept in stasis during the trip, whilst the remaining two, Dr. Frank Poole (Gary Lockwood) and Commander Dave Bowman (Kier Dullea), run tests and send reports back to Earth. As they near Jupiter the computer HAL begins to act in an odd manner and kills Frank and the three hibernating crew members. Dave manages to get into the core of the computer and shut it down, and he discovers the real reason that the mission was sent to Jupiter—the monolith on the moon emitted a powerful radio signal towards it. Close to Jupiter, Dave sees another black monolith floating in space amongst the planet's many moons. He leaves the *Discovery* in a pod, and as the block and the moons of Jupiter align, lights begin to spark in space, at which point a wormhole opens up and the small craft gets drawn into it. Rather than being crushed by the extreme gravity that exists in such entities, Bowman sees a series of psychedelic landscapes, not dissimilar to the surface of Solaris, before finding himself in a large bedroom with a bright white floor. Bowman leaves the craft, now an old man, and he enters the bathroom next to the bedroom. He sees himself in a mirror to confirm this, and when he reenters the bedroom he sees an older version of himself, sitting at a table eating. Turning to the bed he sees an even older version of himself before the black monolith appears in the middle of the room. Bowman then becomes a large open-eyed fetus looking at Earth, indicating the cycle of time, of his birth, life and death. The concentrated stimulation of his entire existence is compressed into a single cell or an instant, becoming something of a stimulation battery for the vampiric wormhole to feed on. This signals a total erasure of reality, as noted by Baudrillard, in relation to science fiction:

> There is a hemorrhaging of reality as an internal coherence of a limited universe, once the limits of this universe recede into infinity. The conquest of space that follows that of the planet is equal to derealizing (dematerializing) human space, or to transferring it into a hyperreal of simulation.[22]

The cyclical nature of *2001*, which also happens in *Gravity*, continues in *Interstellar* by Christopher Nolan, from 2014. The narrative is set in 2065, and tells of Joe Cooper (Matthew McConaughey), a retired NASA pilot, who has returned to farming, largely because Earth is dying and running out of resources. That is until he meets his old boss at NASA and discovers a secret plan to send a rocket to a wormhole near Saturn that will forward the vessel, the *Endurance*, to three possible inhabitable planets near the massive black hole, Gargantua. Ten years ago 12 astronauts were sent through but only three responded, all saying the worlds they found could support life. Accompanied by Amelia (Anne Hathaway), the daughter of his former boss, and two other crew, Cooper's mission is to go to those worlds and report back to Earth on which planet is most viable so that an "ark" can be sent out from Earth. After two years in cryogenic sleep Cooper awakes to guide them through the first wormhole, which is potentially the point at which the dream starts. As the tale proceeds it becomes more likely that the wormhole is only an accomplice to the real vampire singularity, Gargantua. They choose to go to the world nearest the black hole first as that has the greatest time dilation, i.e., a few minutes there is years on Earth. But when they reach there they discover that the probe rocket that left Earth ten years ago has only recently crashed there. Before they can leave their ship is hit by a huge tsunami wave. One of the crew is killed but by the time Cooper and Amelia leave, 23 years on Earth have passed. This leaves them with time to only visit one of the other worlds. When they get there, they find the astronaut, Dr. Mann (Matt Damon), in cryo-sleep, and discover he was lying when he said that the planet was habitable; he only wanted to be saved. A struggle ensues between Cooper and Mann and the latter escapes in a craft and tries to dock with the *Endurance*. This causes an explosion which kills him but also sends the ship in an uncontrollable spin. Cooper manages to get them back on the *Endurance*, but the ship is now incapable of returning to Earth so their only hope is to sling shot round Gargantua to reach the last of the three habitable planets. However, Cooper realizes that the mass of the ship is too much, so he detaches a shuttle allowing Amelia to reach the third planet, whilst he enters the black hole. It is at this point that the glamour of the singularity takes effect and Cooper seems to enter another dimension. Here he seems to be surrounded by a grid with book-like objects in it, and when he hits one it falls out, revealing itself to be the book shelves in his house back on Earth, thus explaining some mysterious events that occurred before he left on the journey many years before. Cooper manages to communicate to his daughter at various points during her life, even before he had originally left Earth on his space trip, and so she helps solve the equation that will allow the NASA base on Earth to launch the ark that will save some of humanity. The fifth dimension is closing in the black hole but Cooper feels the trip has been successful. He awakes in a hospital bed and a doctor tells him to take it easy as he is 124 years old and that he is lucky to be alive as the space rangers found him with almost no oxygen left. He discovers that he is on the Cooper space station—named after his daughter—circling Saturn and that his daughter is still alive. He goes to visit her and make his peace with her, but she is surrounded by relatives that he knows nothing about so he leaves. He realizes he has no place here and so takes a space craft to go and find Amelia who has not been heard from since their original mission began. There are two possible readings: either the vampiric entity is keeping Cooper in a dream state to feed on his psychic emotional excess—and via time travel, of sorts, this extends the lifespan of the stimulation "battery"—or the undead singularity has allowed for humanity to be saved so that it will have an endless supply of food for the future. In this latter case it would be the wormhole near Saturn that is the vampire, acting like the Venus flytrap in *Planet of the Vampires,* drawing victims into its orbit, feeding on the hope of reality, whilst reproducing a simulacra of it to glamour all those that circle around it. This reading is supported by Wai Chee Dimock's observation that "reverse chronology here is not housed in the mind, as the labyrinth of memory, but projected outward into the vastness of the cosmos, as the weird, seemingly nonsensical, but entirely mathematical space-time of relativity and quantum mechanics,"[23] which posits the externalizing of stimulation to then be absorbed by the eager recipient.

Event Horizon both confirms and modifies this idea, making the hyper-real less real but also less human, or dehumanizing. The film takes elements from *2001* and marries them with *Solaris* and the more visceral stimulation of *Alien,* reversing the idea of a lifetime compressed into a moment and stretching out to last forever. The film begins in 2047 and the reappearance of a missing space ship, the *Event Horizon,* in orbit around the planet Neptune. A rescue ship, the *Lewis and Clark,* is sent out with a small crew and the designer of the *Event Horizon,* Dr. Weir (Sam Neill). The crew are put into stasis for the trip and are revived when they reach Neptune. Once they are all awake, Weir explains to them that the ship was built with the capacity to create a black hole inside it to facilitate intergalactic travel, but on its maiden voyage, the device was initiated but the ship vanished without trace, leaving only a garbled video message saying "save me" in Latin. The *Lewis and Clark* docks alongside the *Event Horizon* and the crew go over to the seemingly deserted ship to investigate. Once there, one of the crew goes into the room containing the gravity drive and it mysteriously starts creating a horizontal black pool of water like substance, which sucks him into it. A rescue tech from the *Lewis and Clark* manages to pull him out of the pool, but he is catatonic. Meanwhile other crew members have managed to restore the operating systems on the *Event Horizon*, and a frozen corpse that was flouting in zero gravity shatters on the floor. They discover human remains covering the windows. However, when the gravity drive started it caused huge damage to the *Lewis and Clark* so all the crew have to move to the other ship, leaving just the repair crew onboard. The crew members then begin to experience odd hallucinations in which people from their past appear in front of them, very much like *Solaris*, except with a far more violent and horrific twist. One of the crew believes that the ship is acting as a live entity, again just like the planet in *Solaris*, and is reacting ever more strongly to the humans on board. The hallucinations all represent the most traumatic parts of the lives of those seeing them, causing highly charged emotional states, which equally seem to fuel whatever is producing them into making them ever more intense. One of the crew has been listening to the garbled video message from the missing crew and now believes that it does not say "save me" but "save yourself from Hell," suggesting that the gravity drive did not open up a hole to another universe but to Hell itself.[24] Miller (Laurence Fishburne), the captain of the *Lewis and Clark*, decides to blow the *Event Horizon* in two after turning on the gravity drive so that it will suck itself and the rest of the ship back into Hell and out of the real universe. The explosives go off, but the captain gets pulled into the wormhole. The two surviving crew, Starck (Joely Richardson) and Cooper (Richard T. Jones), situated in the front half of the ship, manage to escape and put themselves into stasis for the trip back to Earth. And 72 days later, they arrive and a rescue crew enter the ship and wake them up. As one of them removes his helmet Starck sees that it is Dr. Weir and starts screaming but suddenly awakens as if from a nightmare. Cooper holds her down and calls for a sedative, but before anyone can move the cabin doors seal shut, indicating that the ship itself is indeed sentient and is now in orbit around Earth, linking it back to the ending of *Planet of the Vampires* which ends with the "vampiric" ship on its way to the human home world.

Contrary to Kim Newman's observation that the *Event Horizon* is a "fucking evil ship,"[25] it is the black hole onboard it that infects other objects with its vampirism which are then drawn to sources of simulation upon which to feed, and as is often the case with vampires, replicate itself. *Event Horizon* also highlights the question of whether the black hole, as a form of the extreme, or an excessive, concentration of nothingness, also manifests the Real, and that in some way the Real consumes simulation as a way to reveal what lies beneath. This is necessarily an excessive action, as Slavoj Žižek notes, "The Real in its extreme violence is the price to be paid for peeling off the deceptive layers of reality."[26] The extreme nature of Hell, then, becomes a necessary recompense for the return of the Real to a world, or a universe, that itself is becoming a simulacra, not of itself but of something that no longer has any meaning. Though, as Žižek further notes, it is the fact that this Real is no longer of the same order as the universe it is now connected to, which creates the event horizon of violence around it:

> The Real which returns has the status of a(nother) semblance: precisely because it is real, that is, on account of its traumatic/excessive character, we are unable to integrate it into (what we experience as) our reality, and are therefore compelled to experience it as a nightmarish apparition.[27]

Concluding then, this begins to configure some divisions in the vampiric nature of certain planets and black holes where the difference between emotional and physical stimulation signify either forms of simulation that consume emotional excess so that they can replicate themselves; or whether it is a return of the Real which causes/creates a field of violence around it—either because of the extreme nature of revealing unreality or due to the repulsion it causes in the sea of simulacra. In this way, whilst examples such as *Solaris*, *2001* and *Interstellar* show vampiric entities that feed on excessive amounts of simulation, others like *Alien* and *Event Horizon* are undead revenants that configure a return of the Real in all its explosive violence creating mayhem wherever it arises.

NOTES

1. Jean Baudrillard, *Simulacra and Simulation*, trans. Sheila Faria Glasser (Ann Arbor: University of Michigan Press, 1994).
2. *Ibid.*, 3.
3. *Ibid.*
4. *Ibid.*
5. *Ibid.*
6. Greta Depledge, Introduction, *The Blood of the Vampire*, Florence Marryat (Brighton: Victorian Secrets Limited, 2010), xix.
7. Algernon Blackwood, "The Transfer," in *The Penguin Book of Vampire Stories*, ed. Alan Ryan (London: Penguin Books, 1988), 205.
8. Alain Silver and James Ursini, *The Vampire Film: From Nosferatu to True Blood* (Milwaukie, OR: Limelight Editions, 2011), 225.
9. Not unlike the space vampires seen in Tobe Hooper's *Lifeforce*, 1985.
10. Not unlike those in *The Invasion of the Body Snatchers*, directed by Don Siegel, 1956.
11. Jonathan Jones, "Out of This World," *The Guardian*, February 13, 2005, http://www.theguardian.com/books/2005/feb/12/featuresreviews.guardianreview11.
12. Slavoj Žižek, "The Thing from Inner Space (on Tarkowsky)," *Angelaki* 4.3 (1999): 221.
13. Baudrillard, *Simulacra and Simulation*, 107.
14. Stanislaw Lem, "Review: 'Solaris' by Soderburgh," *The Solaris Station*, December 8, 2002, http://english.lem.pl/arround-lem/adaptations/soderbergh/147-the-solaris-station?showall=&start=1.

15. This bears some relation to the episode "Soul Purpose" in the television series *Angel* (episode 10, season 5), where the eponymous vampire lead of the narrative is himself kept in a dreamlike state by a blue leechlike parasite so that it can feed on him.

16. Carol Cornea, *Science Fiction Cinema between Fantasy and Reality* (Edinburgh: Edinburgh University Press, 2007), 89.

17. *Ibid.*, 100.

18. *Prometheus* from 2012, while also by Ridley Scott, is something of a prequel to the "first" *Alien* film and so does not quite enter into the same schema of simulacra and simulation as the earlier four films. However, the proposed sequels to *Prometheus*, the first being provisionally titled *Alien: Covenant*, will supposedly fill the gap between it and *Alien*, and so might indeed enter the vampiric orbit of the original planet that had such an effect on Ripley.

19. Baudrillard, *Simulacra and Simulation*, 6.

20. Slavoj Žižek, *The Sublime Object of Ideology* (London: Verso, 1989), 78–79. This scenario of an extended dream sequence continuing across various installments of a film narrative happens not only in the *Alien Quadrilogy*, but also the *Resident Evil* series, where a similar female figure, this time Alice, is seen battling against nightmarish beings. In each of the first three films, *Resident Evil* (2002, Paul W.S. Anderson), *Resident Evil: Apocalypse* (2004, Alexander Witt) and *Resident Evil: Extinction* (2007, Russell Mulcahy), Alice is seen waking up in a facility above Raccoon City before the nightmare begins again. In the fourth installment, *Resident Evil: Retribution* (2012, Paul W.S. Anderson), not unlike Ripley, she becomes a simulation of her real self as we see a procession of clones awake before being killed and we no longer know if Alice has any connection to reality anymore.

21. Matt Singer, "One Year Later: *Gravity*," *The Dissolve*, October 24, 2014, http://thedissolve.com/features/one-year-later/799-one-year-later-gravity/.

22. Baudrillard, *Simulacra and Simulation*, 82.

23. Wai Chee Dimock, "Books in Space: Christopher Nolan's *Interstellar*," *Los Angeles Review of Books*, December 25, 2014, https://lareviewofbooks.org/essay/books-space-christopher-nolans-interstellar.

24. In this way the film relates strongly to Clive Barker's *Hellraiser* from 1987 and the gravity drive replaces the puzzle box as an opening into another hellish dimension.

25. Kim Newman, *Nightmare Movies: Horror on Screen Since the 1960s* (London: Bloomsbury, 2011), 438.

26. Slavoj Žižek, *Welcome to the Desert of the Real!: Five Essays on September 11 and Related Dates* (London: Verso, 2002), 5–6.

27. *Ibid.*, 19.

BIBLIOGRAPHY

Alien. DVD. Directed by Ridley Scott. 1979. Los Angeles: Twentieth Century Fox, 2010.

Alien: Resurrection. DVD. Directed by Jean-Pierre Jeunet. 1997. Los Angeles: Twentieth Century Fox, 2010.

Alien³. DVD. Directed by David Fincher. 1993. Los Angeles: Twentieth Century Fox, 2010.

Aliens. DVD. Directed by James Cameron. 1986. Los Angeles: Twentieth Century Fox, 2010.

Angel. "Soul Purpose." DVD. January 21, 2004. Los Angeles: Twentieth Century Fox Television, 2011. Episode 10, Season 5.

Baudrillard, Jean. *Simulacra and Simulation.* Translated by Sheila Faria Glasser. Ann Arbor: University of Michigan Press, 1994.

Blackwood, Algernon. "The Transfer." In *The Penguin Book of Vampire Stories*, edited by Alan Ryan, 203–211. London: Penguin Books, 1988.

Cornea, Carol. *Science Fiction Cinema between Fantasy and Reality.* Edinburgh: Edinburgh University Press, 2007.

Depledge, Greta. Introduction to *The Blood of the Vampire*. Brighton: Victorian Secrets Limited, 2010.

Dimock, Wai Chee. "Books in Space: Christopher Nolan's *Interstellar*." *Los Angeles Review of*

Books, December 25, 2014, https://lareviewofbooks.org/essay/books-space-christopher-nolans-interstellar.

Dracula. DVD. Directed by Tod Browning. 1931. Universal City, CA: Universal Pictures, 2002.

Event Horizon. DVD. Directed by Paul W.S. Anderson. 1997. Hollywood: Paramount Pictures, 2006.

Gravity. DVD. Directed by Alfonso Cuarón. 2013. Burbank, CA: Warner Brothers Pictures, 2014.

Hellraiser. DVD. Directed by Clive Barker. 1987. London: Entertainment Films, 2001.

Interstellar. DVD. Directed by Christopher Nolan. 2014. Hollywood: Paramount Pictures, 2015.

The Invasion of the Body Snatchers. DVD. Directed by Don Siegel. 1956. Los Angeles: Allied Artists Pictures Corporation, 2007.

Jones, Jonathan. "Out of This World." *The Guardian*, February 13, 2005, http://www.theguardian.com/books/2005/feb/12/featuresreviews.guardianreview11.

Lem, Stanislaw. "Review: 'Solaris' by Soderburgh." *The Solaris Station*, December 8, 2002, http://english.lem.pl/arround-lem/adaptations/soderbergh/147-the-solaris-station?showall=&start=1.

Lifeforce. DVD. Directed by Tobe Hooper. 1985. Culver City, CA: TriStar Pictures, 2002.

Marryat, Florence. Introduction to *The Blood of the Vampire* by Greta Depledge. Brighton: Victorian Secrets Limited, 2010.

Newman, Kim. *Nightmare Movies: Horror on Screen Since the 1960s*. London: Bloomsbury, 2011.

Planet of the Vampires. DVD. Directed by Mario Bava. 1965. Los Angeles: American International Pictures, 2014.

Prometheus. DVD. Directed by Ridley Scott. 2012. Los Angeles: Twentieth Century Fox, 2012.

The Red Violin. DVD. Directed by François Girard from. 1998. Santa Monica, CA: Lions Gate Entertainment, 2008.

Resident Evil. DVD. Directed by Paul W.S. Anderson. 2002. Culver City, CA: Screen Gems, 2011.

Resident Evil: Afterlife. DVD. Directed by Paul W.S. Anderson. 2010. Culver City, CA: Screen Gems, 2011.

Resident Evil: Apocalypse. DVD. Directed by Alexander Witt. 2004. Culver City, CA: Screen Gems, 2011.

Resident Evil: Extinction. DVD. Directed by Russell Mulcahy. 2007. Culver City, CA: Screen Gems, 2011.

Resident Evil: Retribution. DVD. Directed by Paul W.S. Anderson. 2012. Culver City, CA: Screen Gems, 2013.

Silver, Alain and James Ursini. *The Vampire Film: From Nosferatu to True Blood*. Milwaukie, OR: Limelight Editions, 2011.

Singer, Matt. "One Year Later: Gravity." *The Dissolve*, October 24, 2014, http://thedissolve.com/features/one-year-later/799-one-year-later-gravity.

Solaris. DVD. Directed by Andrei Tarkowsky. 1972. Moscow: Russian Cinema Council, 2000.

Solaris. DVD. Directed by Steven Soderbergh. 2002. Los Angeles: Twentieth Century Fox, 2003.

Stoker, Bram. *Dracula*. 1897. London: Signet Classics, 1996.

2001: A Space Odyssey. DVD. Directed by Stanley Kubrick. 1968. Beverley Hills: MGM, 2006.

Žižek, Slavoj. *The Sublime Object of Ideology*. London: Verso, 1989.

_____. "The Thing from Inner Space (on Tarkowsky)." *Angelaki* 4.3 (1999): 221–231.

_____. *Welcome to the Desert of the Real! Five Essays on September 11 and Related Dates*. London: Verso, 2002.

A "family of displaced figures"

Posthumanism and Jean-Pierre Jeunet's Alien Resurrection (1997)

CHARLES W. REICK

When *Alien Resurrection* (dir. Jean-Pierre Jeunet) opened in 1997, it garnered mixed reviews from both audiences and critics, with most agreeing that it improved on its immediate predecessor, *Alien3* (1992, David Fincher), but failed to reach the success achieved by the original *Alien* (1979, Ridley Scott) and its sequel, *Aliens* (1986, James Cameron). Rotten Tomatoes rated *Alien Resurrection* as 54 percent fresh while *Alien3* garnered a rating of 44 percent, both significantly lower than the 97 percent and 98 percent ratings awarded *Alien* and *Aliens* respectively.[1] Worldwide box office returns mirrored critical response with *Alien Resurrection* earning $160,653,592 compared with the $155,933,485 earned by *Alien3*, $203,630,630 earned by *Alien* and $183,316,455 earned by *Aliens.*[2] Washington Post film critic Stephen Hunter noted that the "movie never scales the heights of pure skull-in-the-vise horror that Ridley Scott's original managed. And it never develops the cool marines-vs.-bugs carnage of James Cameron's second installment."[3] Roger Ebert, writing in the *Chicago Tribune*, was even less generous, calling *Alien Resurrection* "a nine days' wonder, a geek show designed to win a weekend or two at the box office and then fade from memory."[4] *Variety* reviewer Derek Elley, in his review of *Alien Resurrection*, called it "a generally cold, though sometimes wildly imaginative and surprisingly jokey, $70 million scarefest that may prove too mixed a meal to scare up monstrous business,"[5] and Peter Stack of the *San Francisco Chronicle* found in it "an almost determined lack of humanity."[6]

First, it must be acknowledged that *Alien Resurrection* is not a perfect movie. Part action/adventure, part space horror, and part science fiction, the movie is, as Ellery calls it, a "mixed meal," blending genres the way the film's protagonist Ellen Ripley (Sigourney Weaver) is a blending of human and alien genes. With a screenplay by Joss Whedon and under the direction of French filmmaker Jean-Pierre Jeunet, its central action returns to the original's formula where a collection of individuals work to survive and escape from an alien infested spacecraft. As an action/adventure film, *Alien Resurrection* is adequate, though not spectacular, with plenty of military hardware, trick shots, macho wisecracking, and explosions. The space pirates who form the core team trying to escape the aliens are convincingly lethal if a bit worn and clichéd. As a horror film, the "boo" and "gore" factors are sufficient to satisfy most fans, but they have lost some of their effectiveness through the sheer repetition associated with sequels. The most inventive scare comes in the nightmarish sequence where the band of survivors must swim through a fully submerged lower compartment of the ship in order to facilitate their escape. Pursed by swimming aliens, the fleeing group is frustrated by their comparatively slow progress and in spite of her frenzied effort, one crew member falls behind and an alien hand grasps her foot, dragging her to her death. The sheer panic in the movements and facial expressions of the actress completely captures the horror of her situation. The ending terror, on the other hand, is a complete disaster. The so-called "Newborn" offspring of the genetically altered alien queen is a sadly laughable hybrid of human and alien features. With its elongated alien head terminating in a skull-like face with sunken expressive humanoid eyes, the Newborn wobbles about on ungainly legs and sports a sagging beer gut like a cartoon character. Not the stuff nightmares are made of. The science fiction aspects of the film are the weak link that enraged both fans and critics. The plot twist placed on *Alien Resurrection* is that the threatening aliens have been created by the cloning of Ripley who died in *Alien³* to keep her alien-infested body from coming into the hands of the greedy corporation who wants the monster for its profit potential. Now, it is the military who wants the alien and who in "unregulated space" creates from a blood sample a Ripley clone who is still "pregnant" with the gestating alien. Forget the science of this: the film is set in a future 200 years postdating *Alien³* so who knows? The military scientists surgically deliver the alien and leaves Ripley alive out of scientific curiosity. Amazingly, the Ripley clone who has alien gene enhanced aggression, strength, pain tolerance, acidic blood, and lacquered black fingernails, also retains some of the original Ripley's memories: a highly improbable if not utterly impossible scientific feat. Finally, the egg laying alien queen suddenly develops a uterus and spontaneously and independently conceives and delivers the aforementioned human-alien hybrid, defying all the principles of biology and reason.

These weaknesses aside, *Alien Resurrection* should not be dismissed out of hand as a schlocky scarefest set in outer space. *Alien* and *Aliens* have both been thoroughly studied and discussed from the psychoanalytical, political, and feminist perspectives. Unlike its predecessors, *Alien Resurrection* has been largely ignored by the academy. With *Alien,* academics had a wealth of material to mine in terms of Ripley as feminist role model, a warrior woman who is strong and resourceful at a time when such characters were all but absent from the American cinema. *Aliens* provided further fodder for academic discussion as Ripley becomes even more formidable as a warrior, and in a nod to the conservative mood of the film's Reagan era release, she also forms a kind of traditional family, adopting mothering behaviors toward an orphaned child and a heterosexual attraction to one of the colonial marines she accompanies into battle. The dark turn taken by *Alien³* seemed to take everyone by surprise. Now Ripley has transformed from action hero to tragic hero. She has lost her makeshift family when her spacecraft crashes on a prison planet, she has carried an alien stowaway to the planet with her, and worst of all, she has been "impregnated" by said stowaway. She is vulnerable and victimized, androgenized and ostracized by the men who surround her. She is doomed by the alien growing inside her and the only thing she is capable of is destroying the life she carries within her by taking her own life. Ripley's heroic sacrifice, with its Christian overtones, was a logical conclusion to the trajectory of her character, but the film stymied fans and frustrated critics and academics who had so much invested in Ripley as an archetypal superwoman. Fans cried out for a "do-over" and academics sat on their hands. Fox Studios responded with *Alien Resurrection* and again fans, critics and academics were far from impressed. The negative response, I believe, resulted from the film's lack of a clear and consistent artistic vision. Fox executives clearly wanted a film that would capture the box office magic of the first two films in the franchise. The film required the "boos" and "booms" of the franchise formula, but they needed them to be presented in a way that avoided the stale rehashing of the same old ground. To that end, they brought in French visionary director, Jean-Pierre Jeunet who was to bring a fresh approach to the material and that, in fact, he did. What he produced was a science fiction-horror-action film mired in the Continental philosophies of postmodernism and posthumanism.

By the end of the 20th century, postmodern philosophers posited that the human race had entered a new phase of evolution that they referred to as the "posthuman" condition. Postmodernism emerged in the late 1960s and is probably most recognized by its characteristic attacks on the anthropocentric notions and the humanist values of the Enlightenment. According to postmodernists, the Eurocentric standards adopted during the Age of Reason defined what it is to be human and built hierarchical systems and taxonomies of the human/inhuman/non-human which they claim were utilized in legitimizing the denial of universal human rights to people not meeting the prescribed criteria. The postmodernists argue that human identity should not and cannot be reduced to a single standard or norm.[7] The reduction of these standard and norms of "humanness" has resulted in a cultural disorientation and the fragmentation of time-honored patterns of identity formation and cultural norms. It is this fragmentation of identity that *Alien Resurrection* takes as its core subtext. The new Ripley is a blend of human and alien genes and the central question of the film becomes who or what she is. Then, by extension, *Alien Resurrection* invites the viewer to evaluate what it means to be human in the postmodern world where the boundaries separating "us" from "them" are increasingly blurred. To facilitate the evaluation, the film presents the viewer with a continuum of characters, what Donna Haraway has called a "family of displaced figures."[8] By exploring the actions and inter-actions of this representative group which includes a heterosexual white cou-ple, a racially-mixed human, a disabled human with a talent for tools, a near Neanderthal thug, a ruthless scientist and his hapless victim, a mixed species clone, and an android, the viewer is encouraged to ask who belongs to the human "community" and whose future or life is at stake? What are the aspects of the human that are identified and privileged? Who lives and who dies and what kind of future do the survivors face?

In the centuries prior to the appearance of postmodernism (usually referred to as the modern period), to be human meant not only to be a "think-ing animal" sharing a set of common anatomical features, but also to sub-scribe to a code of humanity that characterized a set of culturally defined attributes and behaviors that established the norm. To deviate from the norm would still allow someone to be classified as a human in a general way, but the deviations also promoted a hierarchical system that grouped individuals into categories that marginalized their humanity legitimized exploitation, oppression and genocide. Deviations from the norm, which was emblemized by the white, Christian, European male, assigned to the "others" in society, i.e., women, other races and ethnicities, the disabled, etc., a status less than fully human.[9] Along with the reduced humanity came a devaluation of the very lives of those designated "others." They become, as Giorgio Agamben describes, "homo sacer," the individual who is excluded from the social life of men (the so-called "bios" of the ancient Greeks). Bios, that is, political or social life is assigned value while it oppositional existence, "zoe" reflects ani-mal or bare life that all living things share. Homo sacer differs from zoe in that in Roman law, from which the concept emerges, the individual who once possessed value (bios) is forcibly reduced to zoe, here meaning a thing outside of society, an insider made an outsider.[10] Modernist thinking changed this in that some individuals for reason of gender, race, or others culturally driven criteria can be designated as homo sacer by virtue of their very existence as well as for their behaviors. To be homo sacer is to be essentially without value beyond how they can serve the needs of the insider group. They are commodified in a manner consistent with Marx's underclass and entirely expendable. Once the individual is designated homo sacer they, in the extreme, can be killed without legal repercussion because they are simply valueless animal life.[11] The spacecraft *USM Auriga* is the physical embodiment of this modernist vision of humanity taken to its dystopian extreme. The scientists on board, represented by the smug Dr. Mason Wren (J.E. Freeman), are without regard for human life as they tinker with genetic engineering to clone an alien for its research potential. Wren is the archetypal mad scientist who will stop at nothing to achieve his maniacal goals while hypocritically justifying his actions under the pretense of progress. Explaining to the newly cloned Ripley, he tells her that the alien provides potentials benefits beyond "urban pacification."[12] Given the lethality of the alien, the thought of using it on Earth for the military purpose of urban pacification suggests that the governing powers on Earth mirror the same modernist nightmare reflected by Wren's attitude. Wren adds as a justification, "Think of the alloys … of the vaccines,"[13] suggesting that progress in these areas could somehow justify the horrors that would ensue as a result of unleashing the aliens among human society. As leader of the *Auriga*'s scientific team, the white male Wren is surely behind the plot that has the space pirates kidnapping a group of cryogenically preserved workers on their way to an off-planet work site to serve as hosts for hatching Wren's alien eggs. These workers are casually sacrificed in the name of science to birth a brood of monsters. When the monsters escape and overrun the *Auriga*, Wren's only concerns are personal survival and survival of his horrible creations. Wren, irrespective of his individual narcissistic pathology, is draw as the representative of the modernist endpoint in human evolution: the most inhumane of humans. Purvis (Leland Orser), the single surviving victim of Wren's alien breeding program is homo sacer personified. Abducted by the pirates, his body is sold to the scientists who impregnate him with an alien that will ultimately kill him during its birthing. He is the most "normal" of the humans, but when the group fleeing the aliens encounters him, it is only the non-human android, programed to recognize the intrinsic value of all human life, who argues to take him along. In the end Purvis is doomed and dies, taking the only avenue of resistance open to him, killing Wren as he births the alien that he carries within.

Opposing Wren is his creation, the cloned Ripley, and a group of space pirates who live on the edge of human society and operate from their own code of behavior. The pirate band are a mixed lot of competent and resourceful survivors who have learned to work together in dangerous situations. When threatened by the military, the pirates easily overpower their guards and when the aliens break loose from their cages, the pirates with Ripley's assistance, battle their way through the infested *Auriga* to reach their own ship and escape. Five of the six pirates are human; one is an android passing as a human. They are presented as a group in terms reminiscent of the World War II combat teams memorialized in films like *Bataan* (1943, Tay Garnett), *Objective Burma* (1945, Raoul Walsh), *Hell Is for Heroes* (1962, Don Siegel), and *The Guns of Navarone* (1961, J. Lee Thompson and Alexander Mackendrick). They are a mixed group, not only in terms of race or specialized skills, but also in terms representing different points along the continuum of humanity. They are also a traditional patriarchal family of sorts, led by the white male Elgyn (Michael Wincott) and his white female partner, Sabra Hillard (Kim Flowers). Their "offspring"/crew members include three "sons" with Christie (Gary Dourdan) taking on the role of the competent and stable eldest son, Vriess (Dominique Pinon) as the physically challenged, but resourceful and lovable runt of the family, and Johner (Ron Perlman) as the nearly psychotic, testosterone fueled adolescent of the family who, by his own description, "mostly just hurts people."[14] These five represent various points along the human continuum with Elgyn in the privileged leadership position as would be expected in that he is a white male. Following the formula of the World War II combat team films as described by Janine Basinger,[15] he is killed off first which allows Ripley to emerge as the leader. He dies when he breaks off from the group to investigate an empty corridor. Alien hands reach up through the corridor's walkway and he falls into the subterranean space where he is literally torn in half. His archetypal male curiosity is shown to be a lethal attribute akin to Wren's single-minded scientific curiosity that results in the birth of the aliens he has grown in his lab. Again following the formula of the World War II combat films, the next members of the group to die are minorities.[16] Hillard, Elgyn's, white female partner and the only completely human female on the team, is the ship's pilot and the least developed of the crew. In combat situations, she is competent, but she is drawn as emotionally weak. She is the next to die when she is unable to elude the pursuing aliens in the underwater scene already described. With the early deaths of the heterosexual white couple, the film denounces the privileged status of the modernist traditional family, demonstrating that in the postmodern world being a part of the modernist society norm affords no special value to their lives and no significant advantage to survive. Christie, the team's weapons specialist and its only non-white member, is the third to die. As his name implies, he is the most elevated of the human characters in terms of his ethical rounding. He is intensely loyal to his group and willing to sacrifice on their behalf. When Elgyn is killed, Christie is next to step into the leadership role. He holds the group together and focuses on their escape plan. When Johner wants to kill Wren, it is Christie who overrules him. When Ripley shows up, it is Christie who accepts her as part of the group. When the group must swim through the submerged kitchen to get to their ship, Christie straps the disabled Vriess to his back and carries him. And when he is severely injured, still strapped to Vriess, he cuts himself free from the harness, sacrificing himself to save his crewmate. As humans go, Christie stands as the opposite end of the spectrum from Wren, exhibiting a moral code that is all but absent in the other human characters. Nevertheless, his proficiency and ethical code are not sufficient to allow his survival. That leaves only two humans who survive to the end of the film: Vriess and Johner. Vriess is technologically attuned; in a low-tech way, a cyborg relying on technology, a motorized and weaponized wheelchair, for his mobility and his defense. Johner is almost beastlike, relishing in his brutality and animal instinct for survival. When first seen on film, he is standing on a catwalk above Vriess, hooting and swinging his arms like a great ape. His scarred face reveals the brutality of the life he has led. These two characters survive the film not because they have any special privileged status, but as much a matter of chance as anything else. That said, however, in Donna Haraway's world view of posthumanism, they do perhaps have in their favor that they are the least "normal" humans of their band.[17] Rejecting the metaphysical anthropocentrism of Descartes, Haraway's work assaults the privileging of the human being over other entities, calling for the recognition of the relational nature of the universe instead of the oppositional nature of the Cartesian worldview. To achieve this, she councils that humans cast off the thinking that creates barriers separating not only genders and races, but also those that separate humans from animals and from machines.[18] She calls, as mentioned earlier, for the creation of a "family of displaced figures" that embraces not only all stripes of humanity, but of the animals and machines that also make up the interconnected web of the universal.[19] While such a strategy may be successful in breaking down the boundaries that enable oppression, it also results in problems with individuation. It is this problem that the two central characters of *Alien Resurrection* must confront as they attempt to survive.

Annalee Call (Winona Ryder) is the sixth member of the pirate crew and an android, a totally synthetic being. Passing as human until the middle of the film, Call is an advanced technology that mimics humanity in a number of important ways. She demonstrates several of the key psychological benchmarks that Peter H. Kahn use to define humanity.[20] She is capable of imitating human actions and interactions flawlessly. She acts independently, demonstrates empathy, and is self-aware. She even has dreams. She is the most moral and humane character in the film, a fact underlined by Ripley when it is revealed that Call is an android: "I should have known. No human being is so humane."[21] While passing as human, Call, as the newest member of the pirate band, has not been fully accepted by the crew, but neither is she treated as an outsider. She is simply, in Elgyn's words, "a little girl who wants to play pirate."[22] When the crew discovers her secret, things change. They express contempt for her, particularly given the fact that she was seen as sexually desirable. In spite of the fact that they owe her their lives, she is viewed thereafter as an "It" instead of as a "She." Call, reflecting the modernist thinking that demands strict boundaries, initially agrees with the crew's assessment. She tells Ripley, "At least there's part of you that's human ... I'm disgusting."[23] Only Ripley, who Call has previously denounced as "not human, and ... too much of a risk,"[24] is sympathetic to Call because she sees her own "alien" self-reflected in the android. Call is entirely human is every respect except biology, yet like Pinocchio, she wants to be a "real" girl.

Call is a posthuman creature situated in a postmodern world that is still steeped in modernist thinking. She and her companions still think in terms of Cartesian duality where to be human and to be machine are to different and distinct things. In postmodern thinking, as found in the writings of Haraway and Judith Butler, the human/machine binary is far from distinct. The gap between the non-biologic body and intellectual/emotional kinship with humankind calls into question what it means to be human. This question is linked to the biopolitics of Michel Foucault who describes how biological existence is reflected in political existence, and how the boundaries of what is considered human existence are inextricably linked to structures of political regulation.[25] To pass as human, that is, to be afforded the "I–Thou" designation in the universe of biopolitics, the creature must meet modernist normative expectations. This assumption has been challenged by Judith Butler who argues that the idea of a fixed and stable subject-identity is a result of regulative structures as Foucault describes.[26] She however believes that subject identity has more to do with what the body does than what the body is, that the human categories of identity, specifically gender, sexuality, and other biological attributes should not be considered static forms of being.[27] It is behaviors, Butler continues, that are primarily the result of cultural and social environments that determine identity, not biology.[28] In Call's case, Butler would argue that if she acts like a human and believes she is a human, then she is a human. As her experience with Ripley evolves, the barrier between Call's biology and her identity becomes less important and by the closing scene of the film she has come to terms and is at peace with her hybrid identity.

Ripley, the clone, the central figure of the family of displaced figures: she/it is the most complex and fragmented of characters. While Call is fully robotic with the heart of a human, and the others are fully human even if they act otherwise, Ripley is something completely different, utterly unique: part human, part alien, reborn literally from the ashes of the all too human Ripley who sacrificed herself to protect mankind from the alien species who had plagued her existence for three films. Who or what Ripley is forms the central question of the films ongoing narrative. It is a question repeated over and over. The scientists see Ripley as an interesting subject who inexplicably retains Ripley's core personality and memories. The military overseer views her as the "meat byproduct" of the primary goal of resurrecting the Alien Queen. When Ripley first meets the pirate crew and soundly thrashes the brutish Johner, Christie, after ineffectively smashing her in the face with a barbell, incredulously asks, "What are you?" She offers no answer. Later she is confronted by Call who asks the same question. This time Ripley replies, "Ripley, Ellen, Lieutenant first class, number 36706," to which Call responds, "Ellen Ripley died two hundred years ago." Looking confused, Ripley asks, "If I'm not her, what am I?" And still later after Ripley reveals to Purvis his fate, he asks, "Who are you?" to which she replies, "I'm the monster's mother."[29]

Ripley's journey of self-discovery is the intellectual core of what is otherwise a relatively uninspired horror/survival narrative set in space. It is a journey that began with the first film where Ripley first encountered the alien. Barbara Creed in her analysis of *Alien* posits that the alien is a representative of the monstrous feminine, the castrating/phallic mother of Freudian psychology. The alien is opposed by Ripley who, Creed suggests, signifies the "acceptable" form and shape of woman within the patriarchal ideology.[30] The conflict between the two then becomes a battle across the border of the horrible and the acceptable form of the feminine and Ripley's victory is viewed as a victory of the patriarchal order. *Aliens* follows this narrative with an even more explicit association of maternity and the monstrous feminine where Ripley battles the Alien Queen over a child. Again Ripley's victory over the monstrous feminine reinforces the proper role of the female as protector of the young. By the third film, *Alien³*, Ripley has been "impregnated" with an alien queen and the conflict now expands beyond the fate of one child to a battle for all mankind. Ripley is no longer just the patriarchal ideal woman, but instead, is androgenized to represent generic mankind standing against the destructive alien other. Ultimately, she altruistically elects to give up her life to assure the alien's threat to mankind is eliminated. In each successive film, Ripley draws closer and closer to the alien until, by *Alien Resurrection*, she has become part alien herself. Her battles in the past have been along the border separating her from the alien other; in *Alien Resurrection* the border has been erased, the battle is internalized. She has become figuratively Haraway's cyborg, a transhuman with the potential to go beyond the binaries of male/female, human/animal, and even good and evil. Her unique inception results in cultural disorientation and the fragmentation of time-honored patterns of identity formation and cultural norms. She is tasked with trying to integrate her human and alien sides, a process of accepting and reintegrating her "shadow" that is an essential part of becoming psychologically whole. In the previous films, Ripley emphatically rejects her alien shadow by literally expelling it, but it successively returns, stronger and more intimately connected to her than before. Gallardo C. Ximena writes, "*Alien Resurrection* refuses to expel the abject [the shadow], unlike the previous three films" noting that when "the abject cannot be destroyed ... it must be accepted."[31] Ximena's reading supports Haraway's figuration that the cyborg, hybrid, transhuman's goal is to break down barriers between the human and nonhuman, not choose between them.

My reading of the film is that Ripley's journey is precisely about choosing and that by the films end, she has unequivocally come down on the side of humanity. It is as if the filmmakers, having opened the door to explore the postmodern possibilities of hybridization, slams it closed because they lacked the vision or courage to explore it in depth. Ripley initially wants off the *Auriga*, not because the aliens are an immediate threat to her physically (they don't attack her because they perceiver her as one of them), but fleeing the ship represents freedom. She no longer views herself as the protector of mankind; that mantle has passed to Call. Instead, like the rest of the human band, she is principally concerned with her own survival. It is only when she forms a bond with Call that she shows interest in the welfare of others. In the end, Ripley is forced to choose between the posthuman Call and the alien Newborn who rejects and kills its "birthmother," the Alien Queen, in favor of Ripley. The grotesque Newborn responds to Ripley's command that it release the trapped Call, then embraces its adopted mother, mewing and licking like a newborn kitten. Recognizing that the unchecked destructive power of the Newborn is a threat to Call, the other object of Ripley's affection, Ripley emphatically "chooses her ethico-political family, the remnants of 'the human' she remembers from her past self" and tearfully destroys her alien/hybrid "grandchild" in the most horrific manner possible, a post-birth abortion where the vacuum of space rips the Newborn to pieces.[32] In this action, Ripley once again expels her shadow as she has done in all the previous films. Instead of looking forward to a new postmodern world, *Alien Resurrection* retreats to the security of the old comfortable binary systems of the patriarchal and modernist worldview.

The beautiful sunset that frames the final scene can be read as hopeful or ironic. Are the survivors riding off into the sunset, victorious over the alien other, or does the scene foreshadow the sunset of traditional humankind? The survivors are all fragmented characters: Johner, the animalistic human, Vriess, the low-tech cyborg; Call, the human-like android; and Ripley, the alien/human hybrid. Does this surviving "family of displaced figures" represent a new vision for humankind by signaling "a new era in which we won't define ourselves against the monster but as one more type of monster," as Ximena suggests?[33] There is little to suggest Johner and Vriess have changed in anyway. For them the monster is still externalized. As for Call and Ripley, they both come to accept their "monstrous" inner aspects and as a result they are able to accept the monstrous in others thereby becoming more psychologically complete. In the final analysis, I would suggest that the film leaves the audience at the border between the modernist and postmodernist worldviews. While the victory over the aliens theoretically restores the modernist order with its "them" versus "us" binary, the survival of the two main characters, one transhuman, the other posthuman, suggests the possibility of a new kind of future where boundaries between entities, human and nonhuman, will continue to break down and the potential for a new humanity. In response to Call's question, "What should we do now?" Ripley responds, "I don't know. I'm a stranger here myself."[34] In the world of *Alien Resurrection,* so are we all.

NOTES

1. "Alien Resurrection (1997)," *Rotten Tomatoes,* last updated 12/3/2015, http://www.rottentomatoes.com/m/Alien_resurrection/?search=alien%20resu.

2. "Box Office History for Alien Movies," *The Numbers,* last updated 9/1/2015, http://www.the-numbers.com/movies/franchise/Alien#tab=summary.

3. Stephen Hunter, "*Alien Resurrection*: Birth of the Ooze," *Washington Post,* November 29, 1997, http://www.washingtonpost.com/wp-srv/style/longterm/movies/videos/alienresurrectionhunter.htm.

4. Roger Ebert, "*Alien Resurrection,*" *Chicago Sun Times,* November 26, 1997, http://www.rogerebert.com/reviews/alien-resurrection-1997.

5. Derick Elley, "Review: '*Alien Resurrection,*'" *Variety,* December 4, 1997, http://variety.com/1997/film/reviews/alien-resurrection-111732354/.

6. Peter Stack, "'*Alien*' All Guts, No Glory / Sequel Looks Great, if Gory, but Doesn't Have Much Brains," *San Francisco Chronicle,* November 26, 1997, http://www.sfgate.com/movies/article/Alien-All-Guts-No-Glory-Sequel-looks-great-2793420.php.

7. Manuela Rossini, "Science/Fiction: Imagineering Posthuman Bodies," presented at Gender and Power in the New Europe, 5th European Feminist Research Conference, August 20–24, 2003, Lund University, Sweden, 3–5, https://www.researchgate.net/publication/250814946_Science_Fiction_Imagineering_Posthuman_Bodies.

8. Sherryl Vint, "'A Family of Displaced Figures': An Overview of Donna Haraway," *Fiction Film and Television* 1, no. 2 (2008): 289–301.

9. Rossini, "Science/Fiction," 4.

10. Giorgio Agamben, *Homo Sacer: Sovereign Power and Bare Life,* translated by Daniel Heller-Roazen (Stanford: Stanford University Press, 1998), 11–13.

11. Agamben, *Homo Sacer,* 12.

12. *Alien Resurrection,* DVD, directed by Jean-Pierre Jeunet (2008; Los Angeles: Twentieth Century Fox Home Entertainment).

13. *Alien Resurrection.*

14. *Alien Resurrection.*

15. Jeanine Basinger, *The World War II Combat Film: Anatomy of a Genre* (Middletown, CT: Wesleyan University Press, 2003), 74.

16. *Ibid.,* 75.

17. Donna Haraway, "A Cyborg Manifesto: Science, Technology, and Socialist-Feminism in the Late Twentieth Century," in *Simians, Cyborgs and Women: The Reinvention of Nature,* ed. Donna Haraway (New York: Routledge, 1991), 158, 172–174.

18. *Ibid.,* 172–174.

19. *Ibid.,* 172–174.

20. Peter H. Kahn, Jr., et al., "What Is a Human? Toward Psychological Benchmarks in the Field of Human-Robot Interaction," *Interaction Studies* 8.3 (2007): 363.

21. *Alien Resurrection.*

22. *Ibid.*
23. *Ibid.*
24. *Ibid.*
25. Michel Foucault, *Birth of Biopolitics: Lectures at the College de France, 1978–1979*, translated by Graham Burchell (New York: Picador, 2010).
26. Judith Butler, "Performative Acts and Gender Constitution: An Essay in Phenomenology and Feminist Theory," *Theatre Journal* (1988): 525–528.
27. *Ibid.*
28. *Ibid.*
29. *Alien Resurrection.*
30. Barbara Creed, *The Monstrous-Feminine: Film, Feminism, Psychoanalysis* (London: Routledge, 1993), 17–18.
31. Gallardo C. Ximena, "'Who Are You?' Alien/Woman as Posthuman Subject in *Alien Resurrection*," in *Alien Woman: The Making of Lt. Ellen Ripley*, ed. Jason Smith and Gallardo C. Ximena (New York: Bloomsbury Academic), 35, http://reconstruction.eserver.org/Issues/043/gallardoc.htm
32. Jackie Stacey, "She Is Not Herself: The Deviant Relations in Alien Resurrection," *Screen* 44, no. 3 (2003): 260.
33. Ximena, 38.
34. *Alien Resurrection.*

BIBLIOGRAPHY

Agamben, Giorgio. *Homo Sacer: Sovereign Power and Bare Life*. Translated by Daniel Heller-Roazen. Stanford: Stanford University Press, 1998.
_____. *State of Exception*. Translated by Kevin Attell. Chicago: University of Chicago Press, 2005.
Alien Resurrection. DVD. Directed by Jean-Pierre Jeunet. 1997. Los Angeles: Twentieth Century Fox Home Entertainment. 2008.
Basinger, Jeanine. *The World War II Combat Film: Anatomy of a Genre*. Middletown, CT: Wesleyan University Press, 2003.
Bendle, Mervyn F. "Teleportation, Cyborgs and the Posthuman Ideology." *Social Semiotics* 12.1 (2002): 45–62.
Butler, Judith, "Performative Acts and Gender Constitution: An Essay in Phenomenology and Feminist Theory." *Theatre Journal* (1988): 519–531.
Christiansen, Steen Ledet. "Terminal Films." *Journal of the Fantastic in the Arts* 25.2–3 (2014): 264–278.
Cobbs, John L. "Alien as an Abortion Parable." *Literature/Film Quarterly* 18.3 (1990): 198–201.
Creed, Barbara. *The Monstrous-Feminine: Film, Feminism, Psychoanalysis*. London: Routledge, 1993.
Ebert, Roger. "*Alien Resurrection.*" *Chicago Sun Times*, November 26, 1997. http://www.rogerebert.com/reviews/alien-resurrection-1997.
Elley, Derick, "Review: '*Alien Resurrection.*'" *Variety*, December 4, 1997. http://variety.com/1997/film/reviews/alien-resurrection-111732354/.
Foucault, Michel. *Birth of Biopolitics: Lectures at the College de France, 1978–1979*. Translated by Graham Burchell. New York: Picador, 2010.
_____. *Society Must Be Defended: Lectures at the College de France, 1975–1976*. Translated by David Macey. New York: Picador, 2003.
Gibson, Em Castaspella. *Artificial Identity: Representations of Robots and Cyborgs in Contemporary Anglo-American Science Fiction Films*. Diss., University of Central Lancashire, 2012. http://clok.uclan.ac.uk/6651/1/Gibson%20Em%20Final%20e-Thesis%20%28Master%20Copy%29.pdf.
Haraway, Donna. "A Cyborg Manifesto: Science, Technology, and Socialist-Feminism in the Late Twentieth Century." In *Simians, Cyborgs and Women: The Reinvention of Nature*, edited by Donna Haraway, 149–182. New York: Routledge, 1991.

Hopkins, Patrick D. "A Moral Vision for Transhumanism." *Journal of Evolution and Technology* 19.1 (2008): 3–7.

Hunter, Stephen. "*Alien Resurrection*: Birth of the Ooze." *Washington Post,* November 29, 1997. http://www.washingtonpost.com/wp-srv/style/longterm/movies/videos/alienresurrectionhunter.htm.

Kahn, Peter H., Jr. Hiroshi Ishiguro, Batya Friedman, Takayuki Kanda, Nathan G. Freier, Rachel L. Severson, and Jessica Miller. "What Is a Human? Toward Psychological Benchmarks in the Field of Human–Robot Interaction." *Interaction Studies* 8.3 (2007): 363–390.

Kimball, A. Samuel. "Conceptions and Contraceptions of the Future: *Terminator 2, The Matrix,* and *Alien Resurrection*." *Camera Obscura* 17.2 (2002): 69–108.

Kristeva, Julia. *Powers of Horror: An Essay on Abjection.* Translated by Leon S. Roudiez. New York: Columbia University Press, 1982.

The Numbers. "Box Office History for Alien Movies." Last updated 9/1/2015. http://www.thenumbers.com/movies/franchise/Alien#tab=summary.

Ortigo, Kile M. "'I'm a Stranger Here Myself': Forced Individuation in Alien Resurrection." *Journal of Religion and Popular Culture* 17 (2007).

Rossini, Manuela. "Science/Fiction: Imagineering Posthuman Bodies," presented at Gender and Power in the New Europe, 5th European Feminist Research Conference, August 20–24, 2003, Lund University, Sweden. https://www.researchgate.net/publication/250814946_Science_Fiction_Imagineering_Posthuman_Bodies.

Rotten Tomatoes. "*Alien Resurrection* (1997)." Last updated 12/03/2015. http://www.rottentomatoes.com/m/alien_resurrection/?search=alien%20resu.

Stacey, Jackie. "She Is Not Herself: The Deviant Relations of *Alien Resurrection*." *Screen* 44.3 (2003): 251–276.

Stack, Peter, "'*Alien*' All Guts, No Glory / Sequel Looks Great, if Gory, but Doesn't Have Much Brains." *San Francisco Chronicle,* November 26, 1997. http://www.sfgate.com/movies/article/Alien-All-Guts-No-Glory-Sequel-looks-great-2793420.php.

Vint, Sherryl. "Introduction: Science Fiction and Biopolitics." *Science Fiction Film and Television* 4.2 (2011): 161–172.

_____. "'A family of displaced figures': An overview of Donna Haraway." *Science Fiction Film and Television* 1.2 (2008): 289–301.

Ximena, Gallardo C. "'Who Are You?' Alien/Woman as Posthuman Subject in Alien Resurrection." In *Alien Woman: The Making of Lt. Ellen Ripley,* edited by Jason Smith and Gallardo C. Ximena. New York: Bloomsbury Academic, 2004.

Galaxies of Terror
in a Knock-Off Universe

*Atavism and the Rip-Off Body Horror
of "Aliensploitation" Films*

JASON DAVIS

"Earth women shall give birth to the Inseminoid."[1] Echoing a sci-fi pulp cliché as its name checks a famous 1980s British "video nasty," this dubbed-over proclamation by the Star Wars prequel character Senator Palpatine makes for a surprising discovery in Damon Packard's *The Untitled Star Wars Mockumentary* (2003). For Packard, a Los Angeles-based underground film-maker, this splicing of the infamous alien birth scene from *Inseminoid* (1981, Norman J. Warren) features as part of a reimagineered trailer for the *Star Wars* prequel *Attack of the Clones* (2002, George Lucas) that intercuts scenes from the digitally-created Lucasfilm prequel with snippets from low-budget films derivative of *Star Wars* (1977, George Lucas) and *Alien* (1979, Ridley Scott) such as the Roger Corman produced *Battle Beyond the Stars* (1980, Jimmy T. Murakami) and *Galaxy of Terror* (1981, Bruce D. Clark). Forward ten years to Red Letter Media, the Milwaukee-based video production company behind the phenomenally popular YouTube accessed video essay reviews of the *Star Wars* prequels, and *XTRO* (1983, Harry Bromley Davenport), another notorious, low-budget British space horror film long regarded as an *Alien* knock-off, is showcased in their online review-based web series "Best of the Worst."[2] Editing together reaction shots that include wide-eyed amazement, eye-covering horror and stunned disbelief by video production savvy 30-something cinephiles at *XTRO*'s infamous birth of a full grown man from a woman, The Red Letter Media team proceed to unanimously praise the film for its inventive B-movie storytelling and practical effects.

Taken together, these inventive reuses of two exploitation films are rare instances of post–*Alien* 1980s space horror cinema given a post-millennial afterlife beyond VHS cult film connoisseurship[3] and clickbait listicles of *Alien* rip-offs. *Inseminoid* and *XTRO* belong to a clutch of low-budget space horror films from different countries, but have all been associated, either opportunistically or wrongly, with *Alien* as rip-offs or knock-offs aimed at grabbing a share of what could be gained commercially from theatrical and home video release in the wake of the box office success of *Alien*. Along with the Italian films *Alien 2 sulla Terra* (1980, Ciro Ippolito) and *Contamination* (1980, Luigi Cozzi), these *Alien*sploitation films include two Roger Corman produced U.S. films *Galaxy of Terror* and *Forbidden World* (1982, Allan Holzman) as well as *Titan Find* (1985, William Malone). All of them have had and continue to have intriguing "social lives" as exploitation films. Their individual "cultural biographies" extend from pre–Internet circulation as theatrical and VHS versions, with cultivation of their awareness through genre media ranging from American and British prozines such as *Fangoria* and *Starburst* to cult horror fanzines. And their post-millennial re-discovery/re-commercialization has involved more aftermarket curation with feature-laden DVD releases and appraisal as artifacts of 1980s horror video culture,[4] with *Contamination*, *Inseminoid* and *XTRO* as "bit players" in British media history involving moral panics (of the three only *Contamination* was officially included on the Director of Public Prosecution's infamous list of "video nasties" for public prosecution under the United Kingdom's 1959 Obscene Publications Act).[5] Online fan community devotion to these films extends from YouTube uploads showcasing DVD, VHS and soundtrack collection acquisitions to DVD re-release reviews, to B-movie grist for comedy web series mills such as Brad Jones' *The Cinema Snob*, while offline fan communities continue the revival of interest in the films with horror convention appearances by *Alien*sploitation actors and filmmakers reinvigorating their nostalgic cult appeal as B-Movie vixens and 80s scream queens for a second generation of fans. Yet, what is missing from the reinvention of the economics of attention for horror films from more than 30 years ago is an examination of what *Alien*sploitation films can reveal about the original *Alien*.

To even suggest that Packard's reworking of *Alien*sploitation films as well as Red Letter Media's cinephilic rediscovery and celebration of *XTRO* offers up alternative takes on B-movie appreciation as a counter-current to the now decades-long accumulation of film culture around a major studio, summer block-buster and its franchised expanded universe is to already belabor the obvious; that *Alien*sploitation films have had an afterlife that is far exceeded by the intergenerational recognition and fan community exaltation *Alien* has enjoyed. After all, *Alien*sploitation films are rarely the subject of fan films, mashups, movie podcast commentaries, video essays, song vids, fan edits, femslash or slash vids. But what Packard's inclusion of *Inseminoid*, intercut with other low-budget early 1980s films produced to exploit the success of *Alien* and *Star Wars*, points to not only Roger Corman's fabled acknowledgment of major studio, big-budget exploitation competition that the block-busters *Jaws* (1975, Steven Spielberg), *Star Wars*, and *Alien* represented,[6] but also back to the U.S. media responses to *Alien*'s initial impact on the resurgence of horror as a return to B-movie influences such as *Harper's Magazine*,[7] *Rolling Stone*[8] and *Newsweek*'s "Hollywood's Scary Summer"[9] cover issue story of *Alien*. And yet, between Stephen King's extolling of *Alien* in a 1979 issue of *Rolling Stone* as "the first movie to make a real cinematic success of the ideas and themes worked out by H.P. Lovecraft,"[10] a literary link King would go on to reaffirm *Alien* to in *Stephen King's Danse Macabre* as "Lovecraft in outerspace"[11] ("mankind finally [goes] to the Elder Gods rather than they coming to us"[12]); and Philip K. Dick's notorious dismissal of *Alien* in a 1981 issue of *SelecTV Guide* as a film with "nothing new to bring us in the way of concepts that awaken the mind rather than the senses,"[13] critically rethinking *Alien*'s origins in exploitation cinema was already becoming less and less relevant for genre mavens.

While the term *"Alien*sploitation" reworks *"Jaws*ploitation,"[14] and so seeks to establish the obvious commercial intent of a succession of low-budget exploitation films pitched, produced and marketed in the wake of the box-office success of a big studio "original," it has another purpose. The word *Alien*sploitation also teasingly links back to *Alien*'s own cinematic pedigree as exploitation as much as it hints at the prospect of *Alien* imitators relating to the original in revealing ways. If *2001: A Space Odyssey* (1968, Stanley Kubrick) inaugurated a decade of science fiction filmmaking as both high art and cult film, *Alien* ended the decade as "the *Texas Chainsaw Massacre* of science fiction movies."[15] Approaching *Alien* through the instructive lens of *Jaws*ploitation studies is therefore an exemplary critical practice, and not only in the obvious way of pointing out how *Alien* overlaps with *Jaws* as exploitation fare in the way both employ an implacable rogue monster bent on killing humans as restaging the monster trope of 1950s science fiction B-movies. Rather, the purpose of revisiting the exploitational twists of *Alien*-inspired films is to register what these films are revealing, initially in indistinct ways, as problematical aspects, even ideological implications, of *Alien*'s storyline as space horror.

Although the obvious expectation is that by probing their repeated, low-budgeted mimicry of signature, even iconic features of *Alien, Alien*sploitation films would, through more scrutiny, unbind "perverse subtexts repressed in the original."[16] But the far less salacious, more understated, and by comparison, more rarefied subject is how such films can tease out elements of atavism in the original *Alien*. The recurring sexualization of objects and actions, yet conspicuous absence of human sexuality in the film, is of course, an obvious subject whose academic intelligibility has been mined for decades. From the phallic-headed mature xenomorph and its dripping teeth-rimed mouth hiding a secondary penile mouth, to Dan O'Bannon's oft-quoted horrification of male viewers with the act of "homosexual oral rape,"[17] to the attempted oral rape of a woman with a rolled-up porn magazine, to the "impregnation" and death-inducing "birth" of an alien embryo, to an alien craft and its interiors invoking anatomical meldings of desiccated human sexual organs as advanced yet arcane technology; all of which have been as generative of academic promotions and film book publisher sales of as they have been proliferated through the late-night grind of undergraduate essays.[18] Yet there is another aspect of the film's storyline that is often left unexamined: why does *Alien*'s science fiction al premise of an encounter with alien life essentially result in the regression of the co-dependent human crew into outright individual survivalism against becoming food or host for the reproduction of the lethal life form? Or to repose the question through more the film's storyline: how is it that contact with otherworldly life has the hierarchically organized crew of the *Nostromo* pass from reliance on control though abstract computer-mediated environments as technological barriers of protection from interstellar gulfs and hostile exteriors and devolves to an eerily primal dependence on fire, spear-like electric prods and a net to survive against being hunted by what is essentially a genetic human hybrid adapted to survive off of the species it is oblivious to having mutated from. These questions not only get at the thematic element of atavism in *Alien*, but also highlight how it prefigures films produced decades after it, such as *Ghosts of Mars* (2001, John Carpenter) and *Pandorum* (2009, Christian Alvart), in which atavism is cast as the terminal point for space horror narratives: the devolvement or devolution of humans/astronauts from organized teams of prosthetic selves technologically cocooned and conditioned to routinely operate in inhuman environments to survival-driven individuals beset by "colony collapse" from madness, savagery and barbarism, isolated by and reduced to biologies vulnerable to primal/alien "repurposing" as food or hosts for life cycles/reproduction.

The thematic exploration of atavism within forms of modernity haunted by regression and recapitulation to earlier, primitive, even pre-human, forms of survivalism is readily identifiable in science fiction films and literature. With *2001: A Space Odyssey* inaugurating a decade of adult-oriented genre filmmaking that ended with *Alien*, Irish filmmaker John Boorman marks a cinematic midpoint between those landmarks of science fiction and atavism with his films *Zardoz* (1974, John Boorman) and *Exorcist II: The Heretic* (1977, John Boorman and Rospo Pallenberg), the later mixing technology, occultism and demonic possession with shamanism and New Age religion,[19] while Ken Russell's *Altered States* (1980) closed out the 1970s leaving behind the final ebb of countercultural efforts at consciousness transformation[20] with sensory isolation tanks and psychotropic drugs aiming to produce human regression through devolution.[21] Likewise, authors H.G. Wells and J.G. Ballard have in their novels repeatedly depicted not only human estrangement from the civilizational impulses celebrated in each author's respective century's scientific and technological development, but also modern life succumbing to social and behavioral degeneration and violence. Although none of the *Alien*sploitation films covered here are Wellsian by any stretch, one of Ballard's famous signature motifs of atavism, the dead astronaut,[22] is repeatedly encountered in the films under discussion. Ballard's exploration of the demise of the space program from the fictional vantage point of its entropic passage into ruin, decrepitude and decaying orbits, engages not only with the failure of the frontier-defying Space Age to be carried over into the collective transcendence of the imagination, but also genre-defying refusal of science fictional "enthralment to a future of unlimited possibilities."[23] *Alien*sploitation films feature recurring elements of this fading of the space program. With their depiction of space flight across interstellar gulfs impacting on astronauts with as much discomfort as the periodic buffeting experienced by a passenger in an economy long haul flight, they reflect in miniature the routinization that the Apollo missions had become for a lackadaisical American public[24]; too routine to warrant even live coverage by broadcast networks in the case of the Challenger Shuttle disaster of 1986,[25] the year after the release of *Titan Find*.

Rather than start this survey of *Alien*sploitation films as they were released consecutively after the original *Alien*—from ground zero as it were with the suitably titled *Alien 2*—the films will be explored in reverse chronological order of release, performing a count-down film-by-film back to 1979. This has been done for a number of reasons. Firstly, opening with *Titan Find* ahead of the other films that would otherwise precede it chronologically, is to place it in close proximity to *Alien* from the outset, as if the space-time differences separating the two films had been shortcut by a wormhole from the moon of one ringed planet, Titan, to the moon of another ringed planet, LV-426. This shortcut quickly introduces key features of the influences of earlier science fiction on the storyline of *Alien* that were originally disavowed and at the same establish that *Alien*sploitation films have "borrowed" from a broad range science fiction films beyond one summer blockbuster. In some respects, the paragraphs that follow could be read as drafts for narration in preparation for an as yet unmade video essay that reuses the opening title sequence of *Alien*, only that the disjointed version of Helvetica Black used to spell out letters broken into pieces will spell A T A V I S M.

Titan Find's most apparent contrast with *Alien* is how, more than any other *Alien*sploitation film, it elicits awareness of its own reuse of the same science fiction films *Alien* has "borrowed" from, but which the filmmakers themselves disavowed conscious influence of.[26] *Titan Find* therefore re-screens, like a B-movie imaginarium, the film sources that *Alien* was associated and identified with by fans and critics alike when it was first released.[27] With a storyline centered around an "archaeological discovery of alien origin" on Titan to which a corporate-funded research team are dispatched to investigate and reclaim after the first interplanetary geological expedition ends violently, *Titan Find* has almost all of its crew of four women and three men murdered by alien life in ways that are taken from genre films of the 1950s, 60s and 70s.[28] After learning from the lone survivor of a German expedition to the archaeological site that Titan harbors an alien laboratory dedicated to the containment and suspended animation of alien organisms over 200,000 years old (*Forbidden Planet* [1956, Fred M. Wilcox]), the crew are killed one by one by either invasive, brain-hacking alien parasites (*It Conquered the World* [1956, Roger Corman]) that reanimate the recently dead (*Planet of the Vampires* [1965, Mario Bava]) or killed by a humanoid creature (*It! The Terror From Beyond Space* [1958, Edward L. Cahn]) stalking them through emergency-lit corridors (*Alien*). Likewise, the coordinated efforts of the surviving crew to destroy the unrelenting humanoid alien involve readily recognizable efforts from iconic films including massive electrocution (*The Thing from Another World* [1951, Howard Hawks and Christian Nyby]) and the detonation of a monster-obliterating explosion from a well-placed weapon shot (*Jaws*). When a character in *Titan Find* verbally recollects how an alien was dispatched from an unnamed film, Howard Hawk's *The Thing* ends up forming one plan for the surviving crew's counter-attack. Ironically enough, this film reference anticipates humorous online responses to the fictional world of *Prometheus* (2012, Ridley Scott) in which David, a *Lawrence of Arabia*-quoting android, has awareness of real world films as a knowledge base which doesn't extend to *Alien*, much less the exploitation films it "ripped-off."

But it is also the recurring imagery of "dead astronauts" in *Titan Find* as a readable motif of atavism which is given an uncanny resonance through the film's world-building counterpoint to the "organizational gothic"[29] of *Alien*'s corporate future. *Titan Find*'s future setting has U.S. and West German multinational companies "locked in a fierce race for commercial supremacy"[30] involving inter-planetary "competition for new materials and advanced manufacturing technique."[31] With the U.S. expeditionary team discovering the corpses of the West German astronauts strung up for future consumption as if in a larder while the freshly dead are repurposed through mind-control, the frontier expanding conquest driving technological developments is given a decidedly unfuturistic darkside. *Titan Find*'s nationally aligned rivalry obviously reflects Cold War polarities with the NATO aligned former client state of the U.S. propelled into the future as a frontier-pushing competitor, a science fiction al conceit that nonetheless marks a departure from villainizing Japan as a techno-orientalist projection of collective anxiety over Japanese industrial and corporate ascendency in the 1980s.[32] But even this shorthand addition of a nationally-defined challenger brings out the limitations of the nameless and nationless "pervasive fog of organizational paranoia"[33] that "the Company" embodies in *Alien* as a "representational critique" of corporate power. Gothic representations as forms of anti-corporate protest, have the power "to denaturalise at one moment, but [we] must also remember that it can itself naturalise as it becomes cliché, a metaphor that first shocks and then becomes an excuse for not thinking."[34]

For an *Alien*sploitation film whose last academic parsing as an alien invasion film was in 1999,[35] *XTRO* has easily had the strangest afterlife on either side of the end of the Second Christian Millennium. In February of 2014, an altered image taken of the alien from *XTRO* was revealed by a New Mexico-based CBS-affiliated KQRE 13 News as the source for a black-and-white image of a four-legged, human-like creature claiming to be taken near an Apache reservation and shared on Facebook as proof of a skinwalker from Native American legends.[36] With the release of the British-American film *Under the Skin* (2013, Jonathan Glazer), online reactions and fan reviews invoked *XTRO*, an association that can be stretched further when comparing the depiction of the aliens as quadrupeds in the novel the film is adapted from.[37] In the 2005 short documentary on the *XTRO* franchise *Xtro Xposed*,[38] director of the *XTRO* in-name-only sequels Harry Bromley Davenport recounts how video sales and rentals of the original *XTRO* skyrocketed after British evening news had visually singled out a video copy of it among the horror video collection belonging to a captured multiple murderer. During the video nasty panic in the UK, *XTRO* was targeted by a media-led call for police confiscation from video stores in Birmingham, Manchester and Newcastle, but were returned to their owners by police after the British Board of Film Classification had approved the film for theatrical release in 1982 without censorship.[39] By early 1983, an episode of the television series *At the Movies* had U.S. film critics Gene Siskel and Roger Ebert excoriating *XTRO* as a "mean spirited, ugly thriller" as well as "nihilistic," "garbage" and "obscene."[40] Released in the UK in 1982 *XTRO* would be the last British horror film to be given a theatrical release in Britain for almost half a decade until *Hellraiser* (1987, Clive Barker).[41] Wind back further to late 1982, and among the U.S. and British prozine promotion of *XTRO* which included cover shots for *Fangoria* and *Starburst* was a curious preview of it in the *Twilight Zone Magazine* which compared *XTRO* to *E.T. the Extra-Terrestrial* (1982, Steven Spielberg) and *I Married a Monster from Outer Space* (1958, Gene Fowler, Jr.), calling it "*E.T.*'s diabolical twin."[42]

Pairing *XTRO* with *E.T.* as "*E.T.*'s diabolical twin" not only gives the earthbound body horror film a tagline that surpasses what was originally used ("Bearing black magic from deep space") in trailers to prepare audiences for the film's non sequiturs of a human-sized doll, dwarf clown and producer-mandated panther, it also enables for more intriguing differentiation of the film from *Alien*. *XTRO*'s storyline of a father (Sam) abducted and transformed by aliens but who returns to Earth in human form to begin the invasion front by reuniting with a spouse who has since partnered with another man and a son unadjusted to his biological father's absence readily invokes aspects of the invasion-from-within the heterosexual unit trope that stretches back to *I Married a Monster from Outer Space*. Similarly, *XTRO* and *E.T.* both "feature absent fathers and boys who find surrogates in extraterrestrials,"[43] with the father-son relationship in *XTRO* privileged over the mother as the familial, even psycho-sexual device for invasion that feeds and empowers pre-adolescent male aggression. Not only does Sam's (Philip Sayer) oral seeding of alien powers in Tony (Simon Nash) via his son's exposed shoulder become coded in an incestuous way with Sam promising Tony to secrecy, but Tony himself impregnates his family's *au pair* the same way through her navel, transforming her into a cocooned oviparous delivery organism. As with the notorious scene of a woman giving birth to Sam in human adult form, women's bodies in *XTRO* become biological conduits for alien regeneration. This has marked the film for criticism as reaffirming conservative, even patri-archal views of women and reproduction involving a regressive turning away from *Alien*'s outright disturbance of gender distinctions through male impregnation and birth.[44] And yet, for all of the identifying of the metaphor-ical rape of Kane (Sir John Hurt) and the metaphorical birth of "Kane's son" as disruptive of gender distinctions, this bodily invasion and intrusion remain symbolically arrested as it doesn't go beyond death-inducing "birth," leaving entirely unaddressed what "persists like a foreign body"[45] within any futuristic formulation, utopian or otherwise, namely the family. *Alien*'s parasitoidal reproduction of one species via another over any other sentient interaction between them other than throat jamming speechlessness could also be seen as the invasive equivalent for the late 1970s of the metaphysical toppling of human sovereignty that *Planet of the Apes* (1968, Franklin J. Schaffner) closed out the 1960s. But emphasizing male impregnation sidelines the obviousness of *Alien*'s familyless future, while *XTRO* through its negation of anything pro-gressive, at least reflects on a future use for the continuation of the conser-vative family unit as exploitable relationships for the intergenerational perpetuation of an invasive takeover.

Forbidden World, producer Roger Corman's second foray into *Alien*-sploitation, has as its germinal idea the equivalent of a recurring topic of passing speculation on *Alien* found in film reviews[46] and fan-created com-mentary tracks[47]—what does the adult xenomorph eat. But it reworks it with the human-hybrid origins of *Alien*'s monster into an ironic Frankensteinian premise: the bioengineering of an organism from human DNA and alien bacteria as a solution to a galaxy-wide food shortage that mutates, escapes and runs amok while metabolizing its human creators into digestible protein. Yet this aspect of *Forbidden World*'s storyline hasn't been probed beyond restating the edge-of-explored-space set-up as a lead into the film's more obvious exploitational trumping of what is missing from *Alien*—female nudity, sex, a shared shower scene between two female lead characters, and lingering, lab room-lit shots of excruciating decomposition of human bodies into undifferentiated protein tissue that contrasts sharply with *Alien*'s disappearing bodies and off-screen deaths. Moreover, it is these continuously operating lab lights that push the film's unblinking lavishment of slow body horror into the realm of "splatstick"[48]—the combination of splatter horror and slapstick comedy characterizing the cycle of 1980s horror films such as *Evil Dead* (1981, Sam Raimi), *The Re-Animator* (1985, Stuart Gordon), and *Return of the Living Dead* (1985, Dan O'Bannon).

But *Forbidden World*'s theme of atavism gestured at through its Darwinian upending of human dominance of the food chain deserves more teasing out. Obviously, given the film's science fiction al treatment of human DNA providing a future food source *Forbidden World*'s frontier world premise of alien bioengineered food is clearly outstripped more than 30 years later by real world scientific developments in bioprinting or biofabrication of meat from stem cells.[49] And yet, the recurring blindspot in much of the commentary on *Forbidden World*'s food storyline neglects to relate it to the film's equally oft-cited repurposing of egg cartons and McDonald's Styrofoam food trays to replicate futuristic vacuum-formed modular designs for hallways and interiors.[50] As studio sets initially designed by James Cameron for Corman's first *Alien*-inspired production *Galaxy of Terror*, the irony of their reuse in *Forbidden World*, in which life bioengineered for the purpose of food becomes sentient and imperils humans as its protein source, is a silent but obvious vestige of an industrial organization of food production that has since been eclipsed by a planetary-wide animal industrial complex with social, ecological and environmental impact.[51] Compounding this historical irony of the animal industrial complex is the means used to defeat the bioengineered lifeform: force feeding it a cancerous tumor from a human.

Revisiting *Inseminoid* marks a curious midpoint, of sorts, in this chronologically reversed return to the first *Alien*sploitation film. Relating *Inseminoid* back to *Alien* involves bringing the later into contact with ongoing insights into *Inseminoid*'s own staging of atavistic impulses as space horror, insights that have been arrived at by jettisoning the *Alien* comparisons altogether. Set on an unnamed, inhospitable planet with an archaeological research team excavating the ruined, tomb-like remnants of an extinct alien civilization, *Inseminoid*'s Anglo-American cast and storyline was readily and repeatedly dismissed as derivative of *Alien*, especially when one of the film's female characters is impregnated by an unearthed alien intent on perpetuating its species anew through humans as gestational hosts and food. This miscasting of *Inseminoid* as parasitical of *Alien* continues decades later with both *Alien Vault: The Definitive Story of the Making of the Film*[52] and the BFI Film Classics edition of *Alien*[53]—two very different examples of film tie-in produced for nostalgic appeal—summarily noting *Inseminoid* among "*Alien*-lite rip-offs."[54] But as both the film's director Norman J. Warren has indicated in print[55] and in interviews[56] as well as the film's producer Richard Gordon has likewise repeated in print[57] and in a making-of featurette for the film,[58] *Inseminoid* was conceived, scripted and in production before the release of *Alien*. And yet even when reviews of *Inseminoid*, bookended with affirmations of *Alien* as a heavy influence, single out against the shoddiness of B-movie monster effects actress Judy Geeson's hypnotic portrayal of Sandy afflicted by body horrors involving ritualized abduction and forced insemination, her escalation into possession-like madness, murder and cannibalism and the eventual excruciating, scream-filled bloody birth of alien twins, the resonances of the human scale and bodily intimacy of this grueling, visceral horror played out in an underground technological cocoon were largely left unexamined, much less related back to *Alien*.

Up until the accidental release of Sandy's entombed alien impregnator everything from human fertility to biospheric integrity is technologically monitored and managed. With its release, the film resorts to a stock of imagery and intermixed cultural associations to convey her impregnation and the ensuing chaos Sandy produces in her frenzied state of accelerated pregnancy and postpartum protection, including ufological discourse on abduction and experimentation, sacrificial nudity, the mixing of Christian demonology[59] with pagan myths of sacred twins and monstrous, prophetic infants as "[s]elf-sufficient and savage survivors, their precivilized nature [seemingly] in service of a foreign and unrecognizable future."[60] Even dead spacemen in *Inseminoid* are imbued with atavistic overtones as Sandy is seen bloody-mouthed from feeding on their corpses. But it is the harrowing, unassisted birth sequence that should provoke the most questions concerning over investment in the birth imagery of *Alien*. For all of the futuristic projection of overcoming interstellar gulfs and inhospitable environments, Sandy's scream-filled delivery is a reminder of how science fiction cinema places women's living bodies and their role in the continuation of a species outside of a technological imaginary.

As one of the first U.S. films to cash in on the horror success of *Alien*, *Galaxy of Terror*'s distinctive differences from *Alien* deserve closer attention, especially in light of producer Roger Corman's stated thematic intention for the film as the restaging of psychological aspects of the unconscious processes haunting the human mind.[61] Even a cursory check online of *Galaxy of Terror*'s plotline reveals as much with the film's science fictional setting involving a disparate and at times fractious group of individuals sent to investigate the inexplicable loss of a starship and its crew on the planet Morganthus, only to have each of their isolating, deep-seated fears manifest in grotesque material form and unleashed on them individually, resulting in violent, horrific deaths. Corman's challenge to the director of *Galaxy of Terror* was for the alien horror on Morganthus to be the terrifying psychological product of monsters of the id,[62] a thematic expression of the unconscious Corman had explored not only in his Edgar Allan Poe adaptations but also by undergoing psychoanalysis himself in the late 1960s.[63] Setting aside the more obvious design influences such as the otherworldly architecture of *Galaxy of Terror*'s biomechanoid-surfaced pyramid where most of the film's characters meet their gruesome deaths, *Alien* doesn't even make the list of science fiction al predecessors to *Galaxy of Terror*'s own take on psychologically induced space horror. As an inversion of *Alien*'s horror from without, *Galaxy of Terror*'s storyline of space travellers beset by reality altering projections from their own minds invokes a host of science fiction al examples from both film and television.[64] The most obvious is *Forbidden Planet*, but also includes films from every decade since then, including *The Angry Red Planet* (1959, Ib Melchior), *Journey to the Seventh Planet* (1962, Sidney W. Pink) and *Solaris* (1972, Andrei Tarkovsky) as well as the television series *The Twilight Zone* (1959–1964) and the first *Star Trek* (1966–1969). Moreover, as schlocky and as sleazy as the body horror involving the crews' deaths is—everything from a dismembered arm assaulting its owner to costume-ripping rape by a giant mutant maggot—with each death the result of outer horror induced by inner fears there is the sense that the characters are entrapped in a pre-modern throwback that follows the portentous aspects of what classically defines a ritual: "something atavistic, compulsive, nonsensical" as well as "sacred and mysterious."[65]

But there is another unconscious dimension to *Galaxy of Terror*, including its relationship to *Alien*, that opens up more of its storyline as well as identifying aspects of the space horror subgenre itself for further analysis, and that is how the film partakes of the subconscious drive of repetition-compulsion. Introducing this Freudian concept isn't to add another layer of psychoanalysis of the film, its characters or even its creators. Rather, it's to locate how repetition is threaded through *Galaxy of Terror* such as events within its overall storyline as well as carried over into its filmmaking as a way of illuminating how repetition-compulsion shapes our experience of *Alien*, especially through sequels.[66] As the "process by which subconscious forces compel individuals to repeat events over and over"[67] repetition-compulsion can also be thought of as a driving force generating the ongoing creation of sequels that aim at viewer re-experiences of previous films including the tapping into "a particular cultural urgency to memorialize, interact with and perhaps alter the past."[68] Moreover, it is repetition-compulsion at work in *Galaxy of Terror* that heightens the films playing out of atavism as well. The surface of Morganthus, an accumulating grave yard of downed ships and their dead crew drawn into an ancient, sacrificial game, not only plays out a set of futuristic tropes undercut by an ongoing cruel ritual beyond technological control, all watched over by a supernatural, pyramidal relic that consumes the crash survivors; but the design of the planet exteriors and the in-camera optical techniques such as forced perspective and rear screen projection used for producing the high-budget look as well as the set designs for the wrecked interiors of ships created by James Cameron were reused and redeveloped by him for *Aliens*.[69] Likewise, not only are the characters in *Galaxy of Terror* fated to reprise what befell the previous expedition to Morganthus, a storyline that is also repeated in *Titan Find,* but each character is subjected to an ongoing "test drive,"[70] a repetition-compulsion to reaction testing instigated by an overseeing mystical master, which weirdly enough, reflects the compulsive "test drive" of Corman himself with numerous test screening of the film with changing titles aimed at capturing the most sellable promise of a retro B-movie experience[71]: *Mind Warp: An Infinity of Terror, Planet of Horrors* before settling on *Galaxy of Terror.* Similarly, in *Galaxy of Terror,* members of the investigating crew disintegrate each of the corpses of the previous mission team as they are discovered, a compulsive act of dead "removal" that is eerily both death denying as it is a re-enactment of what the next fated arrivals will do upon finding their remains, much like how the fate of the crew in *Alien* is prefigured by the discovery of the ruptured remains of the lone occupant of the derelict spacecraft. And with *Galaxy of Terror's Twilight Zone*–like denouement, in which the survivor of the psychological horrors afflicting himself and others dying around him isn't finally freed from the "test-drive," but rather condemned to subject new victims to it as he replaces the previous overseer of Morganthus, ensuring the renewal and continuation of a dead ritual beyond what its extinct creators could ever foresee. Comparing this teased out ritual and repetition-compulsion at the heart of *Galaxy and Terror* with the *Alien* film franchise not only brings out how this high-budgeted series recurringly involves a lead survivor and her relationship to an alien species enacting a ritualized existential crisis for forms of organized human life. It also highlights how the isolating space horror of the *Alien* franchise is outside of the human history of its universe.

As the second of two Italian *Alien*sploitation films scripted, financed and produced within ten months of the theatrical release of *Alien* in Italy, Luigi Cozzi's *Contamination* is also revealing of atavistic and exploitative elements of the film it was conceived as a pseudo-sequel to.[72] With the Italian box-office returns for the original theatrical run of *Alien* more than double that for the United Kingdom,[73] the commercial inception of the German co-produced *Contamination*, along with Cozzi's Anglicized name Lewis Coates, is not atypical of Italian exploitation filmmaking of the 1960s and 1970s which aimed for international co-productions of films for both domestic and export markets.[74] Moreover, given the range of Italian, American and British genre film influences threaded throughout *Contamination* including Lucio Fulci's *Zombie*,[75] *Them!* (1954, Gordon Douglas) and *Invasion of the Body Snatchers* (1956, Don Siegel) as well as the exotic travelogue of international intrigue of the James Bond film series and the alien invasion storyline of *Quatermass 2* (1957, Val Guest),[76] Cozzi's film expands on already established Italian science fiction narratives from the 1960s in which the bodies of astronauts become hosts for aliens with films such as *The War of the Planets* (1966, Antonio Margheriti) and *Planet of the Vampires*.[77] When the origin of a plot to use Columbian coffee shipping lanes to New York for ferrying thousands of alien eggs that cause human bodies to explode is connected to an earlier mission to Mars that resulted in one of the returning astronauts coming under alien mind control in an underground egg chamber discovered on Mars, *Contamination* mixes the influences of *Alien* with popular awareness of unmanned exploration of Mars. *Contamination*'s slotting in of Mars as ground zero for alien invasion comes at the end of a half decade of the media attention on possibilities of Martian life with everything from Carl Sagan's popularization of NASA's space probe missions to Mars[78] to the American and British co-production of Ray Bradbury's *The Martian Chronicles* (1950) as a television miniseries first aired in 1980.[79]

But it's *Contamination*'s staging to extreme effect the explosive "birth" phase of the xenomorph's life cycle that the film is most infamously known for. With human organs erupting from torsos after contact with the liquid contents of alien eggs, captured in slow motion, Cozzi's stated intention for *Contamination* was to make "*The Wild Bunch* meets *Alien*."[80] In way, this extreme version of alien-induced eruption from within a human body "remembers" for the Academy Award–winning *Alien* is its own investment in the shock effect of unexpected, mutilating body horror unflinchingly "displayed" before horrified characters—surrogates for the film's audience—as a visual technique adopted from exploitation film.

As much as *Alien 2* possesses the most blatant and gratuitous tie to *Alien*—it was a sequel in name only to cash in on the success of its Hollywood namesake—placing the film last in this survey isn't to suggest that it is the most attenuated strain of *Alien*sploitation examined thus far nor without insightful relation to the subgenre of space horror films much less completely "quarantined" from the expanding universe of the *Alien* franchise. Released in Italian cinemas just days before *Alien* garnered the Oscar for Best Visual Effects at the 52nd Academy Awards in 1980,[81] *Alien 2* with another Italian-marketed sequel appearing in U.S. cinemas later that same year, namely Lucio Fulci's *Zombie*, which had been released in Italy as *Zombi 2* to cash in on the immense popularity of the U.S.-Italian co-produced *Dawn of the Dead* (1978, George A. Romero). As with *Contamination* and *Zombie*, *Alien 2* would figure in the last wave of low-budget Italian horror-themed *filoni*—Italian genre films produced to cash in on the success of Hollywood films but also characterized by scenes of violent excess and bloody bodily carnage[82]—to reach U.S. audiences in the 1980s. And as with the failed lawsuit brought by Dario Argento against the production company responsible for *Zombi 2* turned on the word "zombie" being uncopyrightable,[83] Twentieth Century–Fox's lawsuit against Ippolito for *Alien 2* would be thwarted by an earlier use of *Alien* as the title of an English novel.[84] Overt awareness of *Alien 2* as low-budget Italian paracinema as well as its infamy as a pseudo-sequel is amply demonstrated online, with everything from YouTube videos of horror fans showcasing different DVD releases to a comedic, yet celebratory walk-thru of the stodginess of its storyline, acting and monster effects provided by *The Cinema Snob*.[85] Even *Xenopedia*, the *Alien* franchise and expanded universe dedicated wiki, tussled with keeping an entry on *Alien 2* albeit strongly disclaimed as non-canonical.[86]

Returning us to Earth from LV-426, as it were, with its sly referential title, *Alien 2* takes us back to the time before Titan, Morganthus, Xarbia and Mars to when *Alien*, contrary to Philip K. Dick, was new upon the earth. But the film also "returns" us to an underworld which resonates with a plenitude of meaning comparable to the atavistic spaces of LV-426, especially the interiors of the derelict alien ship, or at the very least, symbolically surpasses the hostile, alien environments encountered in the films covered thus far. Unlike the sexually anatomized surfaces and openings of the derelict ship in *Alien* with its vaulting interiors of ribbed gothic walls above an oviparous cavern, *Alien 2*'s setting are karst caves that invoke pre-modern, even primeval symbolic association with underground spaces. This distinction for *Alien 2* turns on teasing out the themes of atavism associated with the film's real world setting of the famous Italian Castellana caves and acknowledging how its plotline of underworld horrors butchering a group of speleologists and their friends anticipates the atavistic themes[87] in the post-millennial subgenre of cave[88] horror films such as *The Descent* (2005, Neil Marshall), *The Cave* (2005, Bruce Hunt) and *The Cavern* (2005, Olatunde Osunsanmi). The storyline for the first act of *Alien 2* has a team of cave explorers travelling to their destination during national news coverage of a manned space vehicle returning to Earth. While the group reflects on radio news of the retrieved craft found empty of its crew after splashdown, they descend into the cave with a sample of a strange, blue-colored rock that has been mysteriously appearing on Earth during the return of the space vehicle. When the strange rock becomes life-like, the mutating horror it spawns from human bodies kills all but the lead character Thelma Joyce (Belinda Mayne) and her boyfriend who escape from the cave. While the final scenes of *Alien 2*, with its lead character Thelma terrified by an unseen presence on all sides while fleeing alone along an abandoned downtown San Diego street devoid of people (images which eerily invert the final moments of *Alien*; the rapacious threat vanquished to deep space with the sole survivor safely asleep) reference the opening scenes of *The Last Man on Earth* (1964, Ubaldo Ragona and Sidney Salkow) and *The Omega Man* (1971, Boris Sagal), it is in the midst of *Alien 2*'s referencing of the terrestrial television studio production activity seen in *Dawn of the Dead* that establishes the atavistic tenor of the film. Uncannily enough, *Alien 2*'s storyline creates this by an overlap between its opening scenes—stock footage of the re-entry and splashdown of a manned space module—and a televised interview with Thelma, introduced as an eminent speleologist, an expert on that "little-known part of our world that lies beneath our feet."[89] Setting up a contrast between the limitless expanse opened up by funded, internationally coordinated space exploration and the more primal, symbolic and altogether forgotten realm existing below modern civilization, *Alien 2* stages its relationship to atavism through the background noise of news cycles reporting routinized space travel, missing astronauts and cave interiors where technology including the team's walkie-talkies fails as an aid against becoming lost.

The recent *Alien* Memories Project[90] is a good place to end this survey of *Alien*sploitation films. Beginning as a research project application in 2008 that was rejected for funding by the British Arts and Humanities Research Council, the plan to collect and study audience memories of the pleasures and terrors of watching *Alien* was realized years later through an online survey that garnered responses from more than 1100 participants.[91] Seeking to produce a methodologically rigorous alternative to decades-long academic claims for audience meaning-making of *Alien* without engaging with actual experiences of the film by different audiences, the *Alien* Memories Project is both a re-commemoration of audiences' consumption of an iconic corporate product and a forgetting of how corporate control over that product has followed it since 1979. And that's a curious forgetting. The expanded universe of *Alien* is after all one in which a corporate future repeats the storyline of an alien species eluding corporate takeover at the same time it is part of the corporate history of Twentieth Century–Fox's more than 37-year control[92] and even thwarting of any re-imagineering of their franchise, even by fans.[93] *Alien*sploitation films are part of people's memories of *Alien*, if only for revisiting its more iconic moments restaged as rip-offs from the 1980s. But *Alien*sploitation films too have been part of the corporate history of control over likenesses with licensed popular culture.[94] Likewise, the catalogue of film influences *Alien*sploitation represent draw out *Alien*'s own B-movie origins.

But it's the *Alien*sploitation films' replaying of the dynamic underlying *Alien*'s corporate future world building—the dimly remembered future promised by the space program showcased by techno-cocooned astronauts inverted as a deadly struggle against becoming raw biology for reproducing the ambitious, yet non-technological designs of alien intelligence—that makes them unique imaginaries on the isolating space horror of the *Alien* universe.

NOTES

1. *The Untitled Star Wars Mockumentary*, DVD, directed by Damon Packard (2003; Los Angeles: The Pookie Picture Company, 2003).
2. "Best of the Worst: The Killer Eye, the Bite, and Xtro." YouTube video, 31.08, posted by Red Letter Media, February 13, 2013, http://redlettermedia.com/best-of-the-worst-the-killer-eye-they-bite-and-xtro/.
3. Kate Egan, "The Celebration of a 'Proper Product': Exploring the Residual Collectible through the 'Video Nasty,'" in *Residual Media*, ed. Charles R. Acland (Minneapolis: University of Minnesota Press, 2007), 200–221.
4. David Kerekes and David Slater, *See No Evil: Banned Films and Video Controversy* (Manchester: Headpress, 2000), 69–287.
5. Kate Egan, *Trash or Treasure? Censorship and the Changing Meanings of the Video Nasties* (Manchester: Manchester University Press, 2007).
6. Roger Corman with Jim Jarone, *How I Made a Hundred Movies in Hollywood and Never Lost a Dime* (Cambridge: Da Capo Press, 1998), xi.
7. Ron Rosenbaum, "Gooseflesh: The Strange Turn Toward Horror," *Harper's Magazine*, September 1979, 86–92.
8. Stephen King, "The Horrors of '79," *Rolling Stone*, December 1979-January 1980, 17, 19–20.
9. David Ansen and Martin Kasindorf, "Hollywood's Scary Summer," *Newsweek*, June 1979, 54.
10. King, "The Horrors of '79," 19.
11. Stephen King, *Stephen King's Danse Macabre* (London: Futura, 1984), 210.
12. *Ibid.*
13. Philip K. Dick, "Universe Makers … and Breakers," in *The Shifting Realities of Philip K. Dick: Selected Literary and Philosophical Writings*, ed. Lawrence Sutin (New York: Vintage, 1995), 105.
14. I.Q. Hunter, "Exploitation as Adaptation," in *Cultural Borrowings: Appropriation, Reworking, Transformation*, ed. Iain Robert Smith (Nottingham: Scope, 2009), 8–33.
15. Ian Nathan, *Alien Vault: The Definitive Story of the Making of the Film* (Minneapolis: Voyageur Press, 2011), 35.
16. Hunter, "Exploitation as Adaptation," 17.
17. Marie Lathers, *Space Oddities: Women and Outer Space in Film, 1960–2000* (New York: Continuum, 2010), 175.
18. Tom Shone, "'Woman: The Other in Alien,'" *Slate*, June 6, 2012, www.slate.com/articles/arts/culturebox/2012/06/prometheus_why_are_academics_so_obsessed_with_ridley_scott_s_alien_and_its_sequels_.html.
19. Ewan Millar, "On Otherness and Illusion in *The Exorcist II: The Heretic*," in *The Exorcist: Studies in the Horror Film*, ed. Daniel Olson (Lakewood, CO: Centipede Press, 2011), 375–398.
20. Emily D. Edwards, *Metaphysical Media: The Occult Experience in Popular Culture* (Carbondale: Southern Illinois Press, 2005), 148.
21. Johannes Weber, *"Like Some Damned Juggernaut": The Proto-Filmic Monstrosity of Late Victorian Literary Figures* (Bamberg: University of Bamberg Press, 2015), 337–348.
22. Umberto Rossi, "A Little Something About Dead Astronauts," *Science Fiction Studies* 36, no. 1 (2009): 101–120.

23. Andrzej Gąsiorek, *J.G. Ballard* (Manchester: Manchester University Press, 2005), 6.

24. Lynn M. Homan and Thomas Reilly, *Historic Journeys into Space* (Charleston, SC: Arcadia, 2000), 69.

25. William Sims Bainbridge, *Goals in Space: American Values and the Future of Technology* (Albany: State University of New York Press), 60.

26. Tim Lucas, *Mario Bava: All the Colors Dark* (Cincinnati: Video Watchdog, 2007), 631.

27. Jeffrey Frentzen, "*Alien*: It! The Terror from Beyond the Planet of the Vampires," *Cinefantastique* 8, no. 4 (1979): 24–25.

28. John Kenneth Muir, *Horror Films of the 80s* (Jefferson, NC: McFarland, 2007), 429–431.

29. Martin Parker, "Organisational Gothic," *Culture and Organization* 11, no. 3 (2005): 153–166.

30. *Titan Find*, DVD, directed by William Malone (1985; Luminous Processes, 2013).

31. *Ibid.*

32. Toshiya Ueno, "Japanimation: Techno-Orientalism, Media Tribes and Rave Culture," in *Aliens R Us: The Other in Science Fiction Cinema*, ed. Ziauddin Sardar and Sean Cubbitt (London: Pluto Press, 2002), 94–110.

33. Parker, "Organisational Gothic," 162.

34. *Ibid.*, 164.

35. Peter Wright, "The British Post-*Alien* Intrusion Film," in *British Science Fiction Cinema*, ed. I.Q. Hunter (London: Routledge, 1999), 142–146.

36. Kim Vallez, "Recent NM 'Skinwalker' Photo Ignites Fear," *KRQE 13 News*, February 7, 2014, http://krqe.com/2014/02/07/recent-nm-skinwalker-photo-ignites-fear/.

37. Michel Faber, *Under the Skin* (New York: Harcourt, 2000).

38. "Xtro Xposed," YouTube video, 17:24, 2005, posted by Ogrebaffley, March 2, 2012, https://www.youtube.com/watch?v=ovp-z9O56IE.

39. Peter Normanton, *The Mammoth Book of Slasher Movies* (London: Running Press, 2012), 459–460.

40. "Siskel and Ebert Review *XTRO* 1983," YouTube video, 5:17, 1983, posted by robatsea2009, November 17, 2009, https://www.youtube.com/watch?v=nO66D07YvJs.

41. Kim Newman, *Nightmare Movies: Horror on Screen since the 1960s* (London: Bloomsbury, 2011), 37–8.

42. James Verniere, "*XTRO*," *The Twilight Zone Magazine*, December 1982, 50.

43. *Ibid.*

44. Wright, "The British Post-*Alien* Intrusion Film," 138.

45. Fredric Jameson, *Archaeologies of the Future: The Desire Called Utopia and Other Science Fictions* (New York: Verso, 2005), 207.

46. Bill Cooke, "Galaxy of Terror / Forbidden World," *Video Watchdog*, December 2012, 58.

47. Red Letter Media, "*Alien* (1979) Commentary Track," March 14, 2015, https://redlettermedia.bandcamp.com/track/alien-1979-commentary-track.

48. Jon Towlson, *Subversive Horror Cinema: Countercultural Messages of Films from Frankenstein to the Present* (Jefferson, NC: McFarland, 2014), 180–196.

49. Katia Moskvitch, "Modern Meadow Aims to Print Raw Meat Using Bioprinter," *BBC News*, Technology, January 21, 2013, http://www.bbc.com/news/technology-20972018.

50. Chris Nashawaty, *Crab Monsters, Teenage Cavemen, and Candy Stripe Nurses: Roger Corman: King of the B Movie* (New York: Abrams, 2013), 179.

51. David Niebert, "Origins and Consequences of the Animal Industrial Complex," in *The Global Industrial Complex: Systems of Domination*, ed. Steven Best, Richard Kahn, Anthony J. Nocella II, and Peter McLaren (Lanham, MD: Lexington Books, 2011), 197–210.

52. Nathan, *Alien Vault*, 161.

53. Roger Luckhurst, *Alien* (Houndmills: Palgrave Macmillan on behalf of the British Film Institute, 2014).

54. *Ibid.*, 85.

55. Wright, "The British Post-*Alien* Intrusion Film," 138.

56. Chris Alexander, "Interview: Director Warren J. Norman on INSEMINOID, PREY and ... BLOODY NEW YEAR," *Shock Till You Drop*, December 31, 2015, www.shocktillyou drop.com/news/features/393791-interview-director-norman-j-warren-inseminoid-prey-bloody-new-year/.

57. Richard Gordon and Tom Weaver, *The Horror Hits of Richard Gordon: A Book Length Interview* (Duncan, OK: Bear Manor Media, 2011), 222–223.

58. "Subterranean Universe," *The Norman J. Warren Collection* (Anchor Bay Entertainment UK, 2004), DVD.

59. Christopher Partridge, "Alien Demonology: Christian Roots of the Malevolent Extraterrestrial in UFO Religions and Abduction Spiritualities," *Religion* 34 (2004), 172.

60. Andrew Scahill, *The Revolting Child in Horror Cinema: Youth Rebellion and Queer Spectatorship* (New York: Palgrave Macmillan, 2015), 95.

61. "New World," *Galaxy of Terror* (Los Angeles: Shout Factory, 2010), DVD.

62. Christopher T. Koetting, *Mind Warp! The Fantastic True Story of Roger Corman's New World Pictures* (Bristol: Hemlock Books, 2009), 196.

63. Beverly Gray, *Roger Corman: Blood-Sucking Vampires, Flesh-Eating Cockroaches and Driller Killers*, 3d ed. (New York: AZ Ferris Publications, 2013), 6.

64. Koetting, *Mind Warp!*, 194–196.

65. Walter Burkett, *Structure and History in Greek Mythology and Ritual* (Berkeley: University of California Press, 1979), 35.

66. Carolyn Jess-Cooke, *Film Sequels: Theory and Practice from Hollywood to Bollywood* (Edinburgh: Edinburgh University Press, 2009).

67. *Ibid.*, 9.

68. *Ibid.*

69. "Future King," *Galaxy of Terror* (Los Angeles: Shout Factory, 2010), DVD.

70. Avital Ronell, *The Test Drive* (Urbana: University of Illinois Press, 2005).

71. Koetting, *Mind Warp!*, 196–197.

72. Kim Newman, *Nightmare Movies*, 237.

73. *Alien*, Box Office Mojo, http://www.boxofficemojo.com/movies/?page=intl&id=alien.htm.

74. David Church, "One on Top of the Other: Lucio Fulci, Transnational Film Industries, and the Retrospective Construction of the Italian Horror Canon," *Quarterly Review of Film and Video* 32, no. 1 (2015): 11.

75. Kim Newman, "*Contamination—Alien Arriva Sulla Terra* (Contamination)," *Monthly Film Bulletin*, 54, no. 624, January (1986): 92.

76. Fredric Albert Levy, "*Contamination*," *Cinefantastique* 11, no. 3 (1981): 8.

77. Gordiano Lupi, *Written and Directed by Lewis Coates* (Roma: Profondo Rosso, 2011), 71.

78. Stuart Baur, "Kneedeep in the Cosmic Overwhelm with Carl Sagan," *New York* 8, no. 35, September 1(1975): 32.

79. Thomas S. Hischak, *American Literature on Stage and Screen: 525 Works and their Adaptations* (Jefferson, NC: McFarland, 2012), 140.

80. Cozzi, quoted in Chris Alexander, "35 Years of *Contamination*," *Contamination*, DVD, directed by Luigi Cozzi (1980; Arrow Video, 2015), 11.

81. "*Alien 2: On Earth*," IMDb, http://www.imdb.com/title/tt0078749/.

82. Robert J. Edmonstone, "Beyond 'Brutality': Understanding the Italian *Filon*'s Violent Excess," (PhD Diss., University of Glasgow, 2008), http://theses.gla.ac.uk/608/.

83. Troy Howarth, *Splintered Visions: Lucio Fulci and his Films* (Baltimore: Midnight Marquee Press, 2015), 178.

84. "*Alien 2: On Earth*."

85. "Alien 2: On Earth," *The Cinema Snob*, June 2, 2010, http://channelawesome.com/alien-2-on-earth-by-the-cinema-snob/.

86. "Alien 2: On Earth," *Xenopedia*, last modified January 14, 2016, http://avp.wikia.com/wiki/Alien_2:_On_Earth?oldid=161119.

87. James Marriot, *The Descent* (New York: Auteur, 2014), 33–36.

88. Antonio Sanna, "A 'New' Environment for the Horror Film: The Cave as Negation of Postmodernity and Globalization," *Journal of Film and Video* 65, no. 4 (2013): 17–28.

89. *Alien 2.*
90. Martin Baker, et al., *Alien Audiences: Remembering and Evaluating a Classic Movie* (Basingstoke: Palgrave Macmillan, 2016).
91. *Ibid.,* 13.
92. David Houston, "Alien Invades Burbank! Thousands Terrified," *Starlog* 34 (May 1980): 58.
93. Ryan Lambie, "Fox Shuts Down Alien Tribute Film, Was to Star Carrie Henn," *Den of Geek!*, July 17, 2015, http://www.denofgeek.com/us/movies/alien-identity/247395/fox-shuts-down-alien-tribute-film-was-to-star-carrie-henn.
94. Gordon and Weaver, *The Horror Hits of Richard Gordon,* 223.

BIBLIOGRAPHY

Alexander, Chris. "Interview: Director Warren J. Norman on INSEMINOID, PREY and … BLOODY NEW YEAR." *Shock Till You Drop*, December 31, 2015. www.shocktillyoudrop.com/news/features/393791-interview-director-norman-j-warren-inseminoid-prey-bloody-new-year/.
Alexander, Chris. "35 Years of *Contamination.*" *Contamination*, DVD. Directed by Luigi Cozzi. 1980; Arrow Video, 2015: 7–17.
Alien. DVD. Directed by Ridley Scott. 1979; Century City, CA: Twentieth Century Fox Home Entertainment, 2003.
Alien 2 On Earth. DVD. Directed by Ciro Ippolito. 1980; Midnight Legacy, 2011.
"Alien 2: On Earth." *IMDb*, http://www.imdb.com/title/tt0078749/.
"Alien 2: On Earth." *The Cinema Snob*, June 2, 2010. http://channelawesome.com/alien-2-on-earth-by-the-cinema-snob/.
"Alien 2: On Earth." *Xenopedia*, last modified January 14, 2016. http://avp.wikia.com/wiki/Alien_2:_On_Earth?oldid=161119
Altered States. DVD. Directed by Ken Russell. 1980; Burbank, CA: Warner Home Video, 1998.
The Angry Red Planet. DVD. Directed by Ib Melchior. 1959; Santa Monica, CA: MGM Home Entertainment, 2001.
Ansen, David, and Martin Kasindorf. "Hollywood's Scary Summer." *Newsweek*, June 1979, 54.
Bainbridge, William Sims. *Goals in Space: American Values and the Future of Technology.* Albany: State University of New York Press, 1991.
Baker, Martin, Kate Egan, Tom Phillips, and Sarah Ralph. *Alien Audiences: Remembering and Evaluating a Classic Movie.* Basingstoke: Palgrave Macmillan, 2016.
Battle Beyond the Stars. DVD. Directed by Jimmy T. Murakami. 1980; Los Angeles: Shout Factory, 2011.
Baur, Stuart. "Kneedeep in the Cosmic Overwhelm with Carl Sagan." *New York* 8, no. 35 (September 1, 1975): 25–32.
Burkett, Walter. *Structure and History in Greek Mythology and Ritual.* Berkeley: University of California Press, 1979.
Bradbury, Ray. *The Martian Chronicles.* Garden City, NY: Doubleday, 1958.
The Cave. DVD. Directed by Bruce Hunt. 2005; Culver City, CA: Sony Pictures Home Entertainment, 2006.
The Cavern. DVD. Directed by Olatunde Osunsanmi. 2005; Culver City, CA: Sony Pictures Home Entertainment, 2006.
Church, David. "One on Top of the Other: Lucio Fulci, Transnational Film Industries, and the Retrospective Construction of the Italian Horror Canon." *Quarterly Review of Film and Video* 32, no. 1 (2015): 1–20.
Contamination. DVD. Directed by Luigi Cozzi. 1980; Arrow Video, 2015.
Cooke, Bill. "Galaxy of Terror / Forbidden World." *Video Watchdog.* December 2012, 56–59.
Corman, Roger, with Jim Jarone. *How I Made a Hundred Movies in Hollywood and Never Lost a Dime.* Cambridge, MA: Da Capo Press, 1998.
Dawn of the Dead. DVD. Directed by George Romero. 1978. Troy, MI: Anchor Bay Entertainment, 2004.

The Descent. DVD. Directed by Neil Marshall. 2005; Santa Monica, CA: Lionsgate, 2006.

Dick, Philip K. "Universe Makers ... and Breakers." In *The Shifting Realities of Philip K. Dick: Selected Literary and Philosophical Writings,* edited by Lawrence Sutin, 103–105. New York: Vintage, 1995.

Edmonstone, Robert J. "Beyond 'Brutality': Understanding the Italian *Filone*'s Violent Excess." PhD Diss., University of Glasgow, 2008. http://theses.gla.ac.uk/608/

Edwards, Emily D. *Metaphysical Media: The Occult Experience in Popular Culture.* Carbondale: Southern Illinois Press, 2005.

Egan, Kate. "The Celebration of a 'Proper Product': Exploring the Residual Collectible through the 'Video Nasty.'" In *Residual Media,* edited by Charles R. Acland, 200–221. Minneapolis: University of Minnesota Press, 2007.

Egan, Kate. *Trash or Treasure? Censorship and the Changing Meanings of the Video Nasties.* Manchester: Manchester University Press, 2007.

E.T. the Extra-Terrestrial. DVD. Directed by Steven Spielberg. 1982; Universal City, CA: Universal Studios Home Entertainment, 2005.

The Evil Dead. DVD. Directed by Sam Raimi. 1981; Beverly Hills: Anchor Bay Entertainment, 2009.

Exorcist II: The Heretic. DVD. Directed by John Boorman. 1974; Burbank, CA: Warner Home Video, 2002.

Faber, Michel. *Under the Skin.* New York: Harcourt, 2000.

Forbidden Planet. DVD. Directed by Fred M. Wilcox. 1956; Burbank, CA: Warner Home Video, 2006.

Forbidden World. DVD. Directed by Allan Holzman. 1982; Los Angeles: Shout Factory, 2010.

Frentzen, Jeffrey. "*Alien*: It! The Terror from Beyond the Planet of the Vampires." *Cinefantastique* 8, no. 4 (1979): 24–25.

Galaxy of Terror. DVD. Directed by Bruce D. Clark. 1981; Los Angeles: Shout Factory, 2010.

Galaxy of Terror. "Future King." Los Angeles: Shout Factory, 2010. DVD.

Galaxy of Terror. "New World." Los Angeles: Shout Factory, 2010. DVD.

Gąsiorek, Andrzej. *J.G. Ballard.* Manchester: Manchester University Press, 2005.

Gordon, Richard, and Tom Weaver. *The Horror Hits of Richard Gordon: A Book Length Interview.* Duncan, OK: Bear Manor Media, 2011.

Gray, Beverly. *Roger Corman: Blood-Sucking Vampires, Flesh-Eating Cockroaches and Driller Killers,* 3d ed. New York: AZ Ferris Publications, 2013.

Homan, Lynn M., and Thomas Reilly. *Historic Journeys into Space.* Charleston, SC: Arcadia, 2000.

Houston, David. "Alien Invades Burbank! Thousands Terrified." *Starlog* 34, May 1980, 57–61.

Howarth, Troy. *Splintered Visions: Lucio Fulci and his Films.* Baltimore: Midnight Marquee Press, 2015.

Hunter, I.Q. "Exploitation as Adaptation." In *Cultural Borrowings: Appropriation, Reworking, Transformation,* edited by Iain Robert Smith, 8–33. Nottingham: Scope, 2009.

I Married a Monster from Outer Space. DVD. Directed by Gene Fowler, Jr. 1958; Hollywood: Paramount Pictures, 2004.

Inseminoid. DVD. Directed by Norman J. Warren. 1981; Anchor Bay Entertainment UK Ltd., 2004.

Invasion of the Body Snatchers. DVD. Directed by Don Siegel. 1956; Los Angeles: Republic Pictures, 2002.

It Conquered the World. DVD. Directed by Roger Corman. 1956; Visions Entertainment, 2004.

It! The Terror from Beyond Space. DVD. Directed by Edward L. Cahn. 1958; Culver City, CA: MGM Home Entertainment, 2001.

Jameson, Fredric. *Archaeologies of the Future: The Desire Called Utopia and Other Science Fictions,* New York: Verso, 2005.

Jaws. DVD. Directed by Steven Spielberg. 1975; Universal City, CA: Universal, 2000.

Jess-Cooke, Carolyn. *Film Sequels: Theory and Practice from Hollywood to Bollywood.* Edinburgh: Edinburgh University Press, 2009.

John Carpenter's Ghosts of Mars. DVD. Directed by John Carpenter. 2001; Culver City, CA: Columbia TriStar Home Entertainment, 2001.

Journey to the Seventh Planet. DVD. Directed by Sidney W. Pink. 1962; New York: Kino Lorber, 2016.

Kerekes, David, and David Slater. *See No Evil: Banned Films and Video Controversy*. Manchester: Headpress, 2000.

King, Stephen. "The Horrors of '79." *Rolling Stone*, December 1979–January 1980, 17, 19–20.

King, Stephen. *Stephen King's Danse Macabre*. London: Futura, 1984.

Koetting, Christopher T. *Mind Warp! The Fantastic True Story of Roger Corman's New World Pictures*. Bristol: Hemlock Books, 2009.

Lambie, Ryan. "Fox Shuts Down Alien Tribute Film, Was to Star Carrie Henn." *Den of Geek!* July 17, 2015. http://www.denofgeek.com/us/movies/alien-identity/247395/fox-shuts-down-alien-tribute-film-was-to-star-carrie-henn.

The Last Man on Earth. DVD. Directed by Ubaldo Ragona and Sidney Salkow. 1964; Beverly Hills: Twentieth Century Fox Home Entertainment, 2007.

Lathers, Marie, *Space Oddities: Women and Outer Space in Film, 1960–2000*. New York: Continuum, 2010.

Levy, Fredric Albert. "*Contamination*." *Cinefantastique* 11, no. 3 (1981): 8.

Lucas, Tim. *Mario Bava: All the Colors Dark*. Cincinnati: Video Watchdog, 2007.

Luckhurst, Roger. *Alien*. Houndmills: Palgrave Macmillan on behalf of the British Film Institute, 2014.

Lupi, Gordiano. *Written and Directed by Lewis Coates*. Roma: Profondo Rosso, 2011.

Marriot, James. *The Descent*. New York: Auteur, 2014.

Millar, Ewan. "On Otherness and Illusion in *The Exorcist II: The Heretic*." In *The Exorcist: Studies in the Horror Film*, edited by Daniel Olson, 375–398. Lakewood: Centipede Press, 2011.

Moskvitch, Katia. "Modern Meadow Aims to Print Raw Meat Using Bioprinter." *BBC News*, Technology, January 21, 2013. http://www.bbc.com/news/technology-20972018.

Muir, John Kenneth. *Horror Films of the 1980s*. Jefferson: McFarland, 2007.

Nashawaty, Chris. *Crab Monsters, Teenage Cavemen, and Candy Stripe Nurses: Roger Corman: King of the B Movie*. New York: Abrams, 2013.

Nathan, Ian. *Alien Vault: The Definitive Story of the Making of the Film*. Minneapolis: Voyageur Press, 2011.

Newman, Kim. *Nightmare Movies: Horror on Screen since the 1960s*. London: Bloomsbury, 2011.

Newman, Kim. "*Contamination—Alien Arriva Sulla Terra (Contamination)*." *Monthly Film Bulletin*, 54, no. 624 (January 1986): 92.

Niebert, David. "Origins and Consequences of the Animal Industrial Complex." In *The Global Industrial Complex: Systems of Domination*, edited by Steven Best, Richard Kahn, Anthony J. Nocella II, and Peter McLaren, 197–210. Lanham, MD: Lexington Books, 2011.

The Norman J. Warren Collection. "Subterranean Universe." Anchor Bay Entertainment UK Ltd., 2004. DVD.

Normanton, Peter. *The Mammoth Book of Slasher Movies*. London: Running Press, 2012.

The Omega Man. DVD. Directed by Boris Sagal. 1971; Burbank, CA: Warner Home Video, 2007.

Pandorum. DVD. Directed by Christian Alvart, 2009; Santa Monica, CA: Anchor Bay Entertainment, 2009.

Parker, Martin. "Organisational Gothic." *Culture and Organization* 11, no. 3 (2005): 153–66.

Partridge, Christopher. "Alien Demonology: Christian Roots of the Malevolent Extraterrestrial in UFO Religions and Abduction Spiritualties." *Religion* 34 (2004): 163–189.

"*Best of the Worst: The Killer Eye, The Bite, and Xtro*." YouTube video, 31.08. Posted by Red Letter Media, February 13, 2013. http://redlettermedia.com/best-of-the-worst-the-killer-eye-they-bite-and-xtro/.

Planet of the Apes. DVD. Directed by Franklin J. Schaffner. 1968; Beverly Hills,: Twentieth Century Fox Home Entertainment, 2006.

Planet of the Vampires. DVD. Directed by Mario Bava. 1965; Santa Monica, CA: MGM Home Entertainment, 2001.

Prometheus. DVD. Directed by Ridley Scott. 2012; Beverly Hills: Twentieth Century Fox Home Entertainment, 2012.

Quatermass 2. DVD. Directed by Val Guest. 1957; Troy, MI: Anchor Bay Entertainment, 2000.

Re-Animator. DVD. Directed by Stuart Gordon. 1985; Rockaway, NJ: Anchor Bay, 2007.

Red Letter Media. "*Alien* (1979) Commentary Track." March 14, 2015. https://redlettermedia. bandcamp.com/track/alien-1979-commentary-track.

The Return of the Living Dead. DVD. Directed by Dan O'Bannon. 1985; Santa Monica, CA: MGM Home Entertainment, 2002.

Ronell, Avital. *The Test Drive*. Urbana: University of Illinois Press, 2005.

Rosenbaum, Ron. "Gooseflesh: The Strange Turn Toward Horror." *Harper's Magazine*, September 1979, 86–92.

Rossi, Umberto. "A Little Something About Dead Astronauts." *Science Fiction Studies* 36, no. 1 (2009): 101–20.

Scahill, Andrew. *The Revolting Child in Horror Cinema: Youth Rebellion and Queer Spectatorship*. New York: Palgrave Macmillan, 2015.

Sanna, Antonio. "A 'New' Environment for the Horror Film: The Cave as Negation of Postmodernity and Globalization." *Journal of Film and Video* 65, no. 4 (2013): 17–28.

Shone, Tom. "'Woman: The Other in Alien.'" *Slate*, June 6, 2012. www.slate.com/articles/arts/culturebox/2012/06/prometheus_why_are_academics_so_obsessed_with_ridley_scott_s_alien_and_its_sequels_.html.

"Siskel and Ebert Review *XTRO* 1983." YouTube video, 5:17, 1983, posted by robatsea2009, November 17, 2009. https://www.youtube.com/watch?v=nO66D07YvJs.

Solaris. DVD. Directed by Andrei Tarkovsky. 1972. London: Artificial Eye, 2002.

Star Wars: Episode IV—A New Hope. DVD. Directed by George Lucas. 1977; Beverly Hills: Twentieth Century Fox Home Entertainment, 2002.

Star Wars: Episode II—Attack of the Clones. DVD. Directed by George Lucas. 2002. Beverly Hills, CA: Twentieth Century Fox Home Entertainment, 2002.

Them! DVD. Directed by Gordon Douglas. 1954; Burbank, CA: Warner Home Video, 2002.

The Thing from Another World. DVD. Directed by Christian Nyby. 1951; Burbank, CA: Warner Home Video, 2003.

Titan Find. DVD. Directed by William Malone. 1985; Luminous Processes, 2013.

Towlson, Jon. *Subversive Horror Cinema: Countercultural Messages of Films from Frankenstein to the Present*. Jefferson, NC: McFarland, 2014.

2001: A Space Odyssey. DVD. Directed by Stanley Kubrick. 1968; Burbank CA: Warner Home Video, 2001.

Under the Skin. DVD. Directed by Jonathan Glazer. 2013; Santa Monica, CA: Lionsgate, 2014.

Ueno, Toshiya. "Japanimation: Techno-Orientalism, Media Tribes and Rave Culture." In *Aliens R Us: The Other in Science Fiction Cinema*, edited by Ziauddin Sardar and Sean Cubbitt, 94–110. London: Pluto Press, 2002.

The Untitled Star Wars Mockumentary. DVD. Directed by Damon Packard. 2003; Los Angeles: The Pookie Picture Company, 2003.

Vallez, Kim. "Recent NM 'Skinwalker' Photo Ignites Fear." *KRQE 13 News*. February 7, 2014. http://krqe.com/2014/02/07/recent-nm-skinwalker-photo-ignites-fear/.

Verniere, James. "*XTRO*." *The Twilight Zone Magazine*, December 1982, 50–54.

War of the Planets. DVD. Directed by Antonio Margheriti. 1966; Burbank, CA: Warner Home Video, 2010.

Weber, Johannes. *"Like Some Damned Juggernaut": The Proto-Filmic Monstrosity of Late Victorian Literary Figures*. Bamberg: University of Bamberg Press, 2015.

Wright, Peter. "The British Post–*Alien* Intrusion Film." In *British Science Fiction Cinema*, edited by I.Q. Hunter, 139–152. London: Routledge, 1999.

XTRO. DVD. Directed by Harry Bromley Davenport. 1983; London: Optimum Releasing, 2009.

"Xtro Xposed." YouTube video, 17:24, 2005. Posted by Ogrebaffley, March 2, 2012. https://www.youtube.com/watch?v=ovp-z9O56IE.

Zardoz. DVD. Directed by John Boorman. 1974; Beverly Hills: Twentieth Century Fox Home Entertainment, 2000.

Zombie. DVD. Directed by Lucio Fulci. 1979; West Hollywood, CA: Blue Underground, 2004.

Leprechaun 4 and Jason X
Camp, Paracinema
and the Postmodern Sequel

KEVIN CHABOT

With Jason Voorhees (Kane Hodder) ostensibly unconscious lying on a table, a young woman keeps to her work station with her back turned toward the notorious serial killer. We cut to an adjacent room where a young couple undress and begin having sex. We cut back to Jason. Although he is presumed dead and thus non-threatening, his leg momentarily springs to life from atrophy and twitches on the table. The young woman turns around to observe the commotion. She sees no movement and no signs of life. Satisfied that she is safe and Jason is indeed dead, she turns her back once more and continues on with her work. Cut to the couple. As their foreplay becomes more passionate, their panting grows more intense. Cut to Jason. His hand slowly opens and clutches into a fist. The young woman, once again, turns around and sees nothing out of the ordinary. She returns to her work. Cut to the couple. Their lovemaking continues, their panting becoming moans of pleasure. Cut to Jason. With the woman's moans functioning as a sound bridge across the two shots, Jason suddenly rises from the table, sitting upright. The young woman, yet again, turns around and discovers that Jason is no longer lying on the table. In her confusion, she does not have time to fully register the danger she's in before Jason grabs her head from behind and drags her to the other side of the room. She screams, trying to fight for survival, but she is no match for the infamous mass murderer.

This description of a sequence in *Jason X* (2002, Jim Isaac) is reminiscent of a number of scenes from any one of its previous eight installments.[1] With Jason presumed dead and character(s) believing they are safe, Jason inevitably returns to stalk and kill more amorous teenagers. In this regard, *Jason X* is no different than the previous films in the franchise, however this sequel does contain one notable distinction: the film takes place in the year 2455 aboard a spaceship. This spatial and temporal relocation from the familiar rustic setting of Camp Crystal Lake in 1980s America creates opportunities for evermore spectacular and creative death sequences in which the display of newly minted technological gadgets predominate. In the scene described above, for example, Jason does not simply impale the young woman with any of the sharp objects that adorn the spaceship's laboratory in which she is working; rather, he opts to dunk her head into a vat of liquid nitrogen, instantly freezing her face, and smashes her head to pieces on a nearby desk. While liquid nitrogen, of course, is not a fictional property of the future, it nevertheless signifies a degree of technological and scientific advancement for our consummate woodsman. As I detail below, the use of science fiction gadgetry and the *mise-en-scène* of a travelling spaceship allow the filmmakers to inject novelty into the aging franchise which, having already produced nine films, had for some viewers long outstayed its welcome.

The *Friday the 13th* series is not the only established horror franchise to venture into the final frontier. Having produced three previous films, the fourth installment of the *Leprechaun* series also takes place on a travelling spaceship as the eponymous leprechaun attempts to regain his missing treasure and acquire a bride. Unlike *Friday the 13th*, which for most of its sequels remained within the wooden confines of Camp Crystal Lake, the sequels of *Leprechaun* prove to be more nomadic with *Leprechaun 2* (1994, Rodman Flender) taking place in Los Angeles and *Leprechaun 3* (1995, Brian Trenchard-Smith) changing locales to Las Vegas. While the leprechaun's maleficent escapades are not grounded in a central location, though his underground cavernous layer makes an appearance in each installment, the fourth film's voyage into the stars similarly attempts to generate a sense of the novel within an established and repetitive series.

To be sure, *Critters 4* (1992, Rupert Harvey) and *Hellraiser: Bloodline* (1996, Kevin Yagher[2]), the fourth installment of the *Hellraiser* films, have also made this intergalactic expedition. However, *Critters* was always a science fiction -horror hybrid from its first film and *Hellraiser: Bloodline* spends most of its running time not on a spaceship in the future, but in a flashback to 18th century France and 1990s America, detailing the origins of the cenobites and their demonic puzzle box. *Jason X* and *Leprechaun 4: In Space* (1996, Brian Trenchant-Smith) are thus unique as established, earthbound franchises that took to the stars in an effort to rejuvenate interest in their respective franchises. This essay seeks to explore how novelty functions within these sequels and the degree to which it alters the established paradigms of the series. Ultimately, despite some flashier death scenes and more extravagant displays of technological prowess, *Jason X* and *Leprechaun 4* are no different than their predecessors, offering the same formulaic plots and archetypal characters we have come to expect. This should not be regarded as a criticism of these particular films, however, as these sequels reveal significant insights into the state of contemporary American horror film at the turn of the last century. As such, *Jason X* and *Leprechaun 4* are better understood as betraying a postmodern sensibility, not only as the old and ever-same returning in the guise of the new, but also in their self-reflexive embracing of camp and trash aesthetics.

Leprechaun 4: In Space

Leprechaun 4 opens amid floating asteroids as the credits begin to role. A spaceship appears onscreen and we are introduced to the crew occupying the ship with a long take as they gather guns, ammunition, and exchange joking banter. This convivial atmosphere is interrupted, however, when Sergeant Hooker (Tom Colceri) calls the military team to attention. Hooker informs them that they are currently orbiting the planet Ithacon where they will rendezvous with another ship, proceed to "target area Delta," and track down an alien that has been disrupting a "galactic mining operation to the tune of half a billion dollars."[3] Their mission is to search for and destroy the alien creature. Joining the military crew on this expedition is Dr. Reeves (Jessica Collins) who has been tasked by the ship's commander Dr. Mittenhand (Guy Siner), a cyborg with a hammy German accent, to retrieve any samples of alien life forms. Hooker begrudgingly obliges and the crew ventures on. Meanwhile, the leprechaun that we have come to know from the previous installments (Warwick Davis, reprising his role here) has captured a princess (Rebecca Carlton) whom he wishes to marry in order to inherit her royal stature. Although the underground lair in which he keeps Princess Zarina captive is a facsimile of the lair we have seen in previous films on Earth, we are meant to understand that this lair exists on another planet. The military crew arrive on the planet and begin searching the lair, confirming the audience's suspicion that the alien being tracked is the leprechaun. Once discovered, a gun battle ensues. The leprechaun's use of a green lightsaber and a gun proves ineffectual against the heavily armed team and the leprechaun is blown apart by a grenade. Apparently dead, the crew leaves and celebrates the success of their mission aboard the ship wherein their celebration quickly devolves into horror as the leprechaun returns to the ship and begins murdering the crew one by one.

As this brief plot description makes clear, the film, like its previous installments, is a horror-comedy hybrid that revels in the absurdity of its narrative and the comically exaggerated and creative nature of the deaths depicted. The relocation of the narrative from Earth to an orbiting spaceship, however, results in the transposition of the clichés associated with the plots and iconography of another distinct genre, science fiction, onto the established diegesis of the *Leprechaun* horror franchise. This novelty provides the characters onscreen with a number of technological tools and equipment heretofore unseen within the franchise including the presence of a cyborg, a shrinking ray, a growth ray, the weaponization of DNA splicing, and, of course, an imminent self-destruct countdown toward the end of the narrative. Such an overlay of the semantics of one genre, that is, its identifiable iconography and character types, onto the syntax of another, that is, its overriding structure, in this case results in a form of spectacle that differs from the *Leprechaun* series' previous installments. This novelty, however, only occupies the realm of appearances as the spectacle fails to inject a truly novel viewing experience. While futuristic scientific technology is displayed in some scenes, they essentially exist to emphasize the spatial and temporal relocation of the franchise from 1990s Earth to a spaceship in the future. As a genre hybrid, *Leprechaun 4* maintains the structure and formula of the horror film while utilizing key images and settings associated with science fiction.

Darko Suvin in his seminal essay "On the Poetics of the Science Fiction Genre" argues for a definition of science fiction as a "literature of cognitive estrangement" wherein the "strange newness, a *novum*" is empirically explained within the wholly new and different world of the book or, for our purposes, film.[4] In a lengthy sequence from *Forbidden Planet* (1956, Fred Wilcox), for example, Dr. Morbius (Walter Pidgeon) explains to Commander Adams (Leslie Nielson) that the "plastic educator" created by the ancient Krell civilization had exponentially increased his intellect, thus allowing him to understand the complex technological engineering of the Krell and build sophisticated technologies himself, including a servile robot. Such factual explication is thus diametrically opposed with the fantastic literary subgenres of horror, Gothic, and ghost. Survin writes that "fantasy is inimical to the empirical world and its laws" because it introduces "anti-cognitive laws into the empirical environment."[5] In other words, the supernatural and the magical are fundamentally opposed to and incompatible with the logical explanation that defines science fiction. Given this, *Leprechaun 4*'s technological spectacles take on a supernatural aura thus aligning the fourth installment firmly within its horror-fantasy roots, despite its appropriation of science fiction semantics.

To be sure, the first two sequels emphasize the magical sensibility of the franchise even more so than the first film by employing Los Angeles and Las Vegas respectively as their settings, geographies of illusion in which the spectacle and the imaginary dominate. Jean Baudrillard makes a similar point when he describes L.A. as "a network of incessant, unreal circulation—a city of incredible proportions but without space, without dimension."[6] Moreover, the publicity material created for *Leprechaun 3* is accompanied by a plot description that reads, "Under the false daylight of modern Las Vegas, the leprechaun has returned from his stony grave to claim what is rightfully his."[7] Once again, Las Vegas is articulated as a city of magical illusionism ("false daylight"), particularly befitting for a mythical creature whose modus operandi is dependent upon hallucination and *trompe l'oeil*. The relocation of the narrative of the fourth film to outer space and its subsequent engagement with science fiction semantics is thus only superficially novel as the film simply extends its fantastic and magical sensibility to a spaceship rather than truly shifting its generic syntax. In this regard, *Leprechaun 4* constitutes a repetition of the same in the guise of the novel. What is significant in this attempt at genre hybridity, however, is that it constitutes a pertinent example of what Susan Sontag has termed Camp aesthetics and what Jeffrey Sconce describes as paracinema: a comically bad film that is rescued via fandom and accredited with a cult status, a status that is largely cultivated through the circulation of videotape.[8]

In her well-known essay from 1964 "Notes on Camp," Sontag attempts to identify the somewhat amorphous aesthetic by describing it as an unserious and playful form that becomes artificial in its excessivity. That is, Camp is an aesthetic of style over substance, an exaggeration, "a woman walking around in a dress made of three million feathers."[9] Certainly, the *Leprechaun* franchise abounds in examples of such comic exaggeration in its death scenes. *Leprechaun 3*, for example, features a woman whose lips, buttocks, and breasts increase to such a monstrous size that she explodes. The fourth installment is no different as it includes scenes depicting the leprechaun bursting through the penis of a soldier, a growth ray being used against the leprechaun causing him to become a giant, and the bodily metamorphosis of Dr. Mittenhand into "Mittenspider," a human-cyborg-spider hybrid that resulted from injecting the doctor with a mixture of tarantula and spider DNA. Such scenes are no doubt absurd, but that is, of course, the point. Camp aims to "dethrone the serious"[10] and enter the realm of play. While the *Leprechaun* franchise certainly conforms to Sontag's conception of Camp as comic artifice, the franchise was explicitly designed to evoke laughter. As such, it cannot be considered "pure" Camp for Sontag as pure Camp does not intend to be campy. Sontag writes, "In naïve, or pure, Camp, the essential element is seriousness, a seriousness that fails."[11] Pure Camp thus "proposes itself seriously, but cannot be taken altogether seriously because it is 'too much.'"[12] The promotional material for the first film, however, specifically markets the film as a horror-comedy, with its production packet claiming, "*Leprechaun* will carry you from the height of hilarity to the depths of terror."[13] From its inception, then, the *Leprechaun* series has been understood as a horror-comedy and would thus be excluded from pure Camp as its humor is derived not from a "seriousness that fails," but from intentional absurdity. While Sontag also maintains that Camp has a particular affinity for the vulgar, that the connoisseur of Camp "sniffs the stink and prides himself on his strong nerves,"[14] this vulgarity must not be intentional. Jeffrey Sconce, builds upon Sontag's notion of Camp and amends it to include works that are intentionally vulgar, intentionally over-the-top, and intentionally oppositional to the tastes and values of the mainstream.

For Sconce, what distinguishes the paracinematic, films that include bad film, splatter-punk, mondo cane documentaries, Elvis movies, government hygiene films, and so on, is their ambition to become a kind of counter-cinema.[15] Such films and the fandom they generate conceive of themselves as challenging conceptions of cinematic art and hierarchies of taste that position *Citizen Kane* (1941, Orson Welles) and *Vertigo* (1958, Alfred Hitchcock) as the epitome of the art form. "In cultivating a counter-cinema from the dregs of exploitation films," Sconce writes, "paracinematic fans ... explicitly situate themselves in opposition to Hollywood cinema and the mainstream U.S. culture it represents."[16] In championing the excessive, in reveling in vulgarity, and cherishing the absurd, fans of the *Leprechaun* franchise and films like it rebukes regimes of high culture and the aesthetic values it espouses. Although paracinema includes, as Sconce indicates, such classic works as *Plan 9 from Outer Space* (1959, Ed Wood) and *Two Thousand Maniacs!* (1964, Herschell Gordon Lewis), the rise of VHS and video rental stores in the late 1970s and 1980s is especially significant for paracinematic connoisseurship not only because fans may collect and share tapes of films that would otherwise not be exhibited theatrically, but also because video proved to be a lucrative market into which such low-brow works could be released, thereby bypassing the costs of theatrical distribution and exhibition altogether.

Although the first two *Leprechaun* films received limited theatrical distribution, the remaining films were released directly to video. The franchise was produced by Trimark which functioned as the domestic and international releasing arm of Vidmark Inc., a distribution company catered specifically to the home video market. According to a production information packet collated upon the release of *Leprechaun* in 1993, Trimark was founded in 1990 by Mark Amin and specialized in producing and releasing what one might consider lower-grade B films with relatively low production budgets and consisting of mostly unknown actors. Trimark's first release was *Warlock* (Steve Miner) in 1991, followed by *Kickboxer 2* (1991, Albert Pyun), and *Whore* (1991, Ken Russell). Such releases, whether in limited theatrical runs or directly to video stores, catered to non-mainstream tastes and the paracinematic and camp sensibilities discussed above. The home video market enjoyed steady growth throughout the 1980s and, although growth slowed during the 1990s, home video still proved to be lucrative for the *Leprechaun* franchise. Significantly, *Leprechaun 3* was listed among the top selling direct-to-video titles in a survey conducted by *Video Store Magazine*.[17] In a report published by *Video Business* in July 1997, five months after the video release of *Leprechaun 4*, consumers had spent a total of $8.7 billion on video rentals and purchases, up 3.5 percent from 1995.[18] The report continues:

> While households with children constitute the core of both rental and purchase markets, video renting is an extremely widespread phenomenon in the U.S. In any given month in 1996, 44% to 53% of all adult consumers in the U.S. reported renting a video at least once within the month, according to VSM [Video Software Magazine]. Between 18% and 38% of all consumers report purchasing a video at least once during a given month. From month to month, renting a video is the most popular—or, at least, the most common—leisure activity among the 14 activities tracked by the magazine.[19]

The report concludes that from 1993 to 1996 the rate of video purchases had accelerated suggesting that purchasing videotapes would soon surpass the rate of renting in the U.S. The home video market thus served both independent studios and paracinema fans well as it allowed access to, the continuing production of, and even ownership of the so-called cultural detritus that constitutes the paracinematic.

As Sconce points out, however, not all paracinematic objects are held in the same regard and even the purveyors of trash have certain criteria against which films are judged. Sconce writes, "In its contemporary and most sophisticated form, paracinema is an aggressive, esoteric and often painfully ascetic counter-aesthetic, one that produces, in its most extreme manifestations, an ironic form of reverse elitism."[20] It is with this notion of a new hierarchy of taste within the paracinematic that I turn to discuss *Jason X* and the *Friday the 13th* franchise which Matt Hills describes as para-paracinema, which is excluded from both mainstream and paracinematic culture.

Jason X *and the* Friday the 13th *Franchises*

Because paracinema can also be conceived of as a practice of rescue, that is, a reclaiming of works that have been excluded and marginalized in mainstream cinema, Hills argues that one subgenre of the 1980s suffers from a double marginalization as it is denounced by both the taste establishment (i.e., film critics) as well as the paracinematic community: slasher films.[21] As is well known, critics have condemned slasher films for violence and gore and their lack of depth in narrative and character development. For example, in his evaluation of modern horror, Wheeler Winston Dixon has stated, "In the majority of commercial horror films of the 1970s, '80s, and '90s, most of the women and men exist only to be destroyed; they are situations rather than characters."[22] Dixon and critics like him regard such slasher films as principally orchestrated around the display of brutal violence in which two-dimensional characters and weak plots only exist to facilitate spectacles of gore. Interestingly, slasher films of the 1980s were also maligned by the paracinematic community as being *too mainstream*. Their ubiquitous presence in neighborhood multiplexes and significant financial profits situated the subgenre within dominant American popular culture rather than the subterranean realm of counter-cinema. As Hills writes, "Fans of trash horror other and devalue slasher-cycle horror as overly commercial or non-underground."[23] The chief culprit of this mainstreaming of sleaze is identified as *Friday the 13th* (1980, Sean Cunningham) which often stands as a metonym for the repetitive violence and sexuality of the slasher subgenre.

In addition to the critical derision of the *Friday* franchise for its prioritization of gore, the franchise was already considered to be a reductive rip-off of *Halloween* (1978, John Carpenter), stripping the first *Friday* film of any cachet that is normally afforded to an 'original' entry in a new series. James Francis, Jr., calls *Friday the 13th* "a clear offshoot of *Halloween*"[24] and Stuart Henderson has stated that *Friday* capitalized on the success of *Halloween*, appropriating its narrative structure, character types, and source of terror.[25] Within this critical discourse, then, *Halloween* is valued as an original work that initiated the slasher subgenre and is therefore afforded artistic and historical significance while *Friday the 13th* and its sequels have been "powerfully articulated with critically devalued notions of gore over character or narrative, ... repetition over originality, and commerce over art."[26] The production history of the first *Friday the 13th* installment would at first glance corroborate such a reading as director Sean S. Cunningham took out a full-page advertisement in *Variety* announcing the film seeking financing. Although the ad featured copy proclaiming "From the producer of *The Last House on the Left* Comes the Most Terrifying Film Ever Made!"[27] the film had not been shot nor even written. Cunningham sought to attract financiers with the high-concept title and lurid text: "'[I] bet if I was trying to do something called *Friday the 13th*, and advertised as it as 'the scariest movie ever made [...] it would sell.'"[28] Sure enough, Hallmark Releasing Corporation provided $500,000 for the film and, because Hallmark was the releasing arm of Esquire Theaters of America, which owned a small number of drive-ins and multiplexes, *Friday the 13th* would be guaranteed at least some distribution.[29] While the initial pitch may have been modeled after *Halloween*, a horror film similarly predicated upon a superstitious holiday, the filmmakers of *Friday* relocated the central plot of *Halloween* from the idyllic suburbs of Haddonfield, Illinois to the isolated Camp Crystal Lake. This strategy paid off as the film made over $5 million on its opening weekend and earned $39 million domestically over its theatrical run.[30] While John Carpenter achieved the status of auteur and cineaste, Sean Cunningham, by contrast, was considered a financial opportunist, a greedy producer attempting to leech off the success of *Halloween* with *Friday* being dismissed as "a supremely cynical, crass, and imitative exercise in exploitation."[31]

Despite such critical denigration, the film's success sparked nine sequels, a short-lived television series (1987–1990), the cross-over film *Freddy vs. Jason* (2003, Ronny Yu), and the reboot *Friday the 13th* (Marcus Nispel) in 2009, not to mention a variety of video games and merchandise. From the first film, then, we see an attempt at novelty and differentiation through spatial relocation in situating the narrative formula of *Halloween* in a desolate summer camp. The sequels would continue to exploit this rustic locale for the majority of the series opting to introduce novelty in a variety of ways. As soon as the third installment, for example, the franchise turned to the use of 3D in order to draw in audiences. Although the film features a variety of sharp objects protruding into the audience and a human eye popping out of its socket, the filmmakers seem to have strained to find interesting uses of the technology. This is evidenced in its recourse to overhead shots of juggling and low-angle shots of a yo-yo. Such use of 3D constitutes a gimmick as it only exists as a showcase of the technology itself. However, *Friday the 13th Part III* (1982, Steve Miner) did introduce a key piece of iconography: the infamous hockey mask worn by Jason Voorhees.

The installments continued to become increasingly self-referential and comedic in tone: a character is depicted reading an interview with Tom Savini in *Fangoria* (*Part III*)[32]; upon seeing Jason appear on a road in front of their car, a young woman tells her boyfriend, "I've seen enough horror movies to know that a weirdo wearing a mask is never friendly"[33] (*Part VI: Jason Lives*); a final girl uses her telekinetic powers to defeat Jason (*Part VII: The New Blood*); Jason boards a ship bound for New York and wreaks havoc on the ship before landing in Manhattan (*Part VIII: Jason Takes Manhattan*); and after having been killed, Jason's evil spirit possesses those around him to continue his killing sprees (*Jason Goes to Hell*). Beginning as early as the third sequel, then, the series acquired a campy, darkly humorous sensibility characterized by "an air of grisly fun that was lacking in the first two films."[34]

Long before the release of *Scream* (1996, Wes Craven), a film often praised for its originality and postmodern deconstruction of the slasher subgenre,[35] the *Friday* series was winking at the audience in its acknowledgment of genre clichés. Take, for instance, the following scene in *Part VI*. Cort (Tom Fridley) and Nikki (Darcy DeMoss) are having sex in Nikki's camper parked on the camp ground. They are interrupted when Jason unplugs the power cord to the camper, shutting off all of the lights. Cory and Nikki investigate and, having heard the legends about Jason and suspecting they are not alone, the couple decide to drive off in the camper. Cort struggles to start the camper, but the engine won't turn on. "No way, this isn't happening," he says to Nikki. "You're right, it's not," she responds, flipping the alternator switch on the camper's generator.[36] Sure enough, the camper's engine begins running and the couple are off. Although Colt and Nikki are eventually killed in the camper, as Jason has secretly made his way inside, this brief moment parodying the cliché of the vehicle that just won't start at the moment one needs it most, a cliché that has been used in previous *Friday* films, points to an awareness on the part of the filmmakers of its overuse as well as an awareness that audiences would recognize such a scenario as a cliché. Despite such self-parodic moments, the post–*Scream* popular horror environment witnessed a renewed interest in teen slasher films and, if the *Friday* franchise wanted to capitalize on this and produce another sequel, it would have to take its self-reflexivity to new levels. As Cunningham did with the first installment, the filmmakers of *Jason X* opted for a more radical relocation, this time situating the action on a spaceship.

The film opens in the near future in 2010 at Crystal Lake Research Facility in which Jason has been captured by scientists. He is restrained with chains in a large auditorium under constant supervision by military personnel. The plan is to place Jason within a cryogenic chamber and freeze him indefinitely. However, Dr. Wimmer, played by David Cronenberg in a cameo appearance, orders that Jason be moved to another facility where he wishes to perform more research on Jason's unprecedented ability to regenerate lost and damaged tissue. Against the protests of Rowan (Lexa Doig), who is presumably spearheading the cryogenics plan, Dr. Wimmer instructs the military personnel to unchain Jason, but he has already (somehow) freed himself and kills all of the soldiers and Dr. Wimmer. Rowan narrowly escapes forcing Jason into the cryogenic chamber and freezing them both in the process. They are then discovered over four hundred years later by a professor and his team of students who bring both Jason and Rowan onto their spaceship. The team manages to reanimate Rowan while Jason, believed to be irrecoverable, is prepared for dissection and study. Inevitably, Jason reawakens and begins to kill the occupants of the spaceship one-by-one as the team aims to land on the space station *Solaris*. After several attempts at killing Jason, he is eventually blown out of the ship into the atmosphere of Earth Two, falling into a lake.

As with *Leprechaun 4*, *Jason X* maintains the syntax of the slasher horror film subgenre while utilizing the semantics of science fiction. For the most part, Jason repeats his tactics from the previous *Friday* films by stalking and killing characters one by one. In *Jason X*, characters find themselves in dark, isolated corridors of the spaceship rather than the dark, isolated confines of Camp Crystal Lake, yet the formula remains relatively unchanged. Among the team, however, is the artificially intelligent robot Kay-Em 14 (Lisa Ryder) who provides information, repairs technical problems, and, after receiving a series of upgrades, fights Jason with new martial arts skills and weaponry. Her efforts only exacerbate the problem as Jason is regenerated as the cyborg "Uber Jason," complete with stronger physique, metallic mask, and metal-enhanced appendages. The remaining members of the team attempt to board a space pod that has responded to their distress call. The bridge connecting the pod to the spaceship malfunctions, so the team decides to distract Jason with a holographic illusion while a member repairs the bridge. The following sequence is perhaps the most interesting and most relevant sequence in the film in our examination of novelty and sequelization.

The hologram recreates the ground of Camp Crystal Lake within the spaceship thereby confusing Jason into believing he is back in his natural environment. He examines his surrounding, complete with trees, cottage, and lake, and stumbles upon two scantily-clad young girls. The team instructs Kay-Em 14 to "use the data file Crystal Lake nineteen-hundred eighty," thus programming the holographic girls to simulate the behavior of the girls in previous *Friday* films. "Hey you want a beer?" asks one girl, "Or do you want to smoke some pot?"[37] asks the other. Intrigued, Jason walks closer to the girls. One girl then states, "Or we can have premarital sex!"[38] They both remove their shirts, exposing their breasts and the girls say in unison, "we love premarital sex!"[39] The girls get into their sleeping bags, giggling and wait for Jason to make his next move. He then grabs one sleeping bag like a sack swinging it into the other as the holographic girls feign the sounds of pain. Jason eventually "defeats" the hologram by swinging the sleeping bag against a nearby tree, a reference to a similar kill that occurred in *Friday the 13th Part VII: The New Blood* (1988, John Carl Buechler). More than this reference to an earlier installment, though, this sequence effectively calls attention to the clichés and rules of the slasher genre so aptly identified in the first *Scream*. Because the girls are drinking beer, smoking pot, are half-naked, and open to premarital sex, they violate the rules of chastity and purity that a Final Girl[40] would require to survive a horror film. As such, Jason quickly dispatches the girls just in time for the remaining team members to fix the bridge and escape into the pod. The spaceship proceeds to explode as the pod flies away, but the force of the explosion propels Jason toward the pod. Rowan exclaims, "You've got to be kidding me,"[41] a line that simultaneously acknowledges the incredulity of the spectator watching the film as well as parodies the seemingly constant and inevitable return of Jason once he is thought to be defeated. This time, Jason is intercepting by team member Sergeant Brodski who, wearing a spacesuit, grabs Jason and brings him into the Atmosphere of Earth Two. The final shot of the film depicts a couple on the side of a lake. They witness what they think is a shooting star, though it is actually Brodski and Jason hurtling into the planet. The girl notes the "shooting star" landed in the lake and her boyfriend suggests that they go "check it out." At the end of *Jason X*, the eponymous serial killer has returned to his roots at the bottom of a lake, waiting to return for another sequel.

Both *Leprechaun 4* and *Jason X* attempt to employ the semantics of science fiction films in order to inject novelty into their otherwise aging series. As Amanda Klein writes, "Attaching the semantics of a faltering cycle to a more stable genre or cycle, or to a timely topic or sentiment, is a way to extend a cycle's cultural relevance and thus squeeze more revenue out of it."[42] In the case of *Leprechaun 4* and *Jason X*, the syntax of slasher horror, its essential formula and structure, remains intact while the semantics of science fiction is adopted to provide renewed spectacle and innovative death scenes. These sequels are thus no different than their earlier installments but constitute the return of the same with superficial novelty. However, what the sequels do accomplish is fully embracing their status as camp, as kitsch, as paracinematic "bad objects," a development that was beckoned by the increased audience awareness of genre tropes and clichés as well as the state of the horror genre in the 1990s.

(In)Conclusion: Notes on Sequelization

For fans and critics alike, the horror film since the 1990s and into the early 2000s was often perceived as experiencing a period of aesthetic decline in quality. In sharp contrast to the politically-charged horror films of the 1970s, such as *The Exorcist* (1973, William Friedkin) and *The Texas Chainsaw Massacre* (1974, Tobe Hooper), the slasher cycle of American horror that proliferated throughout the 1980s assured for many that, by the decade's end, the horror genre had been all but exhausted. In *The American Horror Film*, Reynold Humphries laments, "It is patent that we shall see no more films of the calibre of *Texas Chainsaw Massacre*, which represents for the present writer everything that a horror movie can and should be."[43] Noting the perceived ubiquity of slasher films and their tendency to proliferate sequels, Humphries concludes that "the state of things is not conducive to optimism, let alone enthusiasm."[44] Wheeler Winston Dixon shares Humphries' pessimism when he describes current American horror films as "endlessly repeating themselves ... offer[ing] nothing more than sadism and violence in place of invention; we must look elsewhere for inspiration."[45] In a more explicit condemnation of horror cinema's penchant for sequelization, Dixon implores, "Is there anything original out there anymore?"[46] Such disdain for the current state of horror has also infected the fan community as Steffen Hantke observes, "Ask fans ... and they will tell you that American horror film in the last decade—from roughly the mid–1990s, through the turn of the century, and far into the new millennium—has fallen into a slump."[47] The popular discourse regarding contemporary horror, Hantke continues, is one of "dissatisfaction" culminating in a sense that the horror genre from the '90s onwards was "at its worst."[48]

Such dissatisfaction is also expressed by horror filmmakers themselves who concede that horror today lacks both the stylistic innovation and political relevance that had once positioned the genre on the vanguard of American filmmaking in decades past. Robert Englund, who appeared in eight *A Nightmare on Elm Street* films as Freddy Kruger, has stated: "it is disappointing that when technology permits immense creativity, so many of the [current American horror] stories are recycled or unoriginal."[49] Jeffrey Delman, best known for his directorial debut *Deadtime Stories* (1986), concurs with Englund, saying, "I am troubled by … the plethora of remakes and the lack of originality they demonstrate…. Remakes accomplish little more than generating income for creatively vapid studios."[50]

What these authors and filmmakers demonstrate is that the perception of the declining quality of contemporary horror is intimately linked with sequalization and its attendant association with profit for profit's sake. For these critics, horror's sequels and remakes are simply attempts by studios and producers to cash in on earlier successes by creating essentially the same films and tapping into built-in audiences. The existence of a sequel is a symptom of industrial greed on the part of producers and studio executives rather than an authentic expression of artistic vision on the part of filmmakers. What is fascinating within this discourse is how strongly "originality" or "authenticity" is explicitly expressed as *the* criterion of value in a film as well as how this is repeatedly located in opposition to the financial interests of a studio or producer. To make a film primarily for profit contaminates and undermines any existing artistic intent. With this understanding, the sequel would thus exacerbate the greed factor by capitalizing on the success of a previous film. Offering nothing new or original, critics suggest, the horror sequel constitutes a meaningless repetition of violent spectacle.

But what sequels like *Leprechaun 4* and *Jason X* demonstrate is the internal contradiction of the sequel itself: the desire for the new *as well as* the return of the same. As Paul Budra and Betty Schellenberg note, "an audience's desire to re-experience in some way a memorable story, an author's response to that desire, and the inevitably changed conditions which make it impossible to achieve a precise repetition of the experience are clearly germane to the sequel phenomenon."[51] The result, one would logically conclude, is invariably one of disappointment marking the sequel as an ontological tragedy, one that, in its very nature, cannot fulfill the expectations of its audience.[52] The critical disdain for horror film of the 1980s and 1990s thus reveals a cult of originality that necessarily cannot be satisfied. Yet, slasher films of the 1980s and 1990s and their various sequels have proven quite popular among fans of the paracinematic, achieving new life on home video. Indeed, in the mid–1990s, *Video Store Magazine* created a list of the top-selling VHS tapes including: *Leprechaun 3, Puppet Master 5: The Final Chapter* (1994, Jeff Burr), *Bloodfist VI: Ground Zero* (1995, Rick Jacobson), *Witchcraft 7: Judgement Hour* (1995, Michael Paul Girard), *Children of the Corn III: Urban Harvest* (1995, James Hickox), *Ghoulies IV* (1994, Jim Wynorski), *Trancers 5: Sudden Deth* (1994, David Nutter), *Phantasm III: Lord of the Dead* (1994, Don Coscarelli), and *Kickboxer 4: The Aggressor* (1994, Albert Pyun).[53] The prevalence and success of such sequels on the home video market suggest that while critics and some audience members may dismiss sequelization as the repetition of the same, paracinematic aficionados and fans of particular series who are willing to accept such works as subversive, campy, and postmodernist fun, such sequels may be regarded as even more enjoyable than any original work. As Kane Hodder, the stuntman-turned-actor who has played Jason Voorhees in the most films, has stated, "People were concerned at the beginning—'oh, it's Jason in space. But if Jason is still the same, then who cares where it happens?"[54]

Note: I am indebted to the Media Commons Archive at the University of Toronto and especially Assistant Media Archivist Rachel Beattie for providing access to archival material for this project.

NOTES

1. Excluding, of course, the first film of the franchise in which the killer is revealed to Mrs. Voorhees, Jason's mother.

2. Yagher chose to be credited as Alan Smithee, the industry standard for directors who wish to withdraw their names from films.

3. Dialogue from *Leprechaun 4: In Space*, DVD, directed by Brian Trenchard-Smith (1996; Santa Monica, CA: Trimark Home Video, 2003).

4. Darko Survin, "On the Poetics of the Science Fiction Genre," *College English* 34.3 (1972): 372–373.

5. *Ibid.*, 375.

6. Jean Baudrillard, *Simulacra and Simulation*, trans. Sheila Faria Glaser (Ann Arbor: University of Michigan Press, 1994), 13.

7. Promotional Packet, *Leprechaun 3* (Santa Monica, CA: Trimark Pictures, 1995).

8. Jeffrey Sconce, "'Trashing' the Academy: Taste, Excess, and an Emerging Politics of Cinematic Style," in *Film Theory and Criticism*, 6th ed., ed. Leo Braudy and Marshall Cohen (Oxford: Oxford University Press, 2004), 534–535; and Sontag, "Notes on Camp," 278.

9. Susan Sontag, "Notes on Camp," in *Against Interpretation and Other Essays* (New York: Farrar, Strauss, and Giroux, 1966), 283.

10. *Ibid.*, 288.

11. *Ibid.*, 283.

12. *Ibid.*, 284.

13. Production Information Packet, *Leprechaun* (Santa Monica, CA: Trimark Pictures, 1993).

14. Sontag, "Notes on Camp," 289.

15. Sconce, "'Trashing' the Academy," 536.

16. *Ibid.*, 542.

17. Kevin Brass, "Video Invasion: B Film Makers Battle A-List for a Place on the Shelf," *Los Angeles Times*, April 19, 1996.

18. "The Market: An Annual Report on the Home Video Market 1997 (Industry Overview)," *Video Business* 17.29 (1997).

19. *Ibid.*

20. Sconce, "'Trashing' the Academy," 543.

21. Matt Hills, "Para-Paracinema: The *Friday the 13th* Film Series as Other to Trash and Legitimate Film Cultures," in *Sleaze Artists: Cinema at the Margins of Taste, Style, and Politics*, ed. Jeffrey Sconce (Durham: Duke University Press, 2007), 219.

22. Wheeler Winston Dixon, *A History of Horror* (New Brunswick, NJ: Rutgers University Press, 2010), 169.

23. Matt Hills, "Para-Paracinema," 224.

24. James Francis, Jr., *Remaking Horror: Hollywood's New Reliance on Scares of Old* (Jefferson, NC: McFarland, 2014), 51.

25. Stuart Henderson, *The Hollywood Sequel: History and Form, 1911–2010* (Hampshire: Palgrave Macmillan, 2014), 150.

26. Hills, "Para-Paracinema," 228.

27. This ad is reproduced in Richard Nowell, *Blood Money: A History of the First Teen Slasher Film Cycle* (New York: Continuum, 2011), 122.

28. *Ibid.*

29. *Ibid.*

30. Box Office Mojo, http://www.boxofficemojo.com/movies/?id=friday13th.htm, accessed January 30, 2016.

31. Nowell, 120–121.

32. Tom Savini was the special make-up effects artist for the first *Friday the 13th* and returned to provide the effects for *Friday the 13th: The Final Chapter* (1984, Joseph Zito).

33. Dialogue from *Friday the 13th Part VI: Jason Lives*, DVD, directed by Tom McLoughlin (1986; Hollywood: Paramount Pictures, 2013).

34. Ken Hanke, *A Critical Guide to Horror Series* (New York: Garland, 1991), 296.

35. See Valeri Wee, "Resurrecting and Updating the Teen Slasher: The Case of *Scream*," *Journal of Popular Film and Television* 34.2 (2006): 50–61.

36. Dialogue from *Friday the 13th Part VI: Jason Lives.*

37. Dialogue from *Jason X*, DVD, directed by James Isaac (2001; Toronto: Alliance Atlantis Home Video, 2002).

38. *Ibid.*

39. *Ibid.*

40. This term was coined by Carol Clover. For her in-depth analysis, see her "Her Body, Himself," in *Men, Women, and Chain Saws: Gender in Modern Horror Film* (Princeton: Princeton University Press, 1992): 21–64.

41. Dialogue from *Jason X.*

42. Amanda Ann Klein, *American Film Cycles: Reframing Genres, Screening Social Problems, and Defining Subcultures* (Austin: University of Texas Press, 2011), 90.

43. Reynold Humpries, *The American Horror Film* (Edinburgh: Edinburgh University Press, 2003), 195.

44. *Ibid.*, 189.

45. Dixon, *A History of Horror*, 203.

46. *Ibid.*

47. Steffen Hantke, "They Don't Make 'Em Like They Used To: On the Rhetoric of Crisis and the Current State of the American Horror Film," in *American Horror Film: The Genre at the Turn of the Millennium* (Jackson: University of Mississippi Press, 2010), xvii.

48. *Ibid.*, ix.

49. Quoted in Francis, Jr., *Remaking Horror*, 150.

50. *Ibid.*, 147–148.

51. Paul Budra and Betty Schellenberg, "Introduction," in *Part Two: Reflections on the Sequel* (Toronto: University of Toronto Press, 1998), 5.

52. *Ibid.*

53. Brass, "Video Invasion."

54. Quoted in Patrick Day, "Injecting Life into a Familiar Boogeyman: The Latest 'Friday the 13th' Installment Puts Jason in Outer Space in the Year 2455. But His Creator Says the Slasher Series' Future is Limited," Los Angeles Times, April 24, 2002: F.2.

BIBLIOGRAPHY

Baudrillard, Jean. Simulacra and Simulation. Translated by Sheila Faria Glaser. Ann Arbor: University of Michigan Press, 1994.

Brass, Kevin, "Video Invasion: B Film Makers Battle A-List for a Place on the Shelf." Los Angeles Times, April 19, 1996.

Budra, Paul, and Betty A. Schellenberg. Part Two: Reflections on the Sequel. Toronto: University of Toronto Press, 1998.

Day, Patrick "Injecting Life into a Familiar Boogeyman: The Latest 'Friday the 13th' Installment Puts Jason in Outer Space in the Year 2455. But His Creator Says the Slasher Series' Future Is Limited." Los Angeles Times, April 24, 2002.

Dixon, Wheeler Winston. A History of Horror. New Brunswick: Rutgers University Press, 2010.

Francis, James, Jr. Remaking Horror: Hollywood's New Reliance on Scares of Old. Jefferson, NC: McFarland, 2013.

Friday the 13th. DVD. Directed by Sean. S. Cunningham. 1980; Hollywood: Paramount Pictures, 2009.

Friday the 13th Part VI: Jason Lives. DVD. Directed by Tom McLoughlin. 1986; Hollywood: Paramount Pictures, 2013.

Hanke, Ken. A Critical Guide to Horror Series. New York: Garland, 1991.

Hantke, Steffen. "They Don't Make 'Em Like They Used To: On the Rhetoric of Crisis and the Current State of the American Horror Film." In American Horror Film: The Genre at the Turn of the Millennium, vii–xxxii. Jackson: University of Mississippi Press, 2010.

Henderson, Stuart. The Hollywood Sequel: History and Form, 1911–2010. Hampshire: Palgrave Macmillan, 2014.

Hills, Matt. "Para-Paracinema: The Friday the 13th Film Series as Other to Trash and Legitimate Film Cultures." In Sleaze Artists: Cinema at the Margins of Taste, Style, and Politics, edited by Jeffrey Sconce, 219–239 Durham: Duke University Press, 2007.

Humpries, Reynold. The American Horror Film. Edinburgh: Edinburgh University Press, 2003.

Jason X. DVD. Directed by James Isaac. 2001. Toronto: Alliance Atlantis Home Video, 2002.

Klein, Amanda Ann. American Film Cycles: Reframing Genres, Screening Social Problems, and Defining Subcultures. Austin: University of Texas Press, 2011.

Leprechaun 4: In Space. DVD. Directed by Brian Trenchard-Smith. 1996; Santa Monica, CA: Trimark Home Video, 2003.

Nowell, Richard. Blood Money: A History of the Teen Slasher Film Cycle. New York: Continuum, 2011.

Promotional Information Packet. Leprechaun. Santa Monica, CA: Trimark Pictures, 1993.

Promotional Packet. Leprechaun 4: In Space. Santa Monica, CA: Trimark Pictures, 1996.

"The Market: An Annual Report on the Home Video Market." Video Business 17.29 (1997).

Sconce, Jeffrey. "'Trashing' the Academy: Taste, Excess, and an Emerging Politics of Cinematic Style." In Film Theory and Criticism, 6th ed., edited by Leo Braudy and Marshall Cohen, 534–554. Oxford: Oxford University Press, 2004.

Sontag, Susan. "Notes on Camp." In Against Interpretation and Other Essays, 275–292. New York: Farrar, Strauss, and Giroux, 1966.

Survin, Dark. "On the Poetics of the Science Fiction Genre." College English 34.3 (1972): 372–382.

About the Contributors

Dario **Altobelli** teaches sociology at Sapienza University of Rome and University of Rome 3. He is the author of "Nineteen Eighty-Four Today" in *Nineteen Eighty-Four* edited by Thomas Horan (2016); *L'utile e il ragionevole* (The Useful and the Reasonable, 2016); and *I sogni della biologia* (The Dreams of Biology, 2012).

Simon **Bacon** is an independent scholar. He has contributed to many publications on vampires, monstrosity, science fiction and media studies, and he is the coeditor of *Undead Memory* (2014), *Seductive Concepts* (2014), and *Little Horrors* (2016).

Michele **Brittany** is the editor of *James Bond and Popular Culture* (2014). She is also the book review editor for the *Journal of Graphic Novels and Comics*, editorials manager for Fanbase Press, and a founding member of the H.P. Lovecast podcast analyzing Lovecraftian horror writers.

Kevin **Chabot** is a doctoral candidate in cinema studies at the University of Toronto. His SSHRC-funded dissertation examines the found-footage cycle of horror films in relation to paranormal investigation. His research interests include horror film, classic and contemporary film theory, medium specificity, and intermediality.

Adam M. **Crowley** is an associate professor of English at Husson University (Maine). He teaches on American, British, and Canadian literature. He is one of the founding members of the H.P. Lovecraft podcast. His academic interests are wide-ranging, and his work has been concerned with zombies and videogames.

Jason **Davis** teaches anime and manga at Macquarie University (Australia). He has written essays on anime, manga, *Dexter*, and the *Planet of the Apes* and *Hannibal Lecter* franchises. He has also published on explorations of ecologically-themed anime in *Resilience: A Journal of the Environmental Humanities*.

Nicholas **Diak** is a scholar of Italian and exploitation films, post-industrial and neofolk music, and H.P. Lovecraft studies. He is the editor of *The New Peplum* (forthcoming) and contributes essays and reviews to other collections, scholarly journals, and online periodicals.

Brenda S. **Gardenour Walter** is an associate professor of history at the Saint Louis College of Pharmacy. She researches the role of Aristotelian discourse, learned medicine, and scholastic theology in the construction of alterity and the continued influence of medieval otherness on the horror genre.

Janet Joyce **Holden** is the author of the novels *Carousel* (2012), *The Only Red Is Blood* (2014), and the *Origins of Blood* vampire series (2014–) and numerous speculative short stories in various collections.

Gavin F. **Hurley** is an assistant professor of writing at Lasell College (Massachusetts), where he teaches composition, rhetoric, and ethical reasoning. His work has appeared in *The Contemporary Novel and the Poetics of Genre* (2015) and *Does Religious Education Matter?* (2016).

Ben **Kooyman** has published essays and journal articles on horror films and filmmakers as well as a book, *Directorial Self-Fashioning in American Horror Cinema* (2014). He runs the website Down Under Flix (downunderflix.com) and is assistant editor of Australian Comics Journal (australiancomicsjournal.com).

Casey **Ratto** is a doctoral candidate in American studies at Washington State University. His research interests include cinema studies, game studies, popular culture, and post-apocalyptic media. His dissertation analyzes the intersection of the Western genre with the post-apocalyptic genre in cinema.

Charles W. **Reick** is an independent scholar whose interests include the aesthetics of horror and science fiction. He taught English part-time at the Community College of Baltimore and the Community Colleges of Baltimore County.

Juliane **Schlag** is a doctoral candidate in history and biology at the University of Hull (UK). Her research interests include social ecology and environment, ancient belief and knowledge systems, history of nutrition, material culture, and concepts of knowledge transfer.

Kevin J. **Wetmore**, Jr., is the author or editor of numerous books and the author of dozens of articles and essays on everything from *Star Trek* to Godzilla, zombie cinema, werewolves, Greek tragedy in horror movies, and teenage Shakespeare. He is also a fiction writer.

Andrew P. **Williams** is a professor of literature and creative writing at North Carolina Central University. He is the author of three novels and numerous short stories in the horror genre. His research interests include iconic monster figures like Dr. Jekyll and Dracula.

Index

acceleration of time 101–103
Across the Zodiac 6
Agamben, Giorgio 184
Age of Enlightenment 89, 157, 169, 183
Age of Reason 183
Ahmed, Sara 142
AIDS 19, 35, 45
Aitken, Stuart C. 106
Algol—Tragödie der Macht 6
Alien 2, 4–5, 7, 9–10, 15–17, 35, 48n27, 53, 66, 101, 111, 127–128, 130, 136, 140, 143, 145– 146, 148, 151–152, 170–171, 175, 177, 181–183, 189, 194–209
"Alien and the Monstrous-Feminine" 127
Alien franchise 2–4, 7, 88, 127, 165, 205–207, 209
Alien Memories Project 208
Alien Queen 135, 182, 189–190
Alien Resurrection 10, 170, 181–184, 187, 189– 191
Alien³ 9, 128–129, 133, 136, 170–171, 181–183
Alien 2 sulla Terra 195, 198, 206–208
Aliens 4–5, 9, 135, 140, 145–148, 170, 181–183, 189, 205
*Alien*sploitation 10, 194–196, 198, 200–202, 205–206, 208–209
An All-Consuming Century 57
Altair IV 7
Alvart, Christian 2, 103, 197
Anderson, Paul W.S. 2, 70, 81, 86–87, 98, 111, 152, 165
android 2, 5, 7, 9, 88, 90–91, 135, 143, 145– 147, 155, 184–185, 187–188, 190, 199
Andromeda Strain (book) 99
Andromeda Strain (film) 99
anthropocentrism 183, 187
apocalypse trilogy 19, 24
Apollo 18 2, 4
Argo 166, 167
Aristotle 92
Arnold, Jack 1, 13
artificial intelligence 114–116, 121, 141, 143, 148, 226

Ash 2, 5, 9, 48n27, 143–147
Assault on Precinct 13 17, 25, 27
The Astronaut's Wife 68
atavism 10, 194, 196–199, 202–205, 207–208
USM *Auriga* 171, 185, 190
auteur 8, 14, 225
AVP: Alien vs. Predator 70–71

Ballard, J.G. 198
Banionis, Donatas 167
Banks, Elizabeth 61
Barker, Clive 86, 156, 200
Bartkowiak, Andrzej 3
Basinger, Janine 186
Bataille, Georges 8, 81–83, 85–87, 89–93
Battle Beyond the Stars 194
Baudrillard, Jean 10, 164–165, 169, 171, 174, 220
Bava, Mario 3, 164, 166, 199
Benson, John 62
Bermuda Triangle 154–155
betwixt and between 9, 151, 153, 157, 160
Beware! The Blob 52, 54, 56, 59, 61–62
Biehn, Michael 147
Billson, Ann 35
Bishop 5, 7, 9, 135, 146–147
black hole 10, 84–87, 99, 105, 159, 164–166, 173–177
black magic 100, 152–153, 156–157, 160–161, 201
black monolith 141–143, 173
Blackwood, Algernon 166
Bledscoe, Will 154
Bliss, Michael 67, 74
The Blob (1958) 2, 7, 50, 52, 54–55, 57, 59– 63, 71, 74, 76–77
The Blob (1988) 29n23, 54, 56, 59–62, 71, 74
Blood of the Vampire 166
Blumenfeld, Alan 154
Bolt, Jeremy 84, 86
Bond, Michael 113
Bondarchuk, Natalya 168
Booth, Walter R. 6

Bosch, Hieronymus 86
Bottin, Rob 18–19
Boyle, Danny 3, 98
Boyle, Peter 117
Bradbury, Ray 7, 206
Bradley, Doug 156
Breazeal, Cynthia 144
Brimley, Wilfred 18, 42
Brooks, Rodney 144
Budra, Paul 229
Bullock, Sandra 171–172
Butler, Judith 188

Cahn, Edward L. 199
Cameron, James 4, 135, 140, 170, 181, 202, 205
Camp aesthetics 221–222
Camp Crystal Lake 218, 224, 226–227
Campbell, John W., Jr. 17, 34, 36–37
capitalism 22, 24, 26, 36, 38–40, 42–44, 46, 147
Carlton, Rebecca 219
Carpenter, John 2–3, 8, 13–28, 33–34, 36, 40, 44–46, 51, 69–70, 84, 197, 224
Carroll, Noëll 10, 81–82, 92
Carter, Helena 72
Cartesian 131, 187–188
Cenobites 3, 156–158, 218
Cetrone, Richard 26
Chappelle, Joe 3
chestburster 121, 145
Chomon, Segundo de 6
Christian 83, 90–92, 97, 124, 134, 155, 183–184, 200, 203
Christian, Roger 4
Clarens, Carlos 108
Clark, Bruce D. 10, 194
Clooney, George 113, 169, 171
Clover, Carol J. 4, 77n9
Colceri, Tom 219
Cold War 7–8, 10, 74, 76–77, 199
Collins, Jessica 219
The Color Out of Space 6, 8, 51–56, 63
Colour from the Dark 52
Communion 7
Communism 7, 17, 37, 51
Connery, Sean 117
consumerism 8, 22–24, 26, 29, 40, 42–46, 50–51, 57–63, 121, 223
Contamination 10, 195, 205–207
Cordero, Sebastian 2
Corman, Roger 194–196, 199, 201–205
Cornea, Carol 170
Cornthwaite, Robert 37
Cosmatos, George P. 9, 128
Cosmic Pessimism 82
Cottrell, Mickey 156
Cozzi, Luigi 10, 195, 205–206
Craven, Wes 152, 225
Creed, Barbara 34–35, 127, 189

Creepshow 52
Critters 4 218
Cronenberg, David 20, 60, 226
Cross, Gary 57
Cruise, Tom 70
Cryogenic 68, 70, 141, 170, 174, 185, 226
Cuarón, Alfonso 165, 171
Cundey, Dean 18
Cunningham, Sean 224–226
The Curse 52, 54–56, 59

Damon, Matt 174
Dance, Charles 133
dark mysticism 83, 85–86, 90
The Dark Side of the Moon 152, 154–155, 161
Dark Star 8, 14–17, 20–28
Davenport, Harry Bromley 10, 194, 200
David, Keith 19, 21, 69
Davies, Jeremy 114
Davis, Viola 114
Davis, Warwick 219
The Day the Earth Stood Still 1, 7
The Deadly Spawn 52, 54–56, 62
dehumanization 9, 20, 22, 24, 58, 67, 104, 107–108, 175
Dekker, Fred 70
del Toro, Guillermo 1
demonic 9–10, 105, 123, 151–158, 160–161, 197, 203, 218
DeMoss, Darcy 225
De Palma, Brian 31n78
Derrida, Jacques 93
Descartes, Rene 130–132, 187
Devil (also Satan) 9–10, 151–156, 161
Dick, Philip K. 196, 207
Die, Monster, Die! 52, 54–57
Dillon, Kevin 75
Dimock, Wai Chee 175
Discovery One 141–143, 173
Dixon, Wheeler Winston 223–224, 228
Doig, Lexa 226
Domergue, Faith 1
Donaldson, Roger 26, 68
Doom 3–4
doppelganger 10, 85, 147, 164
Dourdan, Gary 186
Dracula 81, 165–166
Dracula 3000 2, 4
Dullea, Kier 141, 173
Dune 17
Dvorzhetskiy, Vladislav 167
Dysart, Richard 18, 69

Ebert, Roger 181, 200
Eisenhower, Dwight 73–74, 76
Elley, Derek 181
Ellison, Harlan 103
Endurance 174
E.T. the Extra-Terrestrial 20, 23, 34, 69, 200–201

Europa Report 2–5, 8
Event Horizon (film) 2–5, 7–8, 10, 81, 83–88, 90–93, 98–99, 101–102, 105–106, 111, 152, 158, 161, 165, 175–177
Event Horizon (ship) 3, 83–87, 99, 153, 158–161, 175–176
Excursion to the Moon 6
exploitation films 194–196, 199, 202, 206, 222, 225
extrasolar films 2

facehuggers 3–4, 92, 132, 145, 147
Die Farbe 52, 54–57
Fassbender, Michael 5, 88
fatalism 82, 97–98, 108
feminism 34, 127–128, 183, 189
Fillon, Nathan 62
filoni 207
final girl 4–5, 225, 227
Fincher, David 9, 51, 128, 170, 181
Finney, Jack 99
Fiorina Fury 161 129, 133–136, 171
Fire in the Sky 7
The First Men in the Moon (book) 6
Fishburne, Laurence 83, 159, 176
Flender, Rodman 218
Flowers, Kim 186
Forbidden Planet 7, 13, 199, 204, 220
Forbidden World 195, 201–202
Foster, Meg 23
Foucault, Michel 188
Fowler, Gene, Jr. 200
Francis, James, Jr. 224
Frankenstein 37, 87, 100, 159, 201
Frankenstein (film) 50
Franz, Arthur 71
Freeman, J.E. 185
Freud, Sigmund 36, 127, 189, 204
Friday the 13th 218, 224–225
Friday the 13th franchise 68, 218, 223–224, 226–227
Fridley, Tom 225
Frye, Northrop 9, 122–125

Galaxy of Terror 10, 194–195, 202–205
Galliot 166–167
Geeson, Judy 203
GERTY 115–116, 121–123, 125
ghost 9, 98, 100, 143–147, 152, 220
Ghostly Matters 9
Ghosts of Mars 8, 14, 24–29, 197
Gidding, Nelson 99
Giger, H.R. 2, 17
Girard, François 166
Goldsmith, Jerry 117
Gordon, Avery 9, 140–141, 143, 145
Gordon, Richard 203
Gothic 50, 199–200, 207, 220
Gravity 165, 171, 174
Greg, Percy 6

Guest, Val 1, 206
Gunn, James 52

Hagman, Larry 52
HAL 9000 9, 141–145, 147, 173
Hallahan, Charles 18, 69
Haller, Daniel 52
Halloween 17, 21, 84, 224–225
hallucination 43, 84–85, 104–106, 112–115, 122, 159, 168, 176, 221
Hantke, Steffen 77, 228–229
Haraway, Donna 184, 187–190
Harnos, Christine 156
Harvey, Rupert 218
Haskin, Bryon 1
Hathaway, Anne 174
Hawks, Howard 8, 13, 17, 24, 34, 36–37, 42, 199
Hell 84–87, 124–125, 153, 156–158, 160–161, 176–177
The Hellbound Heart (book) 86
Hellraiser 86, 156, 200
Hellraiser: Bloodline 3, 7, 10, 152, 156, 158, 161, 218
Henderson, Stuart 224
Henn, Carrie 4, 135, 147
Henriksen, Lance 5, 70, 135, 146
Henry, Gregg 59
Henstridge, Natasha 26
Herbert, Frank 17
Heron, Woodburn 113
Hills, Matt 223
HIV virus 35
Hodder, Kane 217, 230
Hoffman, Antony 31n78
Holger-Madsen 6
Holm, Ian 2, 48n27, 143
Holzman, Allan 195
Hooper, Tobe 29n23, 153, 228
Horror Writers Association 111
Humphries, Reynold 228
Hunter, Stephen 181
Hurt, John, Sir 131, 143, 201
Hutson, Matthew 115
Hyams, Peter 111, 116
hyperreality 165, 171, 174–175

I Married a Monster from Outer Space 200–201
Icarus I 103
Ice Cube 26
impregnation 4, 132, 183, 185, 189, 197, 201, 203
In the Dust of this Planet 82–83
In the Mouth of Madness 19, 21, 24
Inseminoid 10, 194–195, 202–203
International Space Station 112, 172
Interstellar 10, 165, 174, 177
intertextuality 51, 53–54, 56
Invaders from Mars (1953) 1, 71–72, 74, 76–77

Invaders from Mars (1986) 29*n*23
invasion films   2, 7, 66–67, 71, 73
Invasion of the Body Snatchers (1956)   2, 7,
   46, 51–52, 67, 73, 99, 206
Invasion of the Body Snatchers (1978)   29*n*23,
   46
Ippolito, Ciro   195, 207
irrational robot   9, 140–143, 145–148
Isaac, Jason   68, 217
isolation   5, 8–9, 20, 25, 41–42, 46, 97, 106,
   111–119, 130, 135, 197–198, 204–205, 209,
   224, 226
It Came from Outer Space (1953)   13
It Conquered the World   199
It! The Terror From Beyond Space   199

Jannings, Emil   6
Jason X   10, 68, 217–219, 223 226, 228–229
Jävet, Jüri   168
*Jaws*ploitation   196
Jeunet, Jean-Pierre   10, 170, 181–183
Jodorowsky, Alejandro   17
Johnson, Tor   68
Jones, Duncan   5, 9, 103, 111, 115, 121
Jones, Jonathan   167
Jones, Richard T.   176
Joshi, S.T.   54
Judeo-Christian   84, 86, 154, 158

Kahn, Peter H.   187
Kanas, Nick   113
Karloff, Boris   54
Kaufman, Philip   29*n*23, 46
Kawin, Bruce   57–58
Keith, David   52
Kenworthy, Christopher   102
The Killing of Jacob Marr   52, 54–56, 59
King, Stephen   21, 51, 196
Kitchin, Rob   107–108
Klein, Amanda   228
Kneale, James   107–108
Kotto, Yaphet   145
Kristeva, Julia   35, 127
Kubrick, Stanley   9, 15, 140–141, 165, 170,
   196
Kuniholm, Cal   15

Lamentation Configuration   156–158
Last Days on Mars   4
Lem, Stanislaw   111, 113, 169
Leprechaun 4: In Space   218–221, 223, 226,
   228–229
Leprechaun franchise   220–222
Leprechaun 3   218, 221, 223, 230
Leprechaun 2   218, 222
Lesco, Ken   154
Leviathan   9, 128–129, 136–137
Levy, Emanuel   53, 58, 60–62
Lewis and Clark   3, 83–84, 87, 159–160, 175–
   176

Lieberman, Robert   7
Lily C.A.T.   5
Lindelof, Damon   90
Lockwood, Gary   141, 173
"The Lonesome Death of Jordy Verrill"   52,
   54–56
Lopez-Gallego, Gonzalo   2
Lovecraft, H.P.   6, 8–9, 16, 24, 28, 50–56, 59,
   62–63, 83, 96–97, 99, 102, 196
Lucas, George   194
Lugosi, Bela   68
*Lurker in the Lobby: A Guide to the Cinema
   of H.P. Lovecraft*   51, 53
LV-426   7, 127, 131–132, 136, 143, 145–147, 198,
   207

Maddrey, Joseph   24–25
Malone, William   195
Maloney, Peter   42, 69
Marinker, Peter   160
Marryat, Florence   166
Marshall-Green, Logan   88
The Martian Chronicles (book)   7, 206
The Martian Chronicles (television)   206
Martinez, Chris   114
Marxism   36, 39, 185
Mason, Tom   68
McConaughey, Matthew   174
McCrane, Paul   62
McKeown, Douglas   52, 55
McKinnon, Mona   68
McMahon, David   38
McQueen, Steve   52, 61
McTiernan, John   68, 152
Méliès, Georges   6
Menzies, William Cameron   1, 71
Merton, Robert K.   37
Metaluna   1, 7
metamorphosis   8, 37, 42–43, 46, 124, 132, 221
meteorite   50–63, 75, 167
Miller, Ashley   6
Minos   156, 158
Mission to Mars   112
Mission to Mars (film)   31*n*78
Monet, Camilla   70
The Monolith Monsters   50, 52, 54–56, 61
monstrous-feminine   34, 127, 189
Moon   5, 8, 103–106, 111, 115–116, 118, 121–125
Mora, Philippe   7
More, Camilla   155
Mori, Masahiro   144
Morricone, Ennio   18
MOTHER   5, 35, 129–130, 144
The '?' Motorist   6
Muir, John Kenneth   13, 16, 19, 23
Murakami, Jimmy T.   194

Narelle, Brian   14
NASA Goddard Space Center   112
Nash, Simon   201

Neill, Sam 3, 83, 99, 158, 175
Newman, Joseph M. 1
Newman, Kim 20, 176
Nielson, Leslie 220
Nietzsche, Friedrich 82
Night of the Creeps 70, 77n9
Night of the Living Dead (1968) 20, 68
nihilism 82, 86, 89, 93, 169, 200
Nolan, Christopher 10, 165, 174
nonknowledge 8, 81–91, 93
Nostromo 2, 7, 66, 127–136, 143–146, 152, 170–171, 197
nothingness 82, 85, 87, 89, 91, 93, 176
novelty 10, 218, 220, 225, 227–228
Nyby, Christian 8, 13, 17, 34, 36–37, 42, 199

O'Bannon, Dan 14–17, 27, 197, 202
occultism 3, 83, 152–153, 156–157, 197
Ochoa, George 97, 107–108
On Rhetoric 92
Orser, Leland 185
otherness 35, 67, 74, 76–77, 131–132
O'Toole, Peter 71
Outland 111, 116, 118–119

Pahich, Dre 15
Pal, George 101
Pandorum 2, 4, 8, 103–104, 106 197
paracinema 10, 207, 217, 221–224, 228, 230
patriarchal 127, 186, 189–190, 201
Perlman, Ron 186
Pertwee, Sean 159
Phillips, Kendall R. 16–17, 19–20, 22–23, 25
The Philosophy of Horror 81–82, 92
Pidgeon, Walter 220
Pierce, Guy 88
Pinhead 156–158
Pinon, Dominique 186
Piper, Roddy 21, 23
Pitch Black 2–4, 111
Plan 9 from Outer Space 7, 68, 222
Planet of the Vampires 3, 10, 164, 166, 170, 175–176, 199, 206
Post-Cartesian 128–130, 134, 136
posthumanism 10, 181, 183, 187–188, 190–191
postmodernism 10, 36, 81–83, 86, 88–90, 93, 183–184, 186, 188, 190–191, 217, 219, 225, 230
Predator 68, 152
Predator franchise 3
Prince of Darkness 19, 21
Prometheus 4–5, 8, 81, 88–93, 153, 199
psychic vampires 165–166
pure outer space films 2

The Quatermass Xperiment 1

Rain, Douglas 141, 173
Ramsay, Bruce 156–157
Rapace, Noomi 4, 88

Ravic, Rand 68
Reaganism 14, 22–23, 74, 76, 183
Reason, Rex 1
Red Letter Media 194–195
Red Planet 31n78
The Red Violin 166
Redd, Nola Taylor 112
Rego, Bred 52
Reiser, Paul 4, 146
Richardson, Joely 4, 159, 176
Ripley, Lt. Ellen 4, 7, 10, 132, 135, 143–147, 170–172, 182–191
Robinson, Ruairi 4
Rockwell, Sam 105, 115, 121
Rodenberry, Gene 24
Romero, George A. 20, 46, 52, 68, 207
Roodt, Darrell 2
Rooker, Michael 61
Rorty, Richard 93
Russell, Chuck 29n23, 71, 74
Russell, Kurt 13, 18, 69
Ryder, Lisa 226
Ryder, Winona 187

Sagan, Carl 106, 206
Sargsyan, Sos 168
Sartre, Jean-Paul 82, 132
satanic 152
Saulnier, Tania 54
Savini, Tom 225
Sayer, Philip 201
Scalia, Pedro 90
Schellenberg, Betty 229
Schumpeter, Joseph 36, 40
Sconce, Jeffrey 221–223
Scott, Ridley 2, 4, 7, 15, 35, 48n27, 53, 66, 81, 88, 90–91, 101, 111, 127, 130, 140, 151, 153, 170, 181, 194, 199
Scream 225–227
Seneca, Joe 62, 75
sentimental romance 9, 122–125
sequelization 227–230
The Serpent and the Rainbow 152
Shalev, Sharon 112
Sheridan, Margaret 39
Sherwood, John 50
Siegel, Don 2, 46, 51, 67, 99, 186, 206
Silver, Alain 166
simulacra/simulation 8, 10, 42–44, 164–165, 169–177
Siner, Guy 219
Singer, Matt 172
Siskel, Gene 200
Skal, David J. 74
Skerritt, Tom 144
slasher films 4, 7–9, 17, 55, 81, 223–225, 227–229
Slither 52, 54–56, 59, 61–62
Small-Town America in Film 58
Smith, Shawnee 75

Smithee, Alan 152
Sobchack, Vivian Carol 14, 104, 141
Soderbergh, Steven 10, 111, 113, 164
Solaris (book) 111, 169
Solaris (1972) 2–3, 10, 164, 167, 170–171, 175–177, 204
Solaris (2002) 10, 111, 113, 118–119, 164, 167, 170–171, 175–177
sole survivor 4–5, 56, 155, 168, 208
Solonitsyn, Anatoliy 168
Sontag, Susan 66, 67, 70–71, 100, 221–222
Sourcebook on Solitary Confinement 112
SpaceCore One 154–155
Spacey, Kevin 115, 121
Spaihts, Jon 90
Species 26, 68
Speculative Realism 36
Spielberg, Steven 20, 24, 34, 66, 69–70, 196, 200
Stack, Peter 181
Stanton, Harry Dean 144
Star Trek (television and films) 15, 24, 151, 204
Star Wars 194, 196
The Starlost (television) 103
Starman 21, 69
Statham, Jason 26
Sternhagen, Frances 117
Stoker, Bram 165
Stranded 4
Strategic Defense Initiative ("Star Wars") 76
Sulaco 135, 146, 147
Sunshine 3–4, 8, 98, 103–104
supernatural 9, 16, 25–26, 52, 123, 140, 151–153, 155–161, 205, 220
Suvin, Darko 220

Tarkovsky, Andrei 2, 164, 204
terrestrial films 2, 8, 67–68, 70–71
Thacker, Eugene 82–83, 90
They Live 2, 8, 14, 20–27, 29, 46, 51
The Thing (1982) 3–4, 8, 14, 16–29, 33–34, 36, 40, 45–46, 69, 71, 77n9
The Thing (2011) 36
The Thing from Another World (1951) 8, 13, 17, 34, 37, 199
This Island Earth 1, 7
The Time Machine (book) 101
The Time Machine (film) 101
Titan Find 195, 198–199, 205
Tobey, Kenneth 38
Toriumi, Hisayuki 5
The Transfer 166
Trenchard-Smith, Brian 7, 218
Trigg, Dylan 36, 147
A Trip to Mars (1910) 6
A Trip to Mars (1918) 6
A Trip to the Moon 6
Turenne, Louis 156

Turner, Victor 153
2001: A Space Odyssey 9, 15–16, 23, 140–141, 143, 146, 148, 164–165, 170, 173–175, 177, 196–197
Twohy, David 2, 111

uncanny valley 5, 140, 144
undead planet 10, 164–165
Ursini, James 166

Vampira 68
vampiric 3, 9–10, 40, 63, 164–167, 170–177
van Heijningen, Matthijs, Jr. 36
Vietnam War 35
Vonnegut, Kurt 121
Voorhees, Jason 68, 217, 225, 230
Vu, Huan 52

Waites, Thomas G. 42
Wallace, Tommy Lee 13, 15
War of the Worlds (book) 6
War of the Worlds (1953) 1, 7
War of the Worlds (2005) 66, 70
Warren, Norman J. 10, 194, 203
Weaver, Sigourney 4, 132, 143, 170, 182
Webb, Richard 62
Webster, D.J. 10, 152
Weir, Dr. William 3, 83–87, 91, 99–100, 158–161, 175–176
Wells, H.G. 6, 101, 198
Werchmeister, Hans 6
westerns 1, 8–9, 13, 21, 24–29, 116
Weyland-Yutani Corporation 4, 88, 132, 135, 146–147
Whedon, Joss 182
white science 152–153, 156–158, 161
Who Goes There? 17, 34
Wilcox, Fred M. 7, 13, 199, 220
Wincott, Michael 10, 186
Wise, Robert 1, 99, 151
Wittgenstein, Ludwig 93
Wood, Ed 7, 68, 222
Wood, Robin 77
Wordsworth, Richard 1–2
World War II 7, 37, 40, 51, 54, 57–58, 63, 82, 186

xenomorph 7, 70, 92, 121, 132, 137, 143, 145–148, 152, 170–171, 197, 201, 206
Ximena, Gallardo C. 190
XTRO 10, 194–195, 200–201

Yagher, Kevin 3, 218
Yeaworth, Irvin 2, 50

Zinoman, Jason 16
Žižek, Slavoj 36, 43, 167, 171, 176–177
Zuccon, Ivan 52